Modern Training

Running: Man runs because, throughout a long history of development, he has had to depend upon his own body whenever he wanted to go, and sometimes he had to go in a hurry. He had to run and, by running, he acquired a running heart, running lungs, running muscles, running bones. To be what he is, man must run.

Modern
Training
for
Running

Prentice-Hall, Inc. Englewood Cliffs, N. J.

for Running

J. Kenneth Doherty, Ph.D.

Director of Pennsylvania Relays

MODERN TRAINING FOR RUNNING
by J. Kenneth Doherty

© 1964 by

PRENTICE-HALL, INC.
Englewood Cliffs, N. J.

Copyright under International and Pan American
Copyright Conventions

PRENTICE-HALL INTERNATIONAL, INC., *London*
PRENTICE-HALL OF AUSTRALIA, PTY., LTD., *Sydney*
PRENTICE-HALL OF CANADA, LTD., *Toronto*
PRENTICE-HALL OF INDIA (PRIVATE) LTD., *New Delhi*
PRENTICE-HALL OF JAPAN, INC., *Tokyo*

Third printing......August, 1965

Library of Congress
Catalog Card No. 64-15599

PRINTED IN THE UNITED STATES OF AMERICA
C-69924

To those amateurs who run

Primarily because
To run is
Natural,
Fun,
and
Worthwhile
For its own sake;

Who honor the principle
That amateur sports must be
Avocational,
And act
Within the limitations of
Material reward
and
Time for preparation
Which it requires;

And yet,
Who,
Within those limitations,
Strive to their utmost
To run
Ever farther and faster,
And more enjoyably.

Ken Doherty

Preface

More times than not, when I mention to a coach that I am working on a book for distance running, he suggests with at least a hint of exasperation, "Doherty, why not make this one easy and simple. You've been running and coaching and reading and thinking and talking about endurance running for over a quarter of a century now. It would be a lot easier for you and for us if you would write down the gist of it all. Give us the essentials of endurance training and ignore all the whys and wherefores that clutter your books."

I wish I could do that. For one thing, I assume that book sales would increase, with increased gains for readers, publisher, and author. But somehow to me it seems dishonest, as much so as hawking Indian snake oil as a cure-all for human ills from arthritis to xerophthalmia.

There are no such cure-alls; there are no such simple ways to success in endurance running. There are no simply contrived human robots who need only a few turns of the key to keep them running. It is a man that runs. To be sure, it is a man with legs and lungs and a heart that develop automatically just by running, regardless of the whys and wherefores; but equally sure, it is a man with emotions and counterinterests and counterfears, a man with teammates and friends and family and an entire matrix of human society within which he has developed and must run. Whether the coach recognizes these factors or not, they do strongly influence every man's running and every man's training program.

True, a coach or a runner can ask wisely whether he will not achieve more by (1) selecting a country, an institution, a climate, and a terrain which are strongly favorable to running, (2) assuming that these will not create any critical problems and can therefore be taken for granted, and (3) concentrating all energies upon a few, relatively simple essentials of physical training for running.

Yes, such an approach does work, and has worked time and time again, but in my opinion, never to the degree or the extent in time that a broader and more holistic program might ensure. Under certain rare circumstances, a Cerutty can isolate a Herb Elliott from most human distractions by shanghaiing him to a primitive Camp Portsea, and there concentrating him to world-record achievement. But the boy who has guts enough to be a world champion in running also has guts enough to assert his own individuality and live his own life. Not even Cerutty could stop Elliott from marrying, having a son, going to distant Cambridge University, or retiring from all running at the age of 22, when he was just entering the period of maximum running maturity and achievement.

Coaches should understand and anticipate these things as well as the essentials of physical training, and it is such understanding that is the main purpose of this book. Very little is new in this training system I have called holistic. Every successful coach and runner has used it in one way or another. But they have done so on a catch-as-catch-can basis. They have tended to consider these off-the-field and nonphysical factors as being outside the training system. They have failed to plan carefully for them as they plan for the problems of distance-pace. They therefore often have had to face these factors after they have grown to complex and even cancerous proportions.

The primary purpose of this book, then, is to present a broad and sound foundation of related knowledge on which the individual coach and runner can build his own unique system out of the unique influencing factors and his unique personality. If at times it ranges widely, it does so with the assurance that the vertical height to which running achievement can go is directly proportional to the horizontal foundation of knowledge on which it is based.

Needless to say, I can make few claims that such a holistic approach is my own work, in any isolated sense. What is written here is a complex of ideas from many persons, many of whom, like Wendell Johnson who wrote on the semantics of personal adjustment, or Eugen Herrigel and Alan Watts on the ways of Zen, are quite outside the world of competitive running. My indebtedness to such men is most inadequately suggested in the usual page references.

But I have an even greater sense of obligation to those coaches and runners who have published personal accounts of their experiences. I am indebted to them for their words which I have quoted, but far more for the enthusiasm and sense of dedication which I have absorbed during many delightful days of reading their books and personally trying out their methods. I hope some of that enthusiasm has infected the words of this book, as I want very much to express my great admiration and respect for such coaches as Billy Hayes and Bill Bowerman of the United States, Gosta Holmer of Sweden, Armas Valste and Lauri Pihkala of Finland, Woldemar Gerschler of Germany, Franz Stampfl of England, Percy Cerutty of Australia, and Arthur Lydiard of New Zealand; and for such runners as Paavo Nurmi, Roger Bannister, Jim Peters, Herb Elliott, Derek Ibbotson, Gordon Pirie, and Fred Wilt. Perhaps a few others have been even greater performers, but these men took time and pains to write their most intimate running experiences and thus enriched and simplified both the awareness and the efforts of others.

Contents

Modern Training for Running

1 Motivation in Endurance Running

Why Men Run

Why do men run? The wisest answer would undoubtedly be given by a child, or a Zen Master, or a runner—without saying a word, they would each start running. Men do run and that is the most profound reason of all as to why they run. It tells us, beyond all words, that men are made *for* running, and have been made as they are *by* running.

Unfortunately I am not so wise. This book requires words, even though we are certain that words can never answer the question so forcefully as the running.

Why do men run? The answer is twofold: first, because of social need and readiness; and second, because individual achievement turns this social readiness into action.

It is useless to maintain that [social progress] takes place of itself, bit by bit, in virtue of the spiritual condition of a society at a certain period of its history. It is really a leap forward which is only taken when the society must have allowed itself to be convinced, or at any rate allowed itself to be shaken; and the shake is always given by somebody.[1]

---

[1] Henri Bergson, as quoted by Arnold J. Toynbee, *A Study of History* (New York: Oxford University Press, 1947), p. 212.

Great performance in endurance running is like a coin whose positive side is the development and concentration of all the energies (physical-mental-emotional) that are needed for running, and whose negative side is the restraint and removal of all the many life factors that would dissipate those energies. The two sides are inseparable, interacting, and equally essential for best running.

This analogy, however, is oversimplified because it focuses entirely on the runner, as though we could add things to him or strip things from him, without regard to the many influences around his life-situation. True, there are inner distractions and enervations. But the outer ones are so much more basic, complex, and endless. Some, like Gunder Hägg at Völödalen or Herb Elliott at Cerutty's Camp Portsea, avoid these negative factors by withdrawing from city life altogether to a training camp of the utmost simplicity.

If these negative factors return, performance breaks down, even though the runner is physically and mentally mature and capable, and his training schedule of running soundly planned. Herb Elliott was only 22 years old when he retired from running; his best running years were potentially still ahead of him. But his life-situation changed following his world record at Dublin in 1959. He was granted a three-year scholarship to Cambridge University and, along with his regular studies, had to cram a four-year Latin course into nine months. He met and married Ann Dudley, had a son, and often found himself thinking of his family debts while listening to Cerutty's exhortations toward greater running efforts.

Percy and I weren't on the same wave-length. . . . It surely wasn't indolence that kept me from training. It was my realization that as a family man . . . training was not as important in my career. . . . Running was a job that had to be fitted in between my other activities.

Neither Cerutty nor anyone else could have prevented this change in Elliott. Elliott's autobiography makes it clear that he was never cut out to be a running ascetic, such as Gordon Pirie or perhaps Murray Halberg were, with their lasting and complete dedication to athletics. He had wide interests and enjoyments and clearly intended to indulge them. For a short time, Cerutty could hold them back by flaunting the high goal of the world championship before him and by hiding him away at Camp Portsea. It was a glorious time for both Elliott and Cerutty. Cerutty fought to prolong it, but not even Cerutty's fierce energy could change the total situation.

Why do men run? If I were a physiologist I would answer that they run because they have running bodies: running hearts, running lungs, running muscles, running bones. Without a long human history of running, these would not be what they are. Man is a land animal. His use of other animals for transportation has been a limited and part-time thing. His use of machines is a last-minute addition. Whenever he wanted to go, he had to depend upon himself, and sometimes he wanted to go in a hurry. He had to run and by running he became a man-that-runs. Had he stuck to walking he would now be quite different. His maximum pulse rate would probably never have risen to 200 or more beats per minute as it is today and his muscles would have only a fraction of the 317 billion blood capillaries that are now present. Of course there were fighting and loving, but occasionally a little running was helpful even in these.

Why do men run? If I were a biochemist I might answer that man's chemical composition is both the reason for and the effect of his running. His use of oxygen, for example, is truly amazing. When walking, he needs less than two liters of oxygen per minute. But, when running, man has learned how to expend his energies tenfold, to a degree that requires over 22 liters of oxygen for recovery. Not only does this permit him to run farther and faster without harm to his vital organs, but it also provides complete recovery within a very short time. A similar story could be told for his use of glycogen, phosphocreatine, and each of the other related chemicals of the body. Not to run, that is, not to use what he has acquired during ages of effort is, in a sense, to deny what he is, and to court weakness and in the long run disaster.

Now if I were a psychologist, I might answer that men run because running is satisfying, that it gives a sense of doing what is natural, of freedom such as cannot be experienced in any other way, of achievement for its own sake. I might suggest that men run because successful competitive running brings them recognition and at times a sense of power over others.

A historian might reason that men run today because running is deep in our racial history. For example, the marathon was immediately and completely accepted in the modern Olympic Games because it seemed a "natural," even though it was not part of the ancient Games. Our sense of personal involvement with the Greek victory at Marathon made it a "natural." But all peoples have a similar history. Students of the ancient Inca civilization have become aware that the very extensive system of roads throughout the widespread Inca territory was entirely for foot travel and, more specifically, running. They had no horses nor other animals for rapid transportation. Messages were sent by relay runners, each of whom ran about a mile in distance, carrying knotted ropes by which to refresh their memories of the details they were to transmit by word of mouth. Much of this relay running was done at 9000 feet or more over the Andes mountains so that training must have been a matter of studied concern. Many other examples could be cited.

If I were a sociologist I would try to explain man's running on the basis of the strong awareness of need that modern nations have for running, and therefore of the high recognition they give to those who succeed in it. Running is the main activity of all the events and sports of the Olympic Games. It attracts more spectators, more worldwide attention, and more national representatives than any other. The rising new nations of the world, both small and large, are aware of this showcase and that, by the efforts of only one man, they can make known their virility to themselves and the world. It has not been by chance that Abebe Bikila of Ethiopia won the 1960 marathon, that New Zealand and Australia are now hotbeds of endurance running, that Tokyo held the 1964 Olympic Games, or that India has established a National Sports Institute for the training of coaches of track and field.

Why do men run in Finland? To say glibly that the Finnish people are enthusiastic about running is true enough but only a partial answer. We must go further and ask why the Finnish people are enthusiastic about running. Here the answer is not so simple. In part, because the terrain and, during many of the "running" months, the climate are conducive to running. But also, because in the early decades of the twentieth century, Finland was struggling for independence from the heavy hand of Russia and needed desperately some great national achievement with which to focus self-respect and enthusiasm. I have no knowledge of how Kohlemainen and Stenroos arose as runners, but their victories over the Olympic world at Stockholm in 1912 rallied the Finnish people to endurance running, even in villages a hundred miles or more north of the Arctic circle.

If space permitted, we could go further to show how social need is felt at the institutional and group level as well as at the national. Whatever the United States has achieved in endurance running has been primarily through its schools and colleges. These institutions have seen fit to gain recognition by way of running (and of course other sports) and have therefore provided the incentives and means by which their representatives could achieve success. For example, the numerous champions in running that the Catholic high schools and colleges of the Eastern states have developed are much more the result of a policy to fill an institutional need than of some physical or spiritual aptitude for running in Catholic students.

Next, we should briefly mention the small-group needs and interests which influence men to run. England's mile champion, Nankeville, has written of the closely knit group of nonschool running enthusiasts who encouraged and aided him throughout his running career. The running clubs that grew out of the energies of such men as Billy Morton of Dublin strongly influenced the development of such great Irish runners as R. M. N. Tisdall, Ron Delany, and Noel Carroll. To narrow the group even more, it is doubtful that Gunder Hägg would ever have run competitively if his father and his friends had not had a great interest in running. Herb Elliott has written of his father's passion for running fitness and of their jogs on the long beaches when Herb was but a boy of seven. Such examples could be extended almost endlessly.

Finally, the runner himself might mention that he is running because he wants a school letter, or because he wants to make a trip to a championship meet, or because the coach has encouraged him as a runner. It would take a volume to list individual reasons. But surely our point is made and need not be continued.

It is impractical, if not impossible, to try to comprehend the innumerable cross-currents of racial inheritance, social traditions, institutional demands, family expectations, friendly encouragements, aggressions, impulsions, insecurities, and frustrations that can and do motivate a boy to run. Actually there is never a single motive that can be isolated as exclusively responsible. As with other basic activities, men run for a great complex of reasons, limited only by one's ability to abstract them.

One of the most discerning stories of long distance running is called "The Loneliness of the Long Distance Runner" by Alan Sillitoe. When the big race is about two-thirds over, the "hero's" impulsion to prove his worth forced him to pour it on.

So by the haystack I decided to leave it all behind and put on such a spurt, in spite of the nails in my guts, that before long I'd left both Gunthorpe and the birds a good way off.

Yet his sense of what he called honesty and realness would not let him win; or rather, would not let his jailer-trainer win through his efforts. In full sight of the finish line and the crowd, he deliberately slowed down, waited for his opponent to break the tape, then finished with his back straight and his eyes looking disdainfully into those of his trainer.

Few readers will suffer the twisted life that produced such a twisted motivation, but many will run with a similar tangle of likes and dislikes, tenacity and weakness, of which they are quite unaware and certainly could never put into words.

When a boy first starts to run competitively, his motives are probably of as low an order as his performances: to win a medal or a varsity letter, to make the team, to be one of the gang. He understands Derek Ibbotson who says, "I ran because I possessed a natural ability to beat others and this compensated for my failure to make the school football or cricket team." Or Glenn Cunningham who ran as a boy to recover the use of his badly burned leg muscles and later because it was the fastest way to get around on the Kansas prairies. He understands the excitement of

Herb Elliott at the Melbourne Olympics as he watched the great
Vladimir Kuts demolish his opponents.

Motives should be proportioned to the boy just as his amount of
training is. A coach who emphasizes the deeply hidden satisfactions that
lie in hard work and sacrifice will "lose" his boys. To strive for perfection or self-realization, as a sensitive and mature runner like Roger
Bannister might urge, would have little meaning for the beginner. A
boy, like a man, understands only what is but one short step beyond
what he has already experienced. Bannister wrote that running was an
escape at first rather than a satisfaction. He accepted the discomforts of
running as the price of freedom to do what he really wanted to do, to
be active as a musician, actor, student, without suffering the gibes of
his schoolmates. To those of Bannister's mold, such reasons are under-
standable.

In each instance, some inspiration, some challenge, some obstacle becomes the stimulus to begin, Then, like a fly caught in a spider's web,
the more one struggles, the more enmeshed one becomes. Paavo Nurmi
was undoubtedly caught up in the great wave of enthusiasm that swept
Finland following the Olympic victories of Hannes Kohlemainen. Gunder Hägg was lured not only by the wooded paths of northern Sweden,
but also by the dreams of a glorious future in running shared by his
father. And, of course, many a champion first felt the blood run faster
in his leg muscles as he read the life story of a Zamperini or a Zatopek.

But inspiration produces only the first few steps; what is even more
crucial is the continuing sense of a challenge for which one is specially
fitted. For some years, until he was sure Gunder could go it alone,
Hägg's father devised ways, even falsifying times occasionally, to maintain his son's confidence and belief in his continuing development.

A common problem of motivation is a fixation upon a too distant
goal, rather than upon the means to that goal. True, ambition should
be an endless ladder leading upward, but progress comes by concentrating at any given time upon that one next rung. In writing of Emil
Zatopek's early career, Kozik stated,

> At first it didn't occur to Emil, even in his wildest dreams, that he could get
> anywhere near to touching a world record. He always set himself a goal which
> he felt was possible with determined will and training. First to defeat X, then a
> better runner Y, and so on. He didn't believe in lucky wins and wisely recalled,
> "You can't climb up to the second floor without a ladder. . . . When you set
> your aim too high and don't fulfill it, then your enthusiasm turns to bitterness.
> Try for a goal that's reasonable, and then gradually raise it. That's the only
> way to get to the top!" [2]

Space limitations permit little development here of this thought, de-

---

[2] Frantisek Kozik, *Zatopek in Photographs* (Prague: Artia, 1954), p. 78.

spite its importance. A continuing challenge must be present, a goal that is never actually reached, that grows and recedes as the runner's powers and ambitions develop. As Robert Browning wrote, "a man's reach should exceed his grasp, or what's a heaven for?" But how often a fine prospect has quit the sport altogether when his focused eagerness to be a champion became dulled by his sense of slow progress.

I am reminded of the innumerable times when, on various canoe trips in Canada, we decided to cross some large lake. Perhaps the wind was against us; the sun hot; stomachs empty. How distant and unapproachable the far shore seemed; how bored we felt; how aware we were of our aching muscles; how we doubted the wisdom of those who had selected the route; how ineffective each paddle stroke seemed.

In contrast, consider the unawareness of fatigue or boredom when canoeing on a river. Even when the river is almost as sluggish as a lake, the presence of trees and rocks by which to judge the effect of each paddle stroke and the interest in what might be around the next bend make play of what, on the lake, was drudgery.

In writing of the basic elements in human motivation, Alfred Adler said,

> We all wish to overcome difficulties. We all strive to reach a goal by the attainment of which we shall feel strong, superior, and complete. John Dewey refers, very rightly, to this tendency as the striving for security. Others call it the striving for self-preservation. But whatever name we give it, we shall always find in human beings this great line of activity—this struggle to rise from an inferior to a superior position, from defeat to victory, from below to above. It begins in earliest childhood and continues to the end of our lives. . . . The striving for perfection is innate in the sense that it is a part of life, a striving, an urge, a something without which life would be unthinkable.[3]

To those ill-adapted to the demands of running, such a way to achievement and mastery is unnatural, strange, even crackbrained. "They ought to have their heads examined!" But to those specially made for running, the fun lies in the struggle itself. To these men, distance running is a challenge even when it is a hardship; play even when they slave at it; fun even when they hate it. As Cerutty wrote,

> Running at its best is an outpouring, a release from tensions. . . . An hour, two hours of hard training slips away as so many minutes. We become tired, exhaustingly tired, but never unhappy. It is work but it seems only fun. Exhilarating, satisfying fun.[4]

Of course, such attitudes were developed at Camp Portsea, Australia, where men ran along the beautiful seacoast, up the sand dunes, across

---

[3] Heinz Ansbacher and Rowena Ansbacher, eds., *The Individual Psychology of Alfred Adler* (New York: Basic Books, Inc., 1956), p. 103.

[4] Percy Cerutty, *Running with Cerutty* (Los Altos, Calif.: *Track and Field News*, 1959), p. 17.

open country, then back, following Cerutty's uninhibited training methods, to plunge into the sea itself.

It is harder to understand the motivations of a runner such as the Englishman, W. R. Loader, who has described his early training experiences through the sooty brick and stone deserts of Clydeside, Tyneside, and Merseyside which display coke ovens, foundries, shipyards, blast furnaces, and machine shops, but provide little of the inspiration of nature. In particular he tells of running through a certain tough district of his town where the handicaps of terrain were nothing as compared with the derisive jeers of the onlookers, especially of the girls.

"Yah, look at the runner coming . . . ! Mary Ann, look, it's a runner! He's got nae claes on!" Faces rose up all around, derisive, jeering, insulting. A scabby mongrel dog snapped at the heels, delighted for once to find that someone else's life was being made a misery. Urchins sprinted alongside, mocking the runner's strides with their own exaggerated leg movements. It was a torment of the soul far more bitter than any torture of the body. And through it all one had to run with measured step, eyes fixed ahead as if unaware of the tumult, trying to abolish it by ignoring it. . . . But it is a hard thing for youth to set itself alone against spite and hostility. I did that run a number of times and never faced it without a premonitory chill of the spine. Having stood the jeers to the point where I could persuade myself I wasn't giving up through cowardice, I quietly abandoned the practice.[5]

Looking back from the Olympian heights of a completed and almost perfect career as a runner, Bannister wrote in his autobiography,

For nearly ten years I have been running many times a week and my grasp of the reasons why I run continues to grow. Running through mud and rain is never boring. Like 10,000 cross-country runners, their number ever increasing, I find in running—win or lose—a deep satisfaction that I cannot express in any other way. However strenuous our work, sport brings more pleasure than some easier relaxation. It brings a joy, freedom and challenge which cannot be found elsewhere. . . . I sometimes think that running has given me a glimpse of the greatest freedom man can know: the simultaneous liberation of both body and mind.[6]

But somehow, for me, Brutus Hamilton, head coach of the University of California and the 1948 Olympic team, said it best of all.

People may wonder why young men like to run distance races. What fun it is? Why all that hard, exhausting work? Where does it get you? Where's the good of it? It is one of the strange ironies of this strange life that those who work the hardest, who subject themselves to the strictest discipline, who give up certain pleasurable things in order to achieve a goal, are the happiest men. When

---

[5] W. R. Loader, *Testament of a Runner* (London: William Heinemann, Limited, 1960), p. 61. Also published as *Sprinter* (New York: The Macmillan Company, 1961).
[6] Roger Bannister, *The Four Minute Mile* (New York: Dodd, Mead & Co., 1955; London: Curtis Brown, Ltd., 1955), p. 13. Reprinted by permission of the publishers. Copyright © 1955 by Roger Bannister.

you see 20 or 30 men line up for a distance race in some meet, don't pity them, don't feel sorry for them. Better envy them instead. You are probably looking at the 20 or 30 best "bon vivants" in the world. They are completely and joyously happy in their simple tastes, their strong and well-conditioned bodies, and with the thrill of wholesome competition before them. These are the days of their youth, when they can run without weariness; these are their buoyant, golden days, and they are running because they love it. Their lives are fuller because of this competition and their memories will be far richer. That's why men love to run. That's why men do run. There is something clean and noble about it.[7]

Why Men Stop Running

We have stated the point of view that running is an activity inherent in man's individual and social nature. We are fully aware of course that there is a large segment of men whose body structure and chemistry are deterrents to running. But even they run as small children.

From the coach's standpoint it is equally important to understand why men stop running as it is to understand why they run. Again space limits discussion. But a wise coach will ask the question time and again in his search for more and better running.

In summary, it can be stated that men stop running when the conditions of social need or individual satisfaction become negative or nonexistent. Sweden, where running was for a time so prevalent, no longer seems to feel that this is an important means to national renown. The University of Pennsylvania, which between 1900 and 1930, led the nation's colleges in running achievement, now bases its reputation upon more academic activities. Of course individual participation in running may cease for reasons of necessity. But probably 99 per cent of the men that stop running do so for lack of motivation; running fails to bring sufficient satisfaction to make it worth while, or worse, sets up feelings of dissatisfaction and annoyance.

Much has been written about why men climb mountains—to the average man, a foolhardy and dangerous waste of energy and time. The best answer is simple. Because the mountain is there to be climbed! Once this sense of achievable challenge is lost, the climbing ceases, regardless of untouched energies to go higher.

So with distance running and training. This is all very obvious, and yet 90 per cent of the failures of training systems and coaching methods lie in the failure to plan attitudes as carefully as work schedules. Whoever the athlete and whatever his stage of development, the most effective training system is one that plans for and develops the sense of

---

[7] Brutus Hamilton, "Why Men Like to Run," *Coaching Newsletter* (London), II, No. 5 (July 1957), 7.

satisfaction in effort and the zest for each forthcoming competition with just as much care as the amount and intensity of daily work. We run with our minds and our emotions as much as with our legs; to neglect either is disastrous.

As soon as the foothills and mountains beyond endurance training are viewed as not worth the sweat and dust, as being insurmountable, or as more easily climbed by other men, all work schedules break down. This is true for all runners, with no exceptions. It is true for the novice, who, despite a great potential, is carelessly thrown against men of greater maturity or conditioning. From that moment on, running for him is likely to mean failure and avoidance. It is true for the young prospect who, excited by careless praise or the prospect of victory, drives himself in practice beyond his emotional and physical development. For him, the rainbow becomes a sand hill.

It is equally true for the "greats" of running, for the Bannisters, the Elliotts, the Snells, who retire from competition, not because they have achieved their ultimates in performance, not because their training methods were wrong or inadequate, but because their goals have lost their allure, their challenge. They made their great records by believing that achievement in running was worth its cost, however high; they stopped running when they found that success could be won only by paying a price they no longer felt willing to pay. Other goals seemed more attractive: success in their vocations, their schooling, their family life.

Derek Ibbotson wrote that "there's only one way to the top in running—blood, sweat, and sometimes tears." By paying such a price, he gained the world mile record in 1957. Later he wrote, "In the moment of victory I did not realize that the inner force, which had been driving me to my ultimate goal, died when I became the world's fastest miler."

So with Herb Elliott, who, without really intending to retire, allowed a year of study time to usurp his training time until, much as he would have enjoyed meeting the great challenge of Snell, he felt its fascination was no longer worth its hardships. It is a certainty that, physically, Elliott could have done 3:50 or better for the mile. He was only 20 when he ran 3:54.5. But, despite the dramatic and even agonizing appeal of Cerutty's telephone call from Australia to England, despite the unlimited self-confidence that the undefeated always possess, Elliott's mountain had somehow taken on a new face: steeper, less alluring, not quite worth the climbing.

The accomplishment of a coach can, to a significant degree, be measured by his ability to create and maintain motivation. This applies not only to his stars but also to the much greater number of also-rans who are in the long run the real measure of coaching achievement.

Such a coach will understand that men stop running:

When, as beginners, they fail to enjoy the running for its own sake—at first this is the most important of all considerations;

When they lose their belief in future development;

When they begin to lose the elation that comes with supreme fitness for running;

When the price of achievement and victory in competition is no longer felt to be worth the cost of hardship in training;

When competition is beyond their present ability to make a respectable showing;

When training procedures and terrain are monotonously unvaried;

When competition is too frequent;

When competition is consistently tough without intervening easy races;

When men run for the wrong goals and either achieve them or lose interest in them;

When procrastination or weakness in a workout is allowed to go unnoticed and thereby become a habit;

When early season training is neglected and a man finds himself behind and unable to catch up;

Whenever a distraction-to-be-disciplined becomes a primary interest for which running becomes a distraction;

There are a hundred—no, a thousand—other problems, of which every experienced coach is made aware and which, if he is to succeed, he tries to solve—though of course only one at a time.

2

The Role
of the Coach
in
Endurance
Running

On first thought the role of the coach in endurance running seems rather simple and clearly established, hardly worth consideration in a book of this length. Just the other day, I asked a coach of long standing what his job was. At first he laughed the question off, saying his main job was to keep the alumni dissatisfied but not irritated. Then, a little more seriously, he listed (1) to get some good horses, (2) to get them out on the track every day and often twice a day, and (3) to see that they followed the right training system. When I asked what he meant by "training system," he answered, "what the boys do on the track—you know, like interval training."

Well, that's what I used to think too. When in 1949 or so, *Track and Field News* first told us about Swedish fartlek, we realized America's lack of success in endurance running was caused by lack of the right training system. But still we didn't seem to get anywhere. Then, in 1953, we found that European runners hadn't been using fartlek nearly so much as interval training. Here was the secret; use interval training and you couldn't miss.

But when I started trying to write and really think hard about endurance running and training, I found I was asking a lot of questions I'd never asked before. Why did little Finland with a population of only four million win twice as many Olympic gold medals as any other country between 1912 and 1948? Why did Mihaly Igloi, in Hungary in 1955, bring forth, not one, but three world's champions: Roszavolgyi, Iharos, and Tabori? Was it really the training system he followed? What are the real essentials of successful training that lie back of three such contrasting systems as Arthur Lydiard's marathon training, Percy Cerutty's power running on sand dunes and sea beaches, and Woldemar Gerschler's track training at repeated distances under 400 meters. It couldn't lie in the running systems as they are usually described; it must lie in other factors common to all of them.

Before I go ahead to suggest what these factors are, let me suggest five contrasting ways of organizing the coaching and training for endurance running: (1) that of England and Roger Bannister, (2) that of Finland and Armas Valste, (3) that of Australia and Percy Cerutty, (4) that of Hungary and California and Mihaly Igloi, and (5) that of Germany and Woldemar Gerschler.

Bannister, of course, had no coach. When he first went to Oxford, he contacted a coach recommended by Jack Lovelock. But later Roger wrote,

> He seemed upset when I asked him *why* he said this or that. I think he worked intuitively and *I needed reasons for the things I did.* [Italics mine—J.K.D.]

Stampfl is generally credited with being Bannister's coach, but other than having guided his training schedule by way of another runner, Chris Brasher, Stampfl had no direct contact with Bannister until they happened to travel on the train from London to Oxford when Bannister ran his famous mile in 3:59.4. Bannister wrote in his book, *The Four Minute Mile,*

> The day before I left for Vancouver I had a long talk with Franz Stampfl. I knew exactly the type of program that suited me, and so I did not need to see him *while I was training myself* to a peak. But his advice was invaluable in building up my mental approach to the race. I could carry myself almost all the way. Then at the last minute, when I became hesitant, he helped to give me the confidence and aggressiveness that I previously lacked. . . .
>
> The things a man learns for himself he never forgets, and can adapt to many different situations. The things a man does by himself, he does best. . . . I think it is the duty of a coach to encourage resource and initiative in each of us . . . , not merely to help his pupil to achieve a set performance in his event . . . , [but] also to show how, through experiencing the stress imposed by his event, he can understand and master his own personality.[1] [Italics mine—J.K.D.]

To an American this is heresy. No coach to make decisions, to seek aid for financial problems, to arrange travel and hotel reservations, to

---

[1] Roger Bannister, *The Four Minute Mile* (New York: Dodd, Mead & Co., 1955; London: Curtis Brown, Ltd., 1955), pp. 227-28. Reprinted by permission of the publishers. Copyright © 1955 by Roger Bannister.

speak out against one's critics. No coach to procure shoes that fit, to influence the faculty in shifting exam schedules, to suggest that the girl friend might well stay until after the *big* race is over. No coach to avoid the struggle of deciding that this training plan, not that, is best. No coach to know beyond all doubt just how much is enough and how much more is too much. No coach to scare away the heebie-jeebies of doubt and fear by quoting medical authorities that "physical activity, no matter how strenuous, cannot harm a healthy heart or other vital organs of the body."

In fact, we American coaches must feel downright insulted that this all-time great achievement should have occurred within the English tradition, in which the professional coach is on the lower fringe of social respectability. His presence at team meetings or at post-meet celebrations is for the team captain to decide, and he often decides in the negative. His coaching advice, if sought at all, is something for the individual runner to accept or reject. And yet, whether we like it or not, this same English tradition has produced ten Olympic champions in endurance running. The American system, with its thousands of runners and hundreds of professional coaches, brought forth only two more. Incidentally, of these twelve, seven were at the shortest endurance distance, the half-mile.

Of course, in rebuttal we can argue that a system that is sound and workable in a society such as England would break down entirely in a different society, such as our own. And if you think we are not different, read the English book, *Sport and Society*, edited by Alex Natan, or sit down for a few hours with a group of English officials and coaches and talk candidly of the best solutions to basic sports problems.

For example, a large group of influential sports officials in England would cry "Hear! Hear!" to the following words by Ronald Kittermaster, headmaster of the King's School, Worcester:

> Finally, learning both to win and to lose gracefully is an important part of the educational value of games: win or loss mattering nothing so long as each man gives of his best. For this reason the training of athletic champions for national or international sport is entirely foreign to the British educational-athletic tradition. The view that the object of all sport should be competition, to demonstrate that one team or individual may be acclaimed the best, is one that is widely held both in and outside the British Isles, but it is an un-British and anti-educational view, a denial of all that is best in sport.[2]

But the point I wish to make is that national attitudes and facilities do strongly influence individual attitudes and performance, and thus determine in large measure the role that the coach can play. For example,

---

[2] Alex Natan, ed., *Sport and Society* (London: Bowes and Bowes Publishers, Ltd., 1958), p. 87.

Mutual congratulations between Charles Werner (left), former head coach at Pennsylvania State University and one of America's most successful coaches of distance running, and the author (center) on their recognition as honorary members of the *Mestari* (Master's) Club for track and field for Finland. Their lapel pins were presented by Armas Valste (right), former National Head Coach of Track and Field for Finland.

contrast the words of Kittermaster with these by a high political leader of the USSR:

In the mass character of the Soviet athletics lies its great advantage and the guarantee of its future successes. . . . Everybody is training hard, beginning with the Merited Masters of Sports and ending with green novices. And all and sundry cherish one dream—to be allowed to take part in the Spartakiad's final contests. . . . Only the best, those who show excellent results at each of these stages, will defend the colors of their republic at the grand review of the forces of Soviet sport.

How we bristle at the use of such terminology—"the forces of Soviet sport"—and resent the compulsions that seem to lie behind it. But don't sell these men short. They understand very well the high place of flexibility, freedom, and fun in human motivation; in fact, they go so far as to plan for them nationally, from the top down. Incentives and rewards are placed all along the path of development, from the novice at age six or seven to the Honored Master of Sport at age thirty or more. Limited space permits only the summary statement that, in the entire history of world sport, ancient and modern, few, if any, societies have controlled the conditions negative to sports performance or furthered the conditions favorable to it as has the Soviet Union.

Our second example comes from Finland, where national enthusiasm for running, at least between 1912 and 1956, was even higher than that in the USSR, but was achieved more spontaneously and naturally than was the latter's planned system.

Despite its tiny population of four million, despite a more northerly climate than anywhere in the United States, Finland won 18 Olympic gold medals in endurance running between 1912 and 1956, as compared with eight for the United States during this same period. We tend to speak of Finland's pine-needled paths through the woods and around beautiful lakes, as though these were her secret. But this is only from June to September. When, as is much more common, they are covered with ice and snow and the temperature is below zero, they can hardly be considered secrets of success.

The real secret of Finland's success, above and beyond the endless training, lies in her people's enthusiasm for endurance running. Almost every small town throughout Finland has a well-cared-for running track and runners who use it. In 1955, I travelled 100 miles north of the Arctic circle to a town called Sodankyla. This location would be comparable to a point well north of Hudson's Bay in Canada. Why? To see a track meet of course. Over 100 persons took part—sons, fathers, and in one event (the hammer throw), grandfathers as well.

What is the role that Armas Valste, Finland's national coach, has played in all this? How did he try to solve the long list of problems we have presented? Unlike the USSR at the national level and the USA at the college level, Finland cannot bring its best prospects to a single place for year-round training. They are farmers and workmen and must train at home. So Valste went to them, scheduled trips around the country to consult with each of them. He insisted upon their keeping training diaries. He maintained an extensive mail correspondence. Occasionally, he brought runners to one of the sports training institutes, like Vieru-machi or Kuortane, for special coaching and more intensive work. Valste's manner was authoritative and men had confidence in his instructions. But he strengthened his authority through close contacts with such Scandinavian sports physiologists as Drs. Ove Bøje and E. Asmussen.

In summary, most of the essentials for success were present at acceptable levels. The one great asset, however, which overbalanced whatever may have been lacking, lay in the social climate created by the amazing victories of Kohlemainen and Stenroos in 1912 and of Paavo Nurmi and Willie Ritola in 1920. Coming at a time when Finland was fighting for national independence against foreign domination, these proofs of Finnish virility and toughness were of special and lasting significance. In Finland a man first tried to be a runner, or perhaps a skier. If he lacked talent in those events, he attempted other sports. If successful, he was as much the group or national hero as is the baseball or football player in America. Under such conditions, the role of the coach was one of organization more than motivation.

Another example is Australia with Percy Cerutty and his world champion, Herb Elliott. Once again, it was a social climate that aroused a boy's first interest in becoming a great runner. If there had been no Olympic Games in Melbourne in 1956, there would have been no Herb Elliott at Dublin in 1959 or at Rome in 1960. On the other hand, the crucial factor in his development was Percy Cerutty. Cerutty and Elliott were two sides of a single coin of running performances.

Cerutty offended many American coaches on his trip to America with his remarks about our fatness, our smoking and drinking, and our complete inability to demonstrate what we were trying to teach—even worse than that, our unwillingness to make an effort. However, in some respects, he was, and must be still, one of the great coaches of endurance running. His greatness was primarily founded on his complete devotion and complete concentration of his own life to endurance running. It wasn't so much that he belittled other areas of living. Rather, he felt that life's highest realization could be developed through running. Nothing should interfere with it. Elliott's decision to attend Cambridge University in England was to Cerutty a waste of the world's greatest running talent.

Fig. 2.1   Herb Elliott, Percy Cerutty, and the sea and sand at Camp Portsea. Elliott was very self-dependent, but, during his years of running, the piercing intensity of Cerutty's eyes and energy were always with him. (Adapted from an illustration by Hal Higdon in Fred Wilt's *How They Train*.)

To escape the hindrances and distractions of civilized living, Cerutty left Melbourne and set up his home and training quarters along the sea coast at Camp Portsea. Thus, in one action, he eliminated many of the negative factors that beset the life of the ordinary runner. By chance or design, he chose for his personal reading medieval writings on religious asceticism and out of them formed a runner's creed of Stotanism (a derivative of Stoic and Spartan). He believed in strength of mind and body through suffering and tried to convince his runners of its values. He was convinced that the free expression of animals was a better guide to action than the conscious control of human beings. Thus relaxation-in-action is not so much a matter of will power and control as of imagination and expression, of allowing the pains of fatigue to be expressed by muscle groups unrelated to running and thereby concentrating upon the positive aspects of running rather than upon trying to control its negative aspects. For Cerutty, to try consciously to relax is like trying to lift oneself by one's own bootstraps.

Of course Elliott did not accept all that Cerutty taught—no intelligent man could. He was exasperated at Cerutty's uninhibited antics at times, and embarrassed at other times, and told him so. But the truth remains that while they were together, Cerutty controlled all the potentially negative factors in Elliott's running and furthered most of the positive ones—both physical, with his demand for great mileage and great intensity of work, and mental-emotional. Cerutty taught that free and uninhibited running could come only from a free and uninhibited man. Living alone as he did, he could do as he pleased, run naked along the beach, up the sand dunes, into the hills, and finally into the sea itself, the ultimate mother of man and all of life. He would have none of interval training, with its measured and timed distances and constant awareness of just how many yards had been covered and how many yards there were still to go. He thought such planned effort magnified the awareness of effort and fatigue and limited output.

It's interesting, in passing, to contrast this point of view with that of Mihaly Igloi, who uses interval training constantly, but avoids having his runners become overly conscious of effort by insisting that they just do the running and leave the decisions of how much and of what intensity to Igloi. They concentrate on doing well what they are doing now; they leave the worry of what they may do later to Igloi, trusting his judgment that it will be just enough and not too much.

In contrast, then, to the situation in Finland, where the people as a whole created an invigorating sports climate, Cerutty withdrew from what he considered a negative sports climate, the city, and created his own sports climate. His system worked, and Elliott would be the first to agree. Had Cerutty followed Elliott to Cambridge, as he threatened to do, I doubt that they would have succeeded in running any better than Elliott did alone. The magic of Cerutty was in himself at Camp Portsea. There, he was a sorcerer; in Cambridge, he would have been less than an apprentice.

Cerutty avoided the outer distractions of civilized life by taking his runners out of the city to his way of simplicity at Camp Portsea. On the other hand, Mihaly Igloi was a coach who concentrated his efforts on removing the inner distractions—the doubt, indecision, personal responsibility, and initiative in planning. In 1960, after some seven years of training under Igloi, Laszlo Tabori was asked what system of training Igloi followed. His answer, "I don't know. I haven't thought about it. We never do the same thing from day to day or week to week." Granted this was probably a stock answer that grew out of endless boring questions of this kind, it was still a revealing one, the same kind of answer that all of Igloi's runners give. The problems of undertraining versus overtraining, of speed-work versus mileage, of fartlek versus interval training, consume more of runners' nervous energy than is generally recognized. These uncertainties inhibit performance just as effectively as uncertainty during a race. But such problems do not exist for Igloi's men. Their sole job is to run and leave the worrying and thinking and decision-making to him.

When it comes to developing runners, few can doubt that Igloi has been successful. In Hungary, his greatest trio, Tabori, Roszavolgyi, and

Iharos, were all world-record men. In the United States, his pupils included Max Truex, Jim Beatty, Jim Grelle, and many other fine runners. True, all of these men had already had a successful college career when they went to Igloi, but they all reached their best performances under his coaching. Our point, however, lies in his method rather than in his success. In brief it was one of direct and complete authority over the inner man. He told them when, how, and what to run, both during training and during racing. Since his knowledge, experience, and personal absorption in running were of the highest degree, his decisions were invariably sound. His men were often amazed when a race developed just the way Igloi had said it would. Once they were convinced of his ability, they relaxed and placed themselves in his hands without reservation. Shortly before he received the Sullivan award, Jim Beatty answered a question on this point by saying, "I think Igloi is the greatest coach in the world. I believe in him completely. As long as I believe in him, I believe in myself." World history is full of great deeds of endurance and courage by men who have followed strong leadership with no inner reservations.

We should add that when Igloi was in Hungary, he was able to remove the outer distractions as well as the inner ones. Both he and his runners were in the armed services and therefore separated from the endless annoyances and details that fritter away our energies in normal living. Hungarian runners were the best in the world in 1955. When the Hungarian revolution ended in horror and anxiety, all this changed. Melbourne was a nightmare for them. Though they tried their best to recapture their form for Rome four years later, they could no longer secure the concentration and certainty of the earlier years.

The last example of ways in which coaches have served their runners is provided by Woldemar Gerschler, a coach who adds one more mark to the German reputation for thoroughness, for the understanding and use of science, and for a belief in hard work and the uses of authority. Gerschler is generally considered to be the father of interval training, though when I visited with him at his home in Freiburg in 1960 he denied this. Certainly he was the first to organize its elements and use it in training Rudolf Harbig, a world champion, in 1939.

But in my opinion, Gerschler should be known for a much more important reason: for being the first to use the "sports sciences" of physiology and psychology in a consistent and practical way to supplement a coach's experience and judgment in training runners. Others have done this of course, some before Gerschler, but not at the same high level. Actually we should think of the team of Gerschler-Reindell-Schildge. Reindell was the physiologist; Schildge, the psychologist. They have worked with Gerschler for over 20 years now.

The final straightaway of the 1960 Olympic 800-meter final at Rome. From left to right: George Kerr, West Indies (third); Paul Schmidt, Germany (fourth); Peter Snell, New Zealand (first); Roger Moens, Belgium (second); and Christian Waegli, Switzerland (fifth). Snell, badly boxed in at this point, came charging through a narrow gap on the inside to take the lead in the last 15 meters.

Courtesy of *Track and Field News*

Other than Harbig, Gerschler's most successful runners have come from outside Germany: Roger Moens of Belgium, 1956 world-record holder for 800 meters; Josef Barthel of Luxembourg, 1952 Olympic 1500-meter champion; Gordon Pirie of Great Britain, 1956 world-record holder for 5000 meters and other distances. He coached these men mainly by correspondence and therefore had no way of solving their social problems, as was done in Finland or in Australia.

But he undoubtedly went further than any other to solve what can be called the running problems. First, a runner must seek *him;* he does not seek runners. This means that doubts about his competence or challenges to his authority as coach are never a problem. Moreover, his coaching bolsters the runners' faith in him. His protégés must first visit him at the Freiburg Institute of Physical Education, of which he is director. Here is how Gordon Pirie reacted to meeting him and to a similar visit later.

The next landmark in my life was my meeting with Woldemar Gerschler, the great German coach, after the Helsinki Olympics in 1952. *I was immediately impressed with the quiet authority of this man, and soon I unreservedly put myself in his hands.* I have regarded him as my mentor, my inspiration, and my close friend, ever since. . . . For twenty years he has worked closely with Professor Hans Reindell, a heart specialist, and with psychological experts. These two men and their team have built up the Freiburg Institute into one of the greatest scientific research centers for athletes in the world. I could write a book about them and their work; to summarize their achievement, I should say that they proved that athletes could set themselves targets which had never been dared before. By the most vigorous physical and mental tests of every athlete they advised, they discovered his ultimate potential and showed him how to reach it by harder and harder and harder training. Their work on an athlete's breathing alone would entitle them to lasting fame. So would their methods of testing an athlete's concentration. They put me through trials I thought I could never survive. But I did. They knew exactly what they were doing.

Gerschler is an unassuming, modest man as most great personalities are. His wife was German high-jump champion at the age of 39, and they lead a very happy family life. Gerschler was the first man who ever suggested that I could do *more* than I was trying to do. He has never told me how to run a race. That is for the athlete to decide. But he told me how to produce the maximum effort. *His effect on me was to take from my shoulders the enormous responsibility for training which I had borne so far alone.* I didn't know what I was doing until I met him.

Under Gerschler's guidance I soon realized that the training of the mind is as important as physical training. The essence of success is endless repetition without boredom, and a technique for heightening mental, as well as physical, tension.

The first essential is to teach the athlete to enjoy the basic exercise of running by being uninhibited in movement and thought. He will then revel in the mere rhythm of running and never tire of it. If this sounds simple I can assure you it is the hardest barrier of all for the young athlete to surmount, and many never do. This liberated condition is one which you have to experience to appreciate. I can't describe it any more exactly. When it has been achieved the rest comes relatively easily.[3] [All italics mine—J.K.D.]

In the light of these five examples taken from the lives of great coaches of endurance running, how can we summarize the role of the coach? A very broad answer would be that he must so use, adapt, interrelate, and develop the positive factors within the runner and within his environment, both physical and social, that they become strongly dominant; and, at the same time, so limit and nullify the negative factors that they are ineffectual.

At this point, it should be clear that these positive-negative factors which affect performance extend far outside the training system and the training hours. To list them in detail would go far beyond the scope of this book. But some idea of their number and nature can be gained by indicating the areas and relationships in which they arise.

I. Factors that are primarily external:
   A. Directly related to running:
      1. climate, terrain, training system, training time;
      2. optimum rest and nutrition;
      3. group or team morale, institutional sports morale, national sports morale;
      4. the coach's competence, authority, friendliness, sense of humor, dedication to running, patience, fortitude, toughness, and much more;
   B. Less directly related to running:
      1. financial security;
      2. social distractions and sex problems;
      3. academic status (if a student);
      4. job requirements (if working);
      5. home and family conditions (if married);
II. Factors that arise primarily within the runner:
   A. running inheritance (structural, biochemical, mental-emotional);
   B. acquired mental-emotional control in training and competition;
   C. fortitude and stick-to-itiveness;
   D. lack of inhibitions toward running and its effects.

Each of these factors could be assigned a weight for its range of effectiveness. Almost any one of them could become a decisive factor, especially as related to failure or limited success. But in every case, with no

---

[3] Gordon Pirie, *Running Wild* (London: W. H. Allen & Co., Ltd., Publishers, 1961), pp. 18 ff.

exceptions, the total weight of their effect upon the runner must be strongly positive.

What then is the role of the coach? First and above all, it is a role which each coach must select for himself and in which he must train himself just as intelligently and persistently, 24 hours a day and the year round, as he tries to help his runners train themselves. Second, it is a role that is consistent with the social climate within which the coach works. The coach does not, however, merely accept that climate; he does his utmost to change and improve what he can, even if, as in the case of Cerutty, he turns his back on the whole mess and creates his own environment. Third, he constantly thinks and talks and acts in terms of motivation—enthusiasm, self-confidence, goals, positive mental attitude—with even more concern than he has for mileage and intensity of running. He coaches men, not as physical running machines for which physical training is the all-important means to development, but as human beings whose mental-emotional development must be planned just as carefully and practiced just as persistently as heart and leg development. Fourth, he tries to remove from the athlete's shoulders those burdens of everyday living that amateurism in sport would agree should be removed, but at the same time, he strongly encourages self-dependence and initiative by leaving to the runner those responsibilities and decisions that are properly his *alone*. And finally, he keeps aware of the fast-growing number of coaching tools that the related sciences of psychology (and I place it first deliberately), physiology, sports medicine, and space medicine are making available to us and uses them as supplements to his own coaching experience and judgment.

How does he play this role? By acting out his own special version of the strengths and methods of these coaches I have described. He is not likely to coach within an enthusiastic national sports climate such as that in Finland or the USSR. Chances are he does not have his school student body 100 per cent or even 60 per cent behind him and his runners. Probably there is no terrain or climate such as they have in Scandinavia or Australia. It is unlikely that he will ever coach running talents such as those of Bannister, Pirie, Elliott, or Beatty.

But at least he does have himself; he can begin there. If he cannot or will not run himself, as did Cerutty, he can read, talk, and think about the careers of great runners and great coaches almost as though he had lived those lives himself. Gradually, his own enthusiasm, dedication, and knowledge, not merely of training systems but of the boys and men who do the training, will spread to his team, then to the team family—the local alumni and former runners—then to the student body, and finally, who knows—if there are enough others like him—to the entire state or even the country as a whole.

The future of endurance running lies with those who are dedicated, tough, and persistent, but, equally with those who are intelligent and who studiously seek the new and more scientific methods of the future. In my opinion, amazing as present-day records seem to us now, the great period of progress in endurance running is still ahead of us. Those who assume the total role of coach, social organizer, fanatic, taskmaster, friend, and scientist are most likely to be able to keep up with the pace of that progress. If this is too broad an assignment, the coach, like Gerschler, must secure the help of others to supplement his shortcomings.

The
Physiology
3 of
Endurance
Running

Fundamentals of Endurance [1]

Man can live for weeks without food, about eleven days without drink, but hardly a dozen minutes without oxygen. A ready and liberal supply of oxygen to all organs is essential to their sustained activity. Consciousness endures but a second or two after the brain is deprived of oxygen. The first step in securing this oxygen is, of course, its capture by the lungs in ordinary breathing. But breathing ability is no measure of endurance. In fact, athletes with high endurance breathe in less air than others. The crux of the matter is to get the oxygen from the lungs to the oxygen-craving muscles and nerve cells. This requires a powerful heart and an efficient system of arteries, capillaries, and veins.

Infinitely more important than vital capacity of the lungs is the minute-volume of the heart. At rest the average heart

[1] Arthur H. Steinhaus, formerly Dean and eminent physiologist of George Williams College, has very kindly granted permission for this section to be quoted verbatim from his paper, "Health and Physical Fitness," printed in *Toward an Understanding of Health and Physical Education* (Dubuque, Iowa: Wm. C. Brown Company, Publishers, 1963), p. 17.

may put out about four liters of blood per minute, and this is enough to absorb the three hundred cc. of oxygen needed for resting quietly. But when the muscles are working at a rate which requires that they be supplied with ten to fifteen times this amount, the heart must increase its output accordingly if it would not fall too far behind.

Dr. [David Bruce] Dill who has worked extensively in this field, reports that whereas athletes may pump enough blood to transport from three to a maximum of five liters of oxygen away from the lungs per minute, the average inactive person can take in only two liters, and a person with heart trouble

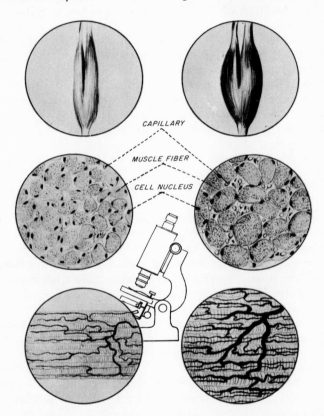

FIG. 3.1   The comparative effects on muscles of strength training and of endurance training. Strength training causes a muscle to increase in size (top circles). Microscopic studies (middle circles) show that this increase in size is caused by an enlargement of individual muscle fibers. The total number of fibers in a given muscle is not increased by training. Blood capillaries are not developed at all by isometric strength training and very little by isotonic strength training (middle circles). Endurance, along with other effects, increases the number and the effectiveness of blood capillaries within the muscle and thus improves its supply of oxygen and fuel (lowest circles).

a half liter or less. This means that the five-liter absorber can do ten times as much work or endure ten times as much as the half-liter cardiac case. He is ten times the distance from bankruptcy. Such extremely high oxygen intakes are possible, first, because the trained athlete's heart is able to pump out almost twice as much blood with each beat as is that of the average person, and second, because his vasomotor system so controls the size of the blood vessels that most of this blood is forced to go through the active muscles where now there may be as many as 2500 capillaries functioning in each cubic millimeter. Here more of the blood's oxygen is unloaded, so it returns to the lungs even greedier than before to reload with oxygen.

It is hardly necessary to add that the same blood which carries the greater supplies of oxygen to the muscles returns with comparable increased loads of carbon dioxide, the waste product which it expels into the lungs. To carry this oxygen and carbon dioxide the blood must be well stocked with red corpuscles bearing hemoglobin. In fact, it takes approximately twenty-five trillion of the former and over a pound and a half of the latter.

If for a brief moment the blood is unable to bring enough oxygen to the working muscles, immediately lactic acid will accumulate. Free lactic acid would cause the muscle to stop. To avoid this the lactic acid is temporarily neutralized by the buffers of blood and muscles. In this way about four ounces of lactic acid can be made harmless pending the advent of oxygen to dispose of it.

To endure, the body must rid itself of the waste product, heat. This usually presents no special problem at normal temperatures, but at high temperatures it appears that the body must learn still another adjustment if it would survive. The heat generated in the muscles is brought to the skin by the blood. Here, also, the sweat glands are stimulated to greater activity. The evaporation of the perspiration takes heat from the skin and the blood coursing through it. Thus even at temperatures of 110-120° F. it becomes possible for a person actually to "refrigerate" himself down to approximately body temperature.

This requires a lot of perspiration and therein lies a danger. Sweat normally contains sodium chloride. With profuse sweating, too much of this salt may be lost and this apparently leads to heart failure. Now it appears, from observations made by Dill (1933) at Hoover Dam and by Professor Lehmann (1935) in the laboratories of the Kaiser Wilhelm Institute in Dortmund, that people who are accustomed to working at these high temperatures learn to hold back the salt and perspire instead almost pure water.

Perfect endurance would mean the ability to maintain top speed of muscle power indefinitely. This is impossible of attainment because of the terrific energy-releasing machines which our muscles are. Instead, we are capable of maximal effort for only brief periods at best. Lesser effort can be longer sustained. Moderate activity by some, and mild activity by most all, can be sustained indefinitely. Thus persons are scattered on the road leading from perfect endurance to the invalid state. The distance which separates them from the latter may be expressed in terms of the following factors:

1. the amount of phosphocreatine and other immediately available fuel in the muscle cell (Note: also adenosine triphosphate);

2. the buffering capacity of muscle and blood;

3. the oxygen and carbon dioxide carrying capacity of the blood measured in hemoglobin, red corpuscles, and alkali reserve;

4. the minute-volume of cardiac output;

5. the amount of carbohydrate and fat stores of liver and muscle;

6. the digestive and absorptive capacity of the digestive system;

7. the vital capacity of the lungs, perhaps the permeability of the lung surface to oxygen (little is known about the latter);

8. the degree of hunger which generally motivates the search for food; and

9. the ability to acquire food.

Heat Exhaustion and Endurance Running [2]

Summary

When exercise is combined with heat stress, the interactions on the body have important implications, particularly for athletes. This arises from the fact that exercise, in addition to imposing an internal heat stress on the body, also has a special requirement for a larger blood flow to the working muscles. As a result, even light work in the heat places a large burden on the cardiovascular system to maintain an adequate blood supply simultaneously to the dilated skin blood vessels, the working muscles, and the brain. Activity which is easily accomplished in cool weather may become impossible during a hot spell due to the inability of the heart to increase its output sufficiently to meet these three requirements for blood flow; consequently dizziness, nausea, and other signs of heat exhaustion supervene, and physical performance is markedly

[2] Elsworth R. Buskirk and David E. Bass, "Climate and Exercise," *Science and Medicine of Exercise and Sports*, Warren R. Johnson, ed. (New York: Harper & Row, Publishers, 1960), pp. 311-38. Copyright © 1960 by Warren R. Johnson. Reprinted with the permission of Harper & Row, Publishers, Inc.

impaired. To an athlete, this means that an excellent state of physical condition may suddenly become inferior if his athletic event occurs during hot weather to which he is unacclimatized.

Of great importance, therefore, is the phenomenon of acclimatization to heat. By working out in a hot room for as little as two to four hours daily for seven to ten days, an athlete can dramatically improve his ability to function in the heat. Performance which might have been reduced as much as 50 per cent on the first day in the heat can be improved almost to that attainable in cool weather by this process. Once attained, acclimatization to heat is well retained for one to two weeks without further heat exposure.

Knowledge of the interactions on the body of heat and exercise suggest several practical considerations for coaches and athletes. Prior acclimatization to heat is one of the most important. Other factors are: maintenance of adequate hydration, use of lighter uniforms, insuring adequate ventilation for evaporation of sweat, scheduling events during the cool hours of the evening in warm latitudes. Attention to these simple precautions, based on physiological considerations, could lead to improved performance and minimize major form reversals due to hot weather.

The Physiology of Heat Regulation

A nude man reclining quietly in a constant temperature room at 85-88° F. is in a neutral thermal state, i.e., he can remain in the room indefinitely without becoming uncomfortably warm or chilled. In a still atmosphere, convective heat loss from the skin surface is negligible, since there are no air currents, and conductive loss is small, since air is a poor conductor. Most of the heat is lost through radiation to the surroundings and evaporation of insensible water. Within the body, heat is brought to the surface largely by convection (by the blood flow) and to a certain extent by conduction through the tissues. If we now increase the room temperature slightly (to 89°), certain physiological responses occur. At first there is a dilatation of the skin blood vessels, heart rate, and cardiac output increase, and blood flow through the skin is increased; as a result there is a higher rate of heat transfer to the skin from the interior. This can be seen in the flushed skin on warm days or with severe exercise. As a result of this increased skin blood flow, the surface temperature of the body is increased and so is radiative loss to the environment. Further increase in ambient temperature imposes a heat load which cannot be met by radiative loss.

As the temperature of the surroundings exceeds that of the skin, the direction of radiation is reversed and the body would actually gain heat from the environment if it did not have in reserve another source of heat loss. This reserve is the elaboration of sweat. The sweat glands provide the major physiological defense against overheating. The body can secrete over three liters of sweat in an hour of strenuous exercise in hot weather; this represents a very large avenue of heat loss, since the evaporation of each liter of sweat removes approximately 580 kcal. from the body. It should be emphasized that only sweat which evaporates possesses "cooling power"; when sweat rolls off the body or is trapped in clothing it contributes nothing to heat loss. This of course accounts for the oppressiveness of "muggy" days, when evaporation is hampered by high humidity. In summary, the protective physiological responses to heat stress are increased skin blood flow and the onset of active sweating. . . .

From the foregoing, it would appear that our body temperature, the familiar 98.6° F., is a jealously guarded "constant." In a sense, however, the term "body temperature" is a misnomer since it obviously is not the temperature of the entire body to which we refer, but that of the body "core" as measured by rectal temperature. The body core can be at 99.0° F. while portions of the skin surface are 60° F. or lower; even in comfortable environments the skin is usually approximately eight to ten degrees cooler than the body core. Although man can survive body core cooling to 77° F. and heating to 108° F., the usual range for optimal physiological function is much narrower; 97°-104° F. Since the healthy individual stays within this range in the face of large fluctuations in heat production and environmental temperature, he is obviously in heat balance, i.e., heat produced equals heat lost. . . .

The homeostatic mechanisms of the body provide a considerable buffer against undue heat stress. For example, metabolic heat production during athletic events (especially track) may increase to values more than 30 times the Basal Metabolic Rate without ill effects. It is interesting to compare this turnover with the total body heat content. Normally the body of a sedentary individual in a comfortable environment contains approximately 2000 kcal (above 0° C.). A thirtyfold increase in metabolic rate would add 2100 kcal to the body in one hour; thus, a well-trained athlete can successfully tolerate a metabolic heat load which in one hour equals the total heat content (above 0° C.) of his body. This does not mean that he maintains heat balance during exercise; indeed, there occurs an actual storage of heat in the body, as evidenced by an increase in body temperature. However, sufficient heat is dissipated both during and after the exercise to prevent excessive rise in body temperature. Most of the heat is lost via evaporation of sweat. Sweat rates as high as 3880 grams per hour have been reported for short, severe bouts of exercise in hot environments. If completely evaporated and sustained for one hour this would extract 2250 kcal, or 32 × basal heat production.

Although the body can successfully tolerate large metabolic heat loads, the extent of its success depends on certain supporting physiological mechanisms. For example, the cardiovascular system, so important in exercise, is equally important in heat regulation. This system not only transports heat to the skin from which it is lost, but it also facilitates the sweating mechanism itself by supporting metabolism of the sweat glands and by providing adequate water for the formation of sweat. . . .

Disturbances of Heat Regulation

When the total heat load on the body exceeds the limit of thermoregulatory compensation, various incapacities occur. These fall into three major categories in order of ascending severity: heat cramps, heat exhaustion, and heat stroke.

The above three categories may overlap or follow each other in sequence. Heat cramps and exhaustion are not dangerous if recognized and if the individual ceases his activity. Heat stroke, fortunately a rare occurrence, can be fatal as a result of irreversible damage to the central nervous system. The average individual will "quit" when heat exhaustion sets in; the athlete who is highly motivated, may overextend himself physiologically during contests in hot weather, and thus expose himself to the danger of heat stroke. Top physical condition and prior acclimatization to heat (*vide infra*) reduces this risk. . . .

Heat and Exercise

When an individual is abruptly exposed to heat . . . [and] required to exercise moderately, e.g., walk at 4 mph, the body is confronted with a requirement to support the exercise. This involves vasodilatation in muscles. As a net result there is a relatively inadequate blood circulation through skin, muscle, and brain. The individual has to stop because of dizziness or faintness. For example, Bass *et al.* found pulse rates as high as 186 in men who walked for the first time at 4 mph at 120° F., 18 per cent R.H. [Relative Humidity], although the

TABLE 3.1

CLASSIFICATION OF DEBILITATING EFFECTS OF HEAT

Disorder	Cause	Symptoms	First Aid
Heat cramps	Excessive loss of salt in sweating.	Pain and muscle spasm; pupillary constriction with each spasm. Body temperature normal or below normal.	Rest. Administer salt and water.
Heat exhaustion	Cardiovascular inadequacy; dehydration.	Giddiness; headaches; fainting; rapid and weak pulse; vomiting; cold, pale, clammy skin; small rise in body temperature.	Rest in shade in recumbent position. Administer fluids.
Heat stroke	Failure of temperature regulatory center due to excessively high body temperature.	High body temperature; irritability; prostration, delirium; hot, dry, flushed skin. Sweating diminished or absent.	Alcohol spray bath or immersion in cold water. Medical emergency requiring physician.

same walk at 77° F. resulted in rates of 115-120. Exercise in the heat involves two stresses, each with a different requirement for blood flow. In an unacclimatized man, the heart cannot meet both demands adequately; as a result, to paraphrase a colloquialism, something must "give." Probably everything "gives" to a certain extent, but the well-known defense against shock—fainting—usually supervenes to halt what could be a dangerous situation. In other words, an unacclimatized man trying to do work in the heat suffers from incipient circulatory shock, qualitatively similar to what he would suffer if he had hemorrhaged.

In addition to and probably as a result of cardiovascular inadequacy, temperature regulation suffers appreciably, since impaired blood flow also means impaired heat transfer from the body core to the skin; hyperthermia becomes a distinct danger. As was pointed out earlier, well-motivated athletes who ignore warning signs of dizziness and faintness may actually become victims of heat stroke because of this vicious circle. A further complication is that the profuse sweat production during work in the heat, so necessary for evaporative cooling, poses the threat of dehydration. Because of its rapid secretion, sweat is formed largely at the expense of blood water, thus further exaggerating the inadequacy of the blood volume. All the initially distressful responses to exercise in the heat—high rectal and skin temperatures, high pulse rates, dizziness, nausea, etc.—are dramatically reduced by repeated daily exposures to work in the heat. This is the result of acclimatization to heat, a phenomenon of great importance to athletes. . . .

Acclimatization to Heat

In general, acclimatization to heat may be characterized by the following summary:

1. It begins with the first exposure, progresses rapidly, and is well developed in four-seven days.

2. It can be induced by short, intermittent exercise periods in the heat, e.g., two-four hours daily. Inactivity in the heat results in but slight acclimatization.

3. Subjects in good physical condition acclimatize more rapidly and are capable of more work in the heat. Tiptop physical condition does not confer "automatic" acclimatization.

4. The ability to perform "maximal" work in the heat is attained quickly by progressively increasing the daily work load. Strenuous exertion on first exposure may result in disability that will impair performance for several days. Care should be taken to stay within the "capacity" of the athlete until acclimatization is well advanced.

5. Acclimatization to severe conditions will facilitate performance at lesser conditions.

6. The general pattern of acclimatization is the same for short, severe exertion as for moderate work of longer duration.

7. Acclimatization to hot-dry climates increases performance ability in hot, wet climates and vice versa.

8. Inadequate water and salt replacement can retard the acclimatization process.

9. Acclimatization to heat is well retained during periods of no exposure for about two weeks; thereafter it is lost at a rate that varies among individuals. Most people lose a major portion of acclimatization in two months. Those who stay in good physical condition retain their acclimatization best.

10. If it is desirable to retain acclimatization, periodic exposures at two-week intervals would be best. . . .

It is of the utmost importance to realize that a well-conditioned athlete who has trained entirely in cool climates is relatively unconditioned if forced to perform in the heat.

In the 1956 Olympic Games, the marathon was run in humid 85° F. air. It was not surprising to hear that the race was won by a French Algerian (Alain Mimoun) who routinely trained in the heat. At the start of the Olympic Marathon, one of our own marathoners, Dean Thackery, reported that Emil Zatopek, the famed long distance runner, summarized his chances in light of the weather with the resigned statement, "Today we die!" . . . Although reliable statistics are not available, it appears that weather frequently benefits the prepared and severely handicaps those who are not. . . .

Dehydration, Water, and Salt

Dehydration should be considered a potential source of debilitation in any events where considerable body sweat is elaborated. Football and basketball players may lose from 3 to 7 per cent of their body weight during the course of a contest. In this situation, larger proportionate loss is sustained by the plasma volume than by other compartments of body fluid. Because of this unequal loss, circulation to working muscle and to the skin is curtailed, which in turn leads to deterioration in performance. It would seem wise, in the absence of contradictory information, to replace body fluid losses at least to the extent of limiting dehydration to no more than 2 to 3 per cent of body weight.[3]

Salt is lost in relatively large amounts in sweat, hence, the individual daily requirement may be increased by 5 to 10 grams under conditions where large amounts of sweat are lost per day. Usually an extra requirement can be met by a few hearty shakes of salt with each meal. The use of enteric coated salt tablets will serve the same purpose, but cases of gastrointestinal upset frequently occur, because concentrated salt irritates the mucosa lining of the gastrointestinal tract. Cachets or salt-containing dough balls (unleavened bread) have been used with some success for experimental purposes. Salt solutions of 0.1-0.2 per cent concentration may also be used. Certain athletes prefer to use bouillon (Oxo) preparations. Although any of the above will provide the necessary extra salt, it is the experience of most investigators that there is no better method of obtaining salt than by merely salting one's food liberally.

---

[3] W. S. S. Ladell, "The Effects of Water and Salt Intake upon the Performance of Men Working in Hot and Humid Environments," *Journal of Physiology*, CXXVII (1955), 11-46.

Individual Differences

A certain number of individuals can be labeled as heat-intolerant. In terms of heat acclimatization, this means that these people will not readily acclimatize to heat or will only partially acclimatize after numerous exposures. Malfunction of the sweating mechanism or thermoregulatory centers is usually associated with heat intolerance. Fortunately, the number of people who are heat intolerant is only of the order of 1 per cent. Of the "normal" 99 per cent, a considerable range in tolerance exists, which is dependent on physical conditioning, body size, build, and composition. . . .

Heat-Stress Indices

The physical components of heat stress have been examined extensively by physicists, physiologists, and psychologists, and in many instances the magnitude of the environmental heat load in terms of expected physiological strain can be determined. Thus far two approaches have been taken in formulating a "heat-strain index"; (1) on the basis of the environment alone, and (2) on the basis of the man-environment interaction.

In athletics it is more desirable to talk about the latter, since the metabolic rate in most competitive athletics is high and therefore a major consideration in any heat-stress index. . . .

In 1947, McArdle et al.[4] formulated a Sweat Rate Index which has been used mainly by British physiologists, who have demonstrated its superiority to previous indices over a wide range of heat stresses. In essence, this index is a prediction of sweat rate from ambient weather information plus the metabolic rate of the man. It has been found that predicted four-hour sweat rate agrees well with actual sweat rate at least under laboratory conditions. Although this index was formulated from empirical data, it does have the advantage of indicating stress in physiological terms, but has the disadvantage in that it applies only to work loads that are much less than those experienced in most competitive athletics.

Recently, attempts have been made to predict physiological heat load of the working man in a given environment from theoretical consideration. Woodcock[5] devised a theoretical model based on physical laws, which shows promise in esti-

[4] B. McArdle, W. Dunham, H. E. Halling, W. S. S. Ladell, J. W. Scott, M. L. Thomson, and J. S. Weiner, "The Prediction of the Physiological Effects of Warm and Hot Environments," *Med. Res. Cncl R.N.P.*, XLVII (1947), 391.

[5] A. H. Woodcock, R. L. Pratt, and J. R. Breckenridge, "A Theoretical Method for Assessing Heat Exchange between Man and a Hot Environment," *EPD Rept. No. 183*, QM Climatic Research Laboratory, 1952.

mating total heat stress. Lee has formulated mathematical equations for predicting the thermal strain over a wide range of hot environments. Lee's equations take into account all variables of the environment except radiation, and include the effect of metabolism. Belding and Hatch[6] have produced a nomogram for securing a Heat Strain Index (HST). Radiation, as measured by a black globe thermometer, is included in this index. Blockley *et al.*[7] have undertaken the most comprehensive analysis of heat stress and have termed it a biothermal analysis system. Their data in terms of time tolerance curves may become extremely useful. Although these theories require the experimental validation which is currently in progress, they represent an important avenue of approach to the heat stress problem. The original sources should be consulted for a further discussion of these indices.

Although the various indices differ in approach, they tend to give similar answers to the question, "How long can a man work at a given rate in a given environment?"

Table 3.2 has been prepared as a rough guide for heat tolerance in composite form from the indices referred to above. These limits should be regarded as approximations for a well-conditioned, heat-acclimatized runner. The runner is working at a rate of 1080 kcal/hr at a work efficiency of 15 per cent for one hour. Radiation is assumed negligible and the effective air movement is 10 mph. Clothing consists of shorts and track shoes.

The approximate limits listed would be altered by individual differences in body composition. Changes in air movement, effective radiation, clothing, etc., would also alter the estimated limits of tolerance.

Table 3.2 emphasizes the important role of the absolute humidity in limiting performance. When the vapor pressure of the environment is close to that of the skin (42 mm Hg), evaporative heat loss is drastically curtailed unless air movement is exceptionally high. Thus wet-bulb temperature as a single parameter may be particularly indicative of the thermal strain imposed by the environment providing the radiant load is low. Wet bulbs over 70° F. should be viewed as close to the tolerance limit for a competitive athletic event involving severe work. Wet bulbs of 80° to 82° F. will indicate tolerance limits for most athletic activities with the possible exception of the relatively inactive sports such as baseball.

---

[6] H. S. Belding and T. F. Hatch, "Index for Evaluating Heat Stress in Terms of Resulting Physiological Strains," *Htng, Piping, and Air Cndting*, August 1955, p. 129.

[7] W. V. Blockley, J. W. McCutchen, J. Lyman, and C. L. Taylor, "Human Tolerance for High Temperature Aircraft Environments," *J. Aviat. Med.*, XXV (1954), 515.

TABLE 3.2

APPROXIMATE LIMITING CONDITIONS FOR A WELL-CONDITIONED, HEAT-
ACCLIMATIZED ATHLETE PERFORMING ONE HOUR OF SUSTAINED RUNNING

Dry Bulb	Wet Bulb	Relative Humidity	Vapor Pressure
° F.	° F.	%	mm Hg
82	82	100	27
83	80	76	25
90	77	55	20
92	73	37	15
96	69	25	11

Dry Bulb (D.B.). Temperature recorded by an ordinary mercury-in-glass thermometer whose bulb is kept dry.

Wet Bulb (W.B.). Temperature recorded by a similar thermometer with a wet wick over the bulb exposed to a current of air moving at least 1000 feet/minute. When D.B. = W.B., the air is said to be saturated and the relative humidity equals 100 per cent.

Relative Humidity. The ratio, expressed as per cent, of the amount of water vapor in the air to the amount that the air could hold at the same temperature if saturated, times 100.

Vapor Pressure. The pressure of a confined vapor that has accumulated above its liquid: it is determined by the nature of the liquid and the temperature.

Higher Altitudes and Endurance Running

Occasionally it becomes necessary for men to compete at altitudes that are several thousand feet higher than those where they normally train. This occurred at the Pan-American Games in 1955 at Mexico City (altitude—approximately 7200 feet) and at the national meets held at Boulder, Colorado, 1957 (altitude—5280 feet) and Salt Lake City, Utah, 1947 (altitude—4390 feet). In all three instances, concensus was reached on these two conclusions: (1) There was little or no noticeable negative effect in races at 880 yards or less, or in field events, but there were marked decreases in performances at distances above one mile. For example, at Mexico City, Wes Santee, who had a best 1500-meter time of 3:45.3 that year, took second place with 3:53.2, and Fred Dwyer, with a best time that year of 3:48.2, took third place with 3:55.8. In the 3000-meter steeplechase, the 1952 Olympic champion, Horace Ashenfelter, who had a best time in the two mile in 1955 of 8:49.6, was able to take only ninth place (no time taken). (2) Individuals vary greatly in their reactions to increased altitudes. Men of apparently similar abilities and physical condition perform very differently. It is reasonable to assume that part of these differences are psychological in nature, but undoubtedly there are also physical differences, just as occur under conditions of high heat and humidity.

No research studies have been reported that deal directly with the problems of distance runners at high altitudes. But Bruno Balke, physiologist at the School of Aviation Medicine, Randolph Air Force Base, Texas, has presented the following conclusions for such runners, based on his research for the Air Force:

There is an important difference in the adaptive state of the blood at a given altitude between chronically and temporarily acclimatized man. . . . Complete acclimatization of the blood is rarely achieved by "newcomers" and is a matter of many years. It was shown, however, by Luft in observations of climbers in the Himalayan mountains that the sea-level values of oxyhemoglobin were regained for any given altitude when the climbers had spent several days [He seems to mean 2-3 weeks. See below—J.K.D.] at altitudes approximately 3000 to 5000 feet higher. Thus complete adaptation of the blood was obtained for an altitude of 10,000 feet after approximately 2 weeks at 13,500 feet, for 14,000 feet after a further 2 to 3 weeks at 19,000 feet, for 17,000 feet after 3 to 4 more weeks at 22,000 feet, and finally, to 19,000 feet after a further stay of 2 weeks at an altitude of 22,000 feet. . . .

All activities which consist of extended or intermittent bursts of muscular efforts over periods longer than about one minute are affected by higher altitudes because of the compensatory demands upon the circulatory and respiratory functions. An adequate period of acclimatization to altitude would become necessary to restore the "normal" performance capacity. As a rule of thumb, a minimal time of one week is required for acclimatizing to an increase of altitude in the order of 3000 feet. If an adequate time for the training at altitude is not permissible, the stay at altitude before the competitive event should be made as short as possible. Soon after the arrival at higher altitude the blood will undergo acid-base changes which will seriously interfere with maximal performance.[8]

We must keep in mind that these conclusions, though scientifically accurate for the conditions studied, do not carry over completely and adequately for the precisely measured conditions of competitive running. A difference of but one second during a four-minute or even a 30-minute race can determine success or failure; to lose a race by only one foot is still to lose. In other words, if we must compete at altitudes some 3000 to 5000 feet higher than normal for us, we must allow an appreciably longer time than would be needed by alpine climbers for what they would consider "complete acclimitization."

Further, though Luft's method of training at altitudes some 3000 to 5000 feet higher than the required altitude seems to hold excellent possibilities, it would be difficult from a practical standpoint to find satisfactory conditions for running, and living, at such altitudes. If we

---

[8] Bruno Balke, "Work Capacity at Altitude," *Science and Medicine of Exercise and Sports*, Warren R. Johnson, ed. (New York: Harper & Row, Publishers, 1960), pp. 339-47.

planned to race at Boulder, Colorado, we might well train at Mexico City. But where would we train if we wanted to race at Mexico City? Apart from such practical questions, the methods and time requirements of training for running at higher altitudes seem to be reasonably well defined.

Nutrition for Endurance Running

It is not within the scope of this book to provide a detailed discussion of proper nutrition for endurance running. But neither are we justified in ignoring the problem altogether when we consider the very strong tendency toward food faddism that exists not only among coaches but also among the pseudoscientists that manage to get their ill-founded conclusions into coaching literature.

Perhaps it all goes back to our common desire to find some easier way to achievement. Physically, one of the basic goals of training is to produce certain chemical changes within our system which will prevent or postpone fatigue impairments. Surely, there must be some easier way to produce these same chemical changes, with less training, by using what Peter Karpovich calls "ergogenic aids" in the various forms of alkalies, vitamins, hormones, phosphates, and all the various special kinds of foods and drugs.

True, there are certain foundations for such a search. Roger J. Williams has made a strong case for his statements that

(1) each human individual has quantitatively a distinctive pattern of nutritional needs, (2) from individual to individual, specific needs may vary severalfold, (3) important deficiencies may exist which have not been discoverable clinically by observing acute outward symptoms, [and (4) these deficiencies "confuse" the wisdom of the body to choose its food wisely.] [9]

Of course, the so-called "wisdom of the body" to choose the right amounts of ‛ e right kinds of food, regardless of any intellectual knowledge of proper nutrition, is normal and therefore possessed by about 95 per cent of us. Such nutritionally normal people will do well on any "well-balanced" diet. But the special needs and deficiencies of the remaining 5 per cent disturb us all with the thought that we may be one of them. After all, Williams did say that these deficiencies are not always discoverable, even clinically. Perhaps we'd better make sure by taking in extras of this or that.

In addition, endurance runners tend to assume that their training makes extreme demands in specific ways upon the nutritional needs of the body, and that the percentage of the nutritionally normal may be

[9] Roger J. Williams, *Biochemical Individuality* (New York: John Wiley & Sons, Inc., 1956), p. 162.

reduced from 95 to 90, or even less. Nutritional deficiencies that would go unnoticed when sedentary might seriously impair maximal performance in running.

Keeping these exceptions in mind, we can still conclude validly that those who have spent their lives in study and research in nutrition are probably best qualified to advise athletes what kinds and amounts of foods should be in their daily diets, and what effects nutritional supplements will have upon performance. True, such research is done primarily with nonhumans or with humans under conditions of normal stress and activity. But the needs of the armed services and of space medicine have greatly stepped up research on nutrition under stress conditions and its conclusions are valid for endurance running.

Unfortunately, the income from advertising influences our magazines to print articles on nutrition and special food supplements by those who have little, beyond enthusiasm and desire for recognition and profit, to support their views. The campaigns for gelatin, for honey, for royal jelly, for apple juice, and recently, for wheat-germ oil are all examples of this.

There are of course historical precedents for such faddism. Written records state that men have swallowed powdered lion's teeth to make them grow strong and lion's heart to give them courage. The fad for extra meat proteins to replace the losses in severe muscular work has been traced back to the Greeks in the fifth century B.C. A recent best seller, *Folk Medicine,* cites the "research" by Lloyd Percival at Sports College in Toronto, showing that "athletes participating in endurance tests showed better performance levels when fed two tablespoonfuls of honey 30 minutes before the test began. Whenever honey feeding was withdrawn, there was a definite decrease in work levels accomplished." We must assume that such conclusions are based upon three sources: (1) "the recorded use of honey from cave-dwelling days," (2) the desire of the researchers to find what they were looking for, and (3) the mental conditioning of the subjects in favor of the special values of honey.

All research workers, no matter how narrowly "physical" their work, agree that mental conditioning does affect performance. For example, Van Itallie and his co-workers state that

awareness on the part of the athlete of having regularly consumed an appetizing diet of wholesome foods at the training table is one of the factors that can have a favorable effect on his morale. A pre-event supplement or meal taken in the belief that it will provide extra energy and thereby enhance performance also may have a beneficial psychological effect.[10]

---

[10] Theodore Van Itallie, Leonardo Sinisterra, and Frederick J. Stare, "Nutrition and Athletic Performance," *Journal of the American Medical Association,* CLXII (November 17, 1956), 1125.

All agree with this statement, but most tend, as we have done, to use it to belittle the argument in favor of training table and special foods. They brush their importance aside as being "merely mental." The fact remains that the athlete and the coach are interested in improving performance—period! Whether such improvement comes by physical or mental or you-name-it means is of little concern. What works, works! Whatever improves performance is worthwhile even though the reasons given for its effectiveness are invalid. If a runner takes a swig of honey prior to a half-mile race in the belief that it has special qualities, and therefore runs better, he cares little whether the aid was chemical and therefore "actual," or mental-emotional and therefore a "delusion."

Further, it can validly be argued that even though of mental origin, it is no "delusion," for psychosomatic medicine has long proved its case that mental-emotional attitudes can bring about chemical and physical changes in the body, both directly and indirectly by "tuning-up" the engine. Steinhaus reports that

the recent findings of two Czechoslovakian workers (E. Gutmann and B. Jakoubek) have shown that the mere placing of rats in the location where they were trained to run, resulted in rises in blood sugar and liver glycogen. This recalls that in 1939 T. Petren of Sweden reported that liver glycogen in guinea pigs regularly rose at the hour when the animals were customarily exercised whereas at other hours it was never higher than in controls.[11]

Here we have cases where "mental" conditioning and no food at all produce chemical changes. However, having said so much in favor of what works even though it be a "delusion," we must add that what works, works even better if it is based upon the truth. To falsify times in a time trial has improved performance time and again, but it has also, time and again, destroyed the trust of the runner in the coach, and that's even more important in the long run. So, a falsehood discovered that relates to nutrition can be equally destructive of faith and respect. A sound coach would be wiser to let the "magical" power of the food lie in its good balance and completeness, rather than in its special ergogenic powers.

To support this reliance upon accepted authorities in nutrition, I shall quote primarily from research studies by such well-known nutritionists as Theodore Van Itallie, Edward D. O'Donnell, and Jean Mayer. These studies are based upon and related directly to the problem of athletics.

Van Itallie [12] remarks that Keys, one of the most respected researchers in this field, "has listed three ways in which special dietaries might influence muscular performance. These involve (1) renewing the supply

---

[11] Steinhaus, *op. cit.*, p. 103.
[12] Van Itallie *et al.*, *op. cit.*, 1122.

of energy-yielding nutrients, (2) facilitating the energy-yielding reactions, and (3) counteracting physical-chemical changes in the body identified with fatigue." Van Itallie then adds, "A fourth way . . . is by reducing any appreciable excess in fat content of the body. Such a decrease in adiposity will result in a proportional decrease in the energy cost of moving the body or its parts." (We have already suggested a fifth way, the nonphysical way of effecting physical reactions, that of producing a beneficial psychological effect. This is implied but not specifically stated in Keys's three points.)

With no known exceptions, serious research workers in nutrition agree that the means for achieving these five methods lie in a varied and well-balanced diet, tastefully prepared and presented at regular meals throughout the life of the person. The energy that is used in endurance running short of six miles or so is supplied to the body over a length of time, not merely in the meal or two before the stress period. Actually, the physical values of the pre-event meal have been greatly exaggerated.

Morehouse states that

the body acts as a homeostatic [same state] mechanism to maintain a constant internal environment during the demands of the competition. As the food passes through the alimentary tract the body is able to select the nutritive components it needs for operation and repair. In some instances when certain elements are lacking in the diet a protective mechanism is triggered off which apparently exerts an influence on the choice of food to meet these needs. The organism has the power to manufacture some of the required nutrient substances from materials in the body if these substances are not provided in the diet.[13]

However, we hardly need add that such "feeding upon oneself" is not a satisfactory way for endurance running.

Psychological Factors

In view of the importance of psychological factors in modifying physical performance, it would be unwise and unjustified to deprecate the psychological value of food, and of the ritual of the training table for the well-being of the athlete.[14]

The food we eat, therefore, influences to a considerable degree, perhaps even more than we realize, our response to emotional factors; and these factors, in turn, must surely have an effect on our nutritional requirements.[15]

If an athlete *thinks* that a certain easily digested food—such as an orange,

---

[13] Laurence E. Morehouse and Philip J. Rasch, *Sports Medicine for Trainers* (Philadelphia: W. B. Saunders Company, 1963), p. 56.

[14] Van Itallie *et al., op. cit.,* 1121.

[15] Edward D. O'Donnell and William A. Krehl, "Diet and the Athlete," *Scholastic Coach,* October 1959, p. 36.

some honey, or a little candy—helps him, it may be well to permit its use, provided it is not eaten too soon before competition. These substances will almost certainly do no harm and may help to keep a competitor in a happy frame of mind.[16] [Italics mine—J.K.D.]

Well-balanced Diet

With all the scientific advancements in nutrition, we now know that these concepts [that special foods provide extra benefits] are essentially false: that the growth, development, well-being, and function of the body depend not on any specific food substance, but on a well-balanced diet which provides all the essentials needed for the various body processes.[17]

There's no uniformity among coaches or dieticians as to what to feed an athlete. This conclusion was reached after an analysis of the actual menus being used by many colleges. Most of the practices seemed to be based upon the coach's particular likes and dislikes.[18]

Supplementation of an adequate diet has not given clearly positive results. . . . It is probable that hard muscular exercise does increase the need for some of the B complex vitamins, but in a balanced diet such increased needs should be met by the increase in food intake secondary to intense exercise.[19]

Number of Meals

In general, it appears that athletes should not eat less than three meals a day. When the sports practiced are particularly protracted and exhausting (such as distance running), up to five lighter meals may be a preferable pattern.[20]

Training Table

Certainly there is no *nutritional* justification for training tables at present. The normal fare of schools and colleges should be wholesome and adequate for all students. Extra needs of athletes can be taken care of by second and third portions and increased bread consumption.[21]

Add to this our earlier comments and those of Van Itallie on the psychological values of training table.

Pre-competition Meal

From the viewpoint of digestion, it makes sense that the last meal preceding an athletic contest should be eaten three hours or so prior to the event. This eliminates the drain on the circulatory system coincidental with active absorp-

---

[16] Warren J. Johnson, "How Good Are Pre-competition Super-foods," *The Athletic Journal,* February 1953, p. 54.

[17] O'Donnell and Krehl, *op. cit.,* p. 36.

[18] *Ibid.,* p. 38.

[19] Jean Mayer and Beverly Bullen, "Nutrition and Athletic Performance," *Postgraduate Medicine,* XXVI (December 1959), 855.

[20] *Ibid.*

[21] *Ibid.*

tion. Conversely, emotions or nervousness felt by the performer prior to entering the contest is less likely to interfere with digestive processes if this last meal is eaten well in advance. (The care and speed with which a small sugar supplement is digested exempts it from such restrictions.) [22]

The chief consideration . . . is the emotional stress that the athlete may experience on the day of the contest. . . . In most cases, the pre-event meal should be consumed not less than three hours before the contest. Individual food preferences should be respected. The athlete knows from experience which foods can be eaten without causing him discomfort. As a general rule, only foods known to be highly digestible should be consumed as part of the pre-event meal.[23]

Calories and Body Weight

Ordinarily, the athlete will spontaneously ingest food in amounts adequate to maintain his weight. Many "overweight" athletes are not actually obese and, for that reason, more informative measurements than those of body weight and stature should be made when the athlete's caloric status is being assessed. Although there is considerable doubt whether manipulation of an adequate diet can enhance performance, there is no doubt whatsoever that performance can be significantly impaired when a less than adequate diet is consumed. The best diet for the athlete is one he enjoys and one that, at the same time, provides a variety of nutritious foods in amounts adequate to maintain his weight at an optimal level.[24]

The athlete's energy requirement may be as much as 100 per cent above that needed by a moderately sedentary individual.[25]

Protein Intake

The importance of meat as a constituent of the diet of athletes has been much debated, but it would appear that an excess of meat at the training table probably has more psychological than physiological value. The requirement for protein is not significantly increased when exercise is performed, unless at the same time an increase in muscle mass is taking place.[26] [As occurs in intensive strength-training, but not in endurance training—J.K.D.]

Wide variations of protein intake do not seem to influence performance. A well-balanced diet easily meets needs for maintenance and whatever muscle growth may take place. Large amounts of meat several times a day are unnecessary.[27]

Historically speaking, protein has always been the chief dietary component of the hard-working individual. . . . Generally speaking, the protein in the diet should be equivalent to about 10 to 15 per cent of the total calories, remembering that protein provides four net calories per gram of protein ingested. . . . It's important to consider the type of protein that is fed. Generally

[22] *Ibid.,* 849.
[23] Van Itallie *et al., op. cit.,* 1125.
[24] *Ibid.*
[25] O'Donnell and Krehl, *op. cit.,* p. 38.
[26] Van Itallie *et al., op. cit.,* 1123.
[27] Mayer and Bullen, *op. cit.,* 855.

speaking, the proteins of animal origin, such as meat, milk, eggs, fish, and cheese, are considered to be the high quality proteins, whereas the proteins of vegetables or cereal sources are considered to be inferior in protein quality.[28]

Keep in mind that these animal proteins are combined with fats, generally considered to be a less desirable source of calories for endurance running.

It is a common experience that an abnormally heavy intake of protein produces an acid residue that must be excreted by the kidneys, a source of irritation and inconvenience during endurance running.

Carbohydrate Intake

In prolonged physical activity, a definite correlation can be observed between symptoms of fatigue and a decrease in blood sugar level. When glucose is administered under these circumstances, the symptoms disappear and the power to work is increased. Christensen and his associates believe that the beneficial effect of administered glucose is a neurophysiological phenomenon and not due to a direct metabolic effect on muscle.[29]

Christensen and Hansen found that a subject could continue strenuous work three times as long on a high carbohydrate diet as on a high fat diet.[30]

Christensen and others believe that, in the last few days before an athletic contest, heavy work should be avoided to allow for maximal filling of carbohydrate stores. However, more experimental work is needed before it can be stated with assurance that this belief is well founded.[31]

After reviewing the literature up to 1942 on the subject of the effect on efficiency of diets high in carbohydrate or fat, Gemmill concluded that muscular efficiency is practically the same on all diets. He states that there is a slight increase in efficiency after a high-carbohydrate diet, which probably does not exceed 5 per cent.[32]

There is . . . evidence showing that in sports requiring endurance and prolonged muscular work, performance is better maintained on a high carbohydrate diet than on a high fat diet (these are meant as the usual diet that is consumed for several days before an athletic event). In such cases, even the slight increase in efficiency with a high carbohydrate diet may well prove decisive. (The minimal figure of 5 per cent has been indicated by many investigators.) [33]

What of sugar, approbated as a readily available source of energy to be taken before a contest? It is conceivable that in a very protracted effort [Normally this assumes distances beyond six miles—J.K.D.] the reservoirs might be exhausted and hypoglycemia occur. But that a special sort of explosive material can be advantageously applied for a maximum effort I do not believe. It is perfectly true that I have given sugar with results that encourage the men to

[28] O'Donnell and Krehl, *op. cit.*, p. 38.
[29] Van Itallie *et al.*, *op. cit.*, 1123.
[30] Mayer and Bullen, *op. cit.*, 850.
[31] Van Itallie *et al.*, *op. cit.*, 1123.
[32] *Ibid.*
[33] Mayer and Bullen, *op. cit.*, 855.

accord no little credit to its service. But the highly strung athlete is so suggest-ible that he will be powerfully influenced by anybody in whom he has con-fidence, in which case it is immaterial what he is given. I have been convinced of this psychological element with substances simpler than sugar and sometimes quite inert.[34]

Fat Intake

In the diet of athletes (as in general), fat, at the metabolic level, acts as an indifferent source of energy. Beyond this it makes no special contribution to muscular performance.[35]

Alkaline Reserves

Keys has concluded tentatively that such changes in the alkaline reserve that may be effected by dietary manipulation will have little influence on the ability of the normal person to perform muscular work.[36]

The evidence of this and related studies seems to indicate that young men in excellent physical condition who have the benefits of a well-balanced diet are provided by nature with whatever emergency fuel and physiological balances are needed for competitive endurance performance. As ordinarily used, the blood alkinizers (including citrus fruit juices) and sugar (including candy and ordinary table sugar) are very likely neither beneficial nor detrimental in meeting the bodily demands for participation in our athletic sports events.[37]

Vitamin Intake

In his review, Keys states that he has been unable to find convincing evidence that supplements of the B complex or vitamins C or E, separately or in com-bination, would enhance the physical performance of apparently well-nourished persons. . . . There is very little evidence to suggest that the requirement for vitamins is appreciably increased during prolonged muscular work. At best, the requirement for certain vitamins may increase in direct arithmetic proportion to the increase in expenditure of energy. In spite of occasional reports of apparently beneficial effects of vitamin supplementation upon athletic per-formance, it remains to be demonstrated convincingly that supplementation of the diet of the athlete in training with vitamins of any sort has a beneficial effect on endurance, muscular efficiency, or coordination.[38]

Fluid Intake

The body requires a constant supply of water. It is utilized in all body processes, including the regulation of temperature by sweating.

---

[34] Sir Adolphe Abrahams, *The Human Machine* (Baltimore: Penguin Books, Inc., 1956), p. 126.
[35] Van Itallie *et al., op. cit.,* 1123.
[36] *Ibid.,* 1124.
[37] Johnson, *op. cit.,* p. 54.
[38] Van Itallie *et al., op. cit.,* 1124.

Excessive sweating during conditions of high heat-humidity works in several ways to speed up the onset of exhaustion, and of course can result in what is commonly called "heat exhaustion" or even "heat stroke." Endurance runners have learned to replace this fluid loss by drinking fluids (water, fruit juices, tea) at intervals during the exercise.

While milk isn't a dietary essential, if the diet is otherwise adequate, it's pretty difficult to assure an adequate supply of certain mineral elements without ingesting milk. The element of most concern here is calcium.[39]

Salt Intake

Keys and associates have found that work capacity in heat is markedly reduced when salt is severely restricted, even when this does not involve heat cramps or heat hyperpyrexia. At least 2 to 3 gms. of sodium chloride must be replaced per liter of sweat lost. Salt tablets may be upsetting to the digestive tract, and many physicians have found a weak solution of sodium chloride to be better tolerated by the individual deficient in salt.[40]

When large amounts of water are lost by sweating, there is also a loss of body salts. The salt loss in activity is especially marked in untrained athletes. [See page 35 for further discussion of this point—J.K.D.] If the salt deficit is not made up in the diet, retention of water in the body is diminished, and dehydration occurs. Dehydration lowers athletic efficiency by reducing the blood volume and causing muscle weakness and cramps. When the athlete performs in hot environments, water and salt should be replaced hourly.[41]

In this marathon training period, it becomes essential for the runner to take liberal quantities of salt with his meals. If he feels fatigued [Lydiard uses this word in the sense of exhausted—J.K.D.] when he comes in from a long run, we at once give him a saline drink with glucose, preferably mixed with a little cordial—not fruit juice—to counter any tendency of the stomach to throw the salt right out again.[42]

The following sample diet for athletes has been added for the purpose of tying the above ideas together. However, this is done with definite reservations. Its value lies primarily in suggesting the variety and the breadth of a well-balanced diet. But social customs as to diet vary so much from area to area and country to country that the specific foods and their distribution among breakfast, luncheon, dinner or breakfast, brunch, tea, and dinner could be greatly changed and still maintain a varied and well-balanced food intake.

---

[39] O'Donnell and Krehl, *op. cit.*, p. 38.

[40] Van Itallie *et al.*, *op. cit.*, 1125.

[41] Morehouse and Rasch, *op. cit.*, p. 67.

[42] Arthur Lydiard and Garth Gilmour, *Run to the Top* (London: Herbert Jenkins, Ltd., 1962; New Zealand: A. H. & A. W. Reed, 1962), p. 72.

TABLE 3.3

SAMPLE DAILY MENUS FOR ATHLETES [43]

	Breakfast	Luncheon	Dinner
I.	One-half grapefruit	Vegetable soup	Soup with meat stock
	Oatmeal	Lamb chops	Baked fish
	Crisp bacon	Baked potatoes	Mashed potatoes
	Eggs	Tomatoes	Baked yellow squash
	Sweet rolls	Bread	Cottage cheese and peach salad
	Milk or cocoa	Milk or tea	Bread
		Pudding	Beverage
			Ice cream and cake
II.	Baked apple	Chicken noodle soup	Soup with meat stock
	Corn flakes	Creamed tuna	Roast beef
	Crisp bacon	Scalloped potatoes	Baked potatoes
	Eggs	Bread	Lima beans
	Toast	Milk or tea	Celery and apple salad
	Marmalade	Fruit	Bread
	Milk or cocoa		Custard
III.	Orange juice	Tomato soup	Soup with meat stock
	Cooked wheat cereal	Beef stew	Roast chicken
	Crisp bacon	Lettuce salad	Candied sweet potatoes
	Eggs	Bread	Peas
	Sweet rolls	Milk or tea	Sliced tomato salad
	Milk or cocoa	Cake	Bread
			Pudding
IV.	Tomato juice	Celery soup	Soup with meat stock
	Rice flakes	Macaroni and cheese	Steak
	Crisp bacon	Carrot strips	Browned potatoes
	Eggs	Bread	Asparagus
	Toast	Milk or tea	Lettuce salad
	Jam or jelly	Custard	Bread
	Milk or cocoa		Fruit

---

[43] Morehouse and Rasch, *op. cit.,* p. 69.

4 Holism in Endurance Running

Holism, as it relates to endurance running, is basically a simple idea. It seeks to understand and use all the positive factors and influences that help a man become a better runner, and at the same time, to eliminate or restrict all the negative factors that might detract from his ability or stop him from running. It is as simple—and as complex—as that.

These factors have already been discussed in Chapter 2 and do not need to be repeated at length. But to summarize, some are environmental: national and group attitudes, physical climate and terrain, economic and educational pressures, etc.; others are personal: over-concern for possible harm from overtraining, physical susceptibility to the stresses of training and competition, or general emotional instability.

Holistic training for endurance running, then, is concerned with all aspects of a man's life that relate to running. Some will protest that no training system could be effective on such a broad front; but when

Some of the material in this chapter is from J. Kenneth Doherty, *Modern Track and Field* (2nd ed.; Englewood Cliffs, N. J.: Prentice-Hall, Inc., 1963), pp. 158-66. Reprinted by permission of the publisher.

a man tries to concentrate his energies upon doing one thing well, there are few attitudes or activities that are unrelated. How and when he sleeps, what and how much he eats, how much stress he experiences from his academic work or from his vocation, how much he worries about money matters, his girl friend, or his wife, how much he feels involved in the cold war with Communism or in desegregation battles in his home town—all these are related to his running.

Should a coach or a training system really attempt to control all these factors when many of them are clearly uncontrollable? Obviously not. There is a little prayer in point which asks for the wisdom to distinguish between the things one can and cannot do something about, for the fortitude to do something worthwhile about the first, and for the peace of mind to endure patiently the second. However, the things related to endurance running about which a coach can do something worthwhile are far more numerous and widespread than most coaches admit.

Further, and this is my main point, these widespread problems should be considered as important in the training system as the problems of mileage and intensity of running. Once accepted as such, they tend to become better understood, better planned, and better executed. I realize, coach, that you are disappointed, that you expected something new and different from this holistic view of training, and that it has suggested only what you have been doing for years. You've been getting board jobs, selecting courses, establishing better public relations, improving the track team's image in faculty minds, curbing the girl friends, playing nursemaid to kids that don't want to grow up, and 101 other trivia. But these matters are usually considered irritating extras, chores beyond the assignments of duty or salary. Naturally they are usually dealt with at the last moment as emergencies, after they are sufficiently serious to be noticeable and complained about. How much easier would be a planned program of prevention.

In introducing a research study on "Some Factors Modifying the Expression of Human Strength," from which they concluded that psychologic rather than physiologic factors determine the limits of performance, Ikai and Steinhaus made these significant comments:

Changes in the central nervous system may be brought on by factors that modify the physicochemical state of neurons and synapses such as oxygen tension, hormones, pharmacologic agents, and temperature changes. Collectively, these may be designated neurologic and physiologic factors. [These have been the main concern of past training systems.—J.K.D.]

The activity of nerve centers and their influence on activity is further determined and modified by the racial history and individual experience of the organism. Individual experiences account in large measure for differences in action between persons and for differences in action of the same person from moment to moment and from day to day.

Although this behavior is always influenced by physicochemical factors already mentioned, its individual character is primarily the result of environmentally induced experiences that include every impact with the animate and inanimate world, including experiences with parents, teachers, and peers.[1] [This is the basic viewpoint of holistic training—J.K.D.]

If such conclusions can be reached in regard to strength, how much more they must be true in regard to the prolonged expressions of endurance.

Contemporary endurance training systems are confined to the hours and problems of running. But even within this narrow scope, they differ greatly in their attitude toward the runner. For example, at one extreme they view him as a running machine, as in a restricted form of interval training that follows an unvarying pattern of distance-slow pace-terrain-recovery interval, with an increasing number of runs as the only variable. At the other extreme would be a kind of fartlek in which freedom and variation would be almost unlimited: terrains of different kinds and challenges, freedom to run where and what and with whom the runner may prefer. But even such a free and flexible system would probably be restricted to the athlete's problems as a runner, and to the hours of running, despite the fact that every experienced coach knows that a runner's success depends primarily upon factors that lie outside the running hours and running problems. It is unlikely that a single distance champion of the past twenty years stopped running because of the limitations of his training system or because he had reached his maximum level of achievement. In every instance, the causes of limited or stopped performance were to be found in the hindrances and distractions outside of training and in the champion's opposing life interests and goals.

Consider the five men who held the world mile record between 1954 and 1963: Bannister, Landy, Ibbotson, Elliott, and Snell. The first four retired at an average age of 24, too young for full running maturity, and after an average of only four years of high-level competition, too few for perfection in tactics or self-control or for competitive staleness. They each retired for two reasons: on the one hand, they found they had attained their goal in running and no longer found the challenge worth its cost; on the other, they had discovered that other concerns were of greater importance.

I agree fully that retirement was probably justified in these cases.

---

[1] Michio Ikai and Arthur H. Steinhaus, "Some Factors Modifying the Expression of Human Strength," *Health and Fitness in the Modern World* (Chicago: The Athletic Institute, 1961), p. 148.

Running as an amateur sports activity is avocational and should not be continued beyond the degree of the importance of an avocation. Actually, I used these champions as examples because they are interesting and because the facts of their lives as runners are available. But if these world champions stop improving, or stop running altogether, for reasons that traditional training systems have ignored, how much more these reasons must apply to ordinary runners who have so much less in the way of motives to urge them on.

Suppose a coach, wise and experienced in the uses of interval training and fartlek, but narrow in his interest in runners as human beings, were to transfer his efforts to the city of Bombay, India. How successful would he be in developing runners when he would have to overcome the apathy toward running, the hot, humid climate, the obstacles to running on the city streets, the lack of running tracks, or the stress of disease and starvation? Obviously he would first have to solve these more primary problems before his skill in coaching running could be of value.

How would I approach such a task? In detail, I don't know of course. But I do know that how I went about it would determine the kind of training system I would have, or better, would actually *be* the system. How we mold the background or framework of our system—what goals we set, what public image we seek, what terrain we choose to run on, what rules of everyday conduct we follow, what freedom from economic stress we establish—all will determine the attitudes and energies of the men when they run, even more than the shrewdness with which the dosages of running work are prescribed. Obviously there should be a unity of approach in all these matters. Let one of them be handled differently or neglected, and it can wipe out all the good that is done in the other areas.

In addition to the broad social problems which should be considered in a holistic system of training, there are other more personal problems. It is amazing how seemingly unrelated persons can sometimes hamper a runner's efforts and the effectiveness of his training system. Years ago I had a great potential champion in distance running, who refused, however, to give that extra ounce of energy in practice and in meets that makes the crucial difference. Years later, he told me of a letter from a hospitalized acquaintance whose doctor claimed he had been driven to heart failure by the high stress of running. One negative letter, whose false assumptions and conclusions could have been easily set aside by proper medical education, held back all the other positive forces for development.

Sometimes a man's own teammates oppose him in ways that make his efforts more difficult and less pleasant. Sometimes his coach unwittingly creates conflicts through his own drives for self-fulfillment.

Sometimes his friends, his sweetheart, his wife, his parents create opposition by direct interference or by innocently placing distractions in his path. Obviously the training system that ignores these opposing forces is limiting its effectiveness.

There is one other aspect of holistic training for endurance running that should be emphasized: that a man runs with his mind and emotions just as much as with his legs and circulatory system, and that the mental-emotional aspects of training should be just as carefully planned as the physical aspects. Contemporary training systems recognize this fact in part, else they would be futile. But they have not recognized it to the extent of assuming that such mental factors as self-confidence or relaxation or competitiveness can be developed just as much as the pulse rate or heart stroke-volume, and that training plans should be made specifically for such development. True mental-emotional attitudes improve quite well without planning, just as a lowered pulse rate occurs by just running without planning of any kind. But they will improve more rapidly, more certainly, and more soundly if the training program is carefully planned with them in mind. Such planning is an essential part of holistic training.

Stated simply, holistic training is based upon an understanding and use of the five W's of running: what, why, where, when, and by whom. Every good training system considers these, of course, but holistic training does so in a different way. For example, it thinks of where and by whom, broadly. The marathon training that works in New Zealand might not work at all in south Texas where the climate is so different. Interval training in Finland might work out quite differently in eastern Canada where, although the physical climates and terrains are about the same, the social climates—the peoples' attitudes—are not at all alike. Similarly, institutions differ from one another; what works at one may not work at all well at another. Don't misunderstand me; holistic training is primarily running—no other way to better running is possible—but unlike other systems of running, it adjusts and interrelates the running, the individual, and the total background within which he functions.

To make our point clearer, we can compare it with the practices of modern industry in its efforts to get a better performance from its more important employees. Formerly the man's personality, abilities, and techniques, as they related directly to his job, were all that were considered vital to his success, or at least, all that were a justifiable area of inquiry and possible action. But, as has been explained in great detail by Vance Packard in his best-seller, *The Hidden Persuaders*, industry today researches all the factors that might either help or hinder performance: the attitudes of the employee's wife, the kind and degree of recognition he needs as an individual, the kind of status symbols that are important to him (a three-drawer desk may be a source of irritation if his associates have four-drawer desks), the emotional tone of his office decor, and many others.

Once these are clearly understood, machinery is set in motion to establish a better interrelationship. In some cases, the man is helped to make adjustments within himself or in his home; in others, the working environment is modified. But unless such knowledge is sought, unless the machinery for using it is integrated within the industrial system, the man may function at half-speed, or even quit his job, for what seems on the surface to be merely on-the-job problems.

So with modern training for endurance running. If performance is the goal, whatever aids performance in a man's 24-hour day and whatever detracts from it are matters of concern—are, in fact, a part of the system that a coach should use to help a man improve his running. This is what we mean by this system called holistic training.

Fatigue and Stress

The Nature of Fatigue as Related to Endurance Running

The problems of fatigue, stress, and relaxation in endurance running might well have been placed in Chapter 3 under the heading of physiology. This, however, would have narrowed our discussion. We have therefore deliberately placed them here and will try to explain them from the viewpoint of holism.

A clearer insight into the nature of fatigue in endurance running will be best assured if we remind ourselves that fatigue is first and above all else a word; further, that it is a word of various meanings not only in everyday use but in the different sciences as well.

Like all words, it itself is never the reality, only the symbol, or approximation of reality, though our ways of speaking, and even thinking, often suggest that the word and the reality are one and the same. When we say, "I'm fatigued!" we might mean that we are actually physically fatigued, but more likely we mean that we only "feel tired," or are disinterested, or dislike what we are doing.

The meaning of fatigue evolved during centuries when men assumed a separation of mind and body. That assumption is still with us, of course, try as we may to escape it and to understand fatigue as a mind-body unity.

In this discussion we shall try to sustain the use of fatigue as meaning "the psychophysical changes arising out of activity which diminish the capacity for more activity." These changes usually occur during activity but their more mental-emotional aspects can precede it, with effects that can be just as deterrent as those derived from physical changes.

There are three key expressions in that two-sentence definition: "psychophysical," "capacity," and "changes . . . can precede it." First, it is our contention that in endurance running, fatigue is mental-emotional as well as physical, and that these more psychic effects of fatigue tend to precede running and are often more deterrent than the physical effects of running. Second, it is the capacity for activity that is diminished by fatigue, not necessarily activity itself. This is in contrast to the assumption of physiology that fatigue is "work decrement" and therefore always measurable in physical terms. Third, the expression, "changes . . . can precede it" reminds us that failure and dissatisfaction from running tend to create aversions that are just as "built in" and effective within the organism as, for example, the heart-rate or the oxygen-carrying capacity of the blood, and therefore will predispose toward decrement even before running begins. It follows that the word "fatigue," without adjectives, should always relate to the person as a mind-body unity. Any more limited use, as in physical fatigue, should be so qualified.

All of this is, of course, an arbitrary point of view, with which traditional physiology tends to disagree. Physiology tends to assume that fatigue, if it is to be a scientific and useful concept, must be "real," that is, physical and measurable, as evidenced by a decrement in work output. It then requires that all other kinds, such as mental fatigue, be so qualified; or better, described in other terms, like boredom or disinterest. But this approach is based upon the old concept of a duality of body and mind.

The point of view presented here [2] permits great flexibility in our use of the word "fatigue." Used alone, without adjectives, it always relates to the whole person. But with adjectives there can be as many aspects of fatigue as there are aspects of a person; even more, since there are numbers of persons and each person experiences fatigue in his own way. John Smith's experiences of fatigue are never the same as those of Harry Jones, even though all related factors seem to be identical. Physical fatigue is that diminished capacity for continued activity whose causes are primarily physical. Oxygen debt fatigue is that diminished capacity for continued activity which is caused primarily by oxygen debt. Similarly, mental fatigue relates primarily to mental causes; emotional fatigue to emotional causes; motivational fatigue to motivational causes; small-muscle fatigue to small-muscle causes, and so on—endlessly.

We have stated that each person is unique in his experience of fatigue,

---

[2] For this point of view we are greatly indebted to S. Howard Bartley and Eloise Chute, *Fatigue and Impairment in Man* (New York: McGraw-Hill Book Company, Inc., 1947).

as he is unique in all other aspects of his being.[3] But more than this, as each person matures and changes, his sensitivities and reactions to the various aspects of fatigue will also mature and change. That is, not only does he develop physical powers to resist and postpone fatigue; he also develops a callousness against its mental-emotional effects. By callousness we imply several things: a mental-emotional resistance to the feelings of fatigue, a control over their effects, and even more, an insensitivity or indifference to them. As Zatopek wrote, "Is it raining? It doesn't matter. Am I tired? That doesn't matter either . . . I practiced regardless, until will power was no longer a problem."

Physical Aspects of Fatigue in Distance Running

Space does not permit a detailed discussion of the physical changes which diminish a man's capacity to keep up a level of severe activity.

To speak of the physical aspects of fatigue rather than of physical fatigue as an entity does not in any way lessen its realities. When the negative effects of fatigue predominate over the positive forces of action, action diminishes and eventually stops. When exhaustion, in the true sense of the word, sets in, no mental motivation, no will-to-succeed can of itself produce continued activity. But the positive-negative forces of action-fatigue concern the person as a whole within a certain physical and social environment. A glance at Table 4.1 may make this clear.

TABLE 4.1

POSITIVE-NEGATIVE FACTORS RELATED TO FATIGUE IN ENDURANCE RUNNING

Physical Condition	Physical Skill	Personal Attitudes	Social Environment	Physical Environment
O$_2$ capacities	Low-high	Interest-distinterest	Friends-rivals	Temperature
Fuel capacities	Relaxation	Confidence-anxiety	Institutional attitudes	Humidity
Heat regulation		Play-drudgery	Community attitudes	Terrain
Capillary development		Competition	National attitudes	Altitude
Heart-lung development		Willed control	Racial attitudes	

Consideration of the various factors in Table 4.1 suggests that it is the totality of these positive-negative factors that determines whether a sustained level of activity or some degree of work decrement will occur

[3] Roger J. Williams, *Biochemical Individuality* (New York: John Wiley & Sons, Inc., 1956).

at any given moment. Physical fatigue is but one of these factors. When action is extreme it may become the determining factor. So fatigue, in the sense of a measurable reduction of work, can be said to be present when the total negative forces of the person-environment are greater than the total positive forces of the person-environment.

Mental-emotional Aspects of Fatigue in Distance Running

In addition to the physical aspects of human fatigue, we can abstract other "mental" aspects, which are equally negative in their effects upon work done, although they are much less objectively observed and measured. The number of these aspects is limited only by our imaginative insight and our ability to verbalize. Bartley and Chute [4] discuss a great many of these aspects, including chronic fatigue, subjective fatigue, voluntary fatigue, combat fatigue, anxiety fatigue, central nervous fatigue, neurotic fatigue, and others.

Again, space limitations cut off full discussion and make referral to the appended references advisable, particularly so since the following material on "stress" is closely related. The main points we wish to make are (1) that the mental-emotional aspects of fatigue are just as "real" and just as effective in producing work decrement as are the so-called physical factors, (2) that control of them is subject to development just as much as the "physical" aspects, and (3) that such development should be understood and planned just as carefully and deliberately as the "leg-work" of training.

Stress and Development

Ideally, development in life occurs gradually by means of small challenges to which the human organism makes an adequate-plus response, a response that more than provides for the needs of the specific challenge. The child may be challenged by a sense of hunger. He responds to this challenge by eating not just enough food to maintain his present state, to keep him alive, but by eating an additional amount to provide growth and development. Or, in a different way, the child feels an impulsion to be active, to play, to run about. Such vigorous action creates a challenge within, a challenge to oxygen supply, to fuel supply, to muscle-nerve coordination, to speed and strength. Again, as with hunger, the organism responds by overcompensation, by providing an oversupply, which more than meets the needs of the present challenge.

This is the pattern of growth and development. So long as the chal-

---

4 Bartley and Chute, *op. cit.*, p. 3.

lenge is within the range of rather easy response, of stretch but not strain, development occurs with no loss to the person. Speaking broadly, it is the pattern of ideal development in distance running, in which workout will stretch but will not strain the endurance resources of the runner.

But training and competition for distance running are seldom so consistently mild in their demands. For many reasons of competition, reward, or ambition, men tend strongly to attempt too much, too intensely, and too soon. They accept challenges for which their present development, if not their full power, is inadequate. They compete on hot, humid days when the stress of heat exhaustion is a serious threat. A desire for team victory may cause individuals to be placed in "unfair" competitions in which an all-out effort to win is the only choice for action. If time permits, worry and anxiety often drain away the nervous energies and contribute to stress even before the competition begins.

Hans Selye on stress. The modern theory of stress, especially that developed by Hans Selye [5] and his associates, is the outcome of a full program of scientific research [6] which has important implications for distance running. As with the word "fatigue," stress is not easily defined. Selye's definition is in fact so technically worded as to be meaningless for our purposes. As an oversimplified compromise, we might define stress as a state or pattern of reaction within an organism by which it seeks to maintain its natural homeostatic balance against "dangerous" aggressions. These aggressions are of many kinds: disease, infection, lack of food, lack of oxygen, extremes of temperature or humidity, over-activity, complete inactivity, and many others. "Homeostatic balance" is a term widely used in biology to describe the limited range of both function and form within which an organism maintains itself despite the forces of change that are present, both in its environment and within itself. The chemical composition of body fluids remains relatively constant, despite extremes of nutritional intake. Body temperature tends strongly to be held within a narrow range despite extremes of external heat or cold.

Selye has concluded from his research that the extent of the reaction to stress is dependent upon the extent of the stressor agent, to use Selye's term. When the stressor agent is local, as in a local infection, the defensive reactions are similarly local; when it is widespread, as in disease or starvation, the defensive reactions become generalized and active throughout the body. Selye calls this generalized reaction the "general

---

[5] Hans Selye, *The Stress of Life* (New York: McGraw-Hill Book Company, Inc., 1956).

[6] Celeste Ulrich, "Stress and Sport," *Science and Medicine of Exercise and Sport*, Walter R. Johnson, ed. (New York: Harper & Row, Publishers, 1960), pp. 251-70. An excellent summary of the problem plus a bibliography of 85 related books and research studies.

adaptation syndrome," and states that the general pattern of this reaction is the same, whether the stressor agent be an invasion by bacteria, hard physical work, exacting mental discipline, or the anxiety of tomorrow's dangers. Obviously the specific reactions would be different but the general pattern is the same. Further, Selye draws the controversial conclusion that the life-supply of this general adaptation energy is limited.

It is as though, at birth, each individual inherited a certain amount of adaptation energy, the magnitude of which is determined by his genetic background, his parents. He can draw upon this capital thriftily for a long but monotonously uneventful existence, or he can spend it lavishly in the course of a stressful, intense, but perhaps more colorful life. In any case, there is just so much of it, and he must budget accordingly.[7]

Adaptation energy is present in what we might call reservoirs of energy. These reservoirs have wide and flexible ranges of capacity. There is today's range, the limits of which are determined by today's maturity, nutrition, climatic temperature, or motivation. But there is also tomorrow's and next year's range of capacity, the limits of which will be determined by the degree of development through training, self-discipline, and will-to-achieve to which the individual subjects himself.

But although the potential capacities of these reservoirs are very flexible and unmeasured in the human organism, it is Hans Selye's conclusion, based almost entirely upon work with small animals, that the reservoirs are limited in capacity. In the case of the white rat, once the limited adaptation energy has been drawn upon beyond the point of further adaptation, the ability to adapt is lost, not only at the highest levels but at the lower levels as well. The tasks that once could be done easily are now beyond accomplishment, not only in terms of the particular stressor that caused the breakdown but also as related to other stressors. The rat, whose adaptation energies are exhausted by muscular exertion, is no longer able to meet the challenges of such other stressors as cold or disease.

According to Selye, adaptation energy can be well trained to serve a special purpose but eventually it runs out; its amount is finite. Selye admits readily that the nature of this adaptation energy is not known.

The term adaptation energy has been coined for that which is consumed during continued adaptive work, to indicate that it is something different from the caloric energy we receive from food; but this is only a name, and we still have no precise concept of what this energy might be.[8]

The stresses that use up our limited adaptation energy can come from different types of agents. They can be environmental: disease, infection,

---

[7] Selye, *op. cit.*, p. 66.
[8] *Ibid.*

hunger, heat, cold. They can be social: competitiveness, city life, social relations. They can be physical: physical fatigue in all its forms and degrees, physical tendencies as in ulcers or malfunctions. Or they can be psychological: anxiety, fear, aggressiveness, doubt about one's "manliness." They can arise both from within and from without. But whatever their nature, Selye concludes that they all draw upon the central supply of adaptation energy, and this is limited.

Stress in sports. The somewhat limited studies of the stress involved in physical activity which have been made to date seem to emphasize the importance of emotional stress rather than that of muscular activity alone. For example, Thorn [9] concluded from a study of stress in rowing, in which he found the decrease in the eosinophil count of the blood of the coxswain was comparable to that in rowing members of the crew, that emotion is more significant than motion in producing stress reactions.

As applied to distance running, this suggests that it is neither the miles nor the pace that determine the state of stress so much as an emotional reaction to the self-discipline, to the hardship, and above all, to competitive elements which tend to be so prevalent in our culture. It should be emphasized that adaptation to emotional stress is physical in nature and similar to that produced by a stressor of a physical nature. Fatigue from emotional causes draws upon the physical energies available for physical work.

In general, emotional stress is thought to be primarily the product of anxiety, that is, of the subjective experience of uncertainty, generalized fear, doubt of personal adequacy, or an inability to reach a definite decision. From the standpoint of adaptation energy, these are the exhausting aspects of competitive sports, beyond the physically fatiguing activity itself.

Further, emotional upsets related to any given stress situation can so condition an individual that the same situation, or even a lesser version of it, can produce a much stronger disturbance at a later encounter. Those who must withstand severe stress for long periods, as during a long season of competitive running, must possess considerable emotional stability. This should be "natural," just as the physical factors of running endurance are natural. But man is born with capacities, not abilities. He is a "natural" in his possession of a high capacity for emotional stability in competition. The level to which that capacity is developed is to some extent determined by carefully assigned overloads of competitive challenge.

---

[9] G. W. Thorn and J. C. Laidlaw, "Studies on the Adrenal Cortical Response in Man," *Transactions of the American Clinical and Climatological Association,* LXV (1953), 179-99.

But, as in most aspects of our modern world, the demands of modern sports make gradual and easy adaptation hard, if not impossible, to arrange. Situations from which great stress arises do occur. Fortunately, apart from its tendency toward homeostasis, the human organism is capable of stretching itself to amazing lengths when emergencies must be met. The history of endurance running is a story of ever greater realization of our "stretchability" as related to the stresses of running. What was deemed humanly impossible in the 1920's is the common performance of boys in their teens in the 1960's. No matter how the alarmists of stress research may warn us against the dangers of wasting a limited supply of adaptation energy, our long-time experience assures us that men are not easily strained in any serious way, that our capacities for adaptation are enormous, and that we have built-in safeguards against excessive work intensities that defy any but the most senseless and extreme efforts. As Celeste Ulrich has written,

> At the present time no value judgment can be passed upon the effect of stress upon the human organism. There is some evidence to indicate that too much stress over a long period of time is detrimental to the body, but the quantitative definition of "too much" or "too great" is relative to each individual.[10]

Having said so much in the way of positive assurance, we must warn again that the conclusions of stress research do have significance and should lead coaches and athletes to the use of caution in all endurance training, especially at the younger age levels. Scientific research should be furthered, especially as it relates to the discovery of a valid and reliable means of determining the effects of various dosages of work and emotional stress upon a given individual. We are now guessing what kind and what intensity of training is best. Our competitive systems have developed with almost no concern for the growth or well-being of the individual competitor. Who can say what proportion of these guesses or these competitions has been helpful, or how many runners have dropped the sport because of their negative effects.

In the not-distant future, coaches on the field will be supplemented by scientists in the laboratory. Personal reactions to the demands of activity on the field will be telemetered to the laboratory for immediate analysis and recommendation sent back to the coach on the field. The values of a training session will be measured by its effects on the person, rather than, as today, on a stop watch. Even then, judgment will be a crucial element in good coaching, but it will be judgment based on facts as well as on feelings and appearances.

Until that time, coaches will do well to exercise caution and patience. They will say, "enough," long before "too much" is a danger. They will

---

[10] Ulrich, *op. cit.*, p. 266.

alternate one or more days of easy work with each day of hard work to be certain that full recovery, emotionally as well as physically, has been achieved. But most of all, they will seek to modify the extremes in both number and intensity of competitions that now exact such a high toll in emotional stress.

One other warning is justified. Stress from endurance training is normally not harmful. But if it occurs at high levels at a time when severe emotional stress is also present from any one of a number of school, home, or personal causes, or when germs or viruses are attacking the body's defenses, then the total stress can be harmful. The man becomes ill. Some might say that the germs caused the illness, the emotional upset was its cause, or overfatigue was to blame. The truth is that whenever the total stress situation rises beyond the capacity of the man to make an adequate response, some form of malfunction occurs. The fatigue alone, the emotional stress alone, or the germs alone will not have made the man ill; it is the combination that proves too much.

The lesson to be gained from this is clear. A wise coach or athlete should avoid hard training sessions when other stresses are present, whether of the mind, the emotions, or the environment. A little patience in such cases may save a long period of forced idleness.

Relaxation in Running

A sound program of holistic training for endurance running emphasizes relaxation. That's a nice-sounding sentence, simple and short, and we think we know what it means. But its simplicity is deceiving. The word, *relaxation,* is used both in and out of sports in so many ways as to make it almost meaningless .The preferred dictionary definition is that relaxation is a "lessening of tension." When applied to lying in bed or to the removal of life problems generally, we have a generalized concept of this meaning. And yet a man such as Dr. Edmund Jacobson has spent a lifetime trying to understand what this kind of relaxation means specifically in terms of muscle action and emotional stimuli. To acquire a working knowledge of his meaning of general relaxation while completely inactive takes an hour or more of practice for many days.[11]

But our interest is relaxation in action. Jacobson defines this as "the minimum of tensions in the muscles requisite for an act, along with the relaxation of other muscles." Again we seem to know what is meant. To bend the elbow we relax the triceps and contract the biceps just enough to bend the arm at the desired speed. It isn't nearly so simple of course

[11] Edmund Jacobson, *You Must Relax* (New York: McGraw-Hill Book Company, Inc., 1957), p. 84.

when we start to run; so many more muscles groups are involved or would like to be. But still we understand reasonably well and can achieve some measure of what is asked.

We understand that relaxation is one way of looking at skill, or coordination, or concentration of effort. As we become more skilled, the extraneous movements (muscle contractions) fall away; that is, we become increasingly relaxed as our skill improves. If I asked you to write your name backwards in three seconds or less, you would contract muscles entirely unrelated to the movement—your face, your neck, and your shoulders probably most of all. After weeks of practice these would be much more relaxed.

We have all experienced and therefore understand this, at least up to the point where fatigue enters the situation. But now things get more complex. It is easy to run relaxed when the pace is slow and easy and the distance well within our staying powers; it is quite a different matter when the breathing is labored, the hearing dulled, the skill uncertain, and the competition unexhausted.

Before possible solutions are suggested, it is essential to remember that many children have no difficulty with relaxation under these conditions. They run with no inhibitions; they are not preconditioned to either discomfort or danger. They get tired and feel tired of course, but they accept this for what it is, without exaggerating either before or after. Their style may be mechanically unsound, but they know nothing of mechanics and care less. They do what they do without concern and without tension.

In suggesting various ways of maintaining relaxation, we face the old paradox of arbitrarily separating what is inseparable. However, it seems helpful to list these four: (1) relaxation by conscious control of the negative; (2) relaxation by positive attention; (3) relaxation by basic relearning; and (4) relaxation by positive abandon or acceptance.

Relaxation by Conscious Control

The first of these, and the most commonly used, is usually related to will power, or better, since psychology no longer admits the will as a special faculty, willed control. By the power of willed control we hold back the rising forces of fatigue. We consciously try to inhibit the growing sense of effort, imperfect control, doubt, numbness, fear, and panic.

A large number of related phrases is in general use. We say that we "make up our minds," "take ourselves in hand," "grit our teeth," "stand firm," "put our foot down," or "take the bull by the horns."

Many coaches and athletes are convinced that they have learned a greater degree of relaxation by this method of inhibiting the growing tensions, pains, and fears. At almost every endurance race, we hear sharp, urgent cries from coaches and other athletes, "Relax!" in a tone of voice that demands, "Force yourself to control yourself!" Derek Ibbotson reminded himself on the last lap of his world-record mile, "Relax, concentrate on your legs and arms; you are on the brink of your greatest victory, but all will be lost if you lose control." Similarly, Elliott's autobiography is filled with self-directed admonitions.

Most athletes imagine themselves at the end of their tether before they're even seventy-five per cent exhausted. I was so determined to avoid this pitfall that if at any time I thought I was surrendering too soon to superficial pain I'd deliberately try to hurt myself more. . . .

Somehow, to me running is a challenge, demanding mastery of the body as well as the winning of races.[12]

In similar fashion, Gordon Pirie wrote,

The athlete has to torture the body, for it will only respond to the same degree as the stimulus applied. Greatest athletes in their races run themselves blind. The body is plunged into the depths of exhaustion and the mind into the depths of despair. . . . You must be a "killer," never giving up till the last ounce is wrung from your inadequate body.[13]

Such a point of view does not express the whole of these runners' attitudes toward relaxation, which I shall develop later, but it is almost invariably an important part.

Before passing judgment on such efforts to relax by direct control of the negative elements, it will be worthwhile to consider the nature of the fatigue that makes relaxation such a problem. Unfortunately, scientific research on fatigue has tended to view it as exclusively physical and has explained it in terms of structural and biochemical changes. Physiologists have tended to define it in such measureable ways as "work decrement," and have located its origins in such physical areas as the motor end plate or the synapse between a sensory and a motor neuron. However, when we are concerned with human fatigue, such concentration upon the physical, when the problem is of the whole person, is less than adequate.

There is an immense force of social suggestion present on every hand —in common talk, in runners' talk, in running literature, in coaches' attitudes and admonitions—which tends to magnify the pains and efforts of fatigue while running. Such words as *agony, suffering, distress, stabbing pain, torture,* and *unendurable* are bandied about as badges of the running fraternity. Young runners come to expect such experiences, and

---

12 Herb Elliott, *The Golden Mile* (London: Cassell & Company, Ltd., 1961), pp. 50, 150. Also published as *Herb Elliott's Story* (New York: Paul R. Reynolds, Inc., 1961).

13 Gordon Pirie, *Running Wild* (London: W. H. Allen & Co., Ltd., Publishers, 1961), p. 22.

as usual, they find what they expect to find, especially when, after it is over, they listen to expressions of sympathy and repugnance from their parents and friends.

I have tried to define fatigue many times—on one occasion, as a relationship between the rising dam of physical impairment and the rising stream of motivation and willed control. In such a situation, many things can happen. The dam can rise to the unsurmountable heights of contracture and exhaustion. Or, at the other extreme, the stream of interest can flow away and dissipate its force, even before it reaches the dam or even though the dam is low. In between these extremes there are many possibilities. The willed control and relaxation of the poor competitor are easily held back and disrupted; those of the great competitor seem to rise resolutely even above what would usually be called physical necessity.

In writing about his famous mile under the four-minute barrier, Bannister said, "I was relaxing so much that my mind seemed almost detached from my body. There was no sense of strain." Then during the last lap of his race,

I had a moment of mixed joy and anguish, when my mind took over. It raced well ahead of my body and drew my body compellingly forward. I felt that the moment of a lifetime had come. There was no pain, only a great unity of movement and aim. The world seemed to stand still, or did not exist. The only reality was the next hundred yards of track under my feet. . . .

My body had long since exhausted all its energy, but it went on running just the same. The physical overdraft came only from greater willpower.[14]

Even though we admit a degree of overstatement and an assumption of the duality of mind and body that is all too common within the medical profession for which Bannister was a student, his attitudes toward the problems of exhausting work and relaxation are typical of those used by runners and coaches generally, with what they have apparently considered as fair success.

Unfortunately, since the primary tool in these efforts is the mind (in the dualistic sense of mind over matter), the consciousness of the growing and potential strength of the enemy is comparable to, and often more than, its consciousness of its own strength to control him. If the enemy is fatigue, it is an old enemy against whom the average runner has fought a losing battle for years. His conditioning toward such an enemy has been primarily negative in terms of defeat, not control. To expect such a man to control what he has learned time and again he cannot control— to make an effort not to make an effort—is unreasonable. Further, he *knows,* though perhaps unconsciously, that it is unreasonable. His mind

---

14 Roger Bannister, *The Four Minute Mile* (New York: Dodd, Mead & Co., 1955; London: Curtis Brown, Ltd., 1955), pp. 213-14. Reprinted by permission of the publishers. Copyright © 1955 by Roger Bannister.

tends strongly to shut out the meaning of the coach's admonition to "relax!" In an effective sense, he doesn't even hear him. Such efforts are always accompanied by emotion. The greater the awareness of effort, the stronger the emotion; the stronger the emotion, the greater the tendency toward tension and uncontrol.

Frequently, this unsuccessful struggle for control occurs under conditions of fatigue or competition which the coach considers trivial or routine. But he should be aware that previous conditioning has produced a linkage, usually unconscious, with past situations that were very stressful to the runner, just as the thought of making a speech to the alumni may cause a coach's heart to race and his muscles to tighten—even though the alumni consider it a trivial or routine speech!

Despite these limitations, however, there is no doubt that verbal suggestions, if made calmly, with no hint of doubt or alarm, do sometimes prove helpful. Above all, they must be cues to relaxation, that is, to letting go, to doing less, and not cues to effort, even though the effort be pinpointed in terms of making less effort. Each individual will select for himself what will serve him as a relaxation cue. Some concentrate on the hands: shake them or drop them or lift them for a few strides, and so change the movement and the effort. This of course produces a beneficial physical change but equally a mental one. Some think of the facial and neck muscles. By awareness of tension and then by a conscious letting go of tension, increased relaxation occurs. Some runners think specifically of a loose lower lip which becomes the cue to greater relaxation in general.

Relaxation by Positive Attention

Our second suggested method of relaxing in action was called "relaxation by positive attention." Probably all great runners are aware that they run their best race when they are least aware of effort: when the eagerness to run, or the absorption in race tactics, or the awareness of competition required their full attention. Of course when they recall such a race, especially for publication, they inevitably bring out its hardships and distress and their terrible struggle to overcome them. But in best running, these are at a second level of consciousness.

Herb Elliott wrote,

Listening for symptoms of fatigue from Geoff, I became oblivious of my own condition.

Or again,

I like to vary my training venues day by day. . . . The change of scenery, the music of the birds and the sight of grazing cattle and sheep is soul-freeing and makes a training session real joy.

Again, in a different way,

He [Cerutty] urged the advisability of impressing an instinct for surging, or galloping, upon my subconscious in the belief that when I became tired during a race I'd react automatically by exerting more effort and making a burst.[15]

We have all experienced the effectiveness of this method in many areas of our lives. We've taken a "long" walk with an interesting companion, and then have been surprised at how short it seemed. Awareness was in positive channels, in the conversation, in the pleasant surroundings. The day may have been hot and humid, but our minds were quite unaware of it. One of the all-time best sellers was Norman Vincent Peale's *The Power of Positive Thinking,* the gist of which was that positive thoughts can prevent negative thoughts from entering the mind. Though Peale's concern was primarily with religion, people apparently found his doctrine to be of wide application.

The literature of research in psychology and industrial management contains endless related studies. The use of music in workshops improves output by distracting attention from effort and boredom. Similarly, the presence of spectators, especially when cheering, has a similar effect upon fatiguing work.

Though it tells us nothing new, a piece of research by Arne Lundervold gives measureable proof of the effects of such direction of attention. Muscle movement—in fact, even the thought of muscle movement—is always accompanied by electrical activity which can be recorded electromyographically. In this study, Lundervold photographed the electrical activity of finger tapping under varying conditions of fatigue and incentive. Action potentials of both related and unrelated muscles were studied. In one photo, he noted that

when persons tested were sharply commanded to concentrate on the task, we sometimes noticed that the (over-all) muscle activity increased. Conversely, fewer electrical impulses were found when the persons' thoughts were diverted from the tapping. . . . During increasing fatigue, the muscle activity [related and unrelated—J.K.D.] increases as well. By psychic stimuli, even such a small one as asking the person how much 4 times 5 is, the muscle activity decreases. Similarly things which occupy the person's thoughts may influence the cerebral activity and in that way the muscular activity as well. Fatigue can . . . be put off in that way.[16]

In a quite different but related area of muscular activity, Wendell Johnson [17] of the University of Iowa has conducted research on the cause

---

15 Elliott, *op. cit.,* p. 49.

16 Arne Lundervold, "The Measurement of Human Reaction during Training," *Health and Fitness in the Modern World* (Chicago: The Athletic Institute, 1961), p. 125.

17 Wendell Johnson, *People in Quandaries* (New York: Harper & Row, Publishers, 1946), pp. 439 ff.

and control of stuttering. Speech is of course a muscular activity which is basically the same as that of other activities, including endurance running. To demonstrate that stuttering is primarily a problem of psychic tension and uncertainty of willed control, Johnson has, upon occasion, provided his stutterers with headphones into which distracting noises could be directed. As long as these stutterers could hear their speaking, they stuttered. But when the noise in their ears was loud enough to cut out their awareness of their speaking, it smoothed out most dramatically. As the sound recedes and their awareness of the method of speaking returns, the stuttering returns also. Some will say we have gone far afield from running, but the lesson is of direct significance.

One can assume that coaches who rely upon the first-named method, that of inhibiting the negative effects of fatigue, confuse it with this second method, that of relaxation by positive attention. But the two are quite different. The first, with its tone of desperate urgency to "relax!" exaggerates the negative phases of control. The second is one of prevention—by directing awareness into positive channels, inhibitions of doubt or fatigue are held below the threshold of consciousness. I once had a distance runner who said he maintained control by silently reciting portions of Kipling's "If" as he ran.

> If you can force your heart and nerve and sinew
> To serve your turn long after they are gone,
> And so hold on when there is nothing in you
> Except the Will which says to them: "Hold on!"

He knew the words perfectly so that required no effort. But he tried to attend to the meaning of each phrase or word, and this effort seemed to keep his mind in positive channels and away from negative ones.

Another device for which a few runners claim some degree of success is to run always within the limits of relaxation: whenever awareness arises that the pace is so fast as to increase tension, it is eased a little; whenever there is awareness that fatigue threatens control, effort is reduced. Gradually and imperceptibly, they are able to run a faster and faster pace without tension and are able to come to terms with fatigue spontaneously.

Some men are able to relax through the complete faith and reliance they place in their coach. We have quoted Gordon Pirie's reaction to Gerschler, "I was immediately impressed with the quiet authority of this man, and soon I unreservedly put myself in his hands." Coaches like Gerschler, or Mihaly Igloi, or Gosta Holmer of Sweden carry an air of complete self-confidence and competence which, like the "darshan" of Gandhi in India, seems to be transferrable to those who merely touch their hands or even see them. They are relaxed deeply within themselves; they may go "all-out" to win, yet hold themselves above the winning—

or the losing for that matter; somehow they maintain a certain quietude or fortitude of mind that holds firm even when, as in Igloi's case, the surface action seems ruffled and even excited at times.

But for most men, the basic cause of tension lies deeper, in what we call the unconscious. Most men cannot let themselves go, as did Pirie with Gerschler, and will need to be reconditioned from within. To achieve a really effective cure, they would be wise to withdraw for a time from the stress of competition and forced training. They should begin again, then progress at their own pace within the limits of unquestioning control and release of inhibitions.

Relaxation by Basic Relearning

Our third suggested method is relaxation by a basic relearning of re-laxation techniques. It is the brain-child of Dr. Edmund Jacobson,[18] whose work has been primarily with hospital patients and sufferers from hypertension and nervous disorders. Relearning is first concentrated on the techniques of relaxing while completely inactive: not only is there no movement but nerve impulses to the muscles are very limited. (Even to "think" an action will produce measureable electrical impulses to the related muscles even though no movement occurs.) Such relearn-ing occurs first with a small muscle group, such as the wrist flexors, but is then extended to the other muscles of the body. Gradually realization occurs that relaxation is not subjectively a positive action but a neutral one, or better, no willed action at all. It is a letting go, a release of tension. The cue to "no tension" (relaxation) is the difference between its feeling and that of deliberately produced muscle tension. "Any effort to relax is failure to relax."

Jacobson warned especially against alerting oneself to possible tension, or allowing others to do so by crying, "Relax! Don't try so hard! Let go!" Not only the words but also the urgency with which they are spoken inevitably produce greater tension rather than the intended relaxation. Whatever suggests tension to the mind is relayed back to the muscles in the form of nervous impulses. If these are in sufficient number, actual contraction will occur.

Having learned inactive relaxation without muscle tension, the pupil must learn by gradual increments of action to perform with the least possible effort. As soon as there is awareness of tension in antagonistic or unrelated muscle groups, action should be decreased until the tension is gone. In running, for example, the man always runs within the limits of complete relaxation and control. Again, he should keep in mind Jacobson's basic rule: "Any effort to relax is failure to relax."

---

[18] Jacobson, *op. cit.*, p. 84.

To many, this method will seem the long way around and will require more time than most runners feel they can devote to it. They tend to concentrate on doing more, effort or no effort, and have little patience with the suggestion of doing more by doing less. However, a few coaches, such as Bud Winter of San Jose State, are convinced that they have derived much of practical value out of such nonexercises (to distinguish them from activities involving effort). Winter schedules practice for his runners in both inactive and active relaxation. When his runners have enjoyed success (and therefore were relaxed), the value of this practice in "letting go" was unquestioned; when doing less well, there were at least a few doubts, especially among his coaching rivals.

One other example comes to mind of the use in endurance running of Jacobson's methods of learning to relax. Though Percy Cerutty probably never heard of Jacobson, his emphasis upon "power running" and "resistance training" tends to produce a result similar to that achieved by Jacobson. Cerutty taught his men to run sometimes while contracting all unrelated muscles with utmost strength and violence: knees high, arms driving, hands tightly clenched. Much of this was done in soft sand, up high dunes, and in knee-deep surf. Though Cerutty argued the values of resistance training in terms of intensity of effort, it may well have taught his men how to relax once such tensions were released.

Relaxation by Positive Acceptance

But there is a fourth method, that of positive acceptance and abandon, which is of increasing interest and use. It is the theory of this method that a man can best concentrate his energies upon the positive phases of running if he accepts the feelings of fatigue as being inevitable, if he relaxes with them, abandons all effort to inhibit them, and comes to terms with them for what they are, but for no more than they are. We have written of Emil Zatopek's practice of holding his breath while walking from one tree to another. He does not speak of doing so to get used to anoxemia or to build up his will power. On the contrary, he wrote, "I practiced holding my breath until will power was no longer a problem." I interpret this to mean that he reached the point where he could relax completely when breath-holding; that is, feelings which we normally associate with discomfort and fear had no such associations for him. He no longer needed to control anything, and therefore "will power was no longer a problem."

Under this theory, we do not need to feel suffering and also inhibit its expression; we do not need to wear out our nervous energies by hiding such feelings from the eyes of others. Rather we learn to accept pain on its own terms, for what it is but no more than it is, to express that pain without inhibitions, and then to concentrate our major efforts and energies in movement, regardless of its concomitants.

Erich Fromm, the eminent psychiatrist, has applied this idea to Western teaching in general.

It is one of the unfortunate aspects of our Western concepts of discipline (as of every virtue) that its practice is supposed to be somewhat painful and only if it is painful can it be "good." The East has recognized long ago that that which is good for man—for his body and for his soul—must also be agreeable, even though at the beginning some resistance must be overcome.[19]

We attain full development whether in running or swimming or what you will, not so much by fighting against opposing forces as by coming to terms with them, by using them as aids to our objective. Without their opposition, we would experience no challenge. In swimming the greatest obstacle to achievement is the resistance of the water. But the swimmer that fights against that resistance achieves little. Rather he must think of the water as being buoyant as well as resistant, as being a friend as well as a foe. He must come to terms with the water, relax with it, discover how it can be used. So with the resistance of distance running.

All runners practice this theory, though quite unconsciously. To run time and again requires acceptance and use of the feelings of fatigue just as the body is required to accept and use, by reconversion, the physical effects of fatigue. Gordon Pirie has been one of the very few to write specifically of its uses.

British runners have been admired because they keep a sort of stiff upper lip even in the agony of a race. They restrain their emotions not to show suffering. The free runner [such as Zatopek] shows in his face and gestures that it is torture and agony to give his last ounce of .energy. How silly to pretend that it is not. Only the British would admire such repression. The restrained runner can never reach the greatest heights. His so-called style is a delusion. . . . British coaches are still trying to produce stylish, instead of uninhibited, athletes.[20]

But the chief advocate of this method was Percy Cerutty. Percy was a volcano of energy, physical and emotional. He could never talk for more than 60 seconds without waving his arms or striding furiously up and down, blaming everyone for his troubles, except his own rebellious nature. If I interpret his somewhat disconnected sentences correctly, Cerutty equated relaxation with uninhibited power and not at all with ease of effort. The latter is a "concept of weakly men and coaches."

Where the science and art of delivering full power without stress and strain is understood, the word relaxation is seldom used. Nor need it be. . . . Zatopek, in his day, was of course the greatest exponent of relaxed uninhibited punish-

---

[19] Erich Fromm, *The Art of Loving* (New York: Harper & Row, Publishers, 1956), p. 111.

[20] Pirie, *op. cit.*, p. 35.

ing effort, despite what the pundits think or say. . . . Relaxation therefore can never be the result of an act of will, nor can it be taught as a technique. It must be the result of, never a thing in itself. . . . For an athlete to attempt to relax by direction or will, the result will be: (1) Further tensions resulting from trying to abolish tension; (2) A weakly nonpositive, noneffectual attitude that militates against high-level performance.[21]

Most coaches decried the agonized facial expressions and the tense upper body of Emil Zatopek as indicating a lack of relaxation. But Cerutty, like Pirie, gained almost the opposite impression. To Cerutty, the primary qualities are indomitable will, all-conquering effort, never-doubting courage. To those who have such qualities, the negative and weakening implications of relaxation as being less than an all-out effort have little interest. To Cerutty then, relaxation meant control, not ease of effort. To one picture of Elliott striding forcefully, arms driving, face determined, Cerutty added the note: "There is no suggestion of ease, as implied by the usual concept of relaxation. Herb did it the hard way. He was strong enough, and resolute enough, to do it that way—success-fully." Cerutty could accept only the relaxation of the natural man, the primitive man who relaxes in and out of action as do the animals of the jungle and not as a result of trained caution or control or through a belief that the easy way is the best way.

The effects of Cerutty's teachings upon his greatest pupil, Herb Elliott, were crucial. Without Cerutty, Elliott could never have run as he did at Dublin and Rome. Elliott once wrote, "Maybe I'm not Herb Elliott, but Percy Cerutty." At any rate, Elliott's autobiography is filled with expressions that could only have been learned from his coach.

Percy helped me . . . by releasing in my mind and soul a power that I only vaguely thought existed. [Page 35]

In apparent conflict with this self-inflicted scourging was Percy's theory that running should be a free expression of the body; that my body in motion, in the words of the song, ought to be doing what comes naturally. [Page 50]

I must have faith in my body and allow it to run instinctively, i.e., without the mind. . . . In races I must let my body go—relax one hundred per cent. [Page 51]

He [Cerutty] introduced me to every book ever written about Francis of Assisi and said, "Walk towards suffering. Love suffering. Embrace it." [Page 38]

Pushing yourself in a thirty-mile run beyond what you thought were the borders of endurance is of great moral benefit. The purifying quality of the pain that has to be suffered is like that in confession.[22] [Page 144]

There are many more such references in Elliott's book and even more in that by Cerutty. Further, they were not alone in this attitude, for every runner has used it to some degree, even though unconsciously.

---

[21] Percy W. Cerutty, *Athletics* (London: Stanley Paul & Co., Ltd., 1960), pp. 82-84.
[22] Elliott, *op. cit.*

Other disciplines where pain, and especially, the expectation and fear of pain, is a problem are becoming active in making a similar approach. Positive education toward the pains of dentistry has been used successfully in some instances. All agree that the pains of childbirth are very severe for most women, though the degree to which this is physical or is mentally preconditioned is not known. There is now a widely used technique of delivery without the use of drugs by which awareness of pain is held to acceptable levels. During the pregnancy the mother is informed in a positive way as to the details of childbearing and birth. By education in a free and calm atmosphere, doubt and possible fear are prevented before they arise. By sharply focussing the mother's attention upon the experience of the uterine contraction itself while dissociating it from the negative and painful feelings implanted by common attitudes and gossip, delivery occurs quite matter-of-factly. So long as the mother regards it as a pain, she will fight against it and thereby magnify it, but if she can regard it as a muscular tension, she can learn how to go with it and relax with it—a technique which is a part of her prenatal exercises.

To shift to another more "distant" discipline, our Western world with its multiplying doubts, confusions, and pains is showing increased interest in the Oriental approach to these problems. On first reaction, this approach seems to be one of detachment and disinterest in human affairs. But the so-called Way of Zen, for example, goes far deeper than this. In writing of this "way," Alan Watts often uses terms very close in meaning to those we use in endurance running.

"Blocking" is perhaps the best translation of the Zen term "nien." . . . Takuan points out that this is the real meaning of "attachment" in Buddhism, as when it is said that a Buddha is free from worldly attachments. It does not mean that he is a "stone Buddha" with no feelings, no emotions, and no sensations of hunger or pain. It means that he does not block at anything. Thus it is typical of Zen that its style of action has the strongest feeling of commitment, of "follow-through." It enters into everything wholeheartedly and freely without having to keep an eye on itself.[23]

This is all very close to the unblocked grimaces of Zatopek which did not so much deny pain as come to terms with it, or to his practice of breath-holding until will power was no longer a problem. In another portion of this same book, Watts writes,

Social conditioning fosters the identification of the mind with a fixed idea of itself as the means of self-control, and as a result man thinks of himself as "I"—the ego. . . . It then becomes almost impossible to see how "I" can let go of "myself," for I am precisely my habitual effort to hold on to myself. I find

---

23 Alan W. Watts, *The Way of Zen* (New York: Pantheon Books, Inc., 1957), p. 148. © Copyright 1957 by Pantheon Books, Inc. Reprinted by permission of Random House, Inc.

myself totally incapable of any mental action which is not intentional, affected, and insincere. Therefore anything I do . . . to let go, will be a disguised form of the habitual effort to hold on. I cannot be intentionally unintentional or purposely spontaneous. . . .

For what I cannot help doing I am doing spontaneously, but if I am at the same time trying to control it, I interpret it as a compulsion. As a Zen Master said, "Nothing is left to you at this moment but to have a good laugh."

In this moment the whole quality of consciousness is changed, and I feel myself in a new world. . . . As soon as I recognize that my voluntary and purposeful action happens spontaneously "by itself," just like breathing, hearing, and feeling, I am no longer caught in the contradiction of trying to be spontaneous. . . . Seeing this, the compulsive, blocked, and "tied up" feeling vanishes.[24]

I have purposely left out the uniquely Zen references and have selected portions related to our topic of distance running. To those who find these comments of interest, I highly recommend not only Watts's writings but even more a little book by Eugen Herrigel, *Zen in the Art of Archery*. Though his purpose was to learn Zen Buddhism, not psychophysical relaxation, his experience in doing so by way of archery under a Zen Master was probably the longest and most intensive concentration on relaxation in action ever conducted. During more than four years Herrigel experienced the mystical exercises related to releasing an arrow from his bow without ever even shooting at a target. When at that point he thought he had gotten through the worst, the Zen Master replied, "He who has a hundred miles to walk should reckon ninety as half the journey."

One day the Zen Master called out, "Stop thinking about the shot! That way it is bound to fail." "I can't help it," Herrigel answered, "the tension gets too painful." The Master then replied in words that have direct meaning for us,

You only feel it because you haven't let go of yourself. It is all so simple. You can learn from an ordinary bamboo leaf what ought to happen. It bends lower and lower under the weight of the snow. Suddenly the snow slips to the ground without the leaf having stirred. Stay like that at the point of highest tension until the shot falls from you. So, indeed, it is: when the tension is fulfilled, the shot *must* fall, it must fall from the archer like snow from a bamboo leaf, before he even thinks of it.[25]

Only when Herrigel had learned to release all worry, disquiet, and tension, to let himself and the arrow go with complete abandon, was he allowed to try a test of archery as we think of it. Few endurance runners will go so far to reach a perfection of relaxation, of what we could then call the artless art of running. But the way to approach the problem, or

---

24 *Ibid.*, p. 142.
25 Eugen Herrigel, *Zen in the Art of Archery* (New York: Pantheon Books, Inc., 1953), p. 71.

should I say, nonproblem, seems to have been cleared for us. We don't have many bamboo leaves to observe, but perhaps an American pine or hemlock will do.

What conclusions should be reached as to these four methods of attaining relaxation in endurance running? First, we should realize that they are never clearly separable, that all runners and coaches, consciously or unconsciously, make use of all of them to some degree. Second, that most men will make greatest use of the first two, as being closer to common sense and accepted practice. Third, that the other two have great potential, though, like endurance training itself, they require patience, practice, and determined persistence. It may well be that the future "world's greatest distance runner" will be a man from the Far East, trained from childhood in the disciplines of Zen, though corrupted by the West's attachment to the rewards of action.

5 Systems of Training

Fartlek

What It is

Fartlek is a system of endurance training which demands hard but untimed efforts over whatever challenges of hill or woods path or sand dune or snow are available; then rests the body with easy jogging and refreshes the mind with the quiet and charm of a lake or wood or twist of road. Fartlek, in English, means "play-of-speed," or "speed-play," which in itself is a happy contrast to our American term "workout." Play is activity for its own sake, activity in which awareness of effort and even of oneself is lost in the doing. The activity of play can be demanding, as much so as any work, but the sense of exertion is lost in the fun of playing.

The advocates of fartlek have pointed out that this is the way young animals and children develop. For a while they play hard—they prefer running to walking—but when they feel tired, they rest. And they rest for only a while until, again, they want to play hard.

Some of the material in this chapter is from J. Kenneth Doherty, *Modern Track and Field* (2nd ed.; Englewood Cliffs, N. J.: Prentice-Hall, 1963), pp. 166-92, 222-23. Reprinted by permission of the publisher.

As Major Raoul Mollett points out,

Fartlek was perhaps the most alluring discovery since the beginning of the century in the realm of training. . . . A window was opened on the forest, and at the same time an idea of training emerged which one would classify as "happy." Fartlek, with its walks, its runs at slow pace through the woods, its short sprints, was able to revolutionize the training of the track world. . . . There is without doubt not a single irreconcilable sedentary person who would not feel a twinge of nostalgia when faced with the thought of a man running barefoot on springy moss, in a setting of forests and lakes reflecting the sky. Faced with this picture, the track world felt an irresistible rise in spirits.[1]

Fartlek has been adopted by men of many countries and of course has been adapted to whatever conditions of terrain were at hand. The English use their rolling hills and dirt side-roads; Americans, their golf courses; Australians, their long stretches of beach sand and bush paths. But whatever the terrain, the primary emphasis remains on getting tired without feeling tired; on multiplying the physical hardships of training while soothing its pains with the balm of everchanging nature.

Its Origins

As one should expect, fartlek evolved. It was not invented by any one person, in any one country, or at any one time. One could argue that Walter G. George, English champion from 1879 to 1884, used a form of fartlek in training at varying speeds over the hills and dales of England. Hannes Kohlemainen, Finnish Olympic champion, 1912, 1920, rarely ran on the quarter-mile track. Gunder Hägg fulfilled all the tenets of fartlek in his training from 1940 through 1945 at a primitive tourist camp in northwest Sweden. (See page 82.) Haakan Lidman writes,

It started about 1938 when in Sweden a fellow called Johnsson from Kaelarna, a little village in the northern part, . . . found out that his training in the forests gave him the strength he needed for the hard races on cinder tracks. He followed what everybody thought was a terrible training-scheme, working out much more than was customary. But he was able to do it without harm, because he was not spoiling his muscles on a hard track.[2]

All agree that the naming of the system and the first writings on its values—one of the best ways of claiming fatherhood—were done by Gosta Holmer, chief coach for the Swedish Olympic Team, 1948. His replies to requests for information from American track coaches were written with a frankness and open-heartedness that are refreshing in contrast to the narrow nationalism in some sports areas. In one of them he said,

My opinion is . . . that it is not the races run that make the runner, but

---

[1] Major Raoul Mollet, "Interval Training," *How They Train*, Fred Wilt, ed. (Los Altos, Calif.: *Track and Field News*, 1959), p. 97.

[2] Haakan Lidman, "Why the Swedes Excel!" *The Amateur Athlete*, March 1947, p. 8.

rather his training methods. Here in Sweden we saw ourselves conquered by the Finns; we gained a certain standard, until I, in the middle of 1930, decided to try to create something new, something that suited our mind and the nature of our country. I rejected the American opinion, that the runners should have fixed distances to run during their daily training-schedule; I realized of course the great importance of that, but I wanted to give the boys a feeling of self-creating, I wanted them to get to understand themselves, and then fix the training according to their own individuality. Speed and endurance are the marks a runner should follow in his training. Following these lines I made up a system, that I call FARTLEK (meaning in English, play-of-speed, or speed-play), and it runs as follows:

The running should be done on cross-country where the surface is soft and springy, although in the large cities, where it is difficult to get to a forest, you should make a path on or around a sports field, and make the path soft by covering it with sawdust.

The athlete should train from one to two hours each day, according to the following schedule:

1. Easy running from five to ten minutes (as a warm-up).
2. Steady, hard speed for one to two km. [⅝ mile to 1¼ mile].
3. Rapid walking for about five minutes.
4. Easy running, broken by wind-sprints of from 50 meters to 60 meters [55 yards to 65 yards] and repeated until you feel a little tired.
5. Easy running with three or four swift steps now and then. (In reality, these swift steps would be like the sudden speeding up of a runner during a race when he tries to fight off a challenger who is trying to pass him. The body suddenly lurches forward, and three or four quick, sudden steps are taken.)
6. Full speed uphill 150 meters to 200 meters [165 yards to 220 yards].
7. Fast pace for one minute following this trial of strength described in (6). The above described work can be repeated until the end of the period of the workout; but every athlete should well remember that he must not feel tired but rather stimulated after the training.[3]

The extent to which this program is followed is of course dependent upon the individual, his time, his energies, and the phase of season. In *Track and Field News,* Cordner Nelson states,

Mid-season training is different. As Fred Wilt pointed out in the third article of this series, some runners use little or nothing except Fartlek. But for those who want to see a fairly typical program as recommended by Holmer, here are schedules for the mile . . . :

Monday—1. Fartlek 45 minutes.
        2. First 440 of race.
        3. Repeat 2 or 3 times. (Easy running for 5 minutes between these runs.)
        4. Walking and easy running to complete 2 hours.
Tuesday—1. Fartlek 20 minutes.
        2. 880 on track (2 seconds per lap slower than race).
        3. Repeat within an hour. (Easy running on sward between and after trials.)

---

[3] Gosta Holmer, "A Training Program," *Track and Field News,* II, No. 3 (April 1949), 6.

Wednesday—Walk in woods 2 hours.

Thursday—Same as Monday, but run uphill 2 to 9 times for 150 yards each time
        during Fartlek.

Friday—Same as Tuesday, but run 4 440's instead of 2 880's, each lap 1 second
        slower than racing speed.

Saturday—Rest.

Sunday—Warm up and run a mile. (First 440 and last 100 at racing speed.
        Middle race to seconds per lap slower than racing pace.)

(Pacing workouts are done at the individual athlete's own pace. Work out
hard once every ten days.)

Remember: these schedules are not blueprints. Each athlete must use his
head. The Swedes are extremely practical about fitting the schedule to the
needs of the individual. For example, Holmer says: "It is wrong to give a
student at Yale the same work in training as a man who, in the struggle of life,
has to walk ten miles." [4]

A further interpretation and development of fartlek is made by S. A.
Tomlin in the British publication *The Athlete*.

The runners practice "Fartlek" twice each week during early training, and
once each week during competitive periods, over the country or on a grass sports
field.

Speed is added by 220 yards bursts on the track two or three times each week.
The runner does a series of such bursts at a speed faster than the average speed
of his race. For instance, a 4 mins. 24 secs. miler runs each 220 yards at an
average speed of 33 secs. His speed training would then be 220 yards in 28/29
secs. He runs 220 yards, walks back to the starting point and repeats, doing
this until he begins to feel weary. The training is then finished off with about
30 minutes of easy running on the soft grass.

On other days the training consists of walking and easy running for 1–2 hours,
the exercise being eased off to suit personal reactions, and stopped before
fatigue occurs.

Gosta classifies the schedule of training into four progressive periods of activity—the months shown being applicable to the Swedish season, which is a little
later than ours:

1. Conditioning period: January to mid-April. Walking, easy running, and
   indoor gymnastic exercises.
2. Pre-season: Mid-April to mid-May. Running work and "Fartlek" with some
   speed training.
3. Early competitive season: Mid-May to early July. Training as above but
   one competition each week.
4. Competitive season: Early July to September. Amount of training according to amount of racing.[5]

---

[4] Cordner Nelson, "Swedish Distance Training Schedules," *Track and Field News*,
II, No. 8 (September 1949), 4.

[5] S. A. Tomlin, "Running Training in Sweden," *The Athlete* (official publication
of the Amateur Athletic Association, 1 Trebeck Street, London, England), Spring
1951, p. 28.

The Uses of Fartlek

Fartlek, in its basic meaning of alternate hard running and recovery running over whatever challenging terrain the local topography offers, has been used in as many ways as there are kinds of coaches and varieties of natural environment. It lends itself easily to every need, but we should be clear and certain that fartlek has as specific purposes and careful organization as interval training. Fartlek is not a carefree "go-as-you-please" system, as some have described it. Certainly it is not an escape from hard work. From a training and performance standpoint, there is no more value in easy running on pine-needled paths than in easy running on a cinder track. To serve its ends, fartlek must be as physically demanding in both mileage and intensity as any system. There is no other way to self-development and success. We repeat—because to misunderstand is to deny the system and follow a fool's path—fartlek may be speed-play but it is such play as climbing Mount Everest or seeking the North Pole by dog-sled.

The fartlek trainer tends to be on his own, with no coach to dictate his movements, with no measuring tape to pin down his distances, with no watch to police his pace. But this does not mean that his plans and outcomes can be similarly happy-go-lucky and disorganized. The freedom and naturalness that are such wonderful assets in fartlek require a high level of self-discipline. In a sense, it does allow a man to run as he pleases, as long as he pleases to run within an intelligent plan and to the limit of his ability and present condition.

Some misinterpret fartlek as training which is not planned. True, the details of training are not as obvious as in interval training. But the requirements of knowing what one is doing and why he is doing it, as well as of doing it no matter what, are just as ironclad as in any system.

The great attractiveness of fartlek and the reason for its past successes lie in its free play under a permissive environment, but this also is its greatest weakness and the reason for its sometimes being discarded in favor of the more exacting conditions of interval training. The fault lies not in the system but in the failure of its followers to understand the whole of it, its rigorous responsibilities, along with its freedom.

Keeping this in mind, we shall consider the various uses that have been made of fartlek. Though the word "fartlek" does not appear in *Gunder Hägg's Dagbok* (training diary), his methods were clearly a forerunner of the system. Study of the 5000-meter training course he set up at Völödalen, shown in Fig. 5.1, discloses three places in which he ran with bursts of energy (*"Ryck"*), four hills (*"Uppfor"*) including one

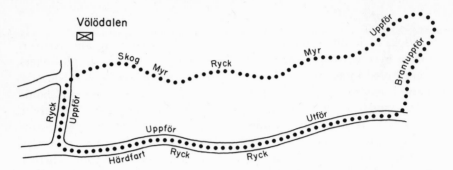

FIG. 5.1   Fartlek training as run on Gunder Hägg's training course at Völödalen in northwest Sweden. Distance: 5000 meters on forest paths, along a river and a lake. Key: *Skog*—woods; *Myr*—peat swamp; *Uppför*—uphill; *Brantuppför*—steep uphill; *Utför*—downhill; *Härdfart*—hard, fast running; *Ryck*—bursts of energy.

steep hill, two bogs or marshy areas ("*Myr*") in which the footing was heavy, and at least one area of hard fast running ("*Härdfart*"). On this course and others of similar merit, Hägg trained for five years, 1940–1945. One need only read his carefully maintained training diary to understand the careful thought that went into planning the exact details of his program and the inexorable insistence upon doing what must be done whether one feels like doing it or not. We are startled by the toughness of Elliott's sand dunes and Snell's marathon training. But often during the long Swedish winter, Hägg had to fight with both arms and legs through drifting snow to complete his 5000-meter course, sometimes in temperatures below zero.

Though most of the great runners of the world since 1940 have used fartlek in varying ways and degrees, the next great advocates of its values were Herb Elliott and his coach Percy Cerutty of Australia. Cerutty mentioned fartlek very seldom in his book, *Athletics,* but this was quite natural when we realize his craving for self-sufficiency and his refusal to be bound by the narrowness of a name or sense of indebtedness to others. Actually, Cerutty's creed of stotanism (a union of *sto*-ic plus spar-*tan*) with its insistence upon hardihood and simple living was but a variation of Hägg's training ideas as developed at Völödalen; his surf running and sand dunes a heightening of Hägg's snow and steep hills in the woods; his demand for repeated wild surges forward a device borrowed from Zatopek and Kuts, which had grown out of Hägg's "*härdfart*" (to make hardy by bursts of speed).

But Cerutty and Elliott added a new dimension to these details of training: a dimension of complete and uninhibited individual freedom in all the ways that a runner may secure it: freedom from the coach even though the coach is loathe to grant it; freedom from the demands of civilized living, civilized foods, civilized clothing and shelter; freedom from the exact and narrow schedules of interval training; freedom from any definite plan for competitive racing. In fact, one wonders how someone who craves freedom to this extent could respond to the rigorous commands of hard training day after day after day. It is fortunate for modern athletics that both men were driven by a common need for mastery of themselves and of others through running. Fred Wilt wrote that when "asked why he runs, Herb said he regards it as a way of expressing himself through pain, and proving himself the better man." Cerutty explained,

As I developed my ideas I almost entirely abandoned the orthodox and traditional way of training for running—that is, running on level ground, tracks, etc., walking or running up hills slowly, i.e., conserving energy, and trying to become faster and stronger by repeated efforts on the track.

In place of these customary athletic activities I "trained" by long walks in our mountains, covering such distances as 220 miles in ten days—as an example—carrying a rucksack with food, tent, etc., and recording eventually 200 miles in five days, two of the five rest, or nonactive days.

Instead of running on hard surfaces I commenced running on soft surfaces, until now much of our training in the winter conditioning period is done running on the soft, dry, loose sand of our Australian beaches. Also we run up the steep sides of sand dunes, and when in urban districts, select the steepest hills in parks or streets and run as vigorously up them as we are able.

Such activities use the body as a resistance, and I hold that for the development of the legs and lungs and heart little or no other exercise for the legs is necessary.[6]

Then, in further explanation,

In his ordinary life he [man] has little chance to escape from the humdrum, the routine. Why then . . . add his exercise . . . to the list of compulsions? Athletics should be, and with me is, a prime means to escape from these imprisoning conditions to exult in our liberty, free movement, capacity to choose. Our training should be a thing of . . . enthusiasm . . . not a daily grind upon a grinding track, artificially hard. . . . How much better to run with joy, sheer beauty and strength, to race down some declivity, to battle manfully to the top of another. . . .

We train as we feel but we rarely feel lazy. Sometimes we go out for long steady runs on the dirt roads—20 miles is common. Elliott has run to 30 miles before exhaustion set in. This was in the heat of our summer. Two days later he won a handicap 880 from scratch, coasting in in 1:51. Strong? I'll say, built in and developed at Portsea, where we haven't a track of any kind at all. It is a truism to say that Elliott never trains on a clay or cinder track and rarely runs in shoes of any kind.[7]

---

6 Percy Cerutty, *Athletics* (London: Stanley Paul & Co., Ltd., 1960), p. 52.

7 Percy Cerutty, *Running with Cerutty* (Los Altos, Calif.: *Track and Field News*, 1959), p. 17.

An interesting description of what can be taken as a fairly typical day for Elliott at Cerutty's Camp Portsea is provided by the Australian track writer, Joe Galli.

Arrived Saturday afternoon. Elliott and two friends had just returned from a 30-mile hike over the rugged terrain, sleeping under the stars at night. A day previously Herb had run a mile in four minutes. We dived into bunks at Cerutty's headquarters and slept nine hours. At 5:00 A.M. we were up. We jogged half a mile to the beach, spent 30 minutes running along the hard sand and plunging into the surf, then back for breakfast. Soon we were off again, running over a sandy, bush track course of just over a mile with two killing climbs. I was proud to break ten minutes for the course. Herb ran it five times, never in more than 6:10. Next—weight lifting. Elliott lifted 200 pounds in the ordinary dead lift, and 125 in the press. Lunch was followed by a discussion of training. Then we tackled a giant 80-foot sandhill. One run up the hill finished me. I found it even hard to walk through its deep loose sand. Elliott scampers up as though it were a moderate grass slope.[8]

Evaluation of Fartlek

Advantages. 1. It develops self-dependent and resourceful runners. No coach is present, no tape has laid out measured distances, no watch forces the pace. The mature runners, who, like Elliott, have "an intensified craving for achievement," find it a paradise of free low-tension running. He alone decides how far and how fast he shall run, and when and where he shall run again. Elliott writes,

Most athletes imagine themselves at the end of their tether before they're even seventy-five per cent exhausted. I was so determined to avoid this pitfall that if at any time I thought I was surrendering too soon to superficial pain I'd deliberately try to hurt myself more.

It's a challenging soil, high in nutrients, in which the deep-rooted, the self-impelled will thrive as under no other system of training.

2. Its proponents claim it is physically challenging and mentally invigorating and refreshing. As young boys in northern Michigan we used to enjoy scrambling to the top of the great sand banks along the shores of Lake Michigan and often raced to see who would be "King of the Mountain." Exhausting? Yes, it probably was, but we did it for the fun and the challenge of it and the question of fatigue just never arose. That's the way of fartlek: it's work, mighty exhausting work, but the challenge of it makes the work seem like play.

Older systems had so many inhibitions: no strength exercises—they'll slow you down; never go swimming during the training season—it'll build

---

[8] Joe Galli, "A Week-end at Portsea," *World Sports* (London: Country and Sporting Publications Ltd.), November 1958, p. 6.

soft muscles; stay away from all other sports and vigorous activities—they'll lead to injury and distraction; never go mountain or hill climbing—it'll stiffen your muscles and shorten your stride. In contrast, fartlek encourages doing anything that is vigorous and demanding of big-muscle energies. Imagine the permissiveness of a system that allowed Elliott to run close to the point of complete fatigue and sometimes heat exhaustion, then plunge into the cold waters of the Pacific for what he called a refreshing swim. Above all else, fartlek first builds men—men capable of handling any task, however unrelated, however tough, under any conditions. While doing this, it builds men that can run.

3. On days when mileage rather than intensity of effort is of primary concern, fartlek provides a pattern of activity that is as natural to young men as it is to young children and animals. They play hard for a while, as hard and as long as it pleases them, then they rest until they are ready to play hard again. So with fartlek.

4. It provides basic endurance training for all endurance events. Four-forty men, half-milers, milers, and two milers can all follow the same basic program. Gradually they come to realize that the demands of their special events are basically the same, that a man of good natural speed who is in shape for a two-mile run is also in shape for a good half-mile run. To say it differently: to improve endurance is not to lessen speed; it will improve the ability to maintain speed when it really counts, during the final struggle to the tape.

5. The daily training session tends to be run on a total time and mileage basis rather than on a number of exact distances and exact times and exact recovery periods. Sometimes, when conditions are enjoyable, even time will slip away and the runner will realize only after the workout how much work he has actually accomplished. Runners cover more miles and yet do not feel so tired. Much of fatigue is related to an attitude of mind—we feel tired because we are aware of how much work we have done. Remove that awareness and fatigue falls away. Fartlek is a way of removing awareness. It thus permits greater physical effort.

6. The softer running surfaces of woods and field paths encourage greater general relaxation of muscles and therefore lead to less muscle soreness. This advantage should not be overvalued, however, for after all, we are preparing ourselves for running on hard surfaces. Better to use softer paths when desirable but then supplement them with other surfaces that prepare the muscles for the hard all-weather tracks that are rapidly being adopted.

7. Fartlek provides a place for practice somewhere, anywhere, at any time of day or night. There need be no cinder track, carefully brushed and rolled. A foot of snow is an opportunity, not a hindrance. If we stumble and flounder, that's good. It just means that more muscles are

being conditioned. One of the athletes we have coached was in medical school. He had almost no opportunity to leave the confines of his school building. Yet he felt he reached a sound basic condition by running up a varying number of flights of stairs; up, then down—sometimes as many as ten floors at a time. Fartlek? Call it what you will.

8. The uncertain footing of open running tends to develop a shorter and more efficient stride—certainly an advantage in the longer distance runs.

Disadvantages. 1. Immature and inexperienced runners may misuse the freedom of fartlek, either by not doing enough, or more likely, by attempting to do too much too fast too soon. They may gain an impression that fartlek training is really "go as you please," and assume there is some magic in the woods or fields that makes it unnecessary to work hard and purposefully. This weakness places a burden on the coach to teach the responsibilities and specific goals of fartlek, not merely in terms of hard work, but more importantly, in terms of just when and why and what kind of hard work is most developmental. At least some of the time the coach usually spends on interval training, closely supervising each runner, should be spent on educating fartlek runners to be intelligent in their training and not merely tough. Better yet, follow Cerutty's example of showing the way. Elliot wrote,

> Percy, for instance, believes that if anyone presumes to show a group of people how to do something he must be prepared first to do it himself. The day before any of my important races he would run four laps of the nearest oval, usually the equivalent of a mile, with all the speed he could muster, and then stagger over to me, eyes bulging and tongue lolling. "Well, you may be able to run faster," he'd gasp, "but tomorrow you can't run any harder than that." [9]

And Percy was in his sixties at the time! Yes, you may feel this is impossible for you, but, to a comparable extent, the inhibitions of your own mind will become the inhibitions of those you teach, especially with regard to the supreme worth of trying.

2. The advocates of fartlek tend to extol the glories of nature: soft pine-needled paths, sea-beaches, and the challenge of a wooded hill. But most of the runners of the world do not have such natural glories at hand. Rather, they have paved streets, reeking with exhaust fumes, concrete walks with strait-laced pedestrians who, as the Englishman Loader writes, are likely to jeer, "Mary Ann, look, it's a runner! He's got nae claes on!" But even the worst cities have cemeteries and river banks and zoos and golf courses which the determined will seek out, even though forced to do so at hours when decent folk—and the police—are indoors.

---

[9] Herb Elliott, *The Golden Mile* (London: Cassell & Company, Ltd., 1961), p. 35. Also published as *Herb Elliott's Story* (New York: Paul R. Reynolds, Inc., 1961).

Interval Training

What It Is

Interval training is a system of repeated efforts in which a distance of measured length is run on a track at a timed pace alternately with measured recovery periods of low activity. For example, ten laps of 440 yards each at a pace of 65 seconds are run alternately with ten recovery laps of relaxed jogging, each requiring three minutes. It is commonly stated that there are five factors in interval training:

1. terrain, which is always a measured, flat running track,
2. a distance to be repeated,
3. the number of times it is run,
4. the pace at which it is run, and
5. the recovery interval of relaxed jogging.

This however is an oversimplification. Other factors can and will be discerned as our understanding of training becomes more specific and complete. For example, a sixth major factor lies in the degree of ease with which a given workout is accomplished. Ease should be interpreted not merely in the sense of being easy but also with overtones of mastery: of freedom from physical and mental tension or strain; of a willed control over the pains and "tying up" of fatigue; of optimum relaxation both physical and mental; of satisfaction in a tough job well done.

The Values of Interval Training

The presence of six or more factors in interval training quickly makes clear its greatest asset: an almost infinite variety and flexibility of workout. Only the flat track is fixed. Theoretically, any one of the other five factors can be made the measure of gradual progress while four are held constant. For example, while running the same distance, pace, recovery interval, at the same degree of relaxation, the number of repetitions of the distance can be gradually increased over months of daily practice. This is the primary emphasis during the early and middle season. Or, holding the other factors constant, the pace at which the distances are run is gradually increased. This is usually emphasized during late season.

This wide range and flexibility of application allows individual choice in selecting a personal system. Each individual coach or runner can choose what appeals to him, physically and emotionally, after careful study of the values inherent in each phase of the system, and, equally important, of his own needs. Each man can do it "my way." This, of course, is one of the best measures of any training system: the degree to which it has a sense of special personal value, meaning, or freshness to a particular runner. This need for freshness cannot be overemphasized. Every system must be based upon procedures that are sound for runners in general. But to this soundness must be added the zest of new discovery, of adventure in untried areas, of unique application.

A system as variable as interval training has values too numerous to cite in detail. In addition to those suggested above, the following values are of special importance:

1. It substitutes frequency of optimum stress conditions for the single steady state of long distance running.

2. During its recovery intervals, it provides many opportunities for the man (mind and body) to overcompensate for the stresses placed upon him and thus develop ever-greater powers to prevent and overcome fatigue.

3. More specifically, it develops the stroke volume (blood output divided by heart rate—a primary concern in endurance running) beyond what is possible by steady running.

4. Distance-pace can be fixed exactly according to what produces optimum stress and development in this particular runner, whereas steady running at longer distances requires a slower-than-optimum pace.

5. Since interval training occurs within the narrow confines of a 440-yard track, it permits a more satisfactory and more frequent use of modern telemetering devices by which the scientist can supplement the judgment of the coach in determining just how much and what kind of work is best. At present writing, increased distances make telemetering much more complex and expensive.

6. It arouses less awareness of the pains or boredom of fatigue because of the short duration and challenge of each run and thus maintains more zest in the workout (this of course is also one of its great weaknesses).

7. It permits training in pace judgment under certain conditions.

8. In terms of total stress, it accomplishes in less than one hour what would require a much longer time when running steadily at a slower pace.

9. It permits a gradual progression in measured work dosages, because it is precisely measurable, or a short spurt in intensity if that is needed.

10. It brings forth its own challenge and attainable goal each day.

11. It allows the individual to build, in measurable quantities, upon the experience of the preceding year.

12. It allows the individual to be largely independent of his coach.

13. It adjusts easily to a year-round training program in which constant changes in the degree of stress minimize boredom and staleness.

There are still other advantages, of course.

The Origins of Interval Training

No one person or country can be credited with the invention of interval training. Runners of the 1920's did "ins and outs," or took a series of "wind sprints," or did "repeated speed work." In somewhat similar fashion, fartlek constantly varies the distance and stress of its faster runs. Like most systems, interval training evolved gradually over a period of ten years and more.

Mihaly Igloi recalled that in 1932 Kusocinski, the great Polish distance runner, proceeded to run 200 meters 15 times on the running track— *following* a cross-country workout. Woldemar Gerschler, guided by physiologist Dr. Herbert Reindell, is generally credited with perfecting the system between 1935 and 1940 in his work with Rudolf Harbig. But in a conversation with the writer in 1960, Gershler denied such sole parenthood, as well as knowledge of the true father. In a paper given at Melbourne in 1956, Carl Diem,[10] honored sports leader in Germany, attributed the origin of interval training to the thinking of Lauri Pihkala, an outstanding Finnish runner before World War I, a leading authority on sports, and organizer of the first Finnish coaching school.

In answer to my own letter of inquiry, Mr. Pihkala wrote a long and delightful letter on June 15, 1962, disclaiming credit for its origin but also writing,

Dr. Diem seems to give credit to me for it due to two chapters I wrote in 1920 for a German work edited by Dr. Krummel titled *Athletics*. Some passages from the chapter "The Rhythm between Work and Rest":

Still more important is the wavelike rhythm in the daily workouts. . . . For instance, an 800- to 5000-meter runner profits more by dashing 130-200 meters four or five times at intervals of 10 to 15 minutes than from running 3000 meters or 5000 meters at moderate pace. . . .

During the progress of training the workouts shall grow shorter but more intensified. . . .

Well, [on re-] reading this . . . these seem to me platitudes, but nobody knows, maybe those speculative Germans discovered [interval training] among my speculative thoughts. Or maybe my artistical metaphorical style impressed the literate Diem and inspired him to see grains which led to the discovery of interval theory.

When I talked with Gershler, he said, I thought, in fun, "Why I always thought you Americans invented Interval Training!" Perhaps he was serious, for Pihkala's letter goes on to say that his thinking was strongly influenced by both the practice and the writing of George W. Orton, University of Pennsylvania track coach and author of *Athletic Training for Schoolboys*. Orton, a great champion runner, was nicknamed "the boy who never walked" and strongly advocated that "speed is the basis for success in track and should be included in the training of all long distance runners."

As a matter of further interest, Pihkala wrote that Paavo Nurmi "cultivated in his practice, during the years preceding the 1924 Paris

---

[10] Carl Diem, "Interval and Looseness," *Report of the World Congress of Physical Education* (Melbourne, 1956), pp. 109-18.

Olympics, long and repeated sprints . . . from 200 to 600 meters . . . as a forerunner of interval training. But according to his nature, Nurmi used to keep his secrets of training for himself, [and] not . . . reveal them to his competitors."

It seems evident that interval training was an evolution to which many contributed. Fortunately, the great measure of its value provides ample credit for everyone.

It seems clear, however, that major credit—for making exact measurements and organizing the various elements in interval training—should go to Woldemar Gershler and Dr. Reindell. World attention first came to their methods when, on July 15, 1939, Rudolf Harbig set his first world record of 1:46.6 for the 800 meters and then again, on August 12, set his second record of :46.0 for the 400 meters. The details of Harbig's training will be described in the section on half-miling and should be read there. In summary, however, not only the over-all pattern but many of the variations of interval training were clearly indicated in Harbig's 1939 training diary, and Gershler, of course, should be credited with inspiring them.

It should be realized that Gerschler has never restricted training of his men to interval training or even to work on the 400-meter track. For example, Harbig's carefully maintained diary [11] details the long-distance woods running that was done throughout the early winter months and intermittently during the later competitive season, as is advocated today by many respected coaches. In fact, on February 16, 1939, he competed in a 2000-meter run, a heretical performance by a 400-meter man. Gerschler's systematic methods are illustrated by a December 16, 1938, workout as follows: (1) 45 minutes running, (2) 1000 meters 3:05 with 15 minutes of jogging, (3) 1000 meters in 3:02 with 10 minutes of jogging; (4) 1000 meters in 3:11. Such work is similar to the repetition running emphasized 17 years later by Franz Stampfl in his book on running. On February 22, 1939, Harbig ran 5 × 300 meters with short rest periods between. Such a pattern became basic in later years, comparable to that of Roger Bannister in 1954.

Similarly on May 2, 1939, three months before he set his 400-meter record, Harbig ran five 200-meter dashes in a total period of 20 minutes in :23.2, :23.8, :24.6, :24.7, and :24.2. On June 1, 1939, Harbig ran what was later called the "funnel system": two runs of 30 meters each; 20 of 50 meters; two of 80 meters; one of 150 meters; one of 200 meters; and a final run of 400 meters. Mihaly Igloi added to this method by also running the reverse, from 400 meters down to 30 meters. In his opinion it is good to start and finish with speed-work. Most tragically, Harbig was

---

[11] *Gunder Hägg's Dagbok* (Stockholdm: Tidens Forlag, 1952), pp. 26 ff.

missing in action during World War II, and no other men of a talent far above that of his contemporaries came under Gerschler's wise teaching. America heard nothing of interval training until after 1953.

The Factors of Interval Training

We have mentioned six factors in the interval training system. Except for the first, the measured flat running track, each of these factors can be particularly emphasized and thus make its unique mark on endurance. As to which is most effective depends on many elements: the time of year in terms of training, the maturity of the runner in terms of endurance, the extent to which terrain is available so that other systems such as fartlek can be used, the competitive distance for which the runner is training, the runner's attitude toward training, etc.

The consensus is that development in distance running is above all else a problem in increased stamina. All that changes is the emphasis—the means by which such stamina is achieved. First, in developing a young runner, first, in each year for all runners, comes stamina of the increased mileage type. This can be achieved by steady running at long distances, by varied running as in fartlek, or by endlessly increasing the number of repetitions of "slow pace-short distance" as in interval training. (See Method 1 in Table 5.1.)

As this kind of stamina is reached to a satisfactory extent, the emphasis gradually shifts to speed-work. (See Method 4 in Table 5.1.) This does not mean stamina is neglected; stamina is still the main concern. But the emphasis within stamina is shifted toward faster pace. Later, as the competitive season nears, speed-work is lessened in favor of pace-work. (See Method 3 in Table 5.1.) But here again, stamina is still the end in view; pace-work is the means to that end, too.

Throughout all this work, development of the mental-emotional aspects of stamina is just as essential as the physical aspects. Each type of stamina (mileage-speed-pace) brings forth special problems in willed control; to neglect the development of this control is to weaken the entire structure of stamina.

TABLE 5.1

CONSTANTS AND VARIABLES IN INTERVAL TRAINING

Method	Constant	Constant	Constant	Constant	Constant	Variable
1.	Distance A	Pace A	Interval A	Ease A		Number X
2.		Pace A	Interval A	Ease A	Number A	Distance X
3.	Distance A	Pace A	Interval A		Number A	Ease X
4.	Distance A		Interval A	Ease A	Number A	Pace X
5.	Distance A	Pace A		Ease A	Number A	Interval X

Note that Table 5.1 is set up within an A level of development. As this level is reached, a shift can be made to a more difficult B level, then to a C level, and so on as high as one can go. For example, when total A distance is sufficient, according to the coach's judgment or the limits of time for each day's practice, a new B pace can be set and a new progression attempted in terms of A distance.

1. The Distance To Be Repeated

Careful consideration reaches the conclusion that there is no one repeated distance in interval training that meets all needs; each has its special values and special limitations. We might say a distance must be long enough to create the kind of stress (and therefore development) that is required by this runner's racing distance. This would mean running that distance in practice. When we define stress broadly—physical-mental-emotional, we realize there is a need for training at such a distance. But to do so exclusively would be like training for strength in shot-putting only by putting the shot, whereas experience has proved that weight-lifting is more effective.

Such scientists as Dr. Hans Reindell and Dr. Joseph Nocker have shown that, from at least a cardiovascular standpoint, there is an optimum distance-pace for each man that will allow him to make an optimum number of repetitions and thus produce maximum development. They have concluded that this distance should not require more than 60 seconds to complete and that the exertion of doing so should permit the pulse rate to drop to about 120-140 per minute at the end of a recovery interval of 40–90 seconds. This would mean something less than 440 yards and, depending upon the pace, as short as 120 yards.

There is a tendency in the United States to use 440 yards as the best training distance. True, 440 yards is long enough to provide a sense of sustained running, of steady rhythm and pace. Its stress effects are certainly more similar to those of distance running than are those of the 100-yard dash. Further, it is short enough to permit running at a rate that is optimum for cardiovascular development. But there is no magic in the exact distance of 440 yards. It happens to be one lap of the track as well as one-half or one-fourth or one-eighth of the runner's competitive distance. That is its main virtue. When working on an 11-lap track, as occurs indoors, two laps (320 yards) would be just as effective a distance and would permit even more repetitions.

Franz Stampfl argues the special values of what he calls repetition training in which mileage is the primary concern and longer distances

(880 yards up to two miles) are repeated at slower than competitive pace. After mileage has reached a sufficient length, the pace is gradually increased. For example, he suggests that a man build up to 6 × ¾ miles in 3-4:00 each, with 10 minutes of jogging between each. Then, over the course of three months of developmental training, the times of this same workout are reduced to 3:35 and then 3:30 for each ¾-mile run.

On September 1, 1955, I observed Pirie doing repetition training when he was at the height of that year's condition. After 30 minutes of warm-up in which he took many easy wind-sprints and a few light stretching exercises, Pirie ran three separate miles in 4:11.5, 4:15.8, and 4:18.9, with 30 minutes of jogging between them. He explained that this kind of workout has benefits, when one is in excellent condition, that cannot be obtained from running shorter distances or when the resting interval is cut to five minutes or less. Certainly fortitude, in the sense of firmness of mind despite fatigue, would necessarily be developed.

Distances can be classified as to their main values, although these depend on the pace and number of runs: (1) speed distances (100 yards up to 220 yards); (2) fast-pace distances (300 yards–880 yards); (3) competitive-pace distances (440 yards–one mile); and (4) slow, steady-pace distances (660 yards–1½ miles). Such classification is obviously uncertain, but it indicates differences that can have helpful applications.

We should keep in mind Dr. Nocker's conclusions (pages 102 and 103), based on physiological research, that these work periods "must not exceed 30 seconds" and that exertions of more than 90 seconds' duration are not successful. On the other hand, such research was concentrated upon heart-capillary effects and did not consider many factors of development, relaxation, and willed control that are also operative.

The question arises as to whether more than one distance should be used in a single workout. Again, Dr. Nocker's conclusions are helpful: that early efforts should be less stressful, that a distance such as 300 meters creates greater stress than one of 200 meters or less, and that therefore early distances might well be at 200 meters or less.

Certainly when a given workout is to be used as a measure of improvement or readiness, as in a time trial, all factors but one, including the distance of each run, should remain constant. The variable on which measurement is based is the only one which should change.

But under all other conditions, the maintenance of interest should come first. If varying the distance, as in the "funnel" system described on page 246, or in any helter-skelter way, makes running refreshing, by all means vary it; that is justification enough. The real secret of success in training for distance running is the ability to have fun while plugging on until your tongue drags on the ground.

2. *The Action and Length of the Interval between Runs*

Though I have tended to call this interval a "recovery interval," the research of Reindell and his associates [12] has clarified the fact that it actually serves the dual role of recovery *and* development. If recovery were the only concern, we would tend to jog until completely rested, then run again. Though Franz Stampfl had a reputation for tough training, he strongly recommended in his book that a man's breathing should return to normal before repeating the run. When he trained Bannister, four minutes were considered to be a rather minimum time for adequate recovery.

But Reindell emphasizes that, from at least the heart's standpoint, the interval between runs is a developmental period as well as a recovery period. During the first 30 seconds or so following each fast run, the heart actually undergoes its greatest stress and, therefore, its greatest development. Maximum heart rates apparently do not increase with training. If greater blood volumes are to be achieved, it must be through an increase in the amount of blood ejected by each stroke. This is achieved in two ways: by hypertrophy and by a more complete emptying of the heart. (Such hypertrophy is entirely normal and healthful—not at all pathological as was at one time implied by the term "athlete's heart.") When the exertion of the run is too great and the heart rate reaches 180 and more, the heart can neither fill nor empty completely. When the rate is below 180, the massaging or "booster-pump" action of the muscles aids the normal means for returning venous blood to the heart. Thus, it is "pressured" into a full expansion and still has time for a complete emptying. Such a stimulus for heart development is present during each interval between runs, up to about 20 times in a single workout. What is true for the heart also tends to be true for the other organs and systems of the body.

From such considerations, Reindell concluded that the most effective time for this recovery-development interval should be between 45 and 90 seconds. In a mature and well-trained man, when the pulse rate fails to return to between 120-140 within about 90 seconds, he has had enough interval running for that day.

Common sense tells us that the number of minutes between runs should be adjusted to a range of individual differences in maturity and condition. A young boy may need 10 or 15 minutes whereas a mature veteran will require only 30 seconds. Judgment based on individual re-actions should decide the length of rest, not the pronouncement of an expert or the reported practice of a champion.

---

[12] Herbert Reindell, Helmut Roskamm, and Woldemar Gerschler, *Das Intervalltraining* (Munich: Barth Publisher, 1962).

As to the kind of activity that should occur during this interval, it is generally agreed that the least effective method is to lie down. However, for purposes of research, Gerschler has experimented by asking his trainees to lie on a horizontal table immediately after running, with both the head and feet elevated. He found that their pulse rates returned to normal by this method just about as quickly as they did when jogging. Gerschler followed this method while working with Gordon Pirie in June 1960, when the latter was training for the 5000-10,000-meter runs at the Rome Olympics. He found that 100 meters at three-quarters speed raised Pirie's heart rate (normal resting rate—38) to about 170, and that about 15 seconds of horizontal rest with feet and head raised brought the rate down to about 120; then, he would run again. But when Pirie was working away from Gerschler, he did the usual jogging between runs.

Undoubtedly some men are experimenting as to just what speed or method of jogging will best aid recovery and development. In terms of venous blood return to the heart we can assume that rhythmical and relaxed action is best. In terms of attitudes and the will to run, enjoyable jogging would be an important consideration.

Occasionally a particular interval training workout is timed as a guide for measuring condition. When this is done, a fixed interval is necessary. For example, Bannister used 10×440 with an exact four-minute interval (total time: 40 minutes) as a test of readiness for his assault of the "4-minute barrier," which the historical limit of mile time was then called.

As an extension, as well as a variation, of such a fixed interval, Tom Courtney (1956 Olympic champion, 800 meters) reported a workout in 1955 by the three Hungarian greats, Iharos, Tabori, and Roszavolgyi under Coach Mihaly Igloi. It consisted of (1) a long warm-up; (2) 5×400 at :55 each with a jog of 400 between; (3) 5×400 at :55 each with a jog of 200 between; (4) 5×400 at :55 each with a jog of 100 between. In this case, as fatigue increased, the recovery interval was decreased!

It is one of the toughest interval training procedures to fix the other factors while gradually decreasing the length of the recovery period. Ibbotson writes,

The originator of the formula which brought me the world mile record was a Russian—Vladimir Kuts. During the winter of 1956-7, when I was training one lunch time with Gordon Pirie and Brian Hewson at Chelsea, we began a discussion on schedules. Pirie said he was going to try the Kuts method of reducing the interval between each set run. . . . My ambition was to become the leading 5000 metre runner in the world and avenge the defeat I suffered from Kuts in the Olympic Games. What could be better than to use his own ideas? It was no easy task reducing the interval of rest between each training run, and after much gruelling application I managed to get down to 45 seconds compared to my usual 90 seconds. Most people, including coaches, thought I was mad, but the results proved I was on the right lines.[13]

But we must remember that these were mature men reaching for world-record performances and driving their bodies and wills toward ever-greater toughness. Try this for your Everest, if you will, but climb a few foothills first.

One further suggestion on recovery jogging. That which works so effectively between runs is even more effective when all the runs are completed. A relaxed jog or even a walk of at least 20 minutes at the end of a workout maintains full circulation and aids both the rate and the degree of recovery. This is one important discovery of modern running. It should be considered as important in sound practice as the warm-up. It aids study during the coming evening, promotes relaxed sleep, and permits another good workout the next day. After a competitive race, such a warm-down furthers effective doubling later. As a further extension of this practice, a long walk on Sunday after a tough race on Saturday aids both mental and physical recovery to the extent that it permits a good workout on Monday.

In summary the determinants of the length of time that is needed for a recovery interval or whether it should be flexible or fixed are maturity, condition, purpose of workout, length of time available for total workout, and the manner in which fatigue is intended to develop during a workout. All these factors must be considered together; and there are others.

Some coaches who emphasize mileage tend to keep the distance-pace at a low level and the interval short. Thus the degree of fatigue within a workout tends to follow a shallow wave of variation. Other coaches who emphasize intensity of work tend to make the distance short, the pace fast, and the degree of fatigue momentarily high. A longer recovery period permits a fresh attack at the repeated distance-pace. Thus the degree of fatigue within this workout tends to follow a high wave of variation. Each method has its uses; each its values and its weaknesses. Most men will derive benefit from both methods during different periods of their careers and of each year's training.

3. Pace

When the emphasis of a given workout is on mileage, the pace is necessarily slow compared to a competitive race. If concern for the distance covered is great, the pace will be very slow. For the 440 it might be 30 seconds slower than a man's best time for that distance. This

---

[13] Terry O'Connor, *The 4-Minute Smiler* (London: Stanley Paul & Co., Ltd., 1960), p. 130.

will allow many repetitions with a minimum of strain. As the runner's condition improves, the number can be greatly increased.

A great deal depends on the number of months that are planned for gradual development. Coaches who strongly advocate mileage, devote about eight months, with variations of course, to this kind of training. These men argue that speed at the finish is not a question of who has the greatest potential speed but rather who has the stamina with which to maintain speed and slow down the least. Much can be said for this point of view.

However, physiologists suggest that there is a positive relationship between speed and endurance. In writing of strength as related to endurance, Laurence Morehouse states,

> The strength of the working muscle is a limiting factor in endurance. A load easily carried by strong muscles may quickly exhaust weak ones. When a strong muscle lifts a comparatively light load, only a relatively few fibers need to be brought into play. As these become fatigued, their threshold of irritability is raised, and they fail to respond to the stimuli. The stimuli then arouse fresh fibers and they take over the work, while the fatigued fibers recuperate in order to resume the burden later on if necessary.[14]

One may assume that, within limits, the greater the number of fiber groups available the greater the endurance of the muscle. The problem then becomes one of activating more and more fiber groups.

All modern distance coaches advocate speed work as a portion of training, although there are differences in their beliefs as to when and to what extent speed is an important factor. In *Franz Stampfl on Running,* pace tends to be kept slower than competitive pace throughout the year's schedule. Speed-work is on a supplemental basis only, as when Bannister ran repeated 150's after his regular workout. In contrast, other coaches feel that training at competitive pace or even faster is essential.

Reindell and Gerschler assumed that during the more strenuous period of a year's training, the stress of each run (distance-pace) should be sufficient to produce a pulse rate of between 120 and 140 at the end of a recovery interval of about 90 seconds or less. This was of course for mature and well-trained men.

4. Number

As with the other factors the answer to the question of what number of repetitions is best in a workout depends upon its intended value.

---

[14] Laurence E. Morehouse and Augustus T. Miller, Jr., *Physiology of Exercise* (3rd ed.; St. Louis: The C. V. Mosby Company, 1959), p. 208.

Number tends to be related to mileage. Most authorities agree that mileage is the first consideration in endurance training. "Best running is the result of more running." "The time in which you can run one mile is directly proportional to the time you've spent running many miles." "You can only find in yourself for a short distance what has already been built there over long distances."

Some successful coaches keep this emphasis on mileage throughout the entire career of a runner and throughout almost all of each year's training. Thus they tend to keep the pace slow and increase the number of repetitions. Other coaches, not so successful at the world level, but who have had success when the number of days and the hours of each day are limited and where tradition is against "marathon" training, have emphasized intensity and so-called "quality" of training. To them, rapidity of development is of greater concern than gradualness. Accordingly, they build up the number of repetitions so that total mileage (runs plus jogging) is from three to five times the distance; then they increase the pace to one that is one or two seconds faster than racing pace. Finally they try to reduce the recovery interval.

We have already mentioned the rule of thumb that a man has run enough repetitions when his pulse rate fails to return to 120-140 within about 90 seconds after running. When I talked with Gerschler in 1960, he seemed to feel that 20 repetitions was a sufficient number to produce optimum development in a single practice. He mentioned that, though he discouraged it, Pirie has run 100 meters 40 times during a single workout. Gerschler was sure this was too much and would work against the best development of a man rather than for it.

5. Degree of Ease

Degree of ease has not previously been listed as one of the essential factors in interval training. Yet its necessity is as obvious as its meaning is simple. One cannot be said to have mastered a given workout or task until one can do that task with relative ease, with full relaxation and certainty of willed control, despite its hardships and the pains of fatigue. To do a thing once is an accomplishment of great value to self-respect and self-reliance. But to do that thing again and again until one is certain of full mastery establishes a fixed base of accomplishment from which one can move safely and surely upward to the next base.

Degree of ease is not so much related to doing a thing easily in a physical sense as it is certainty of control in a mental sense. Any given workout is mastered when one knows with a sense of certainty that one can do it again and again and that it is safely within one's capabilities.

Achievement with relaxation is what is wanted before moving on to the next level.

Stampfl implies this in many ways in his book on running, and says it specifically in this way,

Concentrate on progressing upward by easy stages, never attempting to do that bit more until what you are now doing has become quite easy. Remember that each new rung imposes severe demands on fitness and you will not be able to measure up to them if you are not physically ready for them.[15]

6. Total Distance per Workout

A possible sixth basic factor in interval training is that of total distance covered each day. This might be a matter of the number of repetitions. But regardless of the emphasis in the organized portion of interval training, the runner should gradually increase his daily mileage. He can do it by taking long cross-country or fartlek work as a part of his warm-up, or by finishing up with a long tension-free warm-down after the strenuous workout is finished. Either method, or both for that matter, has much merit.

Other coaches advocate over-distance or "marathon" training as being preferable on a simple mileage basis. Some argue that the main advantage of interval training is that it allows men to rest periodically so they can return to running again and again. They feel the method has been oversystematized with regard to less important factors such as speed and pace. When it comes to training for better performance, they feel that more running is more important than faster running.

Some of the world's best coaches place the main emphasis for eight months of the year on increasing the daily training distance. It is interesting to read that in 1960, when Elliott was at his peak for 1500 meters, he was much disappointed at not having also been selected by the Australian committee to compete in the Rome marathon. His success in practice at running long distances against Murray Halberg and other long distance men had convinced him he was ready for the marathon. Similarly, Snell set a new world mile record on January 27, 1962, of 3:54.4 after only a few weeks of short distance training and just 55 days after having run a full marathon race.

These men speak of total mileages per week instead of specific times at specific distances. Snell was quoted as saying, "Ever since July . . . I've been running a hundred miles a week on roads." Elliott mentioned distances of 25 miles or more in his diary and on one occasion, while

---

[15] Franz Stampfl, *Franz Stampfl on Running* (London: Herbert Jenkins, Ltd., 1955), p. 43.

training en route from England to Sweden, ran ahead of the party bus for 15 miles in one hour and 27 minutes.

This modest performance remained unpublicized; yet personally it was as pleasing as some of my ballyhooed runs, strengthening as it did my secret ambition to be a marathon runner.[16]

Again, we are writing of men of maturity and years of hard training. The point is generally applicable, however, that a gradual and constant increase in the total distance covered in daily practice is probably the most essential factor to success in distance running.

Ways of Using Interval Training

Optimum development in long distance running requires 12 months of activity related to the building of stamina. Two of these months can be "vacations" from serious training but even the vacations should include interesting and vigorous games or activities that contribute to basic endurance. If there are only ten months of running, at least six of those months should emphasize stamina through increased mileage. American school emphasis on competition during about six of a possible ten months has tended to weaken this emphasis. Now, however, we have the example of Peter Snell who competed in a marathon race only a few weeks before setting a world record in the mile. It seems to be well established that mileage-stamina does not reduce speed-stamina.

In any case, shifts from one stage of emphasis to another occur gradually, in a rhythmic wave of change as is shown in Fig. 6.2 on page 130. An occasional workout on speed-stamina might well occur after only six weeks of training even though its period of emphasis is months away.

Note that in Table 5.2 the number of 440's increases up to 12 at 70 seconds each. This schedule assumes that that is a sufficient level of mileage and begins during the ninth week to increase the speed of these 440's to 68 and later, to 66 and 64 seconds. A plan for another runner might well increase the number of 440's to 18 or 20 before increasing the speed. Zatopek gradually increased his number to 60 at a relatively fast pace. Similarly, the number of 880's was increased to six, then the speed was gradually increased to 2:15. We emphasize again that these are merely patterns of development. Actual distances and paces can be decided only in terms of the development of each unique individual runner. Development within the plan of Table 5.2 is very gradual; individual development may well be faster. But be certain that full mastery of a given level of achievement has been gained before moving on to the next one.

---

[16] Elliott, *op. cit.*, p. 95.

TABLE 5.2

EXAMPLES OF DEVELOPMENT IN INTERVAL TRAINING *

About two months of conditioning in cross-country and fartlek are assumed.
Most sessions are preceded by 20-30 minutes of warm-up.

Weeks of Training

	1st	*3rd*	*5th*	*7th*
Mon.	Fartlek	3 × ¾ @ 3:30	8 × 440 @ 70s	Fartlek
Tues.	3 × 880 @ 2:20	Fartlek	Fartlek	12 × 440 @ 70s
Wed.	Fartlek	6 × 440 @ 70s	10 × 440 @ 70s	Fartlek
Thurs.	6 × 440 @ 70s	4 × 880 @ 2:20	4 × 880 @ 2:20	6 × 880 @ 2:20
Fri.	2 × ¾ @ 3:30	Fartlek	3 × ¾ @ 3:30	8 × 440 @ 70s
Sat.	6-8 × 440 @ 70s	8 × 440 @ 70s	Fartlek	4 × ¾ @ 3:30
Sun.	Rest	Easy Fartlek	Rest	Fartlek

	9th	*13th*	*17th*
Mon.	12 × 440 @ 68s	12 × 440 @ 66	12 × 440 @ 64
Tues.	4 × 880 @ 2:20	4 × 880 @ 2:15	4 × 880 @ 2:12
Wed.	12 × 440 @ 68s	3 × 4/4 @ 4:40	3 × 4/4 @ 4:35
Thurs.	Fartlek	Easy Fartlek	12 × 440 @ 64
Fri.	4 × ¾ @ 3:28	12 × 440 @ 66	Fartlek
Sat.	Rest	6 × 330 @ 45s	6 × 330 @ 42s
Sun.	Fartlek	Fartlek	Fartlek

Most sessions are completed by 20-30 minutes of relaxed jogging and walking.
* No man should follow this schedule exactly. It suggests trends, not actual work-outs.

Again, there is no simple answer to the problem of maintaining gradual and sound development within the realities of almost continuous competition in the American school system from October until June. Obviously one must choose between the needs of development and the demands of the week's competition. Theory would of course fit the competitive schedule to the needs of the individual man; practice may find itself driven toward compromise. After all there are few areas in life where the good of the individual rises solitary and supreme above all other considerations. But strive to keep the compromise as minimal and as temporary as possible.

Each individual's schedule should be planned carefully about four weeks in advance so that both development and awareness of development can be maintained. Though a full practice in groups or pairs may occur occasionally, two men would rarely follow the same schedule.

No particular competitive distance was held in mind while making up the schedule of Table 5.2. It might fit the needs of an 880 man as well as those of a three-miler. However, the 880 man might stop his progression in the number of distances at a lower figure and begin the progression in faster pace earlier in the training schedule. In all cases progression should creep during the early weeks of interval training. Later, when the man is ready for it physically and mentally, the overload in daily work will be increased relentlessly. The greatest single danger of interval training lies in its greatest strength: its constant challenge to do one's best and, therefore, to do too much too soon.

In response to an inquiry, Fred Foot, track coach of the University of Toronto and of the phenomenal Bruce Kidd (who at the age of 17 ran two miles indoors in 8:49.2), summarized his training ideas as follows:

Since speed is inborn or innate, we feel that it is next to useless to try to improve our performance through speedwork. Thus in the training time at our disposal we try to build stamina. Under this method sprint times improve because the athlete builds the strength necessary to enable him to utilize his inborn speed over the racing distance.

Our workouts vary from repetitions of 300 yards to one mile under the tyrannical domination of the stop watch at all times. The total workout, including the recovery jogging, usually covers from 5 to 10 miles. We rest one day each week. In our training the emphasis is placed upon the distance covered rather than upon the time the athlete covers the distance. . . . We feel it is better if the weaker athlete completes the full distance of a given workout, but at a slower speed (rather than cutting the distance in order to maintain the speed).

I wish to emphasize that not only our middle distance runners follow this schedule; everyone does it. The sprinters and the newcomers follow perhaps a modified version, but this is only until they build their stamina to the point where they can join in the fun!

The Scientific Basis of Interval Training

In 1960, Professor Joseph Nocker [17] published a review of the physiological bases for modern endurance training from which I have paraphrased the following conclusions:

1. Scientific studies confirm modern endurance training methods in their assumption that training by alternating periods of greater and lesser exertions does produce great development of related organ systems, such as metabolism, circulation, breathing, etc., than can be gained by continuous exertion.

2. A low degree of intensity during the work phase (longer distance–slower pace or short distance–slow pace–many repetitions) produces a high-level adaptation of the circulatory system but a low level of adaptation of the muscle system.

3. A highest level of intensity during the work phase with long recovery periods and few repetitions, as occurs when sprinting, produces a high level of adaptation of the muscle system but a low-level adaptation of the circulatory system.

---

[17] Joseph Nocker, *The Biological Foundations of Improvement through Training,* Don Igelsrud, Lother Schweder, and Dieter Reetz, trans. (Schorndorf, Germany: Verlag Karl Hofmann, 1960), pp. 78-85.

4. The intensity of work must be graded to individual capabilities.

5. The intensity of work must be great enough to obtain adaptation both in the muscles and in the heart. This can be gained by an intensity of exertion of at least 60 per cent and at most 80 per cent of maximal capabilities.

6. Since the related systems function more economically during the later work periods, interval work should not be done in equal doses of intensity. Rather, the early work periods should involve the least stress; later periods, the greatest stress. For example, a workout might well begin with 6 × 200m with increasing burdening and short recovery pauses; then after a longer recovery period of 4 to 6 minutes, a second set of 6 × 300m with short pauses, etc.

7. Scientific studies confirm that the phase of exertion should be relatively short, depending of course upon the rate of work. "I am of the opinion that the work phase must not exceed 30 seconds, assuming correct intensity of exertion. Exertions longer than one and one-half minutes are certainly not successful. Despite these optimums, we can use longer and uninterrupted exertions to develop coordinations and other changes within the muscles. They should not, however, be the main part of the training."

8. The exertion of the heart, as shown by stroke-volume, is greatest immediately after the stopping of work. This period of greatest stroke-volume has a duration of from 30 to 60 seconds, depending upon intensity of work and individual adaptation. We conclude therefore that 30 seconds should be a minimum recovery interval and that, in general, the maximum should not be above three minutes. Frequency of pulse is one valid indicator of recovery. It should not be above 180 at any time and need not be below 120 to 130 at the beginning of the next run.

Evaluation

The values of interval training have already been summarized. The core of such values lies in its almost infinite adaptability to whatever conditions of individual need or coaching attitude may prevail. By emphasizing this or that factor in its program, whether it be mileage, speed, pace, or willed control, a man can shape his development.

Many repetitions have special values. Each period of fatigue is followed by a period of recovery. We can assume, by the very nature of human development, that each recovery process overcompensates for the fatigue that preceded it; that each process builds more structure through use than was there before. Thus, when we run ten separate races in a given interval training workout, as compared with the one or two of other systems, we have in a sense experienced ten developmental periods. This is of course an oversimplification. We cannot assume a comparative value of 10/1 or 10/2 beyond that of steady running. But we can assume that some value derives from this aspect of training.

Interval training lends no ears to the singing of the birds, as is possible in fartlek; no eyes to the beauties of sand, sea, and sky, as did the followers of Percy Cerutty. But the great majority of runners live where such delights are not merely absent but unthinkable. As W. R. Loader writes,

But such settings are not so easy to come by in the modern industrial world. The sooty brick and stone deserts of Clydeside, Tyneside, and Merseyside show few examples of noble mountain peaks or undulating grassy swards or rush-bordered lakesides. On the other hand they can furnish an abundance of coke ovens, foundries, shipyards, blast furnaces, machine shops, and pit shafts. These do not make for the contemplation of beauty. In such surroundings a runner gets no assistance from the inspiration of Nature. He must depend upon his own resources. The greater credit to him that he is able and willing to do so.[18]

But within its limitations of flat and uninteresting terrain, interval training provides maximum incentive for continued practice and development. A man's program for today is always based on previous achievement and therefore establishes goals he knows he can approximate if not actually attain yet. And he can also look ahead into the next four or five weeks and see the pattern of his development.

Weaknesses. But having said so much in favor of interval training, we must recognize that it also has certain limitations and weaknesses. For example, although the short duration of each run permits less awareness of the pains of fatigue, this can be equally a disadvantage. Men must train themselves to come to terms with pain, if need be; to fight on regardless of its hurt. In interval training, they stop to recover before the sharp edge of pain digs deep. In contrast, a man who trains as Herb Elliott did speaks of cultivating one's capacity to hurt oneself deliberately and regularly: "I resisted the impulse to take a breather between efforts, feeling that this was where my methods were superior to interval training."

In preparing for an important race, Elliott used to run on a golf course "to exhaustion" for about four minutes, the estimated time he would have to maintain a hard effort in competition. He and Cerutty felt that the value of such a workout lay not so much in the physical work done as in its training of the mind for control over the body's craving for rest and its terror of exhaustion. During those four minutes Elliott would practice thinking through and feeling through the various problems of each stage of the forthcoming race. "Here is where it will hurt the most. At this point I'll surge forward to prove to my body just who is in control." Control of the will, like that of the body, comes through practice, not avoidance. Men who are specially sensitive to fatigue discomforts may develop the physical requirements for distance running by following interval training methods, but competitive running demands steady hard running, with no breathers between laps. Such men will need

---

[18] W. R. Loader, *Testament of a Runner* (London: William Heinemann, Ltd., 1960), p. 55. Also published as *Sprinter* (New York: The Macmillan Company, 1961).

to include simulations of the mental aspects of competition in their training if they are to reach running maturity.

Second, the shortness of time within which interval training can, apparently, bring a man into competitive condition is both dangerous and deceiving. In attempting too much too fast too soon, it endangers not only muscles and tendons but morale as well. Apparent success in practice is no guarantee of success in competition. The athlete is deluded into a sense of stamina which, in actual fact, can be developed only on a sound base of well-rounded and gradually developed endurance.

Major Raoul Mollet, in an excellent summary of endurance training methods, praised interval training highly but also warned,

> No doubt there will be more and more victims of the method, socially as well as physiologically, for such a way of life has great risks. For every experienced athlete, carefully observed and examined, aided in his training by blood analyses, electrocardiograms, etc., how many other athletes are there, dazzled by the thought of emulation and the spirit of imitation, but deprived of medical advantages and other paraphernalia of champions, who will suffer grave damage to their health? One must be almost regretful at the thought of the passing of fartlek in favor of interval training as the most universally used method of training in world athletics.[19]

A third weakness is related to what is generally considered to be interval training's greatest strength: its systematic analysis of all aspects of the training situation. The total distance covered in practice is divided into a given number of parts, some fast, some slow. At each stage of practice the runner is aware of exactly how many miles have been covered and how many must still be done. He is aware of time throughout, of the time of each separate run as the stop watch ticks off the seconds. He is aware of the presence of the coach, who, friend though he may be, adds one more item of possible tension. Even the style of running tends to be unchanging to conform with a uniformly flat track.

Individuals vary, of course. Some may lose their self-awareness in the details of the system, may anticipate each separate run, and enjoy overcoming its challenge much as Elliott enjoyed each fierce charge up the Portsea sand dunes. But there is at least the danger of drudgery, of the runner getting fed up with the challenges of interval training which face him, day after day. The challenges of fartlek are more permissive; those of interval training tend to be adamant. They therefore tend to make one feel tired.

For this reason most runners who follow interval training vary their workouts from day to day and week to week. One or possibly two workouts are maintained throughout for purposes of measuring development. On other days, the variety of workouts is limited only by the runner's imagination.

---

[19] Mollet, *op. cit.*, p. 97.

But even in such cases, each phase of the situation is broken down into measured parts of which the runner is aware, even though subconsciously. Contrast such a tension-producing situation with the methods of Herb Elliott in which awareness of details, as of self, tend to be lost in the wholeness of things.

> I like to vary my training venues day by day, running on a golf course one day, the next day in a park, then on a race course, up and down the hills flanking the shrine in Melbourne, along the Yarra River and even over cow paddocks. The change of scenery, the music of the birds and the sight of grazing cattle and sheep is soul-freeing and makes a training session real joy.[20]

Don't translate Elliott's words literally. The joy he speaks of is tinged with Elliott's training philosophy of striving for perfection through self-inflicted scourging and suffering. Nevertheless the point of wholeness and unawareness of self is clear. The followers of fartlek tend to speak of so many hours of training rather than so many quarter miles in such a time with so many minutes of rest between.

As one would expect, there is of course a counter-argument to all this. It is a simple one: that, either by inborn temperament or by gradually learned adaptation, the athlete brings himself to accept as desirable and interesting what others might describe as monotonous and "soul-killing." Bruce Kidd wrote that, as a youngster of 17, he had been entirely happy training during four months indoors on a 153-yard, oval, hard track following a daily schedule of repeated distances of two, three, five, or six laps each, all at the same pace of about 68 seconds. Any system and any terrain is mentally satisfactory and challenging if the user feels it to be so. It's all a matter of individual acceptance and affirmation.

Finally, one of the great dangers of interval training is that it can develop excellent interval trainers without developing excellent competitive runners. Men become enamored of the system itself and train as though performance in practice were the primary concern. Both physically and mentally, they find themselves unprepared for the special requirements of competition. The means tend to become the end, important for their own sake. One learns what one practices, physically and mentally; to run 10×440 in 60 seconds is not at all the same as running one mile in four minutes, especially if it is done only a day or so before competition and vital energies are left on the practice track.

The Oregon System of Training

Throughout the discussion of training we have quoted various advocates of this system or that. In addition we plan to give examples of the workout schedules of one or more champions at the various distances.

---

[20] Elliott, *op. cit.*, p. 147.

Bill Bowerman, Head Coach of the University of Oregon, with four of his outstanding distance runners who, on May 12, 1962, set a four-mile world record of 16:09.0. From left to right: Keith Forman, Dyrol Burleson, Vic Reeve, Coach Bowerman, and Archie San Romani.

Courtesy of University of Oregon A. A.

But there is also need for a unifying plan which integrates these systems into one simplified system. We believe we have found such a plan in the following schedule presented by Bill Bowerman of the University of Oregon:

I doubt that we have anything new or even unusual in our workouts. I've tried to learn from and use what others have done. Fartlek is the most important element in our training. I heartily endorse Gosta Holmer's philosophy that the trainee should stop his workout feeling exhilarated and not exhausted. We often use fartlek to complete a workout period; it refreshes both the mind and body after an intensive interval training session.

We have five areas for training. Three are near the campus: two golf courses, very beautiful and very hilly, many large trees, and a stream that meanders where we run; and a wooded park where we can run about three miles without seeing the same terrain. The fourth area is at the beach. I've been to Australia and I assure you that our dunes are at least equal to and our beaches just as challenging as those of Cerutty. The fifth area is in the mountains where an Old Indian Trail runs the length of Oregon and far beyond. It's great in the warm months, but in the winter, the snow is three times as high as the Tall Indian.

During the early stages of training, a coach must spend much time with his men so they will learn that fartlek is not just running; they must learn how to make best use of speed runs and recovery runs, paced runs, challenges and counterchallenges, and do it on many kinds of terrain, and alone. Above all, it's an imaginative and pleasant experience.

We use a separate training schedule for each event and for each man, and each man must keep a training diary.

This training diary is valuable not only for the individual over a three- or four-week period, but even more for comparisons the following year or with the schedules of other men in other years. A sample schedule is given below, as filled out by Jim Grelle for the month of February 1960.[21]

Bowerman provided two schedules: the "B" part as shown in Table 5.3, and an "A" part which to save space we shall summarize as follows. In general, each month's workouts are done at an established pace, beginning at about 75 seconds for October and steadily increasing speed to perhaps 57 by August. All related workouts are done at this pace. Within each month there is a variation in mileage: the first and third weeks call for twice the competitive distance; the second and fourth, three times the competitive distance. During the four weeks of each month, the recovery jogging interval decreases from "full" for the first week, in which a man jogs as far as he runs, to one-half the running distance for the second week, to one-quarter the running distance for the last two weeks. For example, the month of March would be organized in this fashion:

---

[21] Bill Bowerman, "The Oregon School of Running," *Clinic Notes* (National Collegiate Track Coaches Association, 1961), p. 59. This article was supplemented by personal communications with the writer.

Date	Pace	Mileage as Related to Racing Distance	Recovery Interval
March 1	62	2	Full
8	62	2–3	½
15	62	2	¼
22	62	2–3	¼

If a runner is "hung" on a pace, such as 70 seconds, he would not advance to the next month's pace until he has stabilized his condition and can carry his workout with ease. Bowerman has stated that most "green" runners get "hung" on a pace because they try to do too much too fast too soon.

TABLE 5.3

Oregon Training Schedule

Date		Work Done	Recovery		Key to Work Done
1	1	(2 x 9D) (2 x 6C) (2 x 5D) (12) (11)	Full	1.	Warm-up weight work or arm and shoulder work on rope, rings, or apparatus.
2	1	3			
3	1	(10 x 7F) 11		2.	Fartlek
4	1	3		3.	Light fartlek
5	1	3		4.	Repeats: 110s (A-20, B-18, C-16, D-14, E-12, F-11)
6–7	2	(Saturday–Sunday)			
8	1	(1 x 10) (2 x 4D) 11		5.	Repeats: 220s (A-38, B-35, C-33, D-31, E-29, F-28, G-27, H-26)
9	1	3		6.	Repeats: 330s (A-54, B-51, C-48, D-45, E-42, F-39, G-38, H-37)
10	1	(4 x 7F) (4 x 6C) (4 x 5D) 3			
11	1	3		7.	Repeats: 440s (A-75, B-72, C-70, D-68, E-66, F-64, G-62, H-60, I-58)
12	1	3			
13	1	3 8(1 x 3/4@ 64sec.) (1 x 660@ 29sec.)		8.	Repeats: selected longer distances.
14	1	16 2		9.	Sets:
15	1	2			A 1:50 70 34
16	1	3			B 1:45 68 32
17	1	(10 x 7F) 3			C 1:42 66 30
18	1	3			D 1:39 64 29
19	1	(1 x 9D)			E 1:36 62 28
20–21	2	(Saturday–Sunday)			F 1:33 60 27
					G 1:30 58 26
22	1	(4 x 6C) (4 x 5C) 12 9			
23	1	3		10.	Bunches: 2 or 3 660s; 3 to 6 440s; 6 to 10 220s. Use same time as in workout #9.
24	1	(1 x 9) (1 x 14) (4 x 5C) 9			
25	1	3			
26	1	3		11.	Take long recovery run after workout
27	1	8(1 x 3/4@ 64 sec.) (1 x 660@ 29sec.)		12.	Wind-sprints (fast-slow runs)
28	1	3		13.	Reduced interval 440s: run 440-jog 440; run 440-jog 220; run 440-jog 110; run 440. Use letters (times) as in workout #7.
				14.	Alternate sprint 55, shag (jog) 55.
		Name ___ Jim Grelle ___		15.	Up and down hill.

	660	440	220

To illustrate the meaning of this chart, on the 17th of the month, Grelle first warmed up, then did interval training work by running 10 440's in 64 seconds, and completed his workout with light fartlek. On the 27th he first warmed up as suggested in Item 1, then in keeping with Item 8 ran three continuous quarters at a pace of 64 seconds (total time, 3:12), then ran 660 yards at a pace of 29 seconds for each 220.

The Lydiard Training System

To describe the Lydiard system, as has become customary, as "marathon training" is quite unfair and certainly inadequate. Lydiard's ghost-writer, Garth Gilmour, summarizes it much better as "a training system which, reduced to its essentials, is the creation of stamina as the foundation for speed," but even this is not enough.

After a careful analysis of his excellent book, *Run to the Top*,[22] I think the essence of Lydiard's system lies in the carefully proportioned balance with which he has weighed the many essentials of running success. As Gilmour says, he has achieved a wise balance between stamina and speed training. But he has added a proper balance between training and competition (so out of balance in America!); a proper balance between races that are crucial and those that are merely training for these crucial races; a proper balance between mileage and enjoyment; a proper balance between different kinds of terrain; a proper balance between endless training the year round, on the one hand, and maintained motivation through six different kinds of training on the other; a proper balance between steady-pace running and the uneven running of interval training—I could go on.

This is very high praise and I intend it to be just that. The Lydiard training system has acquired an unjustified reputation of endless mileage and grimness, perhaps through use of the term "marathon training." In these few paragraphs we can give only glimpses of its real breadth of work and attitude; only the original book can tell the whole story.

To aid these brief glimpses, I have compiled Table 5.4. This table does two things: (1) it summarizes a year's schedule as it might occur in New Zealand, and (2) it transposes this 52-week schedule to one that might be fitted into an American competitive and training year. I assume that Lydiard would not construct this table just as I have done, though I have based it upon my interpretation of what is in Lydiard's book.

Basic Ideas

Among the more basic of Lydiard's training tenets are the following:

1. Planning must be done carefully for this individual's entire career as a runner.

2. Mileage training up to 100 miles per week forms the soundest foundation for later speed training.

---

[22] Arthur Lydiard and Garth Gilmour, *Run to the Top* (London: Herbert Jenkins, Ltd., 1962; New Zealand: A. H. & A. W. Reed, 1962).

TABLE 5.4

THE GIST OF LYDIARD'S TRAINING SYSTEM

	New Zealand Time Schedule		Adapted to American Time Schedule	
Weeks	Date	Program	Date	Program
0	Mar. 26	Training-off period (3-4 wks.)	June 2	Training-off period (3-4 wks.)
4	Apr. 24	Cross-country (12-14 wks.)	June 30	Time running
		Time running	Jul. 20	Mileage running
		Mileage running	Aug. 15	Marathon training
		Marathon training	Sept. 10	Cross-country training
16	Jul. 17	Cross-country *big race*	Nov. 15	Cross-country *big race*
17	Jul. 19	Road racing (6-8 wks.)	Nov. 17	Marathon training
		Road relay-racing	Dec. 15	Speed hill-training
24	Sept. 15	Marathon training (8-10 wks.)	Feb. 1	Indoor track season
			Mar. 10	Indoor *big race*
32	Nov. 10	Speed hill-training	Mar. 12	Marathon training
40	Jan. 1	Track season (10-12 wks.)	Apr. 1	Speed hill-training
		Repetition training	Apr. 20	Outdoor track season
		Interval training		Interval training
		Trials: over- and under-		Repetition training
		distance		Developmental races
		Developmental races	June 1	Outdoor *big race*
52	Mar. 25	Outdoor *big race*		

Note: Actual dates vary greatly; those given are merely suggestive. The various types of training actually blend into one another and cannot be separated sharply as this table seems to imply. For explanation of the terms in this table, see related article headings.

3. Training occurs seven days a week, 52 weeks a year.

4. From every standpoint, in planning and in practice, in training and in competition, zest must always be equated with zeal.

5. Coaches and runners must distinguish clearly between the few big races on each year's schedule and the many developmental races which, like training, are but means to that end.

6. Variety is essential: in terrain, in pace, in training intensity, in competition.

7. Great stress in training or competition must be followed by days of recovery running.

8. Degree of effort can be stated on a factual time-distance basis and used in making individual assignments.

Time Running (For beginning runners)

Begin by running steadily for a length of time that can be handled easily. Neither mileage nor pace are important. Gradually increase this time until you can run steadily and without severe stress for two hours.

Cross-country

Lydiard divides cross-country into two six-week periods. The first period includes time running and, later, mileage running up to 100 miles per week. The second period includes faster (what Lydiard calls "sharpening") running and time trials of various distances, paces, and efforts. Competition should be delayed until needed as a developmental and motivational device. If a man is well prepared, competition is both fun and an aid to development; if not, it can be deadly.

Train and compete on all kinds of surfaces and under all weather conditions. Alternate steady-pace running one day with repeated speed-work at shorter distances with the tempo of each gradually increased throughout the 12 weeks. As examples of 6¼-mile cross-country schedule: [23]

	First Week		Eighth Week
Mon.	15 miles (¼ effort)	Mon.	12 × 220 (½ effort)
Tues.	880 (¼ effort)	Tues.	Six-mile time trial
	Mile (¼ effort)		
	880 (¼ effort)		
Wed.	10 miles (½ effort)	Wed.	Three miles of 50-yard dashes
Thurs.	Mile (¼ effort)	Thurs.	Three-mile time trial
	Mile (¾ effort)		
	3 × 100 (¾ effort)		
Fri.	6 × 220 (½ effort)	Fri.	3 × 220 (full effort)
Sat.	Competition	Sat.	Three-mile race
Sun.	Jog 20 miles	Sun.	Jog 20 miles

During the eighth week of this 12-week training schedule, Lydiard has placed two time trials and one competition—a strenuous work-load. But he interprets trials, as well as races, in terms of effort, self-control, and improvement, not all-out performance. In fact, he strongly holds back the latter until the few big races on which the entire year's program is based. On all other occasions, the man runs well within himself. He does his "best," but within the limits of control and of doing even better next week and next month.

The Big Race

Before each crucial race—those that have been planned for a full year ahead—Lydiard schedules a full ten days of conserving energy. They run every day, of course, but within the limits of easy effort. Steady-pace work, rather than repeated fast work, is best. If the year's schedule has been well planned, not even psychological conditioning should be a concern—though of course with some men it always is.

---

[23] *Ibid.*, p. 111.

Marathon Training

Lydiard states that 100 miles a week of marathon running is the key to his training system. On a basis of seven days each week, this averages 14 miles per day or better, provides three days of 20 miles each, and four of 10 miles each. If the 20-mile run is exhausting, an easier and shorter run the next day, or even two days, allows time for complete recovery. In addition, for both physical and mental reasons, he varies his terrain between flat running and hill running, and varies the effort that goes into each training run between one-quarter effort and three-quarters effort. Lydiard suggests this schedule [24] as having balanced proportions:

Mon.	10 miles (½ effort)—hilly course
Tues.	15 miles (¼ effort)—easy undulating course
Wed.	12 miles fartlek
Thurs.	18 miles (¼ effort) —easy course
Fri.	10 miles fast (¾ effort)—flat course
Sat.	20–30 miles (¼ effort)—easy course
Sun.	15 miles (¼ effort)—easy course

This marathon training is continued until 18 weeks before the first track competition of some importance.

Road Racing

Lydiard undoubtedly adopted road running and racing because it was already well established in New Zealand. But he also argues its values as being a logical extension of the fence-climbing, changing terrain, and changing pace of cross-country. Road racing requires a steady-pace running on firm surfaces. The races are strenuous, so that training is light and pleasant. Training should still be over all kinds of surfaces in order to maintain the flexible toughness of muscle and tendons gained in cross-country. But since Lydiard recommends the same training during this period that is followed for a two-mile track schedule, we can assume that the lack of this kind of program in our American system is not a critical loss.

Speed Hill-training

This is the most strenuous part of Lydiard's entire year's program of training. He assigned about six weeks to it as compared with about ten weeks for marathon training and about 12 weeks for cross-country. A fairly steep hill (a one-in-three gradient is considered best) is found

---

[24] *Ibid.*, p. 72.

that is about one-half mile long. After a two-mile warm-up jog, the runner springs up this hill on his toes, exaggerating his knee lift. Lydiard emphasizes the springing action rather than speed of running. After about one-half mile of jogging, the man now sprints down hill, with full but relaxed strides. At the bottom he does repeated fast work: perhaps 3 × 220, then 6 × 50 on alternating runs. These are gradually increased in number and speed as condition improves. Each of these efforts totals about two miles of running; the four repetitions that Lydiard recommends, plus the preliminary jogging and warm-down afterward, would total more than ten miles each day. Lydiard cautions that this work must be done thoughtfully and with just the right amount of emphasis on each phase, as this will affect later stages of the training program. Speed, however, is deliberately restricted, since too much would hasten the sharpening of condition which Lydiard reserves for the later crucial races.

Track Training

Lydiard believes strongly in planning both competition and training. The relative importance of races must be clearly and firmly established, and all phases of training, mental and physical, must build precisely toward the *big races*. He is highly critical of shot-gun systems that hope to put runners in shape for the big race by putting them in shape for all the races, as well as of the "peaking" systems that work at minimum levels, then by intensive work, and bring the runner quickly and briefly to a peak performance as was done so well by Roger Bannister.

He therefore divides his track training into two periods of six weeks each. The first period includes speed-work, but it is geared down to what the runner can handle easily and thus reserves the more sharpening, faster runs for the later and more important period. Typical of these workouts are:

1. Overdistance at a steady, easy pace.
2. Underdistance at a faster but controlled pace.
3. The actual racing distance, but at a deliberately slower-than-racing pace.
4. Steady runs at from two to six miles.
5. Repetition running over distances between 220 yards to 880 yards.
6. 15 or 20 × 440 yards.
7. Two or three miles of alternating 50-yard dashes with 50 yards of recovery striding.

The second six-week period continues the balance between repeated speed running and steady-pace running. Speed work is now "all-out" although even here Lydiard pushes or restrains according to how the boy seems to react. To the over- and under-distance work of the first six weeks, he adds time trials. These trials do not attempt to see how

Coach Arthur Lydiard, New Zealand, and his running champions. From left to right: Barry Magee, third, 1960 Olympic marathon; Murray Halberg, 1960 Olympic champion, 5000 meters; Peter Snell, 1960 Olympic champion, 800 meters; and Coach Lydiard. Runner on the right is unidentified.

Courtesy of Track and Field News

fast the runner can cover a certain distance; rather they build on the experience of the first six weeks and provide a certainty of improvement in time as well as of control over tension and fatigue. Improvement is planned so as to continue evenly from trial to trial. Lydiard thinks it is necessary to race twice a week during this last period, but these are mostly under- and over-distance races, so that effort and attitude is focused strongly upon the big race coming later. One becomes fit for racing by running races, not just by running.

Tables of Effort

The tables of one-quarter, one-half, and three-quarters effort for each distance from the 220 to six miles form a very important part of Lydiard's book. For example, in the 440, a man whose best previous efforts average a time of 50 seconds would run 59 seconds for one-quarter effort; 56, for one-half effort; and 53, for three-quarters effort. A man who had a best time of 60 seconds for the 440 would run 69–66–63 for these same degrees of effort. Or, as another example, a man who had a best time of 14:00 minutes for three miles would run 15:30–15:00–14:30, while a man who had run only 16:00 minutes would attempt 17:30–17:00–16:30. Such a schedule of times permits development in terms of each individual on a more precise and fair basis than has previously been provided by such other training systems as fartlek or interval training. The reader is urged to secure a copy of these tables for his everyday use. It would be impossible to follow Lydiard's system without them.

TABLE 5.5
LYDIARD TRAINING SCHEDULES [25]

		Sample 880 Schedule	
	First Week		*Tenth Week*
Mon.	Mile (½ effort) Six starts at 30 yards	**Mon.**	660 (¾ effort)
Tues.	6 × 880 (¼ effort) 2 × 100 (¾ effort)	**Tues.**	880 time trials (improvement without strain) Four starts at 50 yards
Wed.	Competitive sprints 2 or 3 × 300 yards	**Wed.**	4 × 440 at 880 racing speed 2 × 440 (full effort)
Thurs.	Half-mile of repeated 50's 6 × 300 striding 1 × 220 (⅞ effort)	**Thurs.**	Two miles of repeated 50-yard dashes Three starts at 50 yards
Fri.	Two miles (½ effort)	**Fri.**	6 × 220 (½ effort)
Sat.	Six starts at 50 yards 6 × 300 striding 1 × 300 (full effort)	**Sat.**	Compete 880 yards
Sun.	Jog 10-15 miles	**Sun.**	Long jog

25 *Ibid.*, pp. 92 ff.

Sample Mile Schedule

	First Week		*Tenth Week*
Mon.	Two miles (1/4 effort)	Mon.	Mile of repeated 50's: 3 × 100 (full effort)
Tues.	4 × 880 (1/4 effort)	Tues.	One-mile time trial (improvement only)
Wed.	12 × 300 striding 1 × 880 (1/2 effort)	Wed.	Six miles: sprint 100 yards in each 440
Thurs.	Six miles (1/4 effort)	Thurs.	One-mile time trial (improve)
Fri.	6 × 440 (1/4 effort)	Fri.	3 × 220 (full effort)
Sat.	One mile (1/4 effort) One mile (1/2 effort)	Sat.	One-mile competition
Sun.	Jog 15-20 miles	Sun.	Jog over 20 miles

Sample Two-mile Schedule

	First Week		*Tenth Week*
Mon.	Two miles (1/4 effort)	Mon.	50 × 200 (1/4 effort)
Tues.	10 × 300 (1/4 effort) 2 × 100 (3/4 effort)	Tues.	Two-mile time trial (improve)
Wed.	One mile (1/2 effort) Six starts at 50	Wed.	880-yard competition
Thurs.	One mile (1/4 effort) 2 × 880 (1/2 effort)	Thurs.	Two miles of repeated 50-yard dashes
Fri.	6 × 200 (1/4 effort)	Fri.	3 × 220 (full effort)
Sat.	3/4 mile (1/2 effort)	Sat.	Jog 20 miles or more
Sun.	Jog 15-20 miles		

Sample Six-mile Schedule

	First Week (Note that this schedule is same as that for one-mile schedule.)		*Tenth Week*
Mon.	Two miles (1/4 effort)	Mon.	One mile of 50-yard dashes 3 × 100 (full effort)
Tues.	4 × 880 (1/4 effort)	Tues.	Three-mile time trial (improve)
Wed.	12 × 300 striding 1 × 880 (1/2 effort)	Wed.	Six miles with (100-yard sprint) in each 440 yards
Thurs.	Six miles (1/4 effort)	Thurs.	Six-mile time trial (improve)
Fri.	6 × 440 (1/4 effort)	Fri.	6 × 220 (3/4 effort)
Sat.	One mile (1/4 effort) One mile (1/2 effort)	Sat.	Jog of 20 or more miles
Sun.	Jog 15-20 miles		

Training-off Period

The length of the training-off period will vary with the man's yearly program from three to about six weeks. Running during this time consists of 45 to 60 minutes each day of light jogging over varied surfaces at an easy pace, plus, once each week, a long run of about 20 miles easy.

Evaluation: Strengths

We have already emphasized the great strength of Lydiard's system that lies in its precisely balanced emphasis upon such related but contrasting factors as stamina and speed over which coaches have argued for decades and shall not repeat it here. He claims that marathon training (100 miles per week) is the key to his system, in the sense that such "marathon" stamina provides a sound foundation for an even greater emphasis on speed than other systems can provide.

One of the great advantages held by Lydiard, of which he does not seem to be aware, lies in his location in New Zealand where no extensive system of competition was established around which he would have to do all his planning for training. This fact gave him the opportunity to plan a year's program of training exactly in accordance with his theories. The values of competition could be weighed with, not against, the values of training. In fact, he could schedule competition not as the all-important reason for training, but, on the contrary, as a motivator of training. In such competition, winning would have meaning not only in itself but also as it contributed to development and to more zest for more running. I shall write later of the great confusion that now exists in the United States because we have placed 90 per cent of our eggs in the basket of competition. Some of our coaches even think competition during the practice period and within the training group is necessary for best training outcomes. At the school and college levels, we now have about seven months of competition and only three months for training free of competition; in New Zealand this balance is reversed.

This relative freedom meant that Lydiard could start beginning runners from where they were; if they could only run steadily for five minutes they had time in which to do just that and no more. They could then progress gradually—through the various steps of Lydiard's plan: through time training, mileage training, cross-country, road racing, and all the rest. Each new level could be attempted when the preceding level had been not merely tried, but mastered to the point of certainty of control and ease of action.

This freedom from the burden of winning-them-all, which I have attributed to New Zealand, should also be credited to Lydiard's insistence upon first things first, then second things, then third, and so on. He is adamant in looking ahead 12 and 15 months to the big races and in planning the year's program in terms of them. Even more, he insists upon planning an entire career. For example, he wrote,

So in 1953 I started these two nineteen-year-olds [Halberg and Magee] off together, although I still eased back on the work I gave Halberg because I still did not consider him strong enough for the full treatment. It was in the 1953 cross-country season—late in the year—before I finally got to work on him. In July of that year, I predicted publicly that Halberg would be the greatest middle-distance runner New Zealand had known and that he would start cracking world records at twenty-seven—the year he actually won his Olympic title. . . .

I would stress here that they [his training schedules] are not aimed at producing immediate results . . . but at a steady improvement culminating in the athlete's best performances at the age when he reaches his full potential [25 to 30 or more—J.K.D.] [26]

Lydiard believed that mileage training (to use my own analogy) hardens and tempers the steel of development in endurance running, whereas speed training sharpens its edge. He felt that such tempering was best when done gradually over a period of eight or more years of training. By such long-time developmental running, his training steel attained a quality well above that of other world level runners, perhaps even higher than that of such "inhuman" trainers as Vladimir Kuts and Gordon Pirie. Then, since his training steel was properly tempered, he could sharpen its edge with speed training to a keenness beyond that of other systems. He claimed that his men could run faster longer because they were able to train at sprinting speeds more often.

Another great strength of the Lydiard system lies in its variety. For example, it insists upon a variety of terrains—and by terrains we mean not only hills, woods, paths, and running tracks, but also deliberately selected mud and slush, soft sand, fences and stone walls, paved roads, uneven bush country—all for the purpose of establishing a wide and firm foundation of running fitness. On these varied running surfaces, Lydiard planned a variety of training methods: cross-country, road racing, marathon running, speed hill-training, and, when he finally got on the flat running track, he used many of the devices of modern interval training and even of the old American over- and under-distance training with its repeated time trials. I have often criticized the latter because of its overemphasis upon all-out performance in each trial. Lydiard answers this by insisting upon planned increments of improvement: run what you can today, but be certain that you'll be able to improve on it next week and six weeks from now. He even has gone so far as to provide tables of effort on a time basis, as I have already described.

There is of course a serious question as to what degree we in the United States can adopt this kind of precise planning. To do so we shall have to reverse the trends of the past 50 years or more toward

---

[26] *Ibid.*, p. 29.

more and more competition, for its own exclusive sake. Perhaps our school and college coaches can reduce the number of competitions a little. But a more likely improvement can come by a tough concentration upon the few *big races* in the year's competitive schedule and by considering all others as developmental races. On the other hand, the greatly neglected postcollege running program is not so handicapped and is free to develop as it wishes. I am convinced it will do well to follow basically the Lydiard system, though of course our present belief in interval training will lead to our own version of it.

Evaluation: Weaknesses

Though I have tried, and tried hard, I can suggest no important weaknesses in the Lydiard system as used in New Zealand. Unfortunately, the American school and college system of training and competing is not well adapted to its full use. High school coaches are under-pressures to win, and the need to win often is opposed to the need to develop. High school boys judge the coach and his system, as well as their own success, on a basis of achievement this year, this month, and even this week, rather than on how they are developing toward some doubtful goal over the horizon and some seven to ten years away. Lydiard writes,

> You will come to your peak slower than many other runners, and you will be running last when they are running first. But when it is really important to run first, you will be passing them.

Some coaches will find it difficult to sacrifice those early meets.

Lydiard's system uses about six months of training without competition prior to the track season; we now use only about three such months. His system requires 52 weeks each year of some degree of running; ours, only about 36. His system calls for at least six different kinds of terrain and kinds of running; ours, only two or three and in most cities, only one! The relative disinterest of the New Zealand public and newspapers allows him to evaluate the win-loss record of his team as he personally prefers; ours tends to encourage individual development and achievement as long as the team wins.

But despite these and other difficulties, Lydiard's system can be of great help in our effort to improve American running. Adopting its basic tenets will not require us to begin over again. We shall not need to abandon either fartlek or interval training. Actually, Lydiard uses his own versions of both, though he seldom uses the terms as such. Both have their special values. But the clarity with which Lydiard has presented the major goals for training and the step-by-step methods by which those goals can be achieved provide us with a fresh and sure way to running achievement.

Principles of Holistic Training

6

We have just reviewed the methods, strengths, and weaknesses of four systems of endurance training: fartlek, interval training, the Oregon system, and the Lydiard system. Each of these has produced great champions and world records. Each should contain the essentials of endurance training; yet each seems to differ markedly from the others. Further, none of them seems to give specific attention to the broader problems of motivation suggested in our first two chapters They limit their attention to what happens during the few training hours each day and ignore the remaining 20 or more hours, which are often just as effective in determining success in running. In fact, at times, some of the research workers in interval training have seemed to judge a system on the exclusive basis of its effects upon the heart.

Obviously, it is a man that runs; a man with a body to be sure, but also with a mind and emotions that are influenced by many factors of social and physical environment. A sound system of endurance training will consider such a man-environment holistically, that is, will consider the whole situation and all the factors that can make a practical difference.

Some of the material in this chapter is from J. Kenneth Doherty, *Modern Track and Field* (2nd ed.; Englewood Cliffs, N. J.: Prentice-Hall, Inc., 1963), pp. 194-99, 206-208. Reprinted by permission of the publisher.

What then should be the principles of training that should be considered by every system? In trying to answer this question, I have searched exhaustively and widely. As a result, this chapter develops 45 principles—a most wearisome number! A sound coach will understand and use each of these principles, but heaven help the coach—and, even more, his runners—who uses them consciously and openly in his everyday coaching.

A coach should make use of these principles as he makes use of his personal experiences in running, or of his knowledge of biochemistry or mechanics, that is, as a source of sound judgment, of sound advice when asked for and needed, and of sound authority when required.

These are valuable instruments, but their value lies not in their display but in the expert way they are used, unconsciously and without pretension. You will discover that a great violinist is using a Stradivarius only by reading the fine print of the program notes, and often not even there. So with a great coach and his instrument of knowledge. Of him, his runners will say, "What he is and has done, what he knows by personal experience and hard study, speaks so loudly that he needs very few words to express himself—and somehow we understand every word he says."

True, these principles are wordy, but the wordiness is for you, the coach, and not for your runners.

Principle 1

A sound program of training for endurance running should be an organically beneficial and mentally wholesome activity that will build up a boy, not tear him down. It is both natural and healthful for boys to run. Some boys seem made for running, as others seem made for throwing or jumping.

Such a program seeks the conservation of energy through proper use, much as we speak of the conservation of forests. We cut certain trees to allow more and better wood to grow in their places. Similarly, we spend energy today in order to build more energy for tomorrow. We undergo the arduousness of work today in order that tomorrow we can do that same work more easily and enjoyably or at a higher level. By wise use of our powers, both physical and mental, our nature rebuilds them in ever greater abundance.

Energy is present in each of us, not at one level or another, but within a range of possible use and development. This range is both broad and flexible. Its upper limits are far beyond what seems humanly possible and healthful if one considers the limited demands for human energy made by our machine culture. Further, those who reach the upper levels of that range of energy can be active day after day, year after year with no ill effects to their health or longevity. Their organisms develop not only resistance to fatigue but also increase their rate of recovery. Few of these individuals need more sleep than the average; many need less. They have learned to increase their supply of energy, not by saving it, but by using it wisely—gradually building up their demands on it.

Old-time fears of injury to the vital organs have been gradually replaced by a strong reliance on and admiration for human adaptability. For example, the noted British physiologist, Sir Adolphe Abrahams, has been quoted as saying,

You need not entertain the slightest apprehension that ill effects will result from athletic training, nor fear any reduction of life expectation. (There is one proviso: exercise should never be taken during illness, especially if there is a raised temperature. The danger may be minimal but it is definite.) There always will be alarmists who talk of "heart strain," ignorant of the ability of a healthy heart to deal with the greatest stress and meet all demands imposed on it. All heart specialists agree on this latter conclusion.[1]

All of this assumes a reasonably intelligent approach to training, both in the degree of overloading in each day's work and in the intensity of work which ambition arouses in either the coach or the runner.

Principle 2

A sound program of training for endurance running should be preceded by a medical examination designed to measure fitness for the stresses of running and interpreted by a medical doctor who understands sports medicine. The attitudes of the medical profession toward strenuous exercise have progressed greatly during the past half century. Formerly medicine defined health almost exclusively in terms of freedom *from* disease and infirmity; now it adds to this a concept of positive health, the ability to be active regularly at the upper levels of one's range of capacity. Then it considered inactivity as the only treatment for the damaged heart; now it states that "adequate exercise may be as important as adequate rest in the rehabilitation of the cardiac patient." [2] Then it taught the dangers of the "athletic heart"; now the consensus of heart specialists is that the normal healthy heart is invulnerable to the stresses of athletic training.

Athletes who succumb to accidental death in whom cardiac damage was found are rarities. Where it did happen, the past medical histories and physical findings prior to death have been unknown or at least not properly recorded.

In our experience no histopathologic changes were seen attributable to

1 Bert Nelson, ed., *Track and Field News*, XIV, No. 11 (December 1961), 20.
2 Paul Dudley White, "Heart Disease after Sixty-five," *Journal of the American Medical Women's Association*, XII (1957), 127-35.

vigorous physical activity. Professor Chiari, renowned pathologist of the University of Vienna Medical School, told me personally that, despite a wealth of autopsy material and a life-time of experience in post-mortem studies, he never saw a single case of cardiac pathology which could be attributed to sports.[3]

The words "normal and healthy" are crucial. In the presence of active infection or high emotional stress or pathologic chronic fatigue, serious and permanent cardiac damage can occur.

At one time the medical profession assumed that the role of medicine in sports was one of limitation and control; now it adds to this function that of aiding sports performance through regular assessment of the effects of both general and special training measures.

The question arises as to what tests are sufficiently valid, reliable, and simple to warrant inclusion in a medical examination for runners. Unfortunately no final or easy answer can be given. For example many of our best cardiologists believe that a test or a battery of tests which would establish both the condition and the functional capacity of the heart does not exist at present. A. Salisbury Hyman writes,

> It has long been recognized by research cardiologists that there may be little or no correlation between objective evidence of heart disease and functional capacity of that same heart. From the electrocardiogram alone, for example, no estimation of the subject's ability to perform work can be made; no expert in electrocardiography can evaluate possible physical performance from a given tracing. Grossly abnormal records have been found in athletes with better than average physical fiitness and the reverse is also true; normal electrocardiograms do not necessarily indicate good or even normal functional capacity.
>
> Other objective studies of the cardiovascular system show similar poor correlation curves; heart size determined by teleroentgenography or by the orthodiagraphic X-ray method may show marked enlargement in athletes with excellent functional capacity. Individuals with normal or even less than normal heart size may exhibit poor physical performance. In other words, heart size *per se* is no index of physical fitness. Arteriograms and ballistocardiograms taken on athletes also show the same poor correlation; likewise pulse rate, blood pressure, vital capacity, and other physiologic studies may present abnormal findings without an associated loss in functional capacity.[4]

Hyman concludes therefore that certain tests of functional capacity are likely to assume an increasingly important role in differentiating between those who should and those who should not enjoy athletic activity as well as in guarding the development of those who do. Included among these will be tests comparable to the Harvard Step Test, the Cardio-pulmonary Index, the Respiratory Index, and the Schneider Index.

With the rapid growth of sports medicine throughout the world and

---

[3] J. B. Wolffe, M.D., "Cardiovascular Response to Vigorous Physical Activity," *Medicina Sportiva*, XII (1958), 34. Dr. Wolffe is a founder of the American College of Sports Medicine.

[4] A. Salisburg Hyman, "The Cardiac Athlete," *Medicina Sportiva*, XIII (1959), 4.

a corresponding emphasis on doctors specifically trained in the problems of sports, the role of assessment and guidance toward better performance is being added to that of safeguarding health. Heart reactions to the stress of running are now being telemetered directly to the sports medicine laboratory while the athlete is training. The effects of measured dosages of work are being studied by specialists to ascertain what amount and quality of training produces optimum development.

For example, in the Institute of Sport Medicine in Rome, headed by Giuseppe LaCava, long-time president of the International Federation of Sports Medicine, extensive experiments were carried out during the 1956 and 1960 Olympic Games out of which a method of examination was invented and tested on hundreds of athletes. Conclusions were reached that

The assessment of an athlete, and the judgment of his possibilities of actual and potential performance in a sport, cannot be based on a simple clinical examination, but must be supported by morphological findings and functional examinations of various organic systems in their three phases: the static, the dynamic, and the postdynamic, which in combination constitute the whole cycle of sport performance, related to the results and to the biological and mechanical characteristics of the sport that the athlete practices.

In accord with this principle, a series of examinations and functional tests [chain of battery tests] are required, aimed at revealing all the physical and psychical aspects of the complex personality of the subject. It is quite clear that this can be accomplished only in specialized and well-equipped centers by a team of qualified research workers. Their individual opinions will then be analyzed and synthetized in order to trace a medical picture of the subject which will be a guide to doctors and experts directly following the athlete.[5]

However, even such an exhaustive and expensive assessment can be considered valid only for a generalized evaluation of the individual subject, not for his specific fitness for or reactions to his sports specialty.

Obviously general practice of this kind is far in the future of sports. Unfortunately American medical schools do not include specialized training in sports medicine which would enable most doctors to gain a better understanding of the values of exercise and sports and through which many could find a lifetime field for specialization. But as positive health and fitness become a more major concern of medicine, as sports medicine doctors become more numerous, as our methods become more valid and usable, as our machines become simpler and less expensive, we can assume that scientific assessment will gradually supplement the trial-and-error methods that have been our only resource in the past.

Safeguarding the physical and mental health of participants at all levels of achievement will still be the primary function of the medical

---

[5] Giuseppe LaCava, "Clinical Evaluation and Athletic Performance," *Health and Fitness in the Modern World* (Chicago: The Athletic Institute, 1961), p. 214.

doctor and scientist but to that role will be added one of complementing the work of the coach. Improved performance and health, both positive and "negative," if we may use such a term, are actually two sides of one coin: each is necessary to the full development of the other.

Principle 3

A sound program of training for endurance running plans carefully for an effective program of continuous motivation, just as it plans for an effective schedule of work. The various kinds and degrees of motivation for running have already been discussed at length in Chapter 1, and the different methods that coaches have used in Chapter 2. Perhaps they can all be more clearly summarized by the diagram and caption of Fig. 6.1.

All coaches agree on the crucial importance of motivation, but very few agree on the pattern by which it is best achieved. This is almost inevitable when we consider the infinite variety of motivational factors that can be present.

Perhaps the real significance of this principle lies in the words, "plans carefully." When a coach or runner sits down to plan a fortnight or so of work, he should consider the effects of that work upon motivation just as thoughtfully as he does its effects upon the muscles and cardiovascular system. A workout or competition that ends in lowered motivation can reduce future performance just as effectively as one that endangers physical development.

Principle 4

A sound program of training for endurance running recognizes that it is not enough to understand in a bookish sense all the whats and whys of training; the real secret lies in also knowing the hows and the whens. These come only through a coach's personal experience. This experience is best if, as with Lydiard and Cerutty, it occurs by actually running. Lydiard, who was a two-time New Zealand marathon champion at ages 35 and 37, once wrote,

> I still used myself as the principal guinea pig and drove myself to test my body in the extremes of heat and endurance. . . . I was so determined to find just what the human body would stand without actually cracking that I frequently exhausted myself completely and had to walk the last few miles painfully home. But I always made it, one way or another.[6]

A little queer in the head? Impossible? All right for New Zealand crackpots but not for sensible Americans? Then how do you account for

---

[6] Arthur Lydiard and Garth Gilmour, *Run to the Top* (London: Herbert Jenkins, Ltd., 1962; New Zealand: A. H. & A. W. Reed, 1962), p. 25.

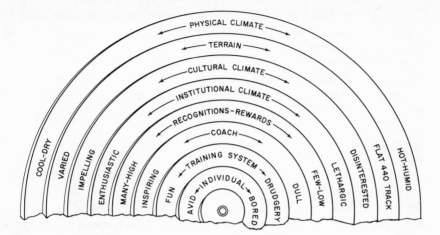

Fig. 6.1 Motivational factors in training for endurance running. This figure contains the essential meaning of holistic training that deserves careful study. Each of the circles represents a motivational factor that can be present at any degree from extremely positive (see adjectives on the left side) to extremely negative (right side).

In life, these factors are interdependent and inseparable, but for purposes of understanding they can be considered separately and their circles rotated independently. For example, we can hold the three inner circles marked "Individual," "Training System," and "Coach" at extremely positive levels, but can rotate the five outer circles until their influences are strongly negative. Obviously, the effectiveness of the total training program would be greatly decreased.

Some of these factors weigh more heavily than others. For example, if the individual runner is sufficiently avid and determined, his success can be considerable, despite the negative influence of all the other factors.

A coach should recognize that his personal influence is but one of many factors, and that it is the total weight of all factors that will determine the success of his runners. He will then realize that his real training system is not merely what and how his men run, as is implied by such terms as "fartlek" or "interval training," but rather is the holistic sum of all related factors as are depicted here. If a training program is to be successful, the total weight of the positive factors, whether few or many, must be much greater than the total weight of the negative factors. In a so-called perfect training program, all factors would be present as suggested by the adjectives on the left side of the figure.

An effective coach will carefully consider each of these factors and do all within his power to make each of them strongly positive.

the down-to-earth common sense and emphasis upon gradual development that Lydiard puts into his coaching? If you are unwilling to make the effort yourself regardless of the achievement, how can you know— more, how can you know in your muscles and your insides—how your runners feel and react? Lydiard states that Halberg's father, Jock, started training after the age of 55 and finished a competitive marathon at 58, just to know how his boy felt. From at least an effort standpoint, can you afford to do less?

To this personal running experience, a coach must of course add personal coaching experience. Within the framework of local traditions and his school or club racing schedule, he must construct a training program that is sound and integrated in terms of the essentials of running development. This will require some years of thoughtful trial-error-and-success, in which he personally is concerned, and even, at times, is the guinea pig.

Principle 5

A sound program of training for endurance running gives first priority to building the stamina that comes from running very long distances. The word, "stamina" is usually defined so that we think of it as a single entity. We then assume we build this entity called stamina whether we run repeated 100-meter dashes, as did Pirie under Gerschler, or run marathon distances as under Lydiard. But there are many kinds of stamina just as, for example, there are many kinds of food. All foods, by definition, are substances having nutritional value, but who would argue that since they all provide nutrition they are all the same. Each food has its own nutritional value, some more basic than others. So with the different ways of running that all produce stamina; each way produces its own unique kind of stamina; and some of these kinds are more basic and therefore must be given priority over other kinds.

This principle states that the kind of stamina that is acquired through running at a comparatively slow pace at very long distances is basic, that is, provides the best possible foundation of running fitness for all other kinds of running. Of course, "very long distances" must be defined within a rather wide range of distances. Individual runners differ in age, in time available, in competitive schedule, and in many other ways. Lydiard would have difficulty justifying his 100-miles-each-week for everyone. Were he to work with boys of 15 to 17 years of age, he would of course approach such distances gradually. But you can be sure that his emphasis would not change.

Actually this principle is recognized by every system. Remember that in 1904 Shrubb trained at 10- and 15-mile distances before he set his two-mile record of 9:09.6. Rudolf Harbig, though basically an interval trainer, did much running in the woods during the early winter months before he set his world records in the 400- and 800-meter runs. I am not aware of a single great distance runner who has failed to include some form of long distance training, call it cross-country, fartlek, hill-and-dale, what you will, especially during the early months of each year's training.

But systems vary greatly in the degree of emphasis they place upon this principle. It is our intent here to place great emphasis upon it. It makes sense from a health and safety standpoint. It makes sense from a developmental standpoint: the runner senses his progress clearly; first in time and then in distance. He is not confused by pace or recovery intervals. He is moving slowly enough to be aware of his surroundings; if they are interesting, he is less aware of his own aches and anxieties. Emotionally, we dislike Lydiard's term "marathon training." He grew up with it and its connotations are satisfying if not actually pleasant. But to us, it suggests monotonous plodding endlessly on hard roads. We need some new term that joins mileage with the enjoyment of running, just as fartlek joined repeated bursts of speed with play.

But the system of building stamina first through long distance running as a foundation for later speed-running is sound, regardless of its name, and we will do well to consider it carefully.

Principle 6

A sound program of training for endurance running is most effective and most healthful when it develops gradually in mileage and intensity over year-round cycles of emphasis. Periods of hard preparatory work swing smoothly into periods of lighter work during the competitive season, and then into periods of rest and relaxation—or better, of "active-rest," to use a Russian phrase. Training always begins at the individual's present level of easy accomplishment and increases as gradually as the demands of competitive schedules will permit. The cycles of development should be thought of as rising on a winding staircase from early youth through the early thirties—or later. By 1962, Finland's distance runners had completed, without layoff, eight years of a continuous program of training. It was concluded that the results were encouraging and the runners' enthusiasms were being maintained. This has not been the pattern of American development, but it is one we must cultivate for the sake of international success and our own maintenance of fitness.

Figure 6.2, on page 130, attempts to suggest the cycles of emphasis that might well be followed in an American school program. The chart should be studied in terms of effort and fatigue, not of mileage or the importance of outcomes. It is equivalent to a single cross section of a winding staircase that would continue to rise from year to year. Note that, from an effort-fatigue standpoint, the fall and early indoor and early outdoor periods are the most difficult. July and August comprise periods of active-rest in which running is continued but at a much lower level of effort. Endurance games, such as soccer or basketball, help to maintain fitness and the habit of daily exertion.

Of course a nonschool program would produce quite a different design. The main competitive seasons would then be during the indoor

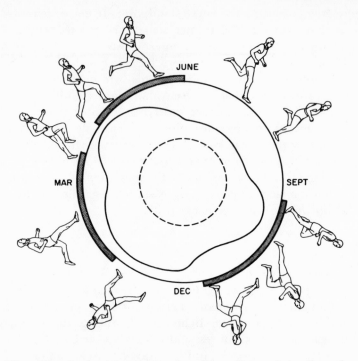

Fig. 6.2   The rhythm of year-round training. Outer circle: line of maximum intensity of training. Inner dotted circle: line of no training (running). Cross-lined areas: competitive reasons (cross-country, indoor track, outdoor track). Wave-like curve: year-round rhythm of training intensity.

This figure is based upon present-day American school schedules. In a more effective year-round program, the line for periods of low training emphasis (June–September) would be held higher than is shown here. That is, so-called periods of rest would tend to bring variety into the training program rather than a decrease in the amount of work done.

season, and again in the midsummer season. The basic plan would be the same, however.

There are of course many different emphases which different systems, different coaches, and different individuals place upon this principle. We have already described Arthur Lydiard's adamant demand for seven-days-a-week, 52-weeks-a-year of training, with about eight months of training for about four months of competition—almost the reverse of the American school system. Now contrast our American postcollege program with little or no competitive cross-country, a limited indoor season in some parts of the country, and a month or less of outdoor competition! No wonder our distance running has been poor!

But whatever the schedule of competition; whatever the emphasis, the principle should be the same and should be clear. As each day swings from periods of activity to recovery to activity, etc., as each week rotates days of hard running with days of restful exercise, so should the seasons of the year bring restful changes of training routines, a rhythmic rise and fall of demand upon the body, a season of heightened competitive tension followed by one of relief from such tension. Vigorous activity never ceases, and, in most instances, running never ceases. Endurance fitness is a way of life, much as walking is a way of life in most countries of the world. But the tensions of fitness will flow and ebb with the fun of fitness. Thus monotony and staleness will be avoided, progress will be maintained, and a freshness of competitive spirit made certain.

Principle 7

A sound program of training for endurance running develops an attitude that running is a matter of supreme importance within the limited hours and energies available to it as an amateur activity. Without full enthusiasm and a sense of commitment, a man can still become a fine runner, even a champion, but he will never attain his full potential. If doubts on this point are present, read the biographies of such men as Zatopek, Peters, Bannister, or Elliott. Read even the light-hearted biography of Derek Ibbotson, *The 4-Minute Smiler.*

Complete commitment, however, does not require full-time work each day. Obviously no amateur could accept such a creed. Rather it requires that during the few hours available for practice each day there be serious concentration on the work to be done. During this short period, all else is distraction: studies, job, love, hobbies, even sleep and food, regardless of the primacy of these factors during the other hours of the day.

Further it implies that self-discipline must become an accepted part of one's daily life. But to discipline other interests and activities does not mean to eliminate them; they need only be maintained in proper proportions. Franz Stampfl states the case well.

The athlete who believes that all normal social life and entertainment must be abandoned in the interests of rigorous and continuous training is a man devoid of imagination and proper understanding of the value of recreation. A colorless, spartan life in which all other interests are sacrificed to a single ideal is no existence for a man intent on achieving mental and physical fitness. Indeed, the relaxation and mental stimulation that hobbies, books, music, and the company of friends provide are as necessary to his well-being and athletic ambitions as the two hours of physical effort that comprise his daily program. Nobody, unless he is a complete moron, can eat, drink, and sleep athletics without the fun that ought to be there giving way to drudgery.

For these reasons every man in training should lead a full life according to his inclinations, only curbing his activities when they adversely cut across the common-sense requirements of his regular routine. Excess in any form is obviously bad, and when it is present, training becomes unproductive and possibly harmful.[7]

Principle 8

A sound program of training for endurance running assumes that better running is primarily the result of more running: more miles per day, more days per year, and more years per career. Such a program emphasizes stamina above all other results, especially during the early years of training and during the early months of each year. The high intensities of stress required by modern competitive performances at all levels— postcollege, college, and high school—require a long build-up of training. The longer it is, the safer and more effective it is likely to be. Consider, for example, the training of Sandor Iharos, as reported by *Track and Field News* for February 1958.

In 1953 Iharos trained 700 times, running from 18 to 25 miles daily. In the winter of 1954 he went still further. Getting up at dawn he ran on the snow-covered, icy paths of a nearby park, frequently in temperatures of about 15 degrees. . . . It was an unending source of astonishment to him what achievements one can drive the body to after proper preparation.

True, this is the schedule of a world-record holder, but he was 24 at the time and had been training regularly for at least six years. Incidentally, eight years later, at the age of 32, Iharos was still training regularly and running effectively with the best. Table 6.1 describes the extent of training by modern champion runners. We can summarize their training as follows:

More years. The average number of years of some degree of training is 10.4. Serious year-round training would probably be less than this. The range of years of training is from 5 years for Ron Delany to 17 for Paavo Nurmi. (Burleson is ignored since his career is not finished.) The average age of first racing was 15.6; that of best running, 26.3. Horace Ashenfelter and Vladimir Kuts did their best running at the age of 29. In contrast, Herb Elliott set a world record of 3:54.5 for the mile in 1958 at the age of only 20; Dyrol Burleson in 1959 at the age of 19 ran a mile in 4:06.7; and Bruce Kidd at 18 years 11 months ran two miles in 8:41.9 and three miles in 13:17.4!

More days per year. These same 20 champions averaged 5.8 days per week and 10.2 months per year during their more than 10 years of training.

More miles per day. Averages for number of miles per day would be difficult to obtain and very confusing to interpret. However, to indicate

---

[7] Franz Stampfl, *Franz Stampfl on Running* (London: Herbert Jenkins, Ltd., 1955), p. 49.

TABLE 6.1

EXTENT OF TRAINING BY MODERN CHAMPIONS

Name		Year Best Run	Age First Racing	Age Best Effort	Differ- ence	Best Effort	Days per Week	Months per Year
Ashenfelter	USA	'52	17	29	12	Olym 3000 SC—8:45.4 (O.R.)	5	10
Bannister	Eng.	'54	11	25	14	Mile—3:59.4 (W.R.)	5	9
Barthel	Lux.	'52	16	25	9	Olym 1500m—3:45.2 (O.R.)	6	9
Brasher	Eng.	'56	16	28	12	Olym 3000 SC—8:41.2 (O.R.)	6	10
Burleson	USA	'59	14	–	–	At 19, mile—4:06.7	6	8
Courtney	USA	'56	16	23	7	Olym 800m and 880—1:46.8	5	10
Delaney	USA	'56	16	21	5	Olym 1500m 3:41.2 (O.R)	5	10
Elliott	Aus.	'60	15	22	7	At 20, mile—3:54.5 (W.R.)	7	12
Hägg	Swe.	'41	17	26	9	Mile—4:01.4 (W.R.)	6	9
Harbig	Ger.	'39	19	28	9	800m—1:46.6 (W.R.)	5	10
Hewson	Eng.	'58	14	25	11	Mile—3:58.9	7	12
Iharos	Hun.	'55	18	25	7	2 mile—8:33.4 (W.R.)	7	12
Kuts	USSR	'56	–	29	–	10000m—28:45.6 (O.R.)	5	11
Landy	Aus.	'54	14	25	11	Mile—3:58 (W.R.)	6	12
Moens	Bel.	'55	17	28	11	800m—1:45.7 (W.R.)	7	10
Nurmi	Fin.	'24	10	27	17	10000m—30:06.1 (W.R.)	7	7
Pirie	Eng.	'56	10	26	16	5000m—13:36.8 (W.R.)	7	12
Reiff	Bel.	'52	18	27	9	2 mile—8:40.4 (W.R.)	5	10
Salsola	Fin.	'58	20	26	6	1500m—3:40.2 (W.R.)	5	10
Zatopek	CS	'52	19	30	11	10000m—28:54.2 (W.R.)	7	12
Average			15.6	26.3	10.4		5.8	10.2

O.R.—Olympic Record
W.R.—World Record

the more extreme examples, Emil Zatopek regularly ran 18 to 25 miles per day, much of which was fast running; Herb Elliott emphasized intensive training but reported that he often covered 20 miles and more of steady running; and the New Zealand "marathon trainers" Peter Snell and Murray Halberg, who were trained by Arthur Lydiard, regularly averaged more than 100 miles a week and often ran 30 miles in one session.

Lydiard strongly claims that such schedules are neither startling nor harmful.

My training system is not the superhuman thing it's made out to be. . . . My system is as simple as it is effective: build up your endurance through marathon training.

In theory, I am trying to develop my runners until they are in a tireless state. In practice, this means I am trying to give them sufficient stamina to maintain their natural speed over whatever distance they are running. Stamina is the key to the whole thing, because you can take speed for granted. No? Look here. Everybody thinks a four-minute mile is terrific, but it is only four one-minute quarter miles. . . . How do you give them the necessary stamina? My making them run and run and run some more, until they don't even think in terms of miles. There is no psychological magic and no pain barrier to be broken through. It is merely a process of long gradual conditioning.[8]

A crucial question now arises, "How much time each day should an endurance runner devote to practice?" One sound answer is: "All the time he can make available. The more time, the more mileage; the more mileage, the better the running."

But many great distance runners believe that even today, when some men train so endlessly, a wise concentration upon quality of training and intensity can still produce great—and even world—records. John Landy, Roger Bannister, and Tom Courtney have affirmed that they required only about 90 minutes per day.

Ken Norris, fine British runner, put it this way:

> I find that in 33 minutes I can run 20 fast 440's in 69 seconds with 110 yards slow jog between each. Even allowing for warming up and warming down and the usual post-mortems, no more than 65 to 70 minutes need be spent on the track.

If amateur sports are to survive, intense work in limited time must be emphasized, instead of a spread of work over unlimited hours.

It must be added that such a daily time limitation places even greater emphasis on the principle of more days per year and more years per career, if training and competitive performances are to approach maximum levels.

Principle 9

A sound program of training for endurance running recognizes that a coach works most successfully when his methods are consistent with the social traditions and social climate that surround him. Men trained and paid to organize sports in a society that believes strongly in competition and in winning will not last long if they agree with the headmaster of the English King's School that winning for the sake of winning is "an un-British and antieducational view, a denial of all that is best in sport."

As one educator said recently,

> I have found that 99 per cent of all communities want you to win. True, they also want you to build character, promote rules of amateurism and good sportsmanship, and be a worthy leader whom young Americans should follow, *but they want you to win.* They believe in character education; they employ

---

[8] Arthur Lydiard, "Why I Prescribe Marathons for Milers," *Sports Illustrated,* March 19, 1962, p. 49. © 1962 Time Inc.

guidance counselors, principals, teachers to build such character, and certainly they do not want the coach to tear it down, *but they want him to win.*

Such consistency of attitude between the coach and the social climate within which he works does not mean he must ignore his own principles. There are small but important ways in which he can throw his weight in his own direction. But no man ever changed the course of a river by rowing upstream.

Principle 10

A sound program of training for endurance running should be a challenge, although the sense of challenge may often be lost in the fog of day-after-day-after-day practice. Usually there will be a feeling of progress or at least of doing something worth doing; and rarely there will be the zestful excitement of achievement and self-discovery. But somehow, despite boredom or temporary loss of faith, there must run the thread of challenge and adventure.

As in all adventure, distance running contains elements of danger and risk: there is the sense of danger in continuing on when every sensitive part of the body warns against doing too much; there is the risk of stepping out in front of a crowd to demonstrate your track powers. But as G. Stanley Hall wrote years ago, "Danger makes us more alive. We so love to strive that we come to love the fear that gives us strength for conflict. Fear is not only something to be escaped from to a place of safety, but welcomed as an arsenal of augmented strength."

Distance running is a paradox of self-inflicted suffering and self-satisfying enjoyment. Both are essential. The pains of running are discussed elsewhere; here we wish to emphasize its satisfactions. Try harder, as you must, but harder within the limits of your own impulses, of your own zest to run. Train, don't strain. Even when you undergo practice runs of great tension, be assured that they will help you run later with less tension. Carry out certain work assignments sternly and to the last inch of distance; they can still be done with a sense of relaxation and competence that is satisfying. Even when Elliott was training his hardest as a junior at age 18, he wrote in his training diary,

I'll train hard and race as I feel. The times will probably come. I'm sure they will, but if they don't, why worry? I'm enjoying my running. . . . I must have faith in my body and allow it to run instinctively, i.e., without the mind. Jesus cured lepers only because they had faith in Him to make their bodies well. In races I must let my body go—relax one hundred per cent.[9]

_____
[9] Herb Elliott, *The Golden Mile* (London: Cassell & Company, Ltd., 1961), p. 51. Also published as *Herb Elliott's Story* (New York: Paul R. Reynolds, Inc., 1961).

Strange as this paradox of suffering and satisfaction may seem, it is the only road to achievement in running. True, each person has his own specific definition of the words "suffering and satisfaction." Some feel suffering is not a sports term at all; that it belongs in hospitals and with religious asceticism. Stone titled his biography of Michelangelo *The Agony and the Ecstasy*. Some runners might prefer those words; others would prefer a less dramatic expression of their feelings: "I get tired but I get a kick out of it."

Coach, did you run as an athlete? Then you know—and more important you can feel—the truth of these words. You have experienced the excitement of discovering power and ease in running, which you didn't know you had. But you, coach, that have never run at distance and pace, you feel these are pretty words that just don't make sense. There's only one answer to you—"Try it!" By all means try it!—or give up your hopes of being a good coach of distance running. If you can't walk a mile in ten minutes, you should still feel the thrill of gradual progress until you can cover a mile, walking and jogging, in some time less than ten minutes. Then you'll coach with conviction; "There's really something in this game after all!" Without that conviction, you'll do the game more harm than good.

Whatever words we use, the over-all attitude while training should be one of relaxed enjoyment. Do this, do that, do what the other fellow is doing, if it interests you or helps him. Do whatever makes you forget the regimentation and tension of daily training. As long as you make demands on the body, let the mind run free. Don't waste time; don't stand around; run, run, run endlessly; but run with a smile in your heart, if not on your face.

Principle 11

A sound program of training for endurance running assumes that maximum performance is possible only when based on a broad foundation of fitness. Few coaches or training systems would disagree with this statement as written, but their interpretations of it would vary greatly. A few die-hards still say, "The key to better running lies in more running." But most modern coaches take a broader view. They try to understand the many factors that might be related to endurance running and the manner and degree to which they are related. For example, some coaches and runners believe in running any distance, anywhere, under any and all conditions of running surface: of hill-and-dale, of sand or surf, of dirt road or concrete walk, of sand dune or stadium steps, in rain or snow, in hot sun or icy cold, in country isolation or crowded city parks. By so doing, these men feel they develop a broad physical endurance as well as mental-emotional toughness that can take anything that might come along. Granted that competition today always takes place under carefully prepared conditions, the self-assurance that comes from broad training carries with it a relaxation and carelessness, in the sense of freedom from worry, that are invaluable.

One might describe this training as "resistance training," to use Cerutty's term. Resistance training would include Zatopek's heavy army shoes, Swedish and Finnish snow-running, and Elliott's running in soft sand and shallow surf. It would include running with weighted vests or belts or ankle wraps, or with weights carried in the hands. In a study of skiing, Christensen and Hogberg found that the use of ski sticks increased maximal oxygen consumption well above that when sticks were not used. Running with light weights or with exaggerated arm action might well bring comparable benefits. Ernst Jokl [10] goes much further than this in suggesting that the hands and arms are not only the most educable parts of the body but that their development has a beneficial effect upon performance that is primarily of the legs. He suggests apparatus gymnastics, calisthenics, wrestling, and even the manual arts such as violin or piano playing as adjuncts to training for running.

Another example of endurance fitness by running is found in Cerutty's idea of "power running," in which a man greatly exaggerates the tension of all muscles while jogging or walking fast. The muscles of the face, neck, shoulders, back, abdomen, arms, hands, are all contracted as hard as the action will permit. One suggestion is to mimic the movements of competitive walkers as tensely as possible. Walk *hard* or jog *hard* in every way that you can. At first the idea seems to have little merit as it seems so opposed to the more important idea of relaxed running. On the contrary, one becomes so conscious of tension everywhere that the periods of relaxation which inevitably follow feel as though they were at a new and more complete level. The discussion of relaxation on pages 63–76 may prove enlightening. Further, this practice should develop both muscle fibers and capillary blood supply. Fibers grow through resistance exercise; capillaries, through repetition. Both are present. If, as some authorities claim, overloads in strength-endurance should be applied in the same movement for which they are intended, then power-running should be helpful.

But this principle of broad fitness should be interpreted beyond the confines of endurance *per se*. There are other related factors that need specific development. Zatopek practiced breath-holding while walking

---

[10] Ernst Jokl, M.D., "Some Physiological Components of Modern Track Training," *Clinic Notes* (NCAA Track Coaches Association, 1956), p. 226.

"until will power was no longer a problem." Woldemar Gerschler once wrote that not only is breath-holding of value but that learning to breathe properly could lead to better world records. As another example, the ability to adjust to high temperatures and humidity is a specific capacity not necessarily related to the capacity to undergo running fatigue. Many times in the past, performances have been determined primarily by this one factor rather than by the over-all running abilities of the contestants. The 10,000 meters at the USA–USSR meet in Philadelphia, 1959, was but one example that will be long remembered by those present. One obvious method of training the heat-regulatory functions is to practice under conditions of higher temperature and humidity. But Dr. Ernst Jokl suggests a more pleasant and generally beneficial method.

I have come to the conclusion that the traditional Sauna bath which all Finnish—and scarcely any American—runners use regularly, combined with the rigors of the long and cold winters (of Finland) . . . is a highly significant adjunct to their athletic training. . . .

The Sauna bath with its dry and steam heat rooms as well as contrast exposure with ice water or snow must be used for several months, twice weekly, before its benefits become effective in terms of performance. . . .

It is suggested that track and field clubs throughout the United States construct Sauna baths. . . . I predict that the introduction in this country of the Sauna bath will lead to a significant performance improvement in long distance running.[11] [Shivers of delight go up and down my spine as I feel the hot blast of Finnish Sauna heat and the cold plunge in a Finnish lake that always follows. What a pity we haven't adopted the custom!—J.K.D.]

To carry the idea of broad fitness a step further, there is the important concept of circuit training [12] used so widely in England. A series of strength and flexibility exercises (squat thrusts, sit-ups, chins, rope-climbing, etc.) are arranged in a circuit. After maximum performances are established, a man goes through the entire circuit of exercises at submaximum levels as rapidly as possible. Circuit training includes competition, measurement of progress, and in the words of its inventors, "a hard core of fitness" that is helpful in sports.

Finally there is the use of strength training exercises. Cerutty and his runners used them regularly and thought them beneficial. Lydiard has been quoted that none of his men do special strength exercises—"We have little enough time for running." Most coaches feel that, within rather narrow limits, such strength exercises as barbell work and isometric contractions are desirable. They strengthen muscles not directly

---

[11] *Ibid.*

[12] R. E. Morgan and G. T. Adamson, *Circuit Training* (London: G. Bell & Sons, Ltd., 1958).

related to running and consequently further a balanced fitness. Even more important, they provide a feeling of fitness and thereby a self-assurance and sense of vitality that the weak-muscled runner can never gain by just running. Almost all agree that such strength exercises should be merely supplementary and done during the nontraining hours.

Principle 12

A sound program of training for endurance running is always of the whole person. This simple and obvious statement tends, unfortunately, to be ignored both by systems of training and by coaches. It has various inferences. First, there is the problem of body-mind relationships already discussed under "Fatigue." No matter how our words declare their inseparable unity, we all tend to act as though the body has its own existence exclusive of the mind and emotions. We all tend to prepare training systems on a simple time-energy basis as though men were machines. We constantly ask clinic coaches or textbooks such as this to tell us "The Way" as though the right system were the crucial element. But it's a man that runs, a whole man, a man with doubts of his abilities, with certain fears of all-out effort, with a sensitiveness to blisters, to a stitch in the side, to vomiting; a man with counterinterests: with a girlfriend, with studies to worry over, with parents who are unhappy or financially destitute; a man who gets little sleep because of the extra job he must maintain to stay in school.

It is such a man that runs, and unless that man finds a way of life according to which he can concentrate his energies on running for a brief two hours or so each day, unless he is able to eliminate those influences that hinder his running and discipline those distractions that lure him to miss practice occasionally or to ease up on its demands, not all the cleverness of the devil's disciple could devise a training system that would be effective.

Further, a sound system of training recognizes that most men come to a new coach, to a new track squad, to a new school, with certain preformed attitudes, loyalties, inhibitions, defeats which tend to block acceptance and progress. His parent may have discouraged, even forbidden, his running as a waste of time and energy. His former coach may have been "a second father," for whom there can be no substitute. Or conversely, both his father and his former coach may have been martinets against whom he has struggled and who form the pattern in his mind for all coaches. He may be using achievement in running as a crutch by which he can prove his worth to his girlfriend, or his classmates, or his brother who has always belittled him.

The autobiographies of such men as Jim Peters,[13] English distance runner of the 1950's, almost always tell of such problems. In Jim's case they were largely related to the counterdemands of his family, a wife and two children. After all, he was 27 when he started to run again after the War. He had a house to pay for, a full-time job to maintain. One wonders how he could even hope to continue in the marathon, especially since his wife was far from sympathetic. Traditional training for the marathon required long, slow runs of three and four hours of time. Peters had only about one hour a day, plus of course his week-ends and vacations. A tradition-bound coach would have said, "It can't be done." But Jim's coach, Johnstone, said, "Let's forget the old ideas. We have nothing to lose. Let's try how much intensity of training we can achieve in about thirty minutes of fast running each week day, then pick up our distance on the week-ends. Everyone says it won't work for the marathon but let's try." As a result, there was no conflict with Jim's job, his peace of mind at home improved greatly, and, incidentally, marathon training has been changed ever since.

Principle 13

A sound program of training for endurance running must always be applied to the specific physical-mental-emotional-social abilities of a specific and unique individual. To believe that the secret of success in distance coaching lies in following a particular system is to court failure. True, knowledge of the essentials of distance training is necessary. True, an understanding of how those essentials apply to men in general is required. But by far the greater knowledge, in fact the only knowledge, that really counts at any one time, lies in the wise application of these essentials to the special characteristics of this unique individual.

Only in recent years have there been serious scientific efforts to discover the endless ways in which individuals vary within themselves and from each other. One of the more exciting of these attempts is summarized in a small book, *Biochemical Individuality,* by Roger J. Williams.[14] At least four of its basic ideas apply to our work.

First, that if our measuring devices were sufficiently sensitive and precise, they would make clear that we differ from each other in all aspects of our being, just as we do in the pattern of our fingerprints.

Second, that though norms and averages are useful and even essential

---

[13] Jim Peters, *In the Long Run* (London: Cassell & Company, Ltd., 1955).
[14] Roger J. Williams, *Biochemical Individuality* (New York: John Wiley & Sons, Inc., 1956).

The 1956 Olympic 800 meters at Melbourne. First, Tom Courtney, U.S.A.; second, Derek Johnson, Great Britain; third, Auden Boysen, Norway; fourth, Arnie Sowell, U.S.A. Sowell held the lead for 600 meters (1:20.4) when Courtney moved alongside. Entering the homestretch, Johnson moved quickly through a gap between the leaders and actually led by a few inches for some 30 yards. Courtney won with a desperate driving burst at the tape in the good time of 1:47.7.

Courtesy of *Track and Field News*

to understanding, the moment one becomes interested in applying that knowledge, individuality becomes the crucial consideration. Many examples are given to confirm this central thesis of the book. For example, norms have been carefully formulated for human eye structure and function, but when any one of us feels the need for eye glasses, we ignore such averages and seek the services of an expert ophthalmologist to prepare glasses fitted to the special needs of our special eyes.

Third, that variability from so-called normality occurs within each person, as well as between persons. There are, speaking accurately, no entirely normal persons, or better, no persons that are normal in all respects. Williams gives many examples of abnormal structures or functions in normal people and assumes that virtually every human being possesses attributes that are abnormal in some respects. Such deviation helps us to understand the so-called peculiarities of athletes. For example, in studying the characteristics of marathon runners, Ernst Jokl [15] and others have reported that though one might describe the typical marathon runner in various aspects of body size, weight, heart action, age, intelligence, blood chemistry, etc., many men evidence characteristics that must be considered deviates from the normal. In each case, success is achieved through compensating factors, including training, which bring balance and effectiveness to the whole.

I conducted research some years ago on the extent to which individuals form a pattern of performance in their willingness to persist in a physical task involving physical discomfort. Here of course motivation would be a critical factor. My conclusion was that performance is always specific and that only a broad pattern of response could be predicted. A man might do well on a series of tests, then fail badly on one that, at least outwardly, was very similar to the others. One concludes that we do not possess general qualities such as sensitivity to pain. Performance is specific to a specific type of pain in a specific situation.

Williams' fourth thesis is that each of these specific attributes is present in each of us within its own range of capacity and that the level of development at any given time depends upon specific development of that attribute. Among such qualities should be included adaptation to conditions of heat, cold, humidity, to specific foods, to infections, to exercise, to various ergogenic aids such as coffee or drugs, and many others. Obviously these ranges of capacity differ from one individual to another. Some possess wide ranges; others relatively narrow. Some are narrow at the upper levels of human capacity; others are narrow at the

---

[15] Ernst Jokl, M.D., "Response of Body to Distance Running," *The Amateur Athlete,* February 1955, p. 24.

lower levels. One conclusion that must be drawn is that coaches are not justified in describing an athlete as being or lacking this or that, or as reacting in a fixed way to certain conditions. Human beings are far too flexible and adaptable to be so narrowly defined.

In contrast, if one were to assume that runners, like chains, are only as strong as their weakest links, our problem has two phases: to discover the many kinds of links upon which training and competition will place stress, and to develop these links to their maximum potential.

In 1959, in the USA–USSR dual meet in Philadelphia, the four competitors in the 10,000 meter run were assumed to be of similar ability and general condition. But performance varied greatly: one man finished strongly, one dropped out, and two were widely separated at various stages of the race. This great variation in performance was brought about by one factor in the situation: their varying capacities to run under the conditions of 85 degree temperature and 58 per cent humidity. The winner, Desyatchikov, held up well, though obviously affected. Bob Soth had some spectators in tears as he fought for several laps in the weird, high-stepping and backward-leaning style of a man undergoing heat exhaustion. He finally dropped and was helped from the track. Pyarnokivi showed similar signs of collapse but stayed on the track to the finish. Truex, more experienced than Soth, slowed down as he felt the effects of heat, then came on with a thrilling sprint at the finish. In summary, their race patterns were specific to their reactions to heat and humidity, not to their over-all conditioning and ability.

In summary of this principle, individual runners must treat themselves and must be treated by their coaches as unique individuals with unique powers and weaknesses. The coach who adopts or creates one system of training as superior to all others, and then expects his individual runners to develop by means of that system, will achieve success only with athletes of a temperament and physical capacity adapted to that system. The others will merely "get by" or even fail. It is a truism that a coach should be judged by his failures as well as by his successes. A good coach is a coach of all the men that come to him, not just of those who happen to conform to the framework of his system.

Principle 14

A sound program of training for endurance running builds the habit of daily exertion as an essential part of year-round living. This may be the most crucial principle of all, more crucial than the training system, more crucial than coaching attitude, more crucial even than the balance between stamina and speed. To run today and tomorrow and tomorrow and every tomorrow that follows will cause most of the other essentials of distance training to fall into line. Coaches have described Zatopek's training as inexorable daily exertion. Ibbotson, the four-minute smiler, once said that if you can't win the inner struggle of "Shall I train or not train today?" you certainly cannot win the outer struggle with your racing rivals. Bill Nankeville wrote,

> No man should go into a sport unless he loves it, and if he loves his sport, he will revel in it. Not only the actual performance of the sport, but the task of practicing towards perfection, and training towards perfect physical fitness.[16]

The habit of daily exertion! Not just the nice days, not just the days you feel like it, but daily, everyday, whether cold or hot or raining or snowing or soggy footpaths or concrete walks—as Zatopek said, "it doesn't matter!" Run until the question of not running just never arises, any more than not sleeping or not eating.

Perhaps the most accomplished writer in modern track and field is the English novelist, W. R. Loader. As you read his words, you know they come from personal experience.

> Two main temptations lie in wait for the runner who has planned a training season of so many evenings or afternoons of work per week for so many weeks or months. The first temptation, when one of those afternoons or evenings comes along, is not to spend it in running. . . . Surely to miss training just this once will not matter? After all there's a long season of it lying ahead. But conscience wags a finger. Conscience points out that to miss training once is to open a breach in the wall of routine. And a single breach will almost certainly be followed by others, to the point where there is no routine left. And then bang goes your ambition to be a runner. Once you have gotten into the habit of enduring torment you must not get out of it.
> A temptation more insidious is to cut a training session short after it has been started. This is insidious because you try to convince yourself you've earned merit merely by turning out, without needing to go through the whole gamut of toil. Such a dishonest suggestion is not always easy to counter. . . . You start off on the first lap or two briskly enough, with your legs moving lightly and your breath coming easily. You say to yourself this is going to be no bother at all. You soon change your mind. An ache develops round the ankles, or in the calves, or shins. . . . All right, you ignore the ache. . . . The aching passes and is replaced by a numbness which indicates that the muscles are still far from happy about the situation but have abandoned further protest as useless. . . .
> By now the runner's respiratory system will be making its protest. . . . The lungs pant as they strive to take in more air. . . . The dead weight in your legs remains. . . . Clammy sweat trickles down your face and body. . . . Your body is a desert of weariness.
> And all the time your mind thoroughly disapproves of the whole, mad, damnable exercise. Or rather, the civilized part disapproves, and asks why in

---

16 Bill Nankeville, *The Miracle of the Mile* (London: Stanley Paul & Co., Ltd., 1956), p. 118.

God's name the stupidity can't be stopped. The other part, more rugged and primitive, tells civilization to shut up and, if it can't make a positive contribution to the work in hand, at least not to sabotage it. . . .

Every stride you take brings you nearer home. Imagine you're a horse perking up when its head is turned toward the stable. What's that? Never mind the bloody stable? You've had enough of this? You're going to stop? By God you're not. Not while I'm in charge. . . . Good show, legs. Soon it'll be only three laps, and then two, and then one. . . . Two laps to go. A mere trifle. . . . You're practically there. You're on the last lap. Now show them what you're made of. Show them you're not half dead. Drive yourself. . . . Keep your shoulders straight. *Sprint in!* [17]

Principle 15

A sound program of training for endurance running uses some form of withdrawal-and-return so long as it is within the agreements of amateurism. This expression may be strange to sport, but its usefulness for us is just as important as for Arnold Toynbee in his historical description of how men and societies revitalize their energies. When men are held back by the endless details and hindrances of normal living, they must for a time, if they hope to progress, withdraw from them, "get away from it all." During this period of withdrawal, they are able to relax, to concentrate their energies without wasting them in fighting distractions, to discover hidden powers and new ways—then to return to normal life, refreshed and armed anew.[18]

This principle has many applications in endurance running. There are the sports training camps, restricted by the International **Olympic** Committee to three weeks of individual attendance out of each year. Some of these are called Sports Institutes, as at Vierumachi and Kuortane in Finland, or at Boson just outside of Stockholm. As such they have a wide use as vacation and educational camps for many groups. Some training camps are called "the armed services" and are maintained by most of the nations of the world. There, through a misuse of the term, "service to country," sportsmen including runners are given extra time and special encouragements to train and compete—as well as fewer duties that hinder performance. Many great champions have written frankly and gratefully of the performance benefits that came through such opportunities. Other training camps, like those conducted by Cerutty at Camp Portsea, Australia, or by Olander in 1945 at Völödalen, Sweden, are individual enterprises.

---

[17] W. R. Loader, *Testament of a Runner* (London: William Heinemann Ltd., 1960), pp. 63-67. Also published as *Sprinter* (New York: The Macmillan Company, 1961).
[18] Arnold J. Toynbee, *A Study of History* (London: Oxford University Press, 1947), pp. 217-30.

Such withdrawal from normal living allows full-time training and related activities and complete freedom from the endless worries and disturbances that eat away our nervous energies. When conducted within the rules of amateurism, they are an effective means to greater development. When conducted beyond those rules, they are an even more effective means to even greater development, but at the same time they are the means to dishonor, whether recognized or not, and to the prostitution of amateur sports.

Principle 16

A sound program of training for endurance running instills in a matter-of-fact way that its paths to achievement are never easy. Greg Rice, outstanding American two-miler of the late 1940's, understood this clearly when he wrote,

The paramount prerequisite for condition, the basis of success, is hard, diligent work. There is no escape. As soon as one no longer desires to make the self-sacrifice necessary for complete preparation he should then forget about winning any races or even competing. . . .

Distance runners themselves prove that work, miles of competition, and training are required as they do not blossom into stars until they have matured. It is not an overnight sport. Years are an important factor in one's developing progress. So do not become too anxious for favorable results, look for a steady and slow betterment and then one day you will discover you are a star. The self-denial and hard work will have left many fond memories.

The darkness of this note seems necessary to me since with the proper attitude one can obtain a much higher objective. Knowledge of what is required makes it easier to overcome the ups and downs of the long period of development without unnecessary discouragement. Discouragement will often face that individual, but his interest will find bolstering from the knowledge of the hardships of others and it will aid him to re-initiate his desire for personal success and better American distance runners.

Preparation, as I remember, even in midseason, was full of personal hardship. After a day in the office, at the five-thirty bell, I would dash into the blackness of the winter's early darkness to the subway entrance to battle the homeward bound human stampede for a standing position to Columbia. Upon arrival, trek to my room, change into my track togs, don an extra heavy sweat suit, and an overcoat to keep out the chill of the night air between sections of my workout since the locker rooms were closed to all activities for the day. The library lights reflected enough rays on the track so one could run without fear of stepping off the track. . . .

The day's training completed, bundle up and return to my room. A shower and if not too tired to eat, out on the streets for a belated dinner. When all was done it was time for sleep and another day.[19]

What meaning should be given to the expression, "hard work"? "Hard

---

[19] Greg Rice, "Work Is the Only Way to Distance Running Success," *The Amateur Athlete*, XX, No. 10 (October 1949), 7.

work" should be interpreted in terms of the degree of stress the work places upon the individual that is doing it. It should not be defined by the number of miles covered or the intensity of the pace run. What is "hard work" to the beginner is obviously "child's play" for the mature and conditioned. We should not therefore be awe-struck at the racing performance of a champion distance runner so much as at the inexorability of his years of daily practice. Such practice is not "hard" for him; otherwise he could not do it day after day with no more rest than the average man gets. His "inhumanness" lies in his determined persistence, rather than in his work-load.

J. W. Alford illustrated this very well in his comments on the training of Zatopek.

I am reminded of the early rather inaccurate accounts of Zatopek's training, and the awe that was felt for the gruelling work we were led to believe he undertook. Zatopek did, of course, train very hard, and nobody is going to become a champion at the distance runs without a great deal of hard work. But his training was not so "inhuman" and "man-killing" as many still believe. *It was a build-up,* and the intensity of the training increased only as he felt himself ready for it.[20]

Principle 17

A sound program of training for endurance running progresses to the next level of effort and achievement, whether of mileage or intensity, only after the present work-level can be carried with sureness and reasonable ease. This is considered so basic in interval training as to be recommended as one of its five factors, degree of ease, along with distance, pace, interval, and number.

Mastery over a given load of stress cannot be claimed the first time the load is carried, but only after it has been carried enough times and with enough freedom from strain to be met with full assurance and minimum stress. Psychological adaptation has now been added to physiological adaptation.

This principle is discussed more fully under "Interval Training" in Chapter 5, but it is basic to all systems, to all sure progress in distance training, as well as to an effective guarantee against staleness. The challenge of doing what one has done before, but doing it more easily, leads to more enjoyable practice.

Obviously this principle has special application to the use of time trials, which in the past have created at least as much emotional stress in runners as the competitive races.

---

[20] J. W. Alford, "Farther and Faster," *Coaching Newsletter* (London), No. 2 (July 1956), p. 5.

Principle 18

A sound program of training for endurance running will plan to nourish and develop competitive spirit just as carefully and thoughtfully as it does the more physical qualities of stamina or skill. The Western world tends to take competitiveness for granted, as being an attribute of all normal men. But the research studies of such social scientists as Margaret Mead [21] and Katherine Horney [22] indicate that this is but one of our social myths to which our individuals must conform or be prepared to make a difficult social adjustment.

Lack of space permits only the broad comment that within the wide range of individuals in every culture there exists a wide range of potential competitiveness as related to a wide range of activities and incentives. It can rarely be said with justification that a man is naturally a great competitor. True, some have learned through successful experience to react "competitively" whenever another person enters the situation; true, some seem to be challenged and energized more than others. But such ability, while based upon inherited assets, is primarily the product of training, cultural and personal.

Throughout his career, Elliott assumed that you can only produce in competition what you have created and suffered through in training. His tactics were simple and largely self-centered: to run his own best race and let the opposition stay with him if they could. This meant that competition was primarily a struggle over himself, that unless his steel was forged in the fires of self-mastery during training, it could never be hard enough to withstand the fierce heat of competition against others.

Somehow, to me running is a challenge, demanding mastery of the body as well as the winning of races. . . . [Then later, as he described his training for the 1960 Olympics:] I set off . . . determined to finish really tired and satisfied. I squibbed on it without realizing it and finished too fresh. It annoyed me. I began to think I had lost the capacity to hurt myself. I must be careful and see that I cultivate this capacity again. I mustn't become a subconscious squib. I was so annoyed that I did three laps of the Shrine hill to finish off.[23]

But, you protest, this is the attitude of a world-renowned athlete who has trained a naturally competitive mind to control a naturally competitive body. What does competitive spirit mean to the beginner, to the inept, to the doubtful?

---

[21] Margaret Mead, *Cooperation and Competition among Primitive Peoples* (New York: McGraw-Hill Book Company, Inc., 1937).

[22] Karen Horney, *The Neurotic Personality of Our Time* (New York: W. W. Norton & Company, Inc., 1937).

[23] Elliott, *op. cit.*, p. 160.

First, it should be repeated that all such traits as competitiveness are present in each of us within a wide range of possible development. True, this range differs in width from one man to another, in the same way though not necessarily in equal measure as such physical qualities as that of endurance. As with endurance, neglect or abuse produces performances at the lower level of this range; desire plus wise and long nurture, at the upper level. But competitiveness is a far more sensitive quality than endurance, more easily bruised, stunted, even destroyed altogether.

Second, competitive spirit is directly related to a conflict between inclination and opposition both within and without, between the anticipation of achievement and the pain of effort, between the will to win and the fear of failure. When competitive spirit fails, a disorganization or loss of control takes place which appears to others to be physical in nature. They say, "He tied up." But they might better say, "His mind lost control."

Third, to show one's competitive spirit is not always feasible in competition; for example, when one faces the alternative of running with the group at a pace that is far too fast or of running at one's own proper pace and falling far behind. Sometimes, coaches, parents and other well-wishers exhort, "Always run to win and therefore maintain contact, whatever the cost," or "You can if you will; anything is possible to the man that won't be beat." Such rules have a nice ring to them, so that some boys give them a literal and almost sacred meaning: to deny them is to betray one's inmost morality.

How many times the writer has regretfully and helplessly watched young men go through four years of college while running under the illusion that if they persist long enough and desperately enough, they are certain to come out on top, though just what "on top" meant was never clear. Even to hint that they should seek other sports or relax and consider their running as a developmental exercise was to insult their deepest faith. "I can't quit now, coach!"

There is no easy way to competitive toughness. Certainly it cannot be achieved by concentrating upon conditioning and avoiding the challenge of others. Just as one learns to run by running, so one learns to compete effectively through closely fought competitions with men one can beat more than half the time. This last point is most important. Few areas of learning are as sensitive to negative results as those that are competitive. Certainly one is not likely to develop confidence in one's ability to win through a long series of defeats. We are all aware of the practice in boxing of arranging matches on a graded scale of competence so that the new prospect is challenged but seldom defeated. To over-match a man is considered poor managing and a certain way of destroying his fighting qualities in the ring.

The problem is no less critical in distance running. Rare indeed is the man who can suffer the punishing blows of repeated defeat and still maintain fortitude and zest. A survey of distance champions discloses records of many victories early in their careers and few defeats. One would expect this, for these men possessed the necessary qualities for victory. Victory was a natural result. But victory was also a cause, a means of developing confidence in oneself and in one's competitive spirit. In our opinion, Bannister's reputation for consistently producing competitive performances beyond what his practice efforts would predict can be attributed to inborn qualities of course but also, in an important degree, to his undefeated record at the mile distance over a period of several years. He had created his own climate of high expectancy and success.

The American school competitive system, with its emphasis upon team success, has led us to take an almost careless attitude toward this problem. Team needs make it impossible to grade competition in terms of individual needs; the individual is forced to compete whatever his chances or whatever the consequences for his future. Only a basically mature person or one guided by a mature coach is likely to make optimum progress under such a system.

Fourth, a firm foundation for competitive spirit can sometimes be best laid by relating progress primarily to oneself. To develop gradually in stamina and willed control over a six months' period or more, to compete when ready against worthy but "beatable" opponents is to attempt a truly developmental program. One of the more desirable practices in certain college conferences in the United States exists in "no interschool competition during the freshman year." Though adopted primarily for academic reasons, this practice permits a gradual and developmental approach throughout the freshman's year which, if properly utilized, can put him into varsity competition strengthened in body and competitive spirit.

One more important consideration in building competitive spirit lies in discovering the exact dosage of work during the days and weeks just prior to major competition that will bring the athlete to his most eager and energetic peak. There are, as always, many bases for judgment, depending on the athlete's program of training and his individual reaction to work and competition. As a rule of thumb, the poorer an athlete's condition, or the lighter the schedule of work he follows, the more rest and mental build-up he will need prior to competition.

After evaluating the performances of English distance runners in the

Rome Olympics, Coach J. W. Alford placed greatest emphasis upon the problem of preparing physically and mentally for major competition.

And now comes the most difficult period. *Strength, speed and stamina will now have been built up to what appears to be their highest level. It needs the nervous impulse of competition to lift them up higher still.* This is where I think many of our best runners have gone wrong. Notwithstanding what one reads of modern "scientific" training, much of what I have seen of some of the training of our top runners has been haphazard, purposeless, and totally lacking in method. *Especially do they fail in their mental attitude to competition, which is, after all, the all-important thing.* Who cares if you can beat everybody in sight on the training track, if you get nowhere in the race? *I believe very strongly that most of our runners underestimate the calls made upon their physical and nervous resources by competition.* And because of this, they neglect to prepare properly for the important races in respect of the way they should husband their energy carefully for a day or two prior to competition, and especially for the last few hours. And they often do not go the best way about giving their systems a chance to recover properly afterwards. This is the one period when it is true to say that the great danger is *overwork;* and the worst way to recover from a bad race is to train twice as hard for the next one.[24] [Italics mine—J.K.D.]

Principle 19

A sound program of training for endurance running distinguishes clearly between the two ideas of strength on the one hand, and endurance or stamina on the other. Strength is often used loosely as when speaking of a strong runner or a strong finish. This is confusing and, for men educated in this field, unjustified. Physiologically, strength is related to the development of muscle fibers; endurance, to the development of blood capillaries. (See Fig. 3.1, page 27.) Any activity has its effect upon both of course. Also, endurance requires the development of more muscles and their capillaries than are needed to carry a certain pace at the start of a run; as one group of fibers tires, another group should be available to take over the action. Therefore speed-work, which requires more strength in the true sense of the word, is advocated to build such "teams" of fibers and the capillaries related to them. This is all helpful to endurance.

But when weight-lifting is advocated for physical reasons to develop "strong" runners, thinking is unclear. Weight-lifting or strength training develops the ability to do a difficult action once, or at most a few times. Obviously, this is not the problem in endurance running. Weight-lifting may help a "scrawny" runner to build a better balanced and more physically fit body; and in many instances, the feeling that one is

---

24 J. W. Alford, "Down to Earth," *Coaching Newsletter* (London), October 1960, p. 9.

physically prepared for anything and everything is a great boost for running morale. But weight-lifting for endurance reasons is no more sound than would be endurance running for weight-lifters.

Principle 20

A sound program of training for endurance running makes effective use of group running. This seemingly innocent statement actually covers a hornet's nest of beliefs and arguments. In America the coach is traditionally the creator and the boss of the track team. The team has little unity except at track competitions, has little time in which to organize for group action, and therefore is willing to let the coach make its decisions. In contrast, in England the professional coach has had little acceptance and the team with its captain has made its own schedules, has prepared its own track, and has settled its own group problems, while leaving individual training to the decisions of the individual.

Competitive running is necessarily an isolated and individual effort, and runners tend to be individualists rather than group-minded. Herb Elliott once wrote,

I rarely like training with anybody. Even if they don't speak, their presence disturbs my concentration, so that my thoughts, which might be valuable if analyzed, are wasted.[25]

But, to an important degree, everyday training can be done in groups whereby younger and less experienced men can gain invaluable encouragement and help, and even the most calloused can find new and better ways. Such group spirit and action does not just happen; it arises out of thoughtful planning that has its own special skills just as does the coach-individual relationship. When properly done, a team morale can grow in which the individual can develop to his maximum performance and still contribute in spirit and action to the group. Of course some individuals, by home or other training, are simply not capable of working with or contributing to the group and thus set up a special problem.

But coaches are increasingly aware of the practical values inherent in science and are seeking the help of psychologists and others in learning to use those values. The first talk of this kind given before the National College Track Coaches Association was that in 1955 by Dr. David Cole, Chairman of the Psychology Department of Occidental College. Among other usable suggestions he related this story:

I had the opportunity this year of watching one team [which] had among its

---

25 Elliott, *op. cit.*, p. 146.

members a very outstanding athlete, a man of championship caliber. . . . The thing that impressed me about this man was the keen interest he showed in the team as a team. He had already competed . . . and won his event . . . , yet all during the course of the meet I saw him talking to one athlete before he started a race, to another after a race, tieing a teammate's shoestring, and so on—just a constant interaction with his teammates. I couldn't help thinking how far this man had gone beyond the concept of track as an individual sport. It appeared that he had really developed a team spirit which had been motivating him all through the afternoon. The man . . . who comes down the last sixty or seventy yards towards the tape, driven on by simply the desire to win for himself, is much more likely to give up than the man driven on by something outside himself—call it Alma Mater, call it team spirit, consider it corny if you wish—it nevertheless is real; and he who is driven by it will probably be able to reach deeper into the reserves that he has, the physical reserves, than the individual [who] lacks it.[26]

A glance at the appended bibliography will disclose that a new science of effective group action is gradually emerging. "Group dynamics" and "sociometric devices" are now common terms in educational, industrial, and political circles, and their uses are becoming more and more accepted and understood. Our present emphasis upon performance and winning in sport makes such an educational approach both doubtful and slow. The winning coach and the winning athlete is publicized endlessly; few questions are asked as to the educational methods by which victory is attained.

But, as our schools take their educational responsibilities in sports more seriously, progress is being achieved. For purposes of understanding, methods of group action can be described broadly as follows:

Laissez faire. Individuals design their own plans without the help of the coach and without reference to group needs or preferences. The group weakens, perhaps falls apart. Hostility develops among members and between some members and the coach. Planning of schedules is less effective. Some individuals are happiest and most effective under this system. They prefer that the coach act only as an advisor who leaves all decisions to them.

Autocratic. The coach determines all policies and details. Future plans are never made known beforehand. Workout details are given piecemeal. Hostility among group members tends to be high. A few successful members believe in the coach; those rejected by him or less successful may come to hate him. Many individuals would prefer to leave the planning and decision making to the coach. They relax under "you do the running; I'll do the thinking." For such men, the system works.

Democratic. The group discusses all policies and details, criticisms

<hr>

[26] David Cole, "Motivation and Performance," *Clinic Notes* (NCAA Track Coaches Association, 1955), p. 17.

of individual action are invited, and decisions are made by the group. The coach makes suggestions and recommendations and discusses possible consequences. Goals and rewards tend to be in terms of the team. Values are related more to individual and group growth than to maximum individual performance or winning for its own sake.

All three of these methods can and have been effective depending upon such factors as group tradition, coaching attitudes and skill in working with groups, and individual backgrounds and attitudes. Contrast the cultural differences between German militarism prior to 1940 in which the individual was a tool of the State and the *laissez faire* of England in which the individual was pre-eminent. Contrast the relationship in Hungary between Coach Igloi and his three great runners, Tabori, Iharos, and Roszavolgyi, all of whom were in the armed services, with that between Bannister and Coach Stampfl, who held the role of advisor to those who cared to seek his advice. Yet each of these cultures and relationships produced great champions.

One must conclude that each sport family must decide just what its real goals are—making records, winning victories, or making men—and must learn the skills of group action that are consistent with those goals.

The following are some suggestions that will be used or rejected depending upon the system of leadership that is selected or imposed:

1. Nothing is worth making that does not make the man. "We're building character this year," is the half-apologetic statement of the losing coach.
2. Competition is for winning. "Nice guys finish last."
3. The most effective help a leader can give is to help a group help itself.
4. Leadership does not reside in a person; it resides in the group.
5. Training in group action should be organized around the tasks the group has set for itself.
6. By planned action, sometimes by unplanned action, a group can make or break almost any one of its members.
7. Some individuals function best when they design and carry out their own plans, without reference to the group needs or interests.
8. Some individuals function best when the planning and the control is left to the coach. "Let's cut out the chatter. Tell us what to do and let's get at it." "It's not what we know but what we do that counts."
9. To contribute to the group requires both good will and skill in group action.
10. Group agreements and actions that encourage one to play the role of the man one wants to be can help one become that man.

Principle 21

A sound program of training for endurance running encourages the individual to be thoughtful and critical of his own goals, his own train-

*ing methods, his own progress, and his own tactics in each approaching
competition.* With few exceptions, thoughtful practice and alert tactics
in racing have characterized the world champions. In his interesting
L'Orgue du Stade André Obey writes of Paavo Nurmi, the great Finnish
champion of the 1920's,

> He never seems to be in trouble, he gets on with the business in hand but
> it never seems to be work for him, that is, he has no difficulties; his inflexible
> stride is gauged to the nearest centimeter, he works like a wonderful machine,
> but *all the time he is thinking of his effort.*

Some months before the actual event occurred, Gunder Hägg predicted
in Sweden that though many men were trying, Roger Bannister would
be the first to break the four-minute "barrier" in the mile, not because
he possessed the greatest physical powers, but because he approached
the problems of training and self-analysis intelligently and with clear
concentration upon what such an effort required. Despite his own problems of self-interest, Percy Cerutty strongly emphasized this aspect of
training in both his writings and his practice.

> Athletes must learn to develop their critical reflective capacities and to
> direct them inwards upon their activities. Athletes must learn to "feel" if their
> training is really benefitting them. . . . Most athletes then go through a pre-
> scribed routine, think little about it as long as they are copying someone else
> who has succeeded, or, what is worse, accepting the views or dictations of some-
> one who purports to know, but probably doesn't. . . .
> It is not sufficient to run, run, run. Milers like Landy spend much of their
> actual training time thinking about it as they run, especially in the recovery
> parts of their routines. It is impossible to think deeply about ourselves, our
> work, and our progress if we train with others. There is a time for chatting
> and comparing of notes, but it is not while training routines are in progress.[27]

True, some successful coaches, by nature and by training, find such
independence upon the part of their athletes both unnecessary and un-
desirable. To be "thoughtful and critical" of one's own methods can
lead to doubt and tension. Similarly, some successful athletes seem to
adapt themselves most easily to endurance training when they simply
follow the dictates of a respected coach. The stress of training and
racing is primarily a mental-emotional problem, not a physical one.
By removing such stress, these athletes tend to relax more, sleep better,
enjoy their food more, and thus concentrate more fully on their running.

These are the facts of our modern society and of up-bringing in our
homes and schools and churches. However, my personal reaction can
best be given by quoting the great physician, Kurt Goldstein.

> The characteristic difference between free peoples and masses consists in the
> fact that the former determine themselves in liberty, bear pain and distress,

---

27 Percy Cerutty, *On Running* (Los Altos, Calif.: *Track and Field News,* 1958), p.
26.

but do this, conscious of necessity, with a free will, with courage. . . . The man in the masses is not free and does not think about what he is doing; yet he may be happy in not needing to think. He does not need courage; he finds protection against his anxiety in the will of other individuals. . . . The more firmly their community is based on the freedom of the individual—that is, the more truly democratic it is—the more individual men will resist such influences.[28]

In a similar way, I admire the approach of a Franz Stampfl.

Franz Stampfl's greatness as a coach rests on his adaptability and patience. He watches and waits for the moment the athlete needs him. Franz once told me of setting a group of boys to the task of traversing a beam suspended above the floor. Some swung along with their hands, some walked upright, some crawled, but none fell off. In each method there was some particular grace derived from the boy's inventiveness. It would have been possible to show them how to cross the beam correctly. Some would have managed it easily, others would have stifled their natural inclination to do it differently and might have come to grief. . . . The things a man does by himself he does best.[29]

The aim of a coach should be not to help his pupil to achieve a certain mark, but to show him how, by undergoing the continuous discipline and stress of his training, he can master himself.

Principle 22

A sound program of training for endurance running selects a man's competitive event on a basis of maximum speed for 220 yards as well as on natural stamina to run longer distances. If in doubt, always select the longer competitive distance. The top half-milers of the world, as well as many college half-milers, can run 220 yards well under 23 seconds. True, the ability to run a 220 can be improved but within a rather narrow range. If your natural speed is so slow that the pace of major competition forces you to run close to your capacity, you cannot run, he will do better if he recognizes the handicap of his slowness now though very slow, if he builds his stamina high enough. But in the long run, he will do better if he recognizes the handicap of his slowness now and chooses the event for which he is best qualified. It is a great burden to know that you are one of the slower men in the race and that you must break away from the field early if you hope to win.

Principle 23

A sound program of training for endurance running includes practice at the specific pace and under similar conditions to those that

---

[28] Kurt Goldstein, *Human Nature* (Cambridge, Mass.: Harvard University Press, 1940), p. 117.

[29] Roger Bannister, *The Four Minute Mile* (New York: Dodd, Mead & Co., 1955; London: Curtis Brown, Ltd., 1955), p. 228. Reprinted by permission of the publishers. Copyright © 1955 by Roger Bannister.

will occur in competition. One learns what one does in a much more specific way than is commonly realized. True, all distances of 100 yards or more involve certain common aspects of endurance. It is a fundamental tenet of modern distance training that men can run anywhere at any pace and achieve a somewhat comparable final product.

On the other hand, a great wealth of research in such related fields as industrial psychology and physiology advocate the value of practicing the specific skill one wishes to learn and at the speed one intends to use it. Running at an 880-yard pace is a specific skill in coordination, rhythm, and adjustment that is different from that of running at the pace of two miles or more. The writer has worked with men who complain that the slower pace is "unnatural" and "not my pace." Certainly the difficulty which half-milers have in shifting from cross-country to the indoor season within a period of a few weeks is proof enough that something more than slow distance is needed for faster work. Similarly there are certain inadequacies of shorter-faster work to prepare for slower paced running.

Specificity of training has intrigued research workers in industry and psychology for many years, and many studies have been made as to degrees of difference between related actions and their relative effects upon desired learning. Research in sports has been more limited. However, Laurence Morehouse draws this conclusion:

> Each athletic event makes specific demands in terms of its pattern of load, rate, repetition, and duration. The neurophysiological adjustments to these demands are also specific. When a new task with a different demand in intensity of load, rate, repetition, or duration is undertaken, an entirely new pattern of neurophysiological adjustments must be acquired. These adjustments are so precise that a slight change in the weight of a club or ball will affect the trained athlete's performance. . . . Although special exercises are valuable to strengthen weak muscles or to improve endurance, performance of the event is the best way to train for the event.[30]

Most runners and coaches solve the problem by using "shotgun" methods, by "spraying" their efforts over and under distance and both faster and slower than pace so that the specific distance-pace is well covered. But until more definitive studies have been made, one will do well to assume that the crucial weeks and even months of a training season should include some work at the exact rhythm and pace of the planned competitive performance. This pace-work can be done while running fartlek off the track and without a watch, as Herb Elliott demonstrated so well, but it is most easily learned, from both a physical and mental standpoint, while setting competitive pace at one-half or even three-quarters the distance.

---

[30] Laurence Morehouse, *Scientific Basis of Athletic Training* (Philadelphia: W. B. Saunders Co., 1958), p. 26.

This principle also relates to the psychology of racing; not only should a man's muscles know specific pace, but his mind and emotions should know the specific feel of the coming competition. Herb Elliott made a practice of "feeling-through" the race one or two days before competition. His legs carried him through the approximate distance on whatever terrain was at hand, while his mind thought through and his senses felt through the various stages and crises of the race. "Here my legs and my lungs will cry, 'Take it easy,' but here I shall pick up the pace." "At this point, I may feel Bill at my elbow, but I'll keep relaxed and in good control." Familiarity breeds control long before it breeds contempt and carelessness.

Principle 24

A sound program of training for endurance running plans to develop mental poise, fortitude, and willed control just as studiously and carefully as it plans to develop the physical aspects of endurance. As with physical endurance, men do not inherit X amount of courage or poise which is always expressed at X level. Rather they inherit ranges of capacity to develop these specific traits—ranges from A-M or A-T. Whether they will be expressed at F level or M level is a matter of the degree of development and motivation.

True, for purposes of understanding and communication, we speak of rather general traits (he is a great competitor, or he has natural self-control) but actual display of such traits is much more inconstant.

For example, a man inherits an unmeasurable range of capacity in willingness to undergo the kind of hardship that occurs in training for distance running. Call it what you will: impulsion to run, desire to achieve by running, competitive spirit as related to running, will power to conquer oneself through running; its display in action is specific to the time and the surrounding conditions and to the degree of development that has been given it.

True, development occurs just by running in about the same way that physical endurance develops just by running with no thought as to the what or how. But like physical endurance it develops most surely, most effectively, and most quickly when it is planned and safeguarded.

The physical qualities related to endurance do not necessarily relate to the mental qualities of endurance. How often the coach spies a "natural" runner among a host of neophytes by the ease and rhythm of his movements, but is disappointed by the blankness or even distaste with which the prospect meets his invitation to join the varsity. Just the other day a football coach in conversation granted that running was worthwhile but expressed complete lack of comprehension as to why men should want to punish themselves in such fashion. To him, though he was built for running, it held out no challenge whatsoever. Such men will avoid running just as they would if their range of cardio-vascular capacity was similarly narrow and low.

But there are many others whose ranges of capacity for running are wide, both physically and mentally, but who, through the great emphasis in our culture upon group sports, have never developed the kind of competitive spirit and willed control required by the solitary sport of running.

Every good coach cultivates a high level of expectancy for performance from his men. Arthur Lydiard wrote, "That is why I never go after a runner. I wait for him to come to me and ask for help. Then I know he really wants to run and I have the upper hand." Such an attitude is undoubtedly effective at the highest levels of coaching, but it would hardly be justified for the uncertain years of high school or perhaps even of college. A good coach at these levels must tolerate low motivation just as he tolerates low physical condition in the early stages of training. Both can be developed, especially if planning is deliberate and coaching carried out with warm-hearted concern.

The goal of course is complete control, control beyond all possible doubt, of panic when the going gets tough, or of maintained relaxation when muscles get tired and tend to "tie-up," just as the goal in learning a physical skill is for automatic and perfect coordination. Some men acquire these traits easily and, we say, naturally. But even for them, not merely practice, but right practice, makes perfect, and right practice is the result of intelligent and deliberate planning.

Even a great "natural" runner like Emil Zatopek replied when asked how he achieved so much,

By self-discipline. When a person trains once, nothing happens. When a person forces himself to do a thing a hundred, more, a thousand times, then. he certainly has developed in ways more than physical. Is it raining? That doesn't matter. Am I tired? That doesn't matter either. Then will power becomes no longer a problem. . . . You not only improve in physical fitness by running but [in] your character as well.

Zatopek's training methods have been described as "inexorable daily regularity." The word "inexorable" is well chosen—"not to be moved from one's purpose." It is such training that this principle seeks.

Principle 25

A sound program of training for endurance running understands that failure, like success, is not so much a matter of specific, factual goals as of personal evaluations. From the standpoint of others, and especially the coach, these often may be illogical and even absurd. Usually they are vaguely defined for their source lies in the emotions rather than in the intellect. But they affect training and performance just as directly as might an injured muscle. I remember one good prospect who valued his every effort in terms of his intention to make the American Olympic team. I could never discover how such presumption started. Perhaps a casual remark by an athlete he admired; perhaps someone had called attention to a mannerism or trait similar to that of an Olympic team member. Perhaps the heroes' tales told him at bedtime started it all; perhaps the father's success or lack of it became imbedded in the boy's mind as a personal challenge; perhaps the exploits of a neighboring athlete had become impelling goals which he must exceed.

Such men seldom disclose the hows and whys or even the goal itself, to the coach for fear he may deride them. And therefore the coach will often be at a loss to understand what is going on in the boy's mind. When such a long reach for achievement exceeds the runner's ability to grasp it, his continuing sense of failure may block even those performances that he can do. His goals take on an emotional value far in excess of their real importance; emotion creates tensions which, directly and indirectly, hold him back.

He may blame himself for his failure. He may blame others. He is quite likely to blame the coach, especially if the coach puts forward other goals, perhaps more reasonable goals, but goals that the boy feels are empty of challenge or, worse, will delay his progress toward the goals *he* thinks are really important.

Many examples come to my mind out of over 30 years of coaching. But space does not permit the full presentation of even one, for such cases of overvaluation of unsound goals are never simple. What is felt and said and done is hidden behind a complex of emotions tied to vaguely defined goals and the what-how-when by which they are attained. One or two suggestions based upon my own errors much more than my successes might be of interest: (1) be personally concerned about the athlete but not personally involved in his frustrations; (2) try to help the athlete define his problems clearly and matter-of-factly; and (3) help him to keep both the problems and their solutions at the simplest level possible. The tendency of a frustrated athlete and an interested coach is to dig deeper than the situation requires. If attention can be concentrated upon doing well today and tomorrow—and enjoying it— for its own sake, the problem will be well on its way toward solution.

Principle 26

A sound program of training for endurance running includes maintenance of a personal training diary or daily record card. Such a record is invaluable for judging progress, for studying reactions to degrees of work and competition, for comparison from one year to the next, and, if the coach has a copy, for comparing the progress of present prospects with that of past champions.

Fred Wilt has made an exhaustive study of such diaries and has compiled a special form for that purpose. (See Fig. 6.3.) The uses of this form are summarized in *How They Train* as follows:

A personal training diary should be accurately maintained by each athlete as an aid to better training. The items recorded daily may include the year, month, day, and day of the week, amount of sleep the previous night, time of day that workout session starts and ends, place of training, body weight before and after training, if known, fatigue index before and after training, brief description of weather including, if known, the temperature, humidity, wind velocity and direction of wind, any unusual events in personal activities such as social life or employment which might adversely affect training, and an accurate description

Month____ Day____Year____
Day of the week: M T W T F Sat Sun

Previous Night's Sleep: ____hours
from ____am pm to____am pm

Morning pulse rate:

Body weight: Before____ After____

Fatigue Index:
Before__; Mid-workout__; After____

Venue of Workout:

Workout period: Hrs ____Mins ____
____ am pm to ____am pm

Breakfast ____am | Lunch ____pm

Dinner____pm | Snacks

TRAINING SURFACE

____ Outdoor ____Indoor
____ Cinder ____Clay
____ Board ____Asphalt
____ Concrete ____Grass
____ X-country ____Other

SURFACE CONDITION

____ Dry ____Fast
____ Wet ____Medium
____ Slick ____Slow
____ Soft ____Uneven

WEATHER

Temperature_____(F)
Humidity_____(%)
____ Bright sun
____ Clear ____Hot
____ Rain ____Warm
____ Showers ____Comf.
____ Cloudy ____Cool
____ Snow ____Cold
____ Damp ____Dry

Wind Direction:
N NE E SE S SW W NW
Speed ____mph
Wind from ____o'clock

ACCURATE DESCRIPTION OF ACTUAL WORKOUT OR COMPETITION

FIG. 6.3

of the actual training. The details of the training should include warm-up, number and distance of repetitions, times, if known, exact description of recovery interval following each fast running repetition, warm-down, any pulse readings taken during training, and description of weight training, swimming, or other activity included in the training. Results of blood tests, description and duration of injuries, daily basal pulse rate, and race results should also appear in the diary. Possible explanations of performances, conclusions, predictions, and recommendations may be made as a result of information accurately recorded in the training diary. Other items could be recorded, but the minimum should be an accurate description of the actual workouts and races. A better understanding of performances in competition may result from including a complete and detailed story of each race in the training diary.

The fatigue index mentioned above is merely a simple, numerical, perhaps vague method by which an athlete may briefly describe in his training diary how he "feels" each workout, for further reference. The fatigue index may range from 1 to 9, with 1 indicating that the athlete feels as good as possible, 5 meaning "average," and 9 referring to extreme fatigue. The numbers between 1, 5, and 9 might serve to more accurately define how the athlete "feels." [31]

Principle 27

A sound program of training for endurance running distinguishes between rate of improvement and quality of improvement. To say that differently, it should distinguish between improvement in performance and improvement in the basic adaptation of the organism itself. It has been emphasized that a gradual approach to training should be made whenever possible. Time is necessary to provide the deep-rooted training effects that are essential to soundness as well as to health and safety. What really matters in an adequate training program is not so much that improvement should be as rapid as possible as that it should be continuous and deep-rooted and should provide a firm foundation for further improvement. It should be noted that the factors in improvement are as much mental-emotional as they are physical.

However there are those who advocate or find themselves forced to adopt a shorter and more intensive approach to training.

McCurdy feels that his type of training is best for the American youth that report to him at Harvard. . . . He feels that Americans are more immediately competitive than Europeans and must get into condition as fast as possible. The European method of slowly building up to a high level is too dull for the impatient American youth. . . . Total miles covered is not too important; it is unnecessary to cover fantastic mileage as do the runners of today. By doing intense hard work they would receive just as much benefit. [32]

---

[31] Fred Wilt, *How They Train* (Los Altos, Calif.: *Track and Field News,* 1959), p. 115.

[32] William Smith, "A Study of the Training Methods for Middle and Long Distance Running of Selected European, Australian, and American Coaches and Athletes." An unpublished dissertation for the Master's Degree in Education, Boston University. Smith is speaking of William McCurdy, Harvard track coach.

It should be added that the above attitude and system grew out of a University program that provides little time for training, either each day or in number of days for premeet preparation. However it also has historical support in the experiences of two great distance runners, Arne Anderson and Gunder Hägg of Sweden.

In telling of the experiences of these two runners, George Smith wrote,

After qualifying as a teacher, Arne Anderson was in 1943 [age: 26] posted to a school outside Stockholm in a suburb called Skrubba. It was here that he discovered "quality" of training to be more important than "quantity." Earlier he had sometimes put in as much as four hours on end, but in the course of his training at Skrubba he found that shorter and rougher periods gave the same if not better results. Like Hägg, he found a forest path where he measured up a lap of about 3000 meters, which he covered either once or twice at various speeds. Also, like Gunder, he forced matters uphill, but unlike his great rival, Arne did a lot of jogging, limbering-up exercises, and often about ten starts with a sprint of 40 yards or so. This speed-work probably led to his triumphs over Gunder, as his victories were usually achieved by a terriffic burst up the home straight. Hägg, on the other hand, often successfully relied on longer, sustained pulls to beat Arne, and for these he trained himself by constantly changing gears.[33]

That a remarkable increase in performance in endurance events can be achieved in about six weeks' time has been demonstrated again and again in both running practice and scientific research. In fact, such a method, whether necessary or simply preferred, has been the prevailing practice of American school sports generally, as well as in track and field. It is very doubtful whether the average length of time between the date of first practice and that of first competition in school sports generally exceeds six weeks and might be nearer to four. Needless to say, under such a system, intensity of practice and maximum rate of improvement in performance become the main concerns.

However, such a system should be justified on a basis of necessity or tradition, not on a basis of desirability or of unique national characteristics. The short-time adaptability of the human body is truly amazing, but such development should be compared to that of the bamboo or the poplar tree which springs up in a few months or years. If one hopes for the durability and height of the oak or the ash, much greater time, patience, and depth of growth is required.

Principle 28

A sound program of training for endurance running assumes that the best equation for success in terms of personnel is: athlete + coach + medical doctor + laboratory scientist = success. The role of the athlete is obvious, but it is important to emphasize that not only what he does

---

[33] George Smith, *All Out for the Mile* (London: Forbes Robertson Ltd., 1955), p. 84.

is important, but also with what degree of independence and integrity he does it and, even more essential, what it does to him. Distance training should produce a man, not a robot or a puppet. The role of the medical doctor is primarily to safeguard the health and well-being of the athlete, but, in addition, his function is positive and helpful toward improved performance. The role of the coach has been discussed elsewhere within a wide range of attitudes and relationships from advisor to dictator, from teacher to organizer of talent, and from personal and lifetime friend to business associate. Cultural patterns, institutional ideals, and personal traits are among the factors which determine just where within these ranges an individual coach will assume his role.

But the newest and therefore most immediately vital element in this formula for success lies in the increasing role of the laboratory scientist. His work as a research person in psychophysiology is essential to our future knowledge of better training for better men. But even more important is his role, either direct or indirect, in maintaining a constant surveillance of the individual athlete's adaptation to the stress of training. Without question, the coach of the future will be so trained in medicine and science as to combine the function of these three persons in most direct contacts with the athlete. When a coach lacks such training, the cooperation among these three essential persons must be constant and close.

One of the better examples of such close cooperation is that among Woldemar Gerschler, Dr. Hans Reindell, and Dr. Schildge, psychologist, at the University of Freiburg, Germany.

These three men of research are trying to discover where the human limit lies and what can be expected in training and performance from the human body. Their development of sport along a scientific basis has helped greatly in transforming the physician into a friend and counsellor of the athlete. . . .

Medical supervision of the athlete is vital. Ill health can have bad consequences when linked to competitive sport, and it can exist before any deterioration in performance leads to the detection of its cause. Coach and physician together shoulder a great responsibility. . . .

Gerschler's view is that the athlete's body can adapt itself to the stresses of more strenuous sporting performances by correct application of scientifically planned training. Too easy a program cannot stimulate the body sufficiently; his schedules are based on knowledge of what the body, and particularly the heart, can stand. The formula is: dosed effort leads to organic adaptation which leads to better performance.[34]

Principle 29

A sound program of training for endurance running is fully aware of the harmful effects of staleness and does something constructive about it. Staleness cannot be brushed aside because modern views explain it as

---

[34] "Woldemar Gerschler: Too Tough? No, No!" *World Sports* (London), September 1958, p. 44.

merely mental. After all, "mental" or "physical" are actually only ways of looking at a man and cannot be placed in separate compartments. In either case performance is affected adversely, and something effective needs to be done. Read this description of staleness by the English writer and former runner, W. R. Loader, and then try to "pooh-pooh" its seriousness.

Our main running at Fenner's in preparation for the annual joust against Oxford was done in the Michaelmas and Lent terms, when the weather is hardly at its best for outdoor athletics. Even so, it is difficult to believe that it could have been so consistently dark and gloomy as it appears in the memory. Much of the gloom must have derived from the state of mind. Training had become an irksome and monotonous chore. The bare branches of the elms sighed mournfully over the cinder circuit of funereal black. Sport had no taste in it, no savor. Legs felt weary long before an afternoon's training stint was over, and not with the weariness of work well done. Competition was approached reluctantly, and with forebodings. That hundred-yard-strip had become a house of little ease. Dully and doggedly one set about digging holes and doing a practice start with a faint scintilla of hope that this time there might be some fire in the running. But it seemed that the fire was out for good.

Desperately trying to convince oneself that the trouble might lie in some fault of technique, studied attempts were made to run straight and smooth and with an almost geometrical precision. But the precision was an artificial thing. You might run direct and steady, your spike marks evenly spaced on the cinders in two lines that could almost have been drawn with a straight-edge. Other fellows simply ran faster.

So often you saw them pulling away from you, moving with relaxed ease while you strained despairingly, tensing your body and arms, feeling your legs going rigid from the effort. The more you tensed and strained, the worse your condition became. Your mind longed to be out there, in front, but some barrier stood in your way. Your feet were weighted down. This wasn't insubstantial air you were driving though, but some more solid, hostile obstacle. Hours, rather than seconds, seemed to have elapsed since the firing of the gun. Defeat stared at you again, somberly. No last-gasp spurt could save you now. In any case, such a spurt didn't come. You passed the winning post when the tape had already been broken by someone else. You felt a fatigue quite disproportionate to the amount of effort normally required over the short sprint. Your heart pounded and your head ached. You went over to pick up your track suit with all the sprightliness of a doddering ancient.

The condition was staleness, but not in the old sense of having overtaxed one's body with physical preparation. In the modern, and correct, view, staleness is a mental condition. The body of a fit young man is capable of physical effort protracted almost indefinitely. It is his mind which revolts from work which it finds boring, tedious, or fruitless. Repeated failure has a depressive effect. Even more depressive is the brooding on the failure, the feeling that no matter how much one tries, this burden cannot be shaken from the shoulders.[35]

Principle 30

A sound program of training for endurance running emphasizes, during the weeks of important competition, the conservation of energy

---

[35] Loader, *op. cit.,* pp. 142-43.

rather than its development by hard training. Common practice is for men to overtrain during this period. They are uncertain that they have done enough work, want to run "just one more" to make sure.

The solution of course is to start training early, in fact, to do it on a year-round basis. Progression should assume there will be delays from injury and outside influence and therefore plan a high level of fitness well before it will be needed. "Peaking" too soon is a bugaboo of minimum trainers who put intensity of work above gradual development. The "peaks" of the year-round runner are rhythmical waves on which one can rise or let down as the situation requires. From a physical standpoint, during the two or three or even more days before major competition, do very little; if your condition is doubtful, do even less.

Principle 31

A sound program of training for endurance running recognizes that human progress and development are never consistently upward along a straight line. For any number of reasons, there are plateaus and valleys in the curve of learning. The athlete and coach may have constructed a sound basic training plan for each month and week, but they can be certain the athlete will not follow it exactly. If cardiovascular tests are being made regularly, there will be periods when no improvement in pulse rates or blood chemistry will be shown. If feelings are the main criterion, the athlete just won't feel right. If the watch is the guide, times may slow up, rather than speed up.

Whatever the basis for judgment, the runner should not be disturbed at "taking it easy" for a few days or perhaps at returning to the training program of the last month or at "firming up" the work that was done then, so that progress, which of course is certain to begin again, will do so from a sound foundation of accomplishment and mental sureness.

In the way of prevention, the principles of always working within the limits of control and a certain ease of action is a wise one. If pace is the constant in interval training, then continue the number of runs up to the point when pace can be maintained; as soon as pace is slowed (as a matter of effort not of judgment), then mileage should cease for that day. Progress in endurance running, like progress in the use of a musical instrument, should not be measured in terms of quantity only— as in the number of miles one can run or of selections one can play— but also in terms of the perfection and ease with which one runs or plays those selections.

Principle 32

A sound program of training for endurance running develops out of coaching that is as much an affair of the heart as of the brain. "Heart" is used here, in keeping with tradition, as the seat of the emotions—of warmth, enthusiasm, passion. Every coach has a certain measure of such emotions as well as of the products of the brain. But few are perfectly balanced; most have more of one than of the other.

For example, one might identify, without too many howls of protest, Gosta Holmer and Percy Cerutty as being primarily coaches of the heart. Holmer, the father of fartlek, often spoke of enjoying the singing of the birds and the beauty of the landscape while running. Fartlek was a well-planned system to be sure, and yet its most basic essential lay in the phrase, "Get tired but don't feel tired." By constantly refreshing the spirit, the fatigue of the muscles could be forgotten.

Similarly, Percy Cerutty could be described as more whole-hearted than clear-brained when it came to creating his system of training. Cerutty planned and planned well—else Elliott could never have achieved what he did—but even more, he burned well, burned with a fiery passion to run and to imbue others with a similar zest to run.

In contrast, much as Gerschler and Lydiard love running, I can't quite put Cerutty's words of feeling into their mouths. With him it was an impulsion out of a heart aflame, sometimes even furiously aflame. With them, though they too could be reckless at times, there always seemed to be an element of calculation and control. Gerschler's methods are masterpieces of planning, both in terms of essentials of training and of individual needs—all within the framework of interval training. Similarly, Lydiard's book is outstanding primarily because his methods are so carefully and clearly worked out, from the triple standpoints of individual differences, of progressive training, and of pointing for the relative high and low peaks of competition—all within the framework of the Lydiard system. Perhaps because it is ghost-written, Lydiard's book is a book about running and training, whereas, in contrast, Cerutty's book is Cerutty, is Cerutty pacing excitedly up and down, emoting his words, not saying them. If he feels like "to hell with the lot of them," he tells us so. I doubt that either Gerschler or Lydiard could feel that way to the same degree, and both would express themselves with at least a trace of inhibition.

But our point is that both the heart and the brain are needed for successful coaching as well as running. Without the heart, there would be no desire to get there; without the brain, there would be no knowing how to go.

Principle 33

A sound program of training for endurance running recognizes that the energy, both physical and mental-emotional, that goes into one's daily work cannot also go into one's training for running. If both make great demands, one or the other must give way—or the man will give out. If the work cannot be lightened, the training must be. However, it is my casual impression that distance runners in world competition tend to carry jobs that do not require strenuous labor or long hours.

Principle 34

A sound program of training for endurance running plans carefully to prevent the mental blocking which tends to arise when attention is focused strongly upon a minor set-back or casual difficulty with a new method. Resolving to fight back, to grit one's teeth and try again in the same way—or being directed to do so—will often merely exaggerate the difficulty. Such forcing of action by the will, whether by the actor or by the coach, is like the parent who tries to correct a speech difficulty by constantly calling attention to it, but instead produces a permanent tendency toward stuttering.

A method more likely to succeed is that of diversion or of withdrawal-and-return. If success seems doubtful today, forget it, shift attention to some other related action, and then return to the action another day in some other way, when the awareness of inhibition has been forgotten or no longer seems to be related. I once had a fine miler who just could not break three minutes for a three-quarter-mile time trial. But one day two lesser men challenged him that they could beat him at a three-quarter mile if they each ran a 660. Time was not mentioned and no 440 times were given. They won by a yard, but he ran 2:58!

Lydiard relates how Barry Magee had established a block in his mind that he could never beat Murray Halberg. When Halberg set his three-mile world record of 13:10.0 at Stockholm in 1961, Lydiard is certain that Magee could have beaten him and his record by taking the lead with three laps to go.

A wise and tactful coach will find ways to avoid such blocks, whether they relate to another runner, to a time or distance, or to a clash of wills between himself and the runner.

Principle 35

A sound program of training for endurance running never risks the trust of the runner in the coach by trying to build self-confidence on a foundation of falsely fast times in time trials. Yes, Gunder Hägg's father got away with it when Gunder was a boy, and so have thousands of coaches. But to be caught just once, even though the runner recognizes the good intentions of the coach, is to bring lingering doubt into a relationship in which complete trust is the very core of its effectiveness.

Principle 36

A sound program of training for endurance running progresses by means of what is usually called the overload principle but what might better be called the optimum-load-rest principle. This principle states that energy systems develop capabilities of doing more work more efficiently when work at the upper levels of present capacity is repeatedly alternated with periods of active rest. The term "overload" has gained general acceptance in physiology and psychology primarily as a way of increasing muscle strength by placing loads on them "which are over and above previous requirements." But its use has widened into the fields of learning skills and increasing cardiorespiratory efficiency, that is, endurance. However, the prefix *over* tends to be interpreted as "too much" and is therefore of doubtful value. Further, both fartlek and interval training have demonstrated beyond all question that work-and-rest cannot be separated. The recovery period—how much and what kind of restful action is taken—is just as crucial for development as is the more vigorous activity that precedes it.

The optimum-load-rest principle, as related to running, is the core of all training systems, whether steady running, marathon running, fartlek, interval training, resistance training, or what you will. We deliberately develop a great variety of stressor agents, to use Hans Selye's term, a great variety of challenges which compel us to rise above them. These stressor agents may be physical in nature: strength, speed, endurance, skill, or more specifically, any phase of these abstractions. They may be, with equal validity, emotional in nature: doubt, anxiety, fear, self-confidence, sensitivity to discomfort and pain, competitive spirit, and many others. To an equally crucial degree, they may be mental in nature: willed control of fatigue, fortitude against the deterrent phases of emotion, concentration upon the task at hand, and discipline of all hindrances and distractions.

But whatever their nature, the principle tends to be the same: we do not so much grow in life as we get stretched. A hill that was only a hill yesterday becomes a hill-to-be-climbed-today and a hill-to-be-rested-from-tomorrow in order that higher hills and even mountains can be climbed next week and next year.

The crucial test of proper use of this optimum-load-rest principle lies in preventing stretch from becoming strain, in selecting hills that can be climbed with difficulty but without injury, in approaching but never reaching—not the breaking point, for we humans are too tough for that—but the breaking-off point, when the goal no longer seems worth the effort.

A recent study of this overload principle by C. Etta Walters [36] listed 20 studies of related research. Such research should be extended, for we have few satisfactory answers for even the simplest questions. What degree of overload has optimum value for development? Is it really true as stated by Muller and others: "If a muscle contracts, even momentarily each day to about 50 per cent of its capacity, it will increase in strength as fast as it can." How many optimum loads in a single workout are of greatest value for development? Is 12×440 yards in 64 seconds with three minutes of jogging of greater value than 10×440 yards in 64 seconds (or 62 for that matter) with three minutes of jogging? Are easier, daily optimum loads more effective, as compared with tougher optimum loads handled only two or three times a week?

Herein lies what today must be called the cunning craft of distance coaching, what tomorrow may be called a science but what will always remain a true art, in which knowledge and experience and full personal commitment will be focused upon the specific needs and interests of the individual.

Principle 37

A sound program of training for endurance running is organized around the truth that training is both general and specific. Better running at any and every distance can be achieved by more running at *any* distance, but *best* running of a distance-pace is achieved by running that distance-pace. A man learns what he does, not necessarily what our minds abstract out of what he does. When a man runs 10×440 yards, his psychophysical organs and systems develop whatever is required of them when he runs 10×440 yards. If what is required is similar to that when running 1×1760 yards, the ability to do the latter will be improved.

Experience has taught us this is true, and therefore we do run repeated 440's in order to run better miles, just as we also do marathon training at ten and twenty miles in order to run better miles. Further, these generalized effects are increased by what we think about them. That we imagine something to be true does have certain beneficial effects. If belief can move mountains, it can also lower heart rates, relax tensions, and run faster miles.

But it is equally true, though experience is less clear and certain, that training is specific. All would agree that many years of piano playing does develop the general ability to play a particular Liszt sonata, but not even the greatest pianist would consider sight reading a concert. He

---

[36] C. Etta Walters, "The Scientific Foundations of the Overload Principle," *Scholastic Coach*, March 1958, pp. 20-22, 57.

practices again and again and again the specific movements, tonal effects, and emotional emphases of that specific sonata. So with running. After we have developed a sound foundation of blood capillaries by means of more running (whether by marathon training or repetition running is relatively unimportant), and after we have developed the needed muscle-fiber groups by means of faster running (whether by Lydiard's fast-hill training or Gerschler's repeated 100-meter dashes is also relatively un-important), then we still need to develop the special requirements of the specific distance-pace-rhythm-relaxation-feeling-attitude-tactics-willed-control of the *big race* we are going to win. This can be done, in part, in training sessions, but it also requires the even more specific training of development races.

Principle 38

A sound program of training for endurance running attempts to bal-ance the values of competition with the values of training. Unfortunately, our competitive society has upset this balance by overemphasizing the values of competition. Let two little boys start throwing stones and within two minutes, one will say, "Mine came closer than yours." Their parents talk that way, their books read that way, their economic system was born that way, above all, their school system is founded and geared and judged that way.

The result is that competition is begun within a few weeks after train-ing begins, long before a man is prepared either physically or mentally-emotionally for competition. Not that this is harmful in itself; our con-cern is that he immediately tends to assume that training is by far the lesser part of sport. He assumes that sport is primarily competition, the more the better; the less training that has to be done, the happier he is. By such an attitude, he not only loses the great values inherent in train-ing but also fails to reach the highest levels of competitive performance.

Of course individuals vary greatly in their attitudes toward competition and training, even when they develop within similar sports organizations. Roger Bannister, for example, planned his year's program carefully. He accepted only enough competitions (12 or so) to enable him to win the two or three major races on each year's calendar. His training was year-round and on a gradual developmental basis that would achieve this same result.

In almost complete contrast, another Englishman, Derek Ibbotson, who also bettered four minutes for the mile (3:57.2), accepted every competition that came along, as many as 70 in one year. Ibbotson also knew the values of training. At one point he said,

But there's only one way to the top in running—blood, sweat and sometimes tears. Whatever success I enjoyed during the summer of 1957 can be traced back to the early months of that year when I trained harder than at any time in my life.[37]

But for him training was always a drudgery, to be avoided whenever possible. Not for nothing was he called the "butterfly of running" and the "four-minute smiler." Even after his lesson in 1957, he laid off during the winter months, then tried to get in shape through competition. As a result, 1958 was a dismal failure.

The point of this important principle is not to decide whether competition or training holds the greater value for sportsmen. Rather it is to understand the different degrees of emphasis that can be placed upon them and to try to choose a balanced program that makes the most of each.

In any developmental program of running, a boy must begin at his own present performance level, not from where the needs of the school or team would like him to be, nor from where his teammates or possible opponents are. From this point of low beginning he should progress gradually and carefully during months of training. He should learn to know himself as a runner, both his strengths and his weaknesses. As he avoids the extremes of strain upon muscles and tendons, so he should also avoid the extremes of stress from competition. This will give him a chance to compete when ready and at a performance level he considers respectable.

The easy way, and the way that American school sports have gone, is to schedule many competitions as soon as possible after the start of training. Some say, "Americans are naturally competitive. Our boys expect many competitions. If you want to kill your sport, ask them to train for months before their first competition. They hate training!" Obviously there's a good deal of truth in this statement. But not nearly as much so as our present competitive program suggests.

Principle 39

A sound program of training for endurance running limits practice time to the level of sport as an avocation, consistent with the tacit agreements of amateurism and the written codes of the Olympic Games. The basic purpose of amateurism in sport is to secure fair competition among men who enjoy an equality of opportunities for maximum performance. These opportunities are of various kinds. Some have to do with the distance that shall be run, others with the implements that shall be used. These are easily measured and precisely fixed so that all men compete under the same conditions. Thus differences in performance

---

[37] Terry O'Connor, *The 4-Minute Smiler* (London: Stanley Paul & Co., Ltd., 1960), p. 129.

arise out of the men themselves and not out of the special advantages they might have. But there are other opportunities for which there should also be some degree of equality—those having to do with time and energy spent in preparation. Amateur sports must always be conducted on an avocational basis; that is, there must always be the more primary demands of one's vocation or school studies. Time for sports preparation is thereby limited to the few hours that remain.

In contrast, professional sports accept no such limitations in either time or energy and, therefore, no limitation of material gain from them. This makes it clear that, despite the almost exclusive attention given to it, limitation of material reward is not the main purpose of amateurism; it is merely the means by which the real purpose of fair competition is hopefully assured.

True, equality of opportunity does not fix an exact number of hours. The number of hours of daily work of the 1900's was often ten or more; those of today are eight or less; those of tomorrow seem certain to be six and less. Actually the number of hours left over for training purposes is not important in itself; what is important—no, essential—is that there be some reasonable degree of world-wide agreement, that such agreement be realistic in terms of world-wide practice, and finally that amateurs, as men of honor, do their best to live up to that agreement.

If amateurism in sports is breaking down, and that now seems to be the case, there are four primary reasons. First, our present codes of amateurism are stated in terms of nineteenth-century English social conditions and attitudes which are not realistic today in the world as a whole. Second, differences in world vocational and educational conditions require different hours and energies of the workers. Third, sports in the different nations of the world serve a wide range of national and institutional purposes. Fourth, the confusion of social conditions, cultural values, and sports values have dulled our sense of honor and concern for the moral values in sport. From these points of view, the problem of material reward is almost a by-product, an effect rather than a cause of the amateur dilemma.

Despite the pessimism of these remarks, there is still reason to believe that amateurism is still alive, even though its true purposes are unclear. A perfect example of this is to be found in Bannister's dashes four or five times weekly to London's more unfrequented tracks at unpredictable times, when he could squeeze in an hour away from St. Mary's hospital. There was never any doubt in Bannister's mind that his profession was more important than his running; yet he was the first to break the four-minute barrier.

As further instance, Cerutty wrote of John Landy in *World Sports,* October 1954,

With a singleness of purpose remarkable in one so young, he marshalled all his capacities and directed them towards his goal. . . . That is the secret of Landy's genius as an athlete. Once his personality came to rest on an objective, it mustered itself behind efforts strenuous, sacrificial, almost fanatical. [Is this to say that Landy placed his running foremost in life and gave it major time and energy? Cerutty says definitely otherwise:] Much of his training was done in the cold and wet of winter nights. Sometimes it was at midnight, because he did not want to interfere with his agricultural science studies at Melbourne University.

Similarly, Landy is quoted in *Track and Field News* for May 1956,

I am sure that five hours a day (as is being done in some quarters) is not necessary to win an Olympic title. Even a daily average of one and one-half hours, with absolute concentration, could achieve the desired result.

Examples of the hardships of amateur runners are on every hand; in fact, the runner free of such hardships is very rare in this country and, according to their protestations, in all the other countries of the world. A newspaper article reacting to Jim Beatty's 1962 world record for the two-mile run of 8:29.8, quoted him as follows:

I'm out running usually at 5 AM on a high school track. I run an hour, sprinting and jogging nonstop from 60 to 600 yards. Then breakfast and by 8 AM I'm on my job as an insurance claims adjuster. At 5:15 PM I'm on the Southern Cal. track, running until dark. On easy days I run 15 miles; on hard ones, about 20.

"Do you really enjoy the training, Jim?" asked a caller. . . .

"I'm no farm mule," laughed Beatty. "Who would enjoy it? But you have to fight it. . . . Something like that two-mile Saturday night makes the grind worth it."

Olympic titles and world records are challenging goals, well worth almost every sacrifice that leads to them. More and more time for preparation is one of the primary means to such goals, but to give such time is to deny the honorable agreements to which amateurs swear allegiance every time they enter Olympic competition or sign a record application blank. To use "stolen" time is just as dishonorable as fouling an opponent or trying to sneak a light-weight implement into competition, and should result in the same disqualification and exclusion from the company of those who believe in fair play.

Principle 40

A sound program of training in endurance running should bring a runner to the start of a race who is intelligently confident of the soundness of his planned tactics. Such confidence is the crucial outcome of all coach-athlete relationships. There are many ways of ensuring its emergence. In some, the coach assumes full authority throughout; in others, the athlete takes the longer and tougher route of self-dependence. But in all cases, regardless of the means by which the runner reaches the starting line, he and he alone can act out the role that lies beyond it. True, the coach can dictate the plan of racing, just as a playwright dictates the role of his actor, but both the runner and the actor must believe in and, in a sense, lose his own identity in his role.

In most cases, not even the wisest coach can predict the pattern of a race. Plans must therefore be kept flexible. But flexibility does not mean uncertainty or confusion of mind. A well-prepared runner will be certain that within the range of possible tactics that may develop he will know what to do and be able to do it. In top-flight competition, even a Vladimir Kuts can get away only once or twice with a plan to run away from the field from the very start.

Coach-athlete relationships vary greatly, of course, but in most instances, the coach will find that calm, tactful persuasion is both safer and surer than dogmatic authority. Of the tactics of a great coach, the athlete should feel, "I believe completely in *my* plan, and the coach agrees with me." It could be argued that Franz Stampfl was one of the greatest of endurance coaches, since the runners that worked with him (not under him), such as Bannister, Chataway, or Brasher, invariably took this attitude toward their racing and his part in it.

To further support this contention, the last words of Stampfl's chapter on "The Coach's Job," are,

And when all the shouting is over, when the senior partner in the firm has broken the record, made the headlines and joined the immortals, the junior partner's reward comes from the satisfaction of a good job well done. Who could ask for more? [38]

Principle 41

A sound program of training for endurance running never allows its men to become bored. The ways of accomplishing this are as many and as varied as the coaches and the runners and the terrain and the systems that are related to them. Gordon Pirie tells us of one such way, the Zatopek way, that is all the more delightful when we think of the latter's reputation for inhuman relentlessness.

He [Zatopek] would jog for hours on the same spot, doing an endless "Knees up, Mother Brown," while reading a book or listening to the radio. Everything was fun to him. On washdays at home he piled all the dirty clothes in the bath and then ran on them for hours. . . . I had the pleasure of meeting him not only on the track but in his home. This was the gayest and merriest home I have ever visited. . . . They [Emil and his wife] used to romp like children. . . . Once in fun he threw her into a stream. . . . Unfortunately her foot hit a rock and she broke an ankle. While she had her leg in plaster, Emil ran

---

[38] Stampfl, *op. cit.*, p. 151.

with her on his back through deep snow for training. . . . Zatopek's sense of fun turned not only his training but his races into a joy. He never seemed to feel the awful tension before a race which lesser mortals endure. His antics often helped to release this tension for others.[39]

Principle 42

A sound program of training for endurance running is aware of the possible conflict between the attitudes and methods of the present coach and those of a former coach or, in some cases, those of the runner's father. Highly favorable associations at the earlier level may, as a matter of mere difference, not of actual merit, lead to an unfavorable reaction to the new coach or method. Or highly unpleasant associations at the earlier level may lead to an assumption of a similar relationship from this one.

What to do about such a conflict is a matter of the coach's make-up and judgment. But at least, he should have knowledge of what these earlier associations have meant to the runner.

Principle 43

A sound program of training for endurance running first and above all else believes in itself. It practices itself persistently and stubbornly and does not shift with every turn of the winds of rumor and the tides of success by others. If you've found a way that makes sense to you, stick to it!

In 1948 or so, fartlek, as interpreted by American runners, had a magic sound; we must play at speed; we must "go-as-you-please." Success was certain as long as we were out in the glories of nature and were enjoying the singing of the birds and the hush of the woods. Gosta Holmer wrote an open letter to American coaches. He opened with words that were as soothing as a warm shower, "When you feel tired then relax by walking in a wood." But we spent so much time under the warm water that there was none left for the icy cold with which he finished his letter, "But don't believe now that fartlek can work wonders. It might open the eyes of American runners and teach them that the road to success is called *work, hard work!*"

Then, when word of interval training finally reached this country after World War II, some 15 years after its first use in Europe, we assumed we had found the great touchstone of running success. "We can't miss this year; we're using interval training at Podunk!" Similarly, in the late 1950's we had to use weights while running if real success was

---

[39] Gordon Pirie, *Running Wild* (London: W. H. Allen & Co., Ltd., Publishers, 1961), p. 50.

to come. In the early 1960's some form of Elliott's sand dune had to be available to assure full development, and later, we were all running "marathons" if we hoped to emulate Halberg and Snell.

Each of these systems was a good system; each produced its share of running success. But not because of the special virtue of the system nearly so much as because it incorporated within itself the fundamental principles of all development in running. It is these fundamental principles that are essential. They are the basic tenets to which each coach and each runner should stick, regardless of what catchy name or magic system is in vogue at the time.

A program is sound if it includes certain essentials of mileage and speed and pace and willed control. A little good judgment as to the weight of emphasis to be placed on each of these will produce a reasonably sound training schedule. Consciously or unconsciously, each individual will learn to compensate for the weaknesses or overemphases of such a program.

The essential thing, the all-important thing, is to stick to what you have, to make the most of it for what it is. The more you study it and worry over it and adjust it here and trim it there, the better integrated it will become, the more skillful you will be in adjusting it to the needs of your unique individuals, and the more they will get out of it.

Obviously some ways are better than others, depending upon the conditions and the attitudes within which they are used. But for you, your way is the best way. Stick to it! Each time you change to a new system, you upset the faith of the runner in himself and in you. And faith runs four-minute miles as well as it moves mountains.

This is not to say that you should deny changes and improvements. That would be foolhardly. But these should be made within the framework of what you already have. A bird in the hand. . . . Remember?

Principle 44

A sound program of training for endurance running keeps things simple. If no problem exists, it does not try to create one. Each problem is kept at its simplest level, not only while stating its nature, but also in outlining steps for its solution. Such a plea for simplicity is almost startling as we review the endless analyses and arguments which infest this book. We repeat: keep things simple—not in the manner of a driver of a bullock cart who uses a goad to hasten the poor beast's plodding steps; but rather with the simple actions of a driver of a complex, high-powered car, who achieves maneuverability and a great variety of speeds by simply pushing a pedal or turning a wheel.

A runner usually only wants to hear the few things that will help him to run a better race. But he will run a better race if those few things are based on knowledge of facts as suggested here and on the experience that comes both from running oneself and coaching others to run.

Yes, keep things simple, but in the way of a well-ordered and understanding mind, not in the manner of an autocrat who knows and dictates only one way. True, most runners want to hear of only one way, but it should be one of a number of possible ways, selected because it is fitted exactly to their unique needs and interests.

When the final count-down for John Glenn's rocket ride around the earth finally reached zero, one simple little button was pressed—one simple little button, but it was the focal point of the work and knowledge of a thousand men and more. It is such simplicity that will send rockets to the moon. It is such simplicity that will reach man's ultimates in distance running.

Keep things simple!

Principle 45

A sound program of training for endurance running laughs freely and gaily at itself while conducting its activities with reckless seriousness. That doesn't make sense? Well, sometimes things don't make sense even though they produce good running. This book is filled with examples of just such non-sense. Balance Zatopek's love of fun as told by Gordon Pirie with his reckless output of energy in his training and racing. Balance the scufflings and the mad dashes into the sea at Camp Portsea by Cerutty and his wildmen with Cerutty's advocacy of Stotanism and medieval asceticism and his pleas to seek suffering. Consider the title of Ibbotson's book, *The 4-Minute Smiler,* and his light-hearted agreement to run just to get a banquet ticket for his fiancée's girlfriend with the abandon he showed a few hours later in driving himself "in a blurred agony of effort and pain" to equal Bannister's "human ultimate" world's record of 3:59.4. No wonder Brutus Hamilton described distance runners as "the best *bon vivants* in the world." Balance Lydiard's tough "marathon" training with his statement that "there are jokes and laughter in training with these boys [Halberg, Snell, Magee], not a grim, gasping grind with an eye on the watch and the mind concentrating on forcing the body to do the mind's bidding."

To recommend that we should "laugh freely and gaily" and yet act "with reckless seriousness" sounds like deliberate exaggeration. It is deliberate, but it is not exaggerated. As I try to get the "feel" of this book as a whole, I doubt that anyone could question its seriousness. Silly as it may sound, there is nothing in life as important as running *while we are running.* True, as an amateur activity, it is only avocational and therefore secondary to other life interests. But if we run naturally, in the true sense of "in accordance with our nature," we run freely and enjoyably, having dropped the worries and doubts that so infest our "educated" minds.

And so, in summary of this wearisome weight of 45 principles of training, I urge you to be serious—recklessly serious. In your running, go all out with no reservations and no inhibitions. Nothing in life is or will be more important than your running is now.

But equally I urge you to laugh—laugh uproariously at times—simply because the joy of doing what comes naturally and what is fun requires an emotional outlet for which laughter is the best answer.

7

Style
and Pace
in
Endurance
Running

Style in endurance running is an individual matter. True, there is an ideal form for each event, which coaches believe produces a perfect balance between maximum speed and maximum economy of effort. But it is always a particular individual's economy of effort that is important. Whatever produces this economy is, for him, good style, whether or not it conforms to traditional concepts of perfect style.

In no other area of track athletics does daily practice for style begin at such an early age. After all, running begins at the age of three or four years, and style is likely to be definitely established by the time a boy reaches high school or college. Any setting or changing of style should therefore be very cautious and always within the range of the individual's own natural and developed habits.

Necessary differences in pace produce natural differences in style at the various distances—the half-mile, the mile, and the two-mile. However, the increased similarity of training that is now commonly practiced for these three events is gradually eliminating these differences to a point where they require no special teaching emphasis.

The elements of proper style can be logically considered under six

Some of the material in this chapter is from J. Kenneth Doherty, *Modern Track and Field* (2nd ed.; Englewood Cliffs, N. J.: Prentice-Hall, Inc., 1963), pp. 209-16. Reprinted by permission of the publisher.

headings: the over-all action, body angle, arm swing, foot placement, rear leg lift, and length of stride.

The Over-all Action

In general, the details of style are unimportant if the over-all action is efficient, smooth, and relaxed. The arms and legs should swing rhythmically and smoothly back and forth and should in no way be driven. In general, all actions should contribute toward movement along a straight line: feet will point straight ahead, shoulders and hips will not swing unduly off center, and arms will move slightly across the body in such a way as to aid balance and the forward movement. A pronounced hip swing does permit a longer stride but detracts greatly from efficiency of action. Without question, overstriding is one of the more serious faults of distance runners.

FIG. 7.1   The rhythm of running. Note how the dotted lines for the head and hips rise very little during this stride. The lowest dotted line follows the right heel as it rises (thus shortening the leg-pendulum) and swings forward.

The so-called picture runner or stylist is undoubtedly so referred to because the style that coaches feel is ideal happens to be natural to him. It is not that he was necessarily "born that way." Rather, his natural physical proportions and muscular structure made it possible for coaching to produce a style that was, at one and the same time, his own and "ideal."

In contrast, one need only recall the awkward arms and the haggard, strained face of the world's greatest distance runner, Zatopek, as he won three Olympic distance titles in Helsinki, to realize that an "ideal" style is not necessary to great success.

Body Angle

In most cases, proper body angle is a natural trait. As a matter of natural balance, the body will begin to lean forward as the pace increases. All human movement is a process of falling with balance, a constant and rhythmic loss and recovery of balance. On this basis, one can hardly prevent the increased angle of speed running. The problem, where it exists, usually lies in maintaining the body as a whole in a straight line. The solution lies in proper placement of the eyes and head. In almost every case, when the eyes are focused at the proper place on the ground ahead, the head is brought into proper position and the correct body angle automatically follows.

Arm Swing

The action of the arms should be a relaxed and rhythmic swing from the shoulders. Balance, rhythm, and ease of movement are the primary considerations and, to most good coaches, the only ones. To aid balance and ease, Arthur Lydiard favors an extended, low-swinging arm action; it seems less tiring.

I find it especially difficult to agree with those who call out to their protégés, "Drive those arms, drive those arms!" In the first place, the forward propelling power of any such movement, in "speeding up the leg action," as they put it, is highly questionable, and certainly, the possible gain is nullified by the loss of rhythm, relaxation, and smoothness. Arm action will of course speed up and become more energetic as pace increases, particularly as the final sprint is unleashed. But such action is a part of the entire body action and should not be given special emphasis.

Foot Placement

The details of foot placement will, like other aspects of form, depend upon (1) the individual and his developed style of running, and (2) his speed and distance. As always, economy of effort is the primary consideration. At all three distances—the 880, the mile, and the two-mile, the landing should be made first low on the ball of the foot. In the 880, the weight will drop only lightly and buoyantly on to the heel; in the two-mile, a greater concern for economy will permit a somewhat greater process of settling and relaxing to occur before bouncing back to the ball and toes. Quite naturally, with a more forward lean of the body in the faster run, there will be a lighter and quicker riding forward of the body weight.

But such differences are a natural aspect of each event, and as modern training methods for the 880, the mile, and the two-mile become more and more alike, they will tend to grow less and less. In a fine talk before the National Collegiate Track Coaches Association in New York City on January 12, 1950, Fred Wilt, noted American distance runner, gave an extensive and sound discussion of this problem of foot placement.

I might mention an incident that occurred last February when the Finnish Olympic Coach, Armas Valste, visited the United States. I asked Valste about this heel and toe type of running which the Finns were supposed to do and he laughed. Valste said, "I can't understand why you foreigners think we in Finland advocate such a type of running."

He said that it is possible to run by allowing the heel to touch the ground first, but it is very slow and it jars the body badly. By these remarks I do not mean to indicate that a middle distance or distance runner should run flat footed. That would be just as serious a fault as allowing the heel to touch the ground first or running exclusively on the toes. . . . While I was in Stockholm during the summer of 1949, Mr. Gosta Holmer, the Swedish Olympic Coach, was watching me take a workout and noticed that I was running too high on my toes. He questioned me as to whether I was having any trouble with soreness in the calves of my legs, and I replied that I was. He stated that I could avoid this if I would lift my toe up just before my foot strikes the ground. This does not mean that I should land flat footed, but it merely means that I avoid pointing my toe down in the normal course of striding and thus relieve my calf muscles of a lot of shock, which is normally incurred if a runner runs too high on his toes.[1]

Arthur Lydiard emphasizes long distance training (six miles and up) as a foundation for all endurance running, including the 880 and even the 440. His point of view as to proper foot placement is therefore slightly different.

Don't run on your toes unless you want to work your calf muscles unnaturally, which is uncomfortable and tiring over distances. It is better to come down with a nearly flat foot, with the heel hitting first. There are many good runners who run on their toes, but I say they would run much better with a nearly flat foot because it is an easier, more natural action for covering long distances. In the half-mile or under, of course, it stands to reason that you will run on your toes.[2]

Rear Leg Lift

At one time in this country there was a considerable weight of opinion that the natural ballistic swing of the rear foot above the level of the

---

[1] Fred Wilt, "Modern Distance Running." An unpublished talk before the National Collegiate Track Coaches Association, January 12, 1950.

[2] Arthur Lydiard and Garth Gilmour, *Run to the Top* (London: Herbert Jenkins, Ltd., 1962; New Zealand: A. H. & A. W. Reed, 1962), p. 56.

knee, as it pushed off and came forward for the next stride, was wasteful of energy and time. And of course, when body carriage is unbalanced or forward lean extreme, there will often be an extremely high swing of the leg, along with a late and short placement of the foot for the next stride.

However, when balance and forward lean are proper, such an upward swing is efficient, natural, and relaxed. It is simply a follow-through or ballistic movement which shortens the weight arm of the leg lever and the length of the leg pendulum as it comes forward. Only in those few extreme cases of poor balance suggested above should there be specific coaching. In general, the less awareness of the action the runner has, the better.

Where coaching is necessary, concentrate on proper body angle, correct foot placement, a balanced swing of the arms, and possibly, on basic flexibility exercises of the hip girdle.

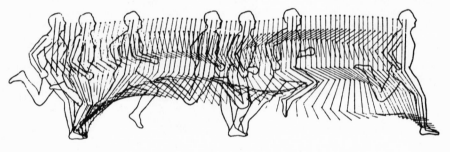

FIG. 7.2   Another example of the rhythm of running.

Length of Stride

Modern training emphasizes sprinting and sprint action. It is inevitable therefore that many runners will employ the high-toed, bouncing, and long-striding action of the sprinter and the quarter-miler. Such a wasteful stride requires correction if distances over one-half mile are to be run successfully. Cross-country work and fartlek will usually take care of the difficulty, but sometimes specific coaching is required.

In offering suggestions to American distance runners, European coaches have placed great stress on the importance of a short economical stride. But with equal emphasis they have spoken of the disrupting effects of any marked change in length of stride. Such a change should be made very early in the year's schedule of training and must be practiced until it both feels and is a "natural" way of running; or rather, until the runner is no longer conscious of it at all. It will require months of running, and to change methods in the middle of a season would ordinarily be very foolish.

Pace

Distance running is primarily competitive, and pace therefore tends to be at that speed which assures success against one's opponents. Pace becomes lost in race tactics. All physiologists conclude that steady running and even pace are, in general, most economical. For example, Morehouse summarizes,

In distance races, whether running, swimming, rowing, or bicycling, energy must be conserved and a steady state established at a dangerously high level of energy expenditure. Under these conditions the race will be finished in the shortest time if the athlete has maintained a speed at which a maximum steady level has been established for the number of minutes required for the event. Then, at the proper distance before the end of the race, he increases the speed so that the maximum energy is expended in the most economical manner.[3]

But time and again we see experienced and knowledgeable runners take off for several hundred yards or even a full lap in a desperate expenditure of energy for the purpose of breaking contact or the will of their opponents.[4] Zatopek's repeated changes of pace and Kuts' bursts away from Pirie in the 1956 Olympic 5000- and 10,000-meter runs are outstanding examples.

But, apart from tactics, best pace tends to be even pace. However, there seems to be one mild modification of this: that the first half of the 880 and mile runs (or their equivalent in meters) should be run slightly slower than the second half. This is the pattern of modern running as is detailed here in the sections on the 880 and mile, a pattern that is probably based on race tactics and human psychology. But it is also based on sound physiology as well, as was explained by Sid Robinson at the first International Track Coaches Association Clinic at Berkeley, California, 1956.

In recent treadmill experiments on a good runner we have found that the energy cost of running is greatly increased by fatigue in the late stages of an exhausting run. . . . Thus the energy cost of running at constant speed was smaller in the middle part of the run than in the first of it and increased greatly as he became fatigued in the last half minute. Associated with these changes in efficiency were increments of lactic acid of 52.7 mg. per cent in the first minute, 40 mg. per cent in the second minute, and 70 mg. per cent per minute during the last 35 seconds. . . .

From the data on hand we are able to make some very interesting deductions

---

[3] Laurence E. Morehouse, *Physiology of Exercise* (St. Louis: The C. V. Mosby Company, 1959), p. 230.

[4] For a fascinating discussion of this point see Franz Stampfl, *Franz Stampfl on Running* (London: Herbert Jenkins, Ltd., 1955), pp. 120 ff. Stampfl relates the dramatic and fierce struggles between Kuts, Chataway, and Zatopek in 1954 in which variation of pace was the crucial tactic.

TABLE 7.1

EVEN PACE IN MIDDLE DISTANCE RUNNING
Even Pace Chart

◄──────────────────────── D I S T A N C E ────────────────────────►

110	220	330	440	600	660	880	1000	¾	1	1¼	1½	2	3
11.0	22.0	33.0	44										
11.2	22.5	33.7	45										
11.5	23.0	34.5	46										
11.7	23.5	35.2	47	1:03.6									
12.0	24.0	36.0	48	1:05.4	1:12								
12.2	24.5	36.7	49	1:06.2	1:13.5								
12.5	25	37.5	50	1:07.8	1:15								
12.7	25.5	38.2	51	1:09.6	1:16.5								
13	26	39	52	1:10.8	1:18	1:44							
13.2	26.5	39.7	53	1:12	1:19.5	1:46							
13.5	27	40.5	54	1:13.8	1:21	1:48							
13.7	27.5	41.2	55	1:15	1:22.5	1:50	2:05						
14	28	42	56	1:16.2	1:24	1:52	2:07						
14.2	28.5	42.7	57	1:17.4	1:25.5	1:54	2:09						
14.5	29	43.5	58	1:18.6	1:27	1:56	2:11	2:54					
14.7	29.5	44.2	59	1:20.4	1:28.5	1:58	2:14	2:57	3:56				
15	30	45	61	1:21.6	1:30	2:00	2:16	3:00	4:00				
15.2	30.5	45.7	61	1:22.8	1:31.5	2:02	2:18	3:03	4:04	5:05			
15.5	31	46.5	62	1:24	1:33	2:04	2:20	3:06	4:08	5:10	6:12		
15.7	31.5	47.2	63	1:25.8	1:34.5	2:06	2:23	3:09	4:12	5:15	6:18	8:24	
16	32	48	64	1:27	1:36	2:08	2:25	3:12	4:16	5:20	6:24	8:32	
16.2	32.5	48.7	65	1:28.2	1:37.5	2:10	2:27	3:15	4:20	5:25	6:30	8:40	
16.5	33	49.5	66	1:30	1:39	2:12	2:30	3:18	4:24	5:30	6:36	8:48	13:12
16.7	33.5	50.2	67	1:31.2	1:40.5	2:14	2:32	3:21	4:28	5:35	6:42	8:56	13:24
17	34	51	68	1:32.4	1:42	2:16	2:34	3:24	4:32	5:40	6:48	9:04	13:36
17.2	34.5	51.7	69	1:33.6	1:43.5	2:18	2:36	3:27	4:36	5:45	6:54	9:12	13.48
17.5	35	52.5	70	1:35.4	1:45	2:20	2:39	3:30	4:40	5:50	7:00	9:20	14:00
17.7	35.5	53.2	71	1:36	1:46.5	2:22	2:40	3:33	4:44	5:55	7:06	9:28	14:12
18	36	54	72	1:37.8	1:48	2:24	2:43	3:36	4:48	6:00	7:12	9:36	14:24
18.2	36.5	54.7	73	1:39	1:49.5	2:26	2:45	3:39	4:52	6:05	7:18	9:44	14:36
18.5	37	55.5	74	1:40.8	1:51	2:28	2:48	3:42	4:56	6:10	7:24	9:52	14:48
18.7	37.5	56.2	75	1:42	1:52.5	2:30	2:50	3:45	5:00	6:15	7:30	10:00	15:00
19	38	57	76	1:43.2	1:53	2:32	2:52	3:48	5:04	6:20	7:36	10:08	15.12
19.2	38.5	57.7	77	1:44.7	1:54.5	2:34	2:55	3:51	5:08	6:25	7:42	10:16	15:24
19.5	39	58.5	78	1:46.2	1:55	2:36	2:57	3:54	5:12	6:30	7:48	10:24	15:36

The T I M E label runs vertically along the left margin with a downward arrow.

Note: This table is adapted from one prepared by Armas Valste, Finland's National Track and Field Coach, 1960.

regarding the purely physical aspects of running middle distance races. It is obvious that the runner should pace himself so as to delay until near the end of the race the sudden increase in energy cost of running associated with great fatigue and high lactic acid concentration. If the first part of the race is run too fast the runner may acquire most of his oxygen debt and be forced to run the remainder of the race with a high lactic acid, with his efficiency greatly reduced, and at a much slower pace. . . .[5]

As will be noted in our discussion of the mile run, most of the miles run under four minutes to date have followed this pattern of a slower first half. Table 8.4 on page 213 shows that the slower miles of the early years of running were run at a faster pace in the first half. It should be added that Robinson concluded that his recommended pattern of pace-running was even more important for the 440- and 880-yard runs than for the longer races.

The data in Table 7.1 make it clear that runners should conserve their anaerobic reserves until the later stages of the race and that the long-held assumption that exactly maintained even pace is most economical physiologically is incorrect.[6]

---

[5] Sid Robinson, "Physiological Considerations of Pace in Running Middle Distance Races," *Clinic Notes, International Track & Field Digest*, 1956, pp. 219-24.

[6] For an excellent summary of research in this field and a related bibliography, see Henry Longstreet Taylor, "Exercise and Metabolism," *Science and Medicine of Exercise and Sports*, Warren R. Johnson, ed. (New York: Harper & Row, Publishers, 1960).

8

A Review of Past Performances and Methods

The 440-yard Dash

History of Improvement in Methods and Time

Very early in the game, before 1870, it was recognized that a man could not sprint all-out for much more than 100 yards and that therefore the 440 should be considered an endurance race. The best tactics were considered similar to those of the 880 or mile, in which one ran easily, with a good deal of speed held in reserve, for the first three-fourths of the race and then finished with what he had left. In general, quarter-milers were not specialists. For example, in 1868, E. J. Colbeck won the English championships in :50.4, after having first taken a second place in the 100-yard dash and a first in the 880 in 2:02, for a new English record. A much more startling example was Lawrence "Lon" Myers, one of the all-time greats of track athletics. Myers held every American record, from the 50-yard dash to the mile. In 1880, he competed in seven races in a single afternoon and won four American championships in the 100, 220, 440, and 880. In 1881, he won the English 440 champion-

---

Some of the material in this chapter is from J. Kenneth Doherty, *Modern Track and Field* (2nd ed.; Englewood Cliffs, N. J.: Prentice-Hall, Inc., 1963), pp. 101-14, 118-19, 230-49, 253. Reprinted by permission of the publisher.

ship in a best time of :48.6. Unquestionably, Myers was capable of better time than this. He had been timed at :05.5 for 50 yards, :10 for 100 yards, and 20.2 for 200 yards, as well as 1:55.5 for the half mile. No times are available for the first 220 of his :48.6 race, a fact which in itself indicates that coaches and athletes were not then conscious of the importance of this knowledge.

However, we do know that Wendell Baker of Harvard ran :23.2 for his first 220 in establishing a record of :47.6 in 1886. This was 1.2 seconds slower than his best time of :22.0 for the 220 and gave him split times of :23.2 and :24.2 for the 440, reasonably close to even pace. In passing, the circumstances and handicaps under which this race and many other similar races of the time were held should prove of interest. Tracks then were not the permanent and precisely "dressed" affairs of today, nor were running shoes so dependable. As a tune-up for the 440-record trial, Baker had just equaled the world record of :10 for the 100-yard dash, but he had burst his left shoe in the effort.

With no spare shoe, and facilities for repairs missing, it was decided to continue. Under the watchful eyes of George Goldie of the New York A.C., G. A. Avery of the Manhattan A.C., and other competent officials, a quarter mile *straightaway* was measured off. *The loose upper surface of the track was scraped,* the temperature was recorded as 81 degrees, a scarcely perceptible wind was noted, the timers took their places, and the trial was on.

Baker was off at the crack of the pistol, running the first 220 yards in :23.2. . . . At the furlong post, G. P. Cogswell of Harvard joined his teammate. His was the task of drawing Baker out to the utmost. With expert judgment and burning speed, Baker passed 350 yards in :37; at 400 yards the time was a shade under :43. At the finish line the officials looked on in amazement, as Baker, running with one shoe, flashed another burst of speed to snap the tape in :47.6. . . .

His left foot bleeding slightly after the race, Baker explained what had happened. At 250 yards he had attempted to kick off the torn shoe; at 285 yards he let it loosen and fly off. With his bare foot digging into the dirt track and the tape 155 yards away, Baker simply grit his teeth and spurted on to a new record.[1] [All italics mine—J.K.D.]

Several items are of importance. First, it is of interest that so-called world records of this period are not official, for the International Amateur Athletic Federation was not organized until 1913. A race with no other competitors running the full distance would not be recognized today. Second, that the track had just been scraped certainly embarrasses our modern standards of surface perfection. But, more to the point, Baker, according to this observer, "flashed another burst of speed . . . and spurted on to a new record." This remark indicates that Baker had been "saving something for the end" and had certainly not been run-

---

[1] "Wendell Baker—Record Breaker," *The Amateur Athlete,* July 1935, p. 7.

TABLE 8.1

OUTSTANDING PERFORMANCES IN THE 440-YARD–400-METER DASHES

Date	Record		Name	Affiliation	Age	Best 220 Time	1st 220 Time	2nd 220 Time	330 Time	Diff. 1st & 2nd	Diff. 1st & Best	Olympic Champion
	440y.	400m.										
1881	:48.6		Lon Myers	New York	25							
1886	:47.6		Wendell Baker	Harvard		:22.0	:23.2	:24.4		1.2	1.2	
1900	:47.8*		Maxie Long	NYAC			:22.8	:25.0		2.2		1900
1904		:49.2	Harry Hillman	NYAC	24							1904
1912		:48.2	C. D. Reidpath	Syracuse								1912
1916	:47.6*	:47.4*	Binga Dismond	Chicago								
1916	:47.4*	:49.6	J. E. Meredith	Penna.	24							
1920		:47.6	B. G. D. Rudd	So. Africa								1920
1924	:47.6		Eric Liddell	Scotland	24	:21.6	:22.2	:25.4		3.2	0.6	1924
1928		:47.0*	E. Spencer	Stanford	22	:21.4	:22.0	:25.0		3.0	0.6	
1928		:47.8	Ray Barbuti	Syracuse	22							1928
1931	:47.4*		Vic Williams	So. Calif.								
1932	:46.4*	:46.2*	Ben Eastman	Stanford	22	:21.6	:21.4	:25.0		3.6	0.2	
1932	:46.5	:46.1*	William Carr	Penna.	23	:21.5	:21.5	:24.7		3.2	0.0	1932
1936		:46.0*	Archie Williams	Calif.			:21.6	:24.5		2.9		1936
1939	:46.4*	:46.0*	Rudi Harbig	Germany	26	:21.6	:22.1	:23.9		1.8	0.5	
1941	:46.3*		Grover Klemmer	Calif.	21		:21.7	:24.3		2.6		
1947		:45.9*	Herb McKenley	Illinois	25	:20.6	:20.9	:25.4		4.5	0.3	
1948	:46.0		Herb McKenley	Jamaica	26	:20.4[1]	:21.0[1]	:24.9		3.9	0.6	
1948		:46.2	Arthur Wint	Jamaica	28	:21.9	:22.2	:24.0		1.8	0.3	1948
1950		45.8	George Rhoden	Jamaica	23	:20.6	:20.9	:24.9		4.0	0.3	
1952		45.9	Herb McKenley	Jamaica	30	:20.7	:22.7	:23.2		0.5	2.0	
1952		45.9	George Rhoden	Jamaica	25	:20.6	:22.2	:23.7		1.5	1.6	1952
1955	45.8*	45.4*	Lou Jones	Manhattan	24	:20.9	:21.2	:24.2		3.0	0.3	
1956	45.8*		Jim Lea	So. Calif.	22	:21.0	:22.6	:23.2		0.6	1.6	
1956		:46.7	Chas. Jenkins	Villanova	25	:21.2	:22.2	:24.5	:33.9	2.3	1.0	1956
1956	45.7*	45.2*	Lou Jones	Manhattan		:20.9	:21.3	:23.9		2.6	0.4	
1958	45.7*	45.6	Glenn Davis	Ohio State	24	:21.0	:22.0	:23.7		1.7	1.0	
1960		45.6	Milkha Singh	India	25	:20.7	:21.6	:23.8	:33.2	2.2	0.9	
1960		45.5	Mal Spence	So. Africa	23	:20.4	:21.3	:24.1	:33.4	2.8	0.9	
1960		44.9*	Carl Kauffman	Germany	24	:21.1	:21.8	:23.1	:33.2	1.3	0.7	
1960		44.9*	Otis Davis	Oregon	28	:21.1	:21.8	:23.1	:33.3	1.3	0.7	1960
1963	44.9	44.9	Adolph Plummer	New Mexico	25	:20.7	:21.7	:23.2	:32.9	1.5	1.0	

[1] Straightaway

* Official world record

190

ning all-out. His times of :10 and :22 for the 100 and 220 support this view.

Although no times for the 220 are available, Maxie Long did hold to a faster pace when he ran :7 for a 440 straightaway in 1900. At the 350 mark he was :36.4; at the 400, :42.2, both of which compare favorably with Myers' .37 and :42.9. Long also had been timed in :10 flat for the 100, so it would appear that his potential speed was not greater than that of Baker. On the basis of these times, one might hazard the guess that Long was about :22.8 at the 220 post.

The first official world record for the 440 was made by Ted Meredith of the University of Pennsylvania—:47.4 in 1916, at 24 years of age. Meredith's record remained for 15 years, unbeaten and untied, and the close association between the 440 and the 880 that he fixed in the minds of coaches and athletes continued to influence their thinking and their methods. All coaching books printed during this period and up to 1932 either include the 440 in their chapter on middle distance events or, if they give it separate consideration, they regard it in middle distance terms.

However, the American custom of running the 440 around only one turn soon changed the event to an endurance sprint. Such a method usually meant a full 220 yards straightaway at the start. There are no lanes and it is a distinct advantage to have the pole position around the curve. Consequently, there was intense competition in a field of six to eight runners to be first at the 220 mark. The first half of the race became more and more rapid—to the point, in fact, where the ordinary 880 man simply could not stay within striking distance of his sprinting rival. Quite naturally, the slow quarter-miler moved up to the 880, where first-lap times were also getting faster, and coaches in desperation were shifting their sprinters to the 440.

The great victory of Eric Liddell, of Scotland, in the 1924 Olympic 400-meter championships provided a clear example of the trend toward sprinters. Liddell was best known as a 100 and 220 sprinter, having best times of :09.7 and :21.4, but when religious scruples led him to refuse to run the 100 trials on Sunday, he shifted his efforts to the 400. With almost no experience in the event, he sprinted all-out to a clear lead at the 200 post in :22.2, and with both form and judgment gone, as it was thought, ripped through the tape in :47.6 for a new Olympic record.

Then, in the Olympic year of 1932, came the tremendous duals between Ben Eastman of Stanford and Bill Carr of Pennsylvania. Eastman had tied the 440 record at :47.7 in 1931 in a great duel with Vic Williams of Southern California and had just broken the world 880 record with a 1:50.9. Then, in late May, in a special record attempt at Palo Alto, he cut the 440 time down to :46.4. But on July 4, the relatively unknown Carr, whose quarter-miling had been almost exclusively in relay events, won the IC4A over Eastman at Berkeley, California, in :47 flat and then in the Olympics made a world record by running 400 meters in :46.2. Quite apart from the great competitive thrills these races provided, which, incidentally, were heightened by old rivalries between the East and West, they also proved a testing ground for the old argument over whether a fast 880 man could defeat a sprinter with endurance and just how each would go about doing it. American coaches, including Richard Templeton of Stanford, have consistently assumed that the half-miler would be forced to set a very fast pace and thus run the "kick" out of the legs of the sprinter. Certainly Eastman attempted just this, for, although he seldom ran the 220 and had a best unofficial time of :21.6, he covered the first 220 of the Olympic quarter in :21.4—unheard-of time and "crazy" pace judgment. Yet Carr stayed on his heels and was able to run faster than Eastman at the finish and thus go on to win. Where was the traditional "float" in such a race? Eastman certainly didn't let down at any point, for he was trying to build up a lead, nor could Carr relax, for he stayed at Eastman's shoulder all the way and must have run within a few tenths of a second of his best previous time. The experts shrugged their shoulders, explained that competitive conditions sometimes force one to ignore economy of effort, and brushed aside the fact that the world record had been broken by 1.4 seconds. Physiologically, a pace of :21.5–:24.7 simply did not make sense.

Both this judgment and the close relationship between the 440 and 880 was strongly supported some seven years later when in 1939 Rudolf Harbig of Germany shocked everyone by setting new world records for the 400 meters (:46.0) and 800 meters (1:46.6) within a period of three weeks. His splits for the 400m were :22.1–:23.9, with a time difference of only 1.8 seconds as compared with Carr's 3.2 seconds. We must keep in mind that Harbig's best recorded time for the 200m curve was :21.6, so that he was running within .5 seconds of his best effort. (For a further discussion of Harbig, see page 204.)

One of the greatest trios of all time, Herb McKenley, Arthur Wint, and George Rhoden, were all natives of the little island of Jamaica with a population of only 1⅓ million people. McKenley first attracted world attention by running :46.2 for the 440 in May 1946, a new world record. The race started on the 220 straightaway and the writer, clocking the 220 time very carefully, was amazed to see :20.9 on his watch dial. Two weeks earlier, McKenley had made his best personal record for the 220 of :20.6, so that, like Harbig, he had run within .3 second of his potential speed. Two years later, on June 5, 1948, at Berkeley, California, McKenley again ran :20.9 for the 220 in establishing a new world record of :46. However, even McKenley thought a slower 220 would bring better results, for he confided to a newspaperman just before the National AAU meet in July that he planned to take it easier this time. Certainly his 220 time of :21.1 was slower, but so was his total time of 46.3.

During the next two years, McKenley broke the :47 flat mark on 53 different occasions, an almost unbelievable record. And in almost every case he piled up a lead by the 220 mark, not merely through superior ability over his competitors but as a matter of running policy. His earlier mark of :20.6 remained his best for the 220. However, the 1952 Olympic final among Rhoden, McKenley, Wint, Whitefield, Matson of San Francisco, and Haas of Germany showed a different pattern. Following the general background as here related, one would have expected a blistering pace during the early stages of the race. However, Rhoden (:22.2), McKenley (:22.7), and Whitfield (:22.9) were content to let 31-year-old Wint set the pace at :21.7. A glance at the quarter-mile record chart (Table 8.1) will show that this is the slowest pace (that is, for Rhoden or McKenley) ever set for a race under 47 seconds. Yet Rhoden, by pouring it on during the third 110 yards, and McKenley, by a tremendous spurt in the final straightaway, were able to come within 1/10 second of the best ever recorded, each with the time of :45.9. Apparently, Wint's pace was 2/10 second faster than he had ever recorded for 200 meters (his best distance was probably over rather than under 400 meters), and he remarked after the race that he had made a great mistake in judgment in going out so fast.

The 1956 Olympic 400-meter final at Melbourne included Lou Jones of Manhattan, who had run :21.3 when he established his world record of :45.2 early that year, Karl Haas of Germany (best 400m–:46.5, best 200m–:20.7), A. Ignatyev of the USSR (best 400m–:46.5, best 200m–:20.7), Mal Spence of South Africa (best 400m–:46.6), Voitto Hellsten of Finland (best 400m–:46.5, best 200m–:21.1) and Villanova junior, Charles Jenkins (best 400m–:46.1 in winning the final Olympic tryout). The experts picked Lou Jones as a clear favorite; Jenkins as a possible place-winner.

In August 1956, D. H. Potts, an astute observer, wrote the following:

I disagree with those who claim that Lou Jones has re-established the Mc-Kenley theory (1948) of how to run the 440. The secret of Jones' success is not running that first furlong at practically top speed as did Hustlin' Herb in the late 40's. What Lou has done is solve the problem of running his own race; that is to say, how to dole out his reserves so as to deplete them at the precise instant of finishing.[2]

But in the Olympic final, Jones led by two meters at 200 meters in

---
[2] D. H. Potts, "U.S. Report," *Track and Field News*, IX, No. 7 (August 1956), 7.

:21.8, with Spence and Ignatyev two meters back, held his lead by one meter at 300 meters (:33.4), then slowed down rapidly to an inglorious fifth place (:48.1). Ignatyev held the lead for a few meters, but Jenkins, strong and relaxed, soon took over and went on to win by a full meter in :46.7 (:22.2—:24.5, time difference—2.3 seconds).

Potts wrote in the December 1956 issue of *Track and Field News,*

Afterwards Jones said he had no excuses. He felt he was physically in condition. . . . He said his defeat was due to the unexpected psychological shock of coming off the turn with Ignatyev practically even with him. He had run the first 300 meters hard and expected to emerge with at least a three- or four-meter lead. He was so unprepared for the possible failure of this strategy that he actually froze mentally. . . . Jenkins attributed his somewhat unexpected win to his coach's last letter, admonishing him to run relaxed, and to his Olympic roommate, Andy Stanfield, who kept him from getting nervous. Jenkins said he followed instructions and ran the first 300 relaxed. . . . I felt very strong after my semifinal, and I was confident I had a chance.[3]

Several comments are in order. First, Jones was the favorite with all the pressures which that term implies. But one wonders why Jones was so confident he would have a lead at 300 yards. True, this had been his experience in American and Pan-American races, but Ignatyev was undefeated since 1952 and had a best 200-meter time of :20.7, as had Karl Haas of Germany. Further, his 200-meter time (:21.8) was some .5 second slower than when he set the world record :45.2. In contrast, Jenkins was picked only to place, concentrated primarily on relaxation both before and during the race, and saw the race work out in terms of his own hopes and plans. That the time was relatively slow means nothing.

The 400-meter final at Rome, 1960, produced a photo-finish between Otis Davis, U.S.A. and Oregon, and Karl Kauffmann of Germany. Both men were credited with "a fantastic world record of :44.9!" Both men had identical 200-meter splits (:21.8—:23.1). The difference between them, and the key to success in the race, lay in their 300-meter time. Usually Davis started his finish as he came out of the final curve, but on this occasion he started earlier than ever before and thus picked up a full three meters at 300 meters (:32.9) over Kauffmann (:33.3). Kauffmann was gaining on Davis all the way to the tape but failed by two inches to catch him. Davis (lane 3) had men ahead of him at 200 meters and therefore a guide for his efforts. He was in front from about 290 meters to the finish. Kauffmann (lane 1) had Davis ahead of him all the way.

How to Run the 440

The most important conclusion that can be drawn from this summary history of the 440 is that best performances occur when both the physio-

---

[3] D. H. Potts, "Jenkins in Upset Victory," *Track and Field News,* IX, No. 11 (December 1956), 5.

logical and psychological conditions are at their best. This statement, which now seems so obvious, will be the key to both training and competing in the 440 during coming decades. I shall write first of optimum physiological conditions.

Optimum physiological conditions. To date, perhaps the most valuable research related to these problems is that done by Franklin Henry [4] in 1952. Among his many conclusions are the following:

1. That men generally reached their top speed about six seconds after leaving the starting blocks.
2. That "it is physiologically impossible for the runner, after he has reached his peak velocity, to maintain it for more than about 15 or 20 yards."
3. That an earlier study by Sergent showed "that the energy cost of running increases as the 3.8th mathematical power of the speed."
4. That "it can be said with confidence that insofar as the *physiological limit* is involved in setting records, a steady pace will result in faster time for the 220 and 440 as well as the half, the mile, and the two-mile."

All related research known to the writer confirms these conclusions and we must therefore assume they are *physiologically* correct. Yet a glance at the time differences between the first and second 220's in Table 8.1 shows that no world records to date have produced even pace. Surprisingly enough, McKenley's second :45.9 produced the least time difference of .5 seconds; Lou Jones' :45.2, the greatest difference of 3.0 seconds. (Note: there is some question as to Jones' 200 time in this race; one observer caught him at :21.9.) The most obvious explanation of this lies in an understanding of competitive tactics and the natural urge to run fast while one feels full of energy.

One of the first men to write on this problem was Godfrey Brown, England's record holder (1951) for the 440. Brown was impressed by the success of the McKenley method but also cited its main weakness.

A third weakness may well lie in the fact that this method usually implies a marked decrease in effort and speed over the third quarter of the race, with a full-out effort to fight off further deceleration in its last quarter. Such a fluctuation seems to constitute an unnecessary qualification of the even-pace law. I admit that there should be an over-all deceleration over the body of the race, but I maintain that the deceleration should be gradual and smooth—like clockwork running down. . . . Obviously deceleration is going to be setting in [during the closing stages of the race—J. K. D.], and the man who finishes strongly will be the man who can fight off this tendency most successfully. This point cannot be stressed too strongly—that in a correctly run 400 meters the strong finisher is the man who slows down least. In a mile race the strong finisher hits up a speed above the average speed at which he runs his race, but the runner who is able to do this at the end of a quarter-mile has run his race badly,

---

[4] Franklin M. Henry, "Research on Sprint Running," *The Athletic Journal*, XXXII, No. 6 (February 1952), 30.

because he has distributed his effort badly [5] [By running too slowly at first, he saves too much for the finish—J. K. D.].

This statement is consistent with the facts of quarter-miling and should be carefully considered by every coach and 440 man. It is an essentially different point of view from the one shown by coaches in their writings, although not by runners in their actions. In a consideration of what pace a particular 440 man should run, the problem has traditionally been put in terms of the total time the athlete is seeking. If the time sought is :52, he is then advised to run his first 220 about two seconds faster than his second, i.e., :25—:27.

The approach of the "maximum speed, minimum deceleration" method is quite different. The first question now is, "What is the maximum speed at which this boy can run 220 or 300 yards?" And the second is, "How little does he need to slow down and relax during the first two-thirds of his race to permit him to finish with a minimum of deceleration during the last 100 yards or so?" This method does not think of the race as having three parts: an initial sprint to the 220, a "float" around the curve, and a finish. Rather, the race is a smoothly co-ordinated unit. Ideally, there is no point at which any change in style or effort occurs. A man simply runs as smoothly, as relaxed, and as fast as possible, all the way.

In 1941, at the meetings of the National College Track Coaches in California, the coaches had been questioning Cliff Bourland, a :46.2 quarter-miler, about the mechanics of his "float." Cliff had implied that there were a few minor form differences between this "float" and his finish. When asked directly, his coach, Dean Cromwell, answered positively that no changes in form occurred, that there was no settling of the body or dropping of the arms. "In fact, Mr. Champion, you merely drop your tension and everything else remains the same." A champion should be able to go all the way, without recourse to a letdown or a time-consuming "float."

In summary, the quarter-mile is an endurance sprint in which maximum acceleration is achieved first and then this momentum is maintained to the finish line with the least possible deceleration. As Brown has stated, the strongest man at the finish is not the one who increases his pace most but rather the one who slows down the least. The problem lies, then, in knowing in each competition just what pace will produce this result.

The graphic curves shown in Fig. 8.1 illustrate this point.

The *A* curve represents the all-out man who sprints as fast as he can as long as he can. He has a long lead at 220 and perhaps at 350 yards,

---

[5] Godfrey Brown, *Athletics* (London: J. M. Dent & Sons, Ltd., 1951), p. 239.

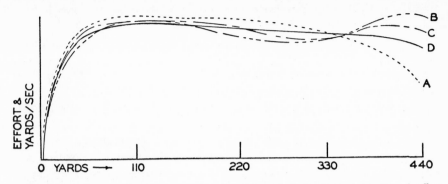

FIG. 8.1   Curves of effort-speed in the 440-yard dash. Both intensity of effort and actual momentum must be considered in interpreting these curves.

but he ties up completely in the homestretch and decelerates very rapidly. This is typical of the "there's one in every race" schoolboy whose determination is greater than his judgment. But even the greatest champions do it occasionally, for example, McKenley versus Wint in the 1948 Olympics or Lou Jones against the field in the 1956 Games.

The B curve illustrates the traditional coaching method. Actual races are seldom run this way, even in ordinary college and high school meets; but coaching books persist in advocating the theory. The excessive floater stays well back throughout the race. He "takes it easy" around the curve, but then "comes from nowhere" and really turns it on down the homestretch to a thrilling and sometimes successful finish. However, in the writer's opinion, success in this case is achieved only because his potential ability is greater than his opponents', or because the latter have failed to maintain the poise and control their methods demand. It should be noted that the B curve is the only one of the four in which there is a true pickup in speed during the last 90 yards. Both C and D may gain on their opponents during the finish, but this is simply because the latter are slowing down even more rapidly.

Curve C is called a modified "float" with a finish. It might also be described as a "coaches' curve," for it suggests to the relatively inexperienced a method that is sound and safe. Note that C stays well up and is probably running within 1 to 1.5 seconds of his best time for the 220. He does "float," but the letdown is merely one in tension, to use Cromwell's phrase, and not in the details of form. No ordinary eye would detect a change, unless it might be a vague feeling of greater relaxation. In most cases, C will be in second place until at least the last 20 yards. Of course, if his opponent bogs down, the C curve will appear more like that of B, but that is a gamble the newcomer must take. As C gains maturity and experience, he will attempt to lengthen the distance over which his top speed can be maintained and he may become a front runner throughout.

This was the tactic followed by Jenkins at Melbourne. While maintaining a reasonable contact with his rivals, he concentrated upon staying relaxed, then turning it on in the final straight. It worked for him. It did not work quite well enough for Kauffmann at Rome, for Davis' staying power was just too much to make up the three-meter lead he held at 300.

Such a method of running the 440 is sound. It combines the fastest pace that is consistent with both physical and mental relaxation and control. It assumes a well-conditioned, somewhat mature, and experienced runner; one who can run within about 2.0 seconds of his best time for the 220 and still maintain self-control to the finish line. As he matures in various ways, this 2.0 seconds could be gradually reduced to 1.0 seconds or even lower, as in the cases of most Olympic finalists and world-record men.

The D curve represents those mature men who maintain the fastest pace for the 220-330 that permits a least possible loss of momentum over the rest of the course. Each runner must discover for himself just what this "fastest pace" is. It will vary with both his physical condition and his mental control. It will increase as he matures, gains experience, acquires poise. Herb McKenley was convinced that if he concentrated on keeping relaxed he could run within .4 second of his best 200 time and still get home in good shape. He attributed his defeat by Wint in the 1948 Olympics to his own failure to relax, especially during the third 100 meters, not to having run too fast a 220 (:21.4), nor to any "fear of Wint." Lou Jones ran his best time when there was a .4 second differential; Otis Davis and Karl Kauffmann when they had differences of .7 and .9 seconds, respectively. As men's physical endurance and mental control mature, their ability to maintain a faster pace will improve. One might argue, therefore, that these time differentials will decrease. But it is equally true that as men mature, they will gain in their power to maintain complete control over mental panic and physical tension during the last two-fifths of the race and will thereby find it possible to run closer and closer to even pace.

Davis at Rome ran :11.1–:10.7–:11.1–:12.0 (21.8–:23.1). It seems clear that his slow-down of .9 second during the last 100 meters was more than would be allowed by the principle of minimum deceleration. One might argue that he should have run the first 200 a little slower, or that he put too much effort into his third 100 meters during which he picked up his three-meter lead. Davis was mature at 28 years of age. But he had had relatively little experience as a top-flight competitor. The poise gained from several more years of tough competition might well have enabled him to maintain greater control and relaxation during the final 100. If we balance the two factors of maximum pace and even pace, we can suppose that a "perfect" Davis might run :21.9–:22.1 for an ultimate time of :44.0. This hypothesis assumes a best 200 time of :21.1. If that time could be improved, then, of course, the rest of the times would be bettered.

One might conclude that two approaches are available for improving men's tactics in running the 440. Theoretically, the two methods would eventually achieve the same perfect result of maximum pace—even pace. In Table 8.2 a theoretical development of this sort is indicated. Each method achieves the same 440 time throughout. Method A assumes a fixed best-ever time for the 220 of :22 seconds. (Note that actually this time would improve under both methods.) Even when immature, the runner following Method A would tend to hold a pace within about 1.5 seconds of his best time for the 220. As he matures and gains self-control, this time would become gradually lower until he can run within about .5 second of his best 220 time and still maintain relaxation and control throughout the final 220. Those following this method would of course train to develop greater speed-endurance, but they would place relatively greater emphasis on the speed factor in achieving such endurance.

TABLE 8.2

COMPARISON OF TWO METHODS OF DEVELOPMENT AND TACTICS IN RUNNING THE 440

| | Method A * | | | | Method B ** | | |
	Best 220 Time	1st 220	2nd 220	440 Time	Best 440 Time	1st 220	2nd 220
Stage 1	:22	:23.3	:25.7	:49	:49	:23.3	:23.7
Stage 2	:22	:23.2	:25.3	:48.5	:48.5	:23.1	:23.4
Stage 3	:22	:23.1	:24.9	:48	:48	:22.9	:23.1
Stage 4	:22	:23.0	:24.5	:47.5	:47.5	:22.7	:22.8
Stage 5	:22	:22.9	:24.1	:47	:47	:22.5	:22.5
Stage 6	:22	:22.8	:23.7	:46.5	:46.5	:24.1	:24.9
Stage 7	:22	:22.7	:23.3	:46	:46	:23.9	:24.6
Stage 8	:22	:22.6	:22.9	:45	:45.5	:23.7	:24.3
Stage 9	:22	:22.5	:22.5	:45.5	:45	:23.5	:24.0

* Method A bases its training development and its competitive tactics upon a man's best time for the 220-yard dash. This time would improve with training but, to keep things simple, we have used a fixed time of :22 for all nine stages of development.
** Method B is based on three factors: (1) best 440 time to date, (2) an effort to maintain as even a pace as possible, and (3) the necessity for maintaining competitive contact with those setting the faster pace of Method A.
Note that the development traced here covers some years of time.

In contrast, those following Method B would emphasize the idea of even pace, though forced by the realities of racing to maintain competitive contact with their rivals, who follow Method A. As greater maturity and control are reached, these men find they can keep more relaxed and controlled during the second 220 and thereby come closer and closer to even pace. Men following Method B will train to develop greater speed-endurance by placing relatively greater emphasis upon the endurance (mileage) factor. The number of their practice runs at a somewhat slower pace will be greater than that of Method A.

Both methods face the common problems of increasing pace and reducing tension. Table 8.2 assumes that both will ultimately achieve the same goal of maximum and even pace. They differ only in the degree of emphasis they place upon the two factors of speed and endurance. Those who follow Method A conform to Woldemar Gerschler's theories on interval training. Those who follow Method B are consistent with the ideas of Arthur Lydiard and Franz Stampfl. Understanding will be aided by reading the related discussions on pages 110 and 256.

Optimum psychological conditions.   The opening sentence in "How to Run the 440," stated that best performances occur when both the physiological and psychological conditions are optimum. The problems of relaxation, control, tension, tying-up, panic, all concern both the body and the mind. Did Lou Jones carry too fast a pace at Melbourne? Physically he tied up in the last 100 meters. Yet he actually ran slower than during his :45.4 and :45.2 efforts. He stated afterwards that "his defeat was due to the psychological shock of coming off the turn with Ignatyev practically even with him." The question naturally arises whether his psychological training had been as carefully and completely planned as his physical training. Jones' case is only one of innumerable examples.

Organization of Practice

A greater change in training for the 440 has occurred since the early 1930's than for any other running event. At that time an Archie Williams or a Bill Carr achieved times of :46.4 while training primarily as sprinters who added a few 220's or 330's at the end of each day's sprint work. Today, the approach is much more similar to that for the mile and 880 than to that for the 220.

The modern quarter-miler understands that today's high level of stamina needed to run under 45 seconds requires some 10 months or more of training. His first concern during the early months is for endurance by means of mileage, or as Lydiard says it, "for stamina as a foundation for speed." He distinguishes between distance-endurance and speed-endurance and knows that the latter can be developed to its fullest extent only when it evolves out of the former. He understands that the extensive bed of blood capillaries within the running muscles, so essential to stamina, are acquired by countless repetitions of muscle movements, and that by running first at a slower pace, the number of such repetitions is likely to be increased. After this foundation of distance-endurance is fully developed, he moves gradually into the faster pace-shorter distance that has been his primary training of the past.

Though as yet no quarter-miler has carried this point of view so far, we should assume that in the near future a man will be trained for the 440 as Peter Snell was trained for the 880. We have already described how Snell competed in a full marathon at over 25 miles only about six weeks before he ran 1:45.1. This is not to say that speed-work is no longer considered important. Quite obviously, the faster the pace of an event, the more speed-work is needed to develop the muscle fibers required for carrying such a fast pace. But such speed-endurance should be based upon and develop out of distance-endurance.

James Elliott, coach of Olympic champion Charlie Jenkins and many other excellent quarter-milers, stated this point very concisely.

> You have to sell quarter-milers on a program of hard work. The only way they can become great runners is by living track 12 months a year, 24 hours a day. How they live and what they do during that time determines the degree of greatness they achieve. . . . They must be convinced that there is no shortcut to success. . . . During the fall our quarter-milers jog a mile before practice and a mile after. We often run repeat 220's, concentrating on relaxation not speed, hitting them in about 28 seconds. . . . At first they can only do five or six 220's but they build up to where they are able to run 13 or 14 of them.[6]

During the competitive season, Elliott's men emphasized hard work during the early days of each week. They often ran repeat 660's on Mondays and repeat 300's on Tuesday. Such a schedule is consistent with that of Jim Lea (former world-record holder for the 440 at :45.8) as reported by Fred Wilt.[7]

Warm-up. Identical for race or workout. Jog 1½ to 2 miles. 5-10 minutes calisthenics. 8-12 × 100 yards fast running, each faster than the last. Walk 120 yards after each. Then directly into workout, or 15 minutes complete rest before race.

Summer Training (April-May). Walk an equal distance for recovery after each of these fast intervals:

Mon.	8 × 330 in 37-39 seconds each.
Tues.	10-15 × 220 in 24-28 seconds each. (Best was 15 × 220 with :23.7 average.)

---

6 Jim Elliott, "The Quarter Mile," in *Championship Track and Field*, ed. Tom Ecker (Englewood Cliffs, N. J.: Prentice-Hall, Inc., 1961), p. 30.

7 Fred Wilt, "Jim Lea, How He Trains," *Scholastic Coach*, XXIX, No. 8 (April 1960), 44.

Wed.	6×440 in 52-55 seconds each.
Thurs.	10-15 $\times$ 150 sprints, usually racing against teammates.
Fri.	In early season, short wind sprints, easy starts, and baton work. During racing season, rest one day before racing; in late season, rest two days.
Sat.	Competition.
Sun.	Rest or 30-45 minutes of easy fartlek.

The Half-mile Run

History of Tactics and Performance

Any history of tactics and outstanding performances in the half-mile run can well begin with the wonderful exploits of Lawrence "Lon" Myers of the Manhattan Athletic Club during the years 1865 to 1878 when he was an amateur and for five years after that when he was a professional. In 1880, he ran seven times in a single afternoon and won the American title in the 100, the 220, the 440, and the 880. In 1886, he defeated the great English runner, W. G. George, in the 880, the three-quarters-mile and the mile. His best time for the 880, 1:55.4, remained as the American record for 11 years, despite his tendency to run many events and seldom to concentrate on one. As long as any of his contemporaries remain alive, they will argue that Myers was the greatest middle-distance runner of all time. Less controversial is the fact that Myers encompassed the breadth of future track training with both over-distance and under-distance work, and his ability to combine speed-work in the sprints with half-mile racing.

With the exception of three men (Cunningham, 1936, 1:49.7m.; Wooderson, 1938, 1:48.4m.; and Snell, 1962, 1:44.3m.) half-milers have doubled in the 440 yards event, and have emphasized speed-work in their training.

The most outstanding of the early champions was Ted Meredith, Pennsylvania '16, and 1912 Olympic champion. This 18-year-old Mercers-burg Academy runner had given excellent performances in both the 440 and the 880 during the 1912 spring season, but he had been unable to win either final in the American Olympic tryouts. In running the 440, he habitually took the lead and carried a very fast pace throughout the first half of the race. However in the half-mile, his superior speed gave him an advantage at the finish and he therefore held back until the final straightaway. In the Olympic final he was running against Mel Sheppard, the 1908 winner in both the 880- and 1500-meter races, against Davenport of the USA, and Braun of Germany, who were both fine quarter-milers. Sheppard, the strongest but also the slowest of the group, took the lead immediately and hit the 400-mark at the then unbelievable time of :52.4.

Meredith was a close second, however, with Braun and Davenport just behind. Not until the final straightaway did Meredith move up and out to take the lead by two feet from Sheppard and a new Olympic record of 1:51.9. Sheppard's strategy was to build up as great a lead as possible during the first 440 and "run the sprint out" of his faster quarter-mile opponents. Theirs was to be up at the 660-yard mark and outsprint him at the finish. As has happened since in many, many races the man with the finishing kick was the winner.

The next great champion, Douglas G. A. Lowe of Cambridge University, England, has undoubtedly, by example, teaching, and writing,

TABLE 8.3

OUTSTANDING PERFORMANCES IN THE 880-YARD–800-METER RUNS

Date	Record 880y.	Record 800m.	Name	Affiliation	Time at 440	Age	Olympic Champion	Related Data
1884	1:55.4		Lon Myers	Manhattan A.C.				
1895	1:53.4*		C. H. Kilpatrick	NYAC		24		
1904		1:56	J. D. Lightbody	USA			1904	
1908		1:52.8	Mel Sheppard	New York		25	1908	
1912	1:52.5*	1:51.9*	Ted Meredith	Mercersburg	:52.5	18	1912	Best 440 :47.4
1916	1:52.2*		Ted Meredith	Pennsylvania	:52.8	22	1920	
1920	1:53.4		A. G. Hill	England				
1926	1:51.6*	1:51.6*	Otto Peltzer	Germany	:54.6	26		
1928		1:50.6*	Sera Martin	France	:52.8			
1928		1:51.8	Douglas Lowe	England	:55.0	26	1924, 1928	
1932	1:50.9*	1:50.0	Ben Eastman	Stanford	:52.0			Best 440 :46.4
1932		1:49.8*	Tom Hampson	England	:55.0		1932	
1934		1:49.8*	Ben Eastman	Stanford	:54.0			
1936		1:49.7*	Glen Cunningham	Kansas	:54.0	27		Best mile 4:06.7
1936		1:52.9	John Woodruff	Pittsburgh	:57.0	20	1936	Best 440 :47.0
1937	1:49.6*	1:49.6*	Elroy Robinson	Fresno State	:53.5			
1938	1:49.2*	1:48.4*	Sidney Wooderson	England	:52.7	24		Best mile 4:06.4
1939		1:46.6*	Rudi Harbig	Germany	:52.2	26		Best 440 :46.0
1948		1:49.2	Mal Whitfield	Ohio State	:54.0	24	1948	
1950	1:49.2*		Mal Whitfield	Ohio State	:50.5	26		Best 440 :46.2
1952		1:49.2	Mal Whitfield	Ohio State	:54.2	28	1952	
1953	1:48.6*		Mal Whitfield	Ohio State	:52.8	29		
1955	1:47.5*		Lon Spurrier	California	:51.6	22		
1955		1:45.7*	Roger Moens	Belgium	:52.4	25		
1956		1:47.7	Tom Courtney	Fordham	:53.0	23	1956	
1957	1:46.8*		Tom Courtney	Fordham	:52.2	24		Best 440 :46.0
1957		1:45.8	Tom Courtney	Fordham	:50.6	24		
1960		1:46.3	Peter Snell	N. Zealand	:52.0	21	1960	
1962	1:45.1*	1:44.3*	Peter Snell	N. Zealand	:51.0	23		Best mile 3:54.4

* Official world record

influenced both training and tactics in the half-mile as much as any other one person. His first emphasis lay in knowing as much about the methods and abilities of the other runners in a race as he knew about himself. In 1924, Lowe won the Olympic title by his superior sprint in the last straightaway, and one might have expected him to follow this tactic indefinitely. Yet, two years later, when he became convinced that Dr. Otto Peltzer of Germany had great speed at the finish, Lowe took the pace at the quarter post and tried to carry the entire last 440 yards. Peltzer kicked past him at the tape, however, to the new world record of 1:51.6. As one consequence of this defeat, Lowe gave exclusive attention to quarter-miling and to greater speed throughout the 1927 season.

In the 1928 games at Amsterdam, Lowe knew the abilities and probable tactics of everyone in the field. Assured by this knowledge, he relaxed in a second-place position during his trial heat of 1:57, whereas Lloyd Hahn, the American champion in both the half-mile and mile, and Sera Martin, the French world-record holder, had to fight hard to win theirs in about 1:53. In the final, Hahn, the miler, tried to run away from the field with a 53-second first quarter. Lowe and Martin, however, stayed at his shoulder, not letting him relax for a moment. At the 660, Lowe surprised the others with a sudden burst of speed and managed to gain the few crucial yards that meant the difference at the finish. His year of training for greater speed had paid off.

From the standpoint of tactics in training and competition, the next great performer was Rudolf Harbig, a pupil of Woldemar Gerschler of Germany, the recognized father of interval training. Under Gerschler, Harbig had been soundly trained for both endurance and speed. Throughout the early winter months he had done much running in the woods and repeated 1000-meter practice runs. Later he ran many repeated 200-meter and 300-meter dashes. He was therefore prepared physically and mentally to race out in front or relax and win from behind. He had already run :21.8 for 200 meters and just two months later set a world record from the 400-meter of :46.0.

On July 15, 1939, a match race was set up between Harbig and Mario Lanzi, the Italian record holder at 1:49.5. Harbig's best time was 1:49.4 so the men were well matched. Lanzi set pace with a fast :52 at 400 meters; Harbig stayed close throughout, and then in the final straightaway, sprinted past Lanzi to what was then an almost unbelievable 1:46.6. This record held for 16 years, until it was broken by Roger Moens of Belgium (1:45.7) in 1955. In a very exhaustive analysis of all related factors, R. L. Quercetani selected Harbig as the greatest of all 800-meter–880-yard men through 1954; Mal Whitfield was considered second, and, surprisingly, Long John Woodruff of Pittsburgh was rated third.

Our next selection in this history of tactics is Mal Whitfield of Ohio

The 1960 Olympic 1500 meters at Rome. From left to right: Zoltan Vamos, Rumania; Michel Jazy, France; Michel Bernard, France; Arne Hamarsland, Norway; Istvan Rozsavalgyi, Hungary; Dyrol Burleson, U.S.A.; Herb Elliott, Australia; and James Grelle, U.S.A. The winner, Elliott, varied his position from third around the first turn, to sixth at 600 meters, to third at 800 meters in 1:58.0. He then spurted suddenly to the lead, ran his last lap in :55.6 and his last 800 meters in 1:52.8, with a world-record time of 3:35.6 for the full 1500 meters.

Courtesy of *Track and Field News*

State, two-time Olympic champion, 1948 and 1952. In 1948 in London, Whitfield faced a most formidable field. Arthur Wint, the 6′ 4″ Jamaican, who had just won the 400-meter Olympic title in :46.2, appeared to be the man to beat. His usual tactic was to outsprint his rivals in the final stretch. Marcel Hansenne, who had recently lowered the French 800-meter record to 1:48.3, was strong in the 1500-meter race and had an excellent kick at the finish. Herb Barten of Michigan was the Big Ten mile champion and had previously beaten Whitfield by outsprinting him in the last 200 meters. Whitfield won, not so much because of his superior ability as his superior tactics. The first lap was slow (:54.0), with Chef d'Hotel and Wint leading and Whitfield running third. Usually he would have relaxed there for another 200-300 meters, but Whitfield surprised the entire field by driving hard throughout the third 200 meters and picked up a full five meters lead around the third turn. Wint, Hansenne, and Barten came up on him rapidly in the final stretch but he had enough lead to hold them off. Had he delayed his bid, a different champion might have been crowned.

At Helsinki four years later, Whitfield and Wint were the favorites, running against other fine competitors, such as Ulzheimer of Germany and Nielsen of Denmark. During the intervening years, Whitfield had done a great deal of 400-meter work and had, in fact, brought his best time down to :45.9. In addition to greater experience and therefore competitive relaxation, he now had greater confidence in his ability to outsprint his rivals. Surprisingly, Wint led at the 400-meter mark in :54.0. This was an easy pace and gave him freedom for his giant strides. Whitfield, "because of the strong wind" lay back in fifth position around the second curve but moved up to Wint's shoulder at the quarter, which he'd run in :54.2. On the back stretch, Whitfield and Wint picked up the pace, with Whitfield barely able to get into the lead before the final curve. On the straight, Wint opened up, came to Whitfield's shoulder, but then faded badly as Whitfield turned it on to win rather easily by two yards. Later Whitfield said, "I played it safe. I felt I could win that way. I had plenty left in the stretch."

In contrast to such highly competitive races, Lon Spurrier had only himself and a few friendly and less-talented rivals to worry about when he set his world record of 1:47.5 in 1955. He planned a 53-55 second pace and actually ran :51.6 for the 440 and 1:19.3 for the 660. Running entirely unchallenged, he maintained control and relaxation all the way, easing off in the last few yards to prevent tying up. His time bettered Whitfield's accepted world record of 1:48.6 by 1.1 seconds, the greatest improvement in 880-yard history.

With that one exception, the pattern for both winning and setting records in the 800-meter—880-yard event remained unchanged through the next two Olympic games at Melbourne and Rome. In 1956, both Tom Courtney, the winner, and Derek Johnson, who was second, came from behind. Sowell led in :52.4 with Courtney second and Johnson fourth. At 600 meters (1:20.4) Courtney moved up to take the lead as he came out of the final turn. Johnson came along fast and actually led for about 30 meters, but lost by inches in the last desperate drive for the tape. Each man in the race had a plan, of course; tactics were an important factor of victory and defeat. But as one looks back, it was not so much tactics as sheer bull-dog determination that made the difference. Both Johnson and Courtney ran themselves out and were extremely fatigued for several hours afterward. Neither had followed the tough training schedules of the Europeans; both drew heavily on some inner "mental" source of power.

Rome produced the greatest upset in Olympic 800-meter history. Roger Moens, world-record holder at 1:45.7 was the clear favorite, and next favored were George Kerr of the West Indies and Paul Schmidt of Ger-

FIG. 8.2   Running style in the 440/880 events. Note the more forceful drive of legs and arms. The foot-placement is higher on the ball and toes; the knees rise higher; the stride is longer.

many. Peter Snell, only 21 years old, was unknown. His best previous mark was 1.49.2. In fact, he revealed after the Games that he had been sent from New Zealand "merely for the experience and to get ready for the 1500 meters at Tokyo in 1964." *Track and Field News* reported that it was a compact five-man race after the first turn, which, for the first time in Olympic history, was run in lanes. All the action, except for a minimum of jockeying, came in the last 150 yards. Waegli of Switzerland held the lead at 400 meters in :51.9, and at the 600-meter point in 1:19.1. Moens was second; Snell, third. With only 100 yards to go, Waegli faltered, Moens moved into what seemed to be a permanent lead. Moens looked around three times in the stretch. With but

25 yards to go, Snell amazingly (to himself as well as to the 70,000 spectators) moved ahead to win by two feet over the bewildered "Snell-
shocked" Moens. Snell's four runs in three days were timed in 1:48.1,
1:48.6, 1:47.2, and 1:46.3 (2.9 seconds under Whitfield's Olympic record
and his own personal record of 1:49.2!). His world-record 800-meter
time of 1:44.3, which came two years later, was almost an anticlimax.
(For the record, the splits on this race were :24.8, :26.2, :25.9, and :27.4
for a 600-meter time of 1:16.9 and a best-ever 800-meter time of 1:44.3.)

Pace in the Half-mile

It has been established beyond all doubt that physiological economy,
which is theoretically crucial, and tactical success in actually running the
half-mile are two very different things. In our discussion of pace for
distance running, we have cited the conclusion of Dr. Laurence Morehouse that "a maximum steady state during the minutes required for
the event" will produce the best time, and also the conclusion of Dr.
Sid Robinson that the first half of a mile or 880 should be about one
second slower than the second half.

Experience has not coincided with these conclusions of science. Analysis of the times given in Table 8.3 on page 203 and the times for other
races under 1:49, which were all run during the period 1948 to 1963,
discloses that every race, without exception, had a faster first quarter,
and only three races had a time difference of two seconds or less. The
average time for the first 440 in 22 races was :52.3; the average for the
second 440, :55.1.

The practical definition of the expression, "race tactics" is "the means
to beating one's opponents." [8] This is something quite different from
making best time. It can be argued that the man who makes best time
will always beat his opponents, but this by-passes the uncertainties of
human emotion and control. Assuming that others run fast first quarters,
as has been done in the past, the man running even pace or slower would
be well back in the pack at the 440-mark and would not get the lead
until late in the final straightaway. He cannot be sure that the way will
be clear enough to allow him to hold his smooth pace. Men jockey for
position and they are not likely to move over just because a man's plans
are scientifically sound.

Occasionally the way is cleared in the 1500 meters or mile. Delany

---

[8] For a fascinating discussion of this point see Franz Stampfl, *Franz Stampfl on
Running* (London: Herbert Jenkins, Ltd., 1955), pp. 120 ff. Stampfl relates the
dramatic and fierce struggles among Kuts, Chataway, and Zatopek in which variation
of pace was the crucial tactic.

ran to win at Melbourne, though he had to run on the outside around
two turns. But the faster pace of the 880 and its shorter distance in which
to maneuver make such a plan foolhardy if more than four men have
a chance to win.

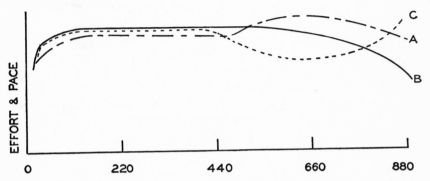

FIG. 8.3   Curves of effort and pace in running the half-mile. Individual *A*
lays back during the first 440, but pours it on for the entire last lap, even though
slowing down in the stretch. *B* sets a more even pace, maintains effort throughout,
but also slows down on the final straightaway. *C* takes it easy during the first 660,
being concerned only with maintaining contact, and then puts all his energy into
the final 220.

It seems certain that the theories of scientists are physiologically sound,
and that ultimate human records will be achieved on a basis of even
pace. But the ultimate is not here yet, and Snell's times were :51.0 and
:54.1 for his 1:45.1 record. Before the ultimate time is recorded, we'll
have a lot of fun and fury trying to beat each other, unmindful of the
niceties of even pace.

One further comment: whatever the number of competitors and whatever the conclusions of the scientists, a man's pace should be set in terms
of what he is certain he can handle. A man can be certain of setting even
pace, or any pace, only when he has run miles and suffered fatigue to
the point where his certainty is of the muscles and the heart and lungs
as well as of the cortex. When such certainty is present, then even the
wild surges of Kuts make sense and win great victories.

Training for the Half-mile

We have already fully discussed training for endurance running and
no repetition is needed here. However, it may be of value to present
three sample training diaries of champions who have had different attitudes and different systems of training.

Training of Rudolf Harbig [9]

Former world-record holder 880 meters, 1:46.6, 1939, and 400 meters, :46.0, 1939. Best marks other events: 1000 meters, 2:21.5 (world record); 200 meters, :21.5; 100 meters, :10.6.

Age 1939—26. Started racing in 1932 at age of 19 as a long distance runner. Coached by Woldemar Gerschler, "father of interval training."

Harbig's carefully maintained diary tells of the long distance woods running that he did throughout the late fall and winter months and intermittently during the later training season.

Sample early season workouts

1. 1¼ mile warm-up. Calisthenics. 1500m run. Jog 15 min. 1000m light running with 6 × 80m fast striding en route. Calisthenics.
2. 45 min. jogging. 1000m in 3:05. Jog 15 min. 1000m in 3:02. Jog 10 min. 10.0m in 3:11.

Sample summer training

1. 30 min. warm-up. 3 × 200m in :23.8, :23.8, :24.3. Walk 5 min. Jog 10 min. 600m in 1:25.3.
2. 30 min. warm-up. 800m in 2:11. Jog 15 min. 800m in 2:02. Jog 10 min. 600m in 1:28.
3. 20 min. warm-up. Crouch starts. 2 × 30m, 2 × 50m, 2 × 80m, 1 × 150m, 1 × 200m, 1 × 400m.

Harbig's great achievement was attributed to (1) his own iron will in self-discipline both on and off the practice field, and (2) the careful planning of his coach, some ten years ahead of his time in training methods.

Training of Tom Courtney [10]

Olympic 800m champion, 1956. Represented Fordham and New York A.C. Best marks: Mile—4:07; ¾ mile—2:56; 1000 meters—2:19.3; 1000 yards—2:08.6; 880 yards—1:46.8 (world record); 800 meters—1:45.8; 600 yards—1:09.5 (world record); 400 meters—45.8; 220—21; 100—9.7. Born August 17, 1933, at Newark, N.J. 6' 2", 183 lbs. Started racing in 1949 at age 16.

Mid-precompetitive season training

Mon.	10 × 300y in 36. Walk 300y after each.
Tues.	6 × 880y in 2:10. Walk 440y after each.
Wed.	10 × 300y in 36. Walk 300y after each.
Thurs.	Light sprints. Acceleration sprints and sprints on grass. Jog 3-4 miles.
Fri.	10 × 300y in 36. Walks 300y after each. "As I got closer to racing season I reduce the number of fast runs and run them faster. My work is on the track and usually not with a watch—only because I have no coach."

---

[9] Taken from Toni Nett, *Ihr Weg Zum Erfolg*, Teil 2 (Stuttgart: Verlag Karl Hoffmann, 1952), as translated by Fred Wilt, *How They Train* (Los Altos, Calif.: *Track and Field News*, 1959), p. 5.

[10] Wilt, *How They Train*, p. 4.

Mid-competitive season training

Mon.   4 × 300y in 32. Walk 300's. ("My fastest 300 in this set of 4 is 29.8.")
Tues.   ¾ mile in 3:00 (60, 65, 55). ("I have run ¾ mile in 58, 60, 58 for 2:56, and in 60, 68, 52 for 3:00.")
Wed.   3 × 300y in 31-32. Walk 300's. ("Sometimes I run 660 yards in 1:18 for pace.")
Thurs.   Rest.
Fri.   Jog 1 mile. 3 × 80y fast. Jog 80y after each.
Sat.   Race.
Sun.   Rest.

Duration of workouts: 1½ hours, starting at 3:00 PM. Virtually self-coached since graduation from Fordham. Very little weight training, but feels it would help runners.

Training of Peter Snell

1960 Olympic 800m champion—1:46.3. World-record holder: 800 meters—1:44.3; 880 yards—1:45.1; mile—3:54.4. Trained by Arthur Lydiard.

Lydiard's schedule for the first and the tenth weeks of Snell's training prior to the Rome Olympics have already been given on pages 116 and 117. As one other example, Lydiard suggests the following for the second week preceding major competition (11th week of speed training):

Mon.   12 × 220y (½ effort).
Tues.   1 × 660y (¾ eort); 4 starts to 50y.
Wed.   1 × 440y (fair speed); 1 × 440y (full effort).
Thurs.   One mile of 50y dashes; 5 starts to 50y.
Fri.   3 × 220y at full effort.
Sat.   Competition at 440y.
Sun.   Jog 10 miles or more.

However, Snell received very little such sharpening work prior to his greatest efforts in 1962. During his short four-year career under Lydiard, Snell's heavy muscles had given him many setbacks. But between April and December of 1961, he had completed the full marathon training as we have already outlined it and the very strenuous sharpening work which Lydiard calls hill training. Amazingly for a half-miler, he competed in a marathon race early in December, stayed with the leaders, including Murray Halberg, for 22 miles, then eased off for the last four!

On January 1, 1962, with only two and one-half weeks of speed-work (other than hill-training), Snell ran a mile in 4:01.3. Then during the following five weeks of competition, he recorded 880 yards in 1:48.3 and 1:47.3, 800 meters in 1:46.2; three days later, a world-record mile in 3:54.4; and one week later, a world-record 800 meters in 1:44.3 and 880 yards in 1:45.1.

Beyond all doubt, this was the greatest middle distance running the world has ever seen. But it was even more amazing when we realize that it was preceded by a marathon competition about seven weeks before, and by less than four weeks of the repeated speed-running on the track that we have thought essential to best 880 running. Normally, Lydiard recommends a full 12 weeks on the track before the *big race*. We should also keep in mind that Lydiard insists upon about 10 days of reduced training prior to a major competitive effort.

We can of course consider Snell as superhuman, or as the exception that proves the rule. Lydiard denies both these assumptions emphatically. More reasonably, most coaches will reconsider the basic structure of their middle distance training programs.

The Mile Run

History of Tactics and Performance

All histories of mile running rightly begin with the exploits of the Englishman W. G. George, who, in 1885, set an amateur record of 4:18.4; then, turning to more lucrative professional racing, which was so prevalent at the time, beat the best of them, W. Cummings, in the amazing time of 4:12.8. In this race, George ran successive quarters in :58.5, :63.3, :66.0, and :65.0. This fast first half, 2:01.8, is a little difficult to understand when one considers that a steady pace over long distances was then the common training method. Training articles written at the time emphasize steady running for two to 20 miles either once or twice a day. Perhaps it resulted from George's efforts to set records at all distances, from 1000 yards to 12 miles. In any case, George's success with this fast first half influenced the attempts of future runners for over a quarter century.

It is of value to note that even during its heyday professional running was hardly an honored practice and that George succumbed to its lure only when there were no further goals to conquer in amateur running and when he discovered that his attempts to be a combined student-athlete had placed him in debt some 1000 English pounds. Apparently his debts were soon cleared, for F. A. M. Webster comments that on the day of George's great race with the professional champion, Cummungs, such a surge of spectators was on hand—about 30,000—that "George was forced to reach his dressing room at the top of the old grandstand by means of a ladder from an adjoining coal yard." [11]

George's amateur record was broken within ten years by Tommy Conneff, of Irish birth but of Boston background, who ran 4:15.6 in 1895. But his professional time was not surpassed for 29 years, until,

---

[11] F. A. M. Webster, *Athletics of Today* (London: Frederick Warne & Co., Ltd., 1929), p. 80.

TABLE 8.4

Date	Record Mile	Record 1500m.	Name	Affiliation	Age	Quarter Times	Olympic Champion
1886	4:12.8		W. G. George	England	28	:58.5-:63.3-:67.0-:65.0	(Professional)
1895	4:15.6*		Thomas Conneff	New York			
1907		3:59.8*	H. A. Wilson	England			
1908		4:03.4	Mel Sheppard	New York	25		1908
1911		3:55.8*	Abel Kiviat	New York	19		
1912		3:56.8	A. N. S. Jackson	England			1912
1913	4:14.4*		John P. Jones	Cornell		:61.8-:67.6-:66.8-:58.2	
1915	4:12.6*		Norm S. Tabor	Brown		:58.0-:67.0-:68.0-:59.6	
1917		3:54.7*	J. Zander	Sweden			
1921	4:13.8		A. G. Hill	England	32	:59.6-:64-4-:67.2-:62.6	1920
1924	4:10.4*		Paavo Nürmi	Finland	26	:58.6-:63.2-:64.9-:63.7	
1924		3:52.6*	Paavo Nürmi	Finland	26	(Held 19 world's records)	1924
1926		3:51.0*	Otto Peltzer	Germany			
1928		3:53.2	Harry Larva	Finland			1928
1930		3:49.2*	Jules Ladoumègue	France			
1931	4:09.2*		Jules Ladoumègue	France		:60.8-:63.4-:63.8-:61.2	
1933		3:49.0*	Luigi Beccali	Italy	25		1932
1933	4:08.7	3:48.8*	William Bonthron	Princeton	22	:61.2-:62.3-:65.1-:40.2	
1933	4:07.6*		Jack Lovelock	New Zealand	23	:61.4-:62.2-:65.1-:58.9	
1934	4:06.8*		Glen Cunningham	Kansas	25	:61.8-:64.0-:61.8-:59.2	
1936		3:47.8*	Jack Lovelock	New Zealand	26	:61.4-:64.1-:62.0-:40.3	1936
1937	4:06.4*		Sidney Wooderson	England	31	:58.6-:64.0-:64.6-:59.4	
1941		3:47.6*	Gunder Hägg	Sweden	23	:59.0-:61.1-:61.4-:44.3	
1942	4:04.6*		Gunder Hägg	Sweden		:57.2-:63.0-:64.0-:60.4	
1942		3:45.8*	Gunder Hägg	Sweden		:58.0-:60.2-:60.7-:46.9	
1943	4:02.6*	3:45.0*	Arne Andersson	Sweden		:58.5-:62.5-:59.8-:44.2	
1944	4:01.6*		Arne Andersson	Sweden	27	:56.6-:59.5-:63.3-:62.2	
1944		3:43.0*	Gunder Hägg	Sweden		:56.7-:59.8-:61.5-:45.0	
1945	4:01.4*		Gunder Hägg	Sweden	27	:56.5-:62.7-:62.2-:60.0	
1947		3:43.0*	Lennart Strand	Sweden	26		
1947		3:44.4	Henry Eriksson	Sweden			1948
1952		3:43.0*	Werner Lueg	Germany	21	:56.6-:62.2-	
1952		3:45.2	Joseph Barthel	Luxembourg	25	:58.2-:63.6-:61.7-:41.7	1952
1954	3:59.4*		Roger Bannister	Oxford	21	:57.5-:60.7-:62.3-:58.9	
1954	3:58.0*	3:41.8*	John Landy	Australia	25	:58.5-:60.2-:58.5-:60.8	
1956		3:40.6*	I. Rozsavölgyi	Hungary	27	:55.7-:53.5-:60.6-:40.8	
1956		3:41.2	Ron Delany	Eire	21	:60.0-:61.4-:61.0-:38.8	1956
1957	3:57.2*		Derek Ibbotson	England	25	:56.0-:60.4-:63.9-:56.9	
1957		3:40.2*	Olavi Salsola	Finland	24	:56.8-:61.1-:60.5-:41.8	
1957		3:38.1*	S. Jungwirth	Czecho.	27	:54.9-:59.3-:59.2-:44.7	
1958	3:54.5*		Herb Elliott	Australia	20	:58.2-:59.9-:60.9-:55.5	
1960		3:36.0*	Herb Elliott	Australia	22		
1960		3:35.6*	Herb Elliott	Australia	22	:58.5-:59.5-:56.0-:41.6	1960
1962	3:56.3**		James Beatty	No. Caro.	28	:55.5-:60.1-:62.4-:58.3	
1962	3:54.4*		Peter Snell	New Zealand	22	:60.5-:59.0-:58.5-:56.4	

* Official world record
** Official American record

213

in 1915, Norman Tabor of Brown recorded 4:12.6 in beating his frequent rival, John Paul Jones of Cornell. The great races between these two men during their three college years were one of the high points of college miling. First, Jones set a new amateur record of 4:15.4. Two years later, in 1913, he won the IC4A championships in 4:14.4.

But, not to be denied, Tabor came back in 1915 with his brilliant 4:12.6, which shattered every mark on or off the books. In so doing, he recorded :58.0, :67.0, :68.0, :59.6 for his four quarters. This is a different pace pattern from that of George, with its slow second quarter, an even slower third quarter, and a blazingly fast final quarter. One thinks of these times as occurring in a large field of runners in which someone runs the first quarter much too fast, then simply relaxes with the field for the middle half-mile, and finally sprints all-out for the full final quarter. It is a method of running that is still prevalent today.

The next stage in both record making and pace making in the mile was dramatized by perhaps the most famous of all distance runners, Paavo Nurmi, the Phantom Finn. He was not primarily a miler, having established 19 world records at 11 standard distances during the 11 years of his career; yet he covered the mile distance in 4:10.4 and even held the 1924 Olympic title and world record for 1500 meters in 3:52.6. The unique emphasis of Nurmi's running was on even pace. His habit at longer distances of carrying a watch and hitting even time for lap after lap was the sensation of the sports world for a full decade.

Yet, when he set his world mile record in 1923, the pace was off, for he found it necessary to remain with his opponents regardless of pace. His rival this time and on many other memorable occasions was an excellent runner named Edvin Wide of Sweden, who completed the first lap in :58.6, and the 880 in 2:01.8. However, Nurmi then took over, hitting 3:06.7 at ¾ mile and :63.7 for his final lap. Nurmi is said to have had in mind a 4:08 mile with even quarters of :62 each, but his opponent's pace spoiled these plans and a slower total time resulted.

Nurmi's daily practice occurred as he ran five miles to and from work. He carried a stop watch at all times, became interested in the relative effects of different pace upon his performance, and thus came to the practice of even pace that has so widely influenced distance running since his time.

But the flawless Nurmi's mile record lasted only seven years. By 1931, a rugged little Frenchman, Jules Ladoumègue, became the first man in history to beat 4:10 for the mile, with a best time of 4:09.2. Had he not been suspended from amateur competition, Ladoumègue undoubtedly would have toughened even further the great competition among Jack Lovelock of New Zealand, Glenn Cunningham of Kansas, and Bill Bonthron of Princeton during the years 1933 to 1936. First, Lovelock, running at the famous Princeton Invitational Meet, beat Bonthron in 4:07.6. A year later, in 1934, Cunningham lowered this record to 4:06.8; yet even this fast time had to give way just three years later to the pattering strides of Sydney Wooderson of England. On this occasion a deliberate attempt to break the record was publicized and carried out with almost flawless precision to a 4:06.2 conclusion.

One of the greatest influences upon training for the mile came through the tremendous finishing pace of the champions of this era. Glenn Cunningham, Bill Bonthron, Charles Fenske, and, most of all, Jack Lovelock had tremendous bursts of speed at the finish, and all were capable of excellent quarter-miles well under 50 seconds. For example, in the 1936 Olympic 1500-meter final at Berlin, Lovelock was close to the leader but still in fourth place 300 yards from the finish. Yet within 100 yards he had a 10-yard lead on the field, and his surprised opponents never fully recovered it. The time for this final quarter was :56.0.

The value of such great speed gradually became more evident and athletes in all countries turned to more and more speed work in their practice sessions. Swedish fartlek and interval training were direct results.

With fartlek came great distance running in Sweden. Rune Persson, Lennart Strand, Rune Gustafsson, Arne Andersson, and Gunder Hägg were all excellent performers, with best mile times under 4:07. The most successful of these were the last two, who by their repeated exploits at many distances surpassed all prior champions. Hägg first attracted attention in August 1941, by breaking Jack Lovelock's 1500-meter record in 3:47.5. A year later, he also set a new mile record at 4:06.2, with Andersson only a yard or so behind. Andersson equaled this time a week or so later, but Hägg, within two months, lowered it again to 4:04.6. Andersson was not to be outdone, however, and the following spring, in 1942, with Hägg absent, he competed against two of his own countrymen. Arne Ahlsen was third in 4:06.6; Rune Gustafsson, second in 4:05.8; and Andersson, the winner in 4:02.6! Furthermore, to complete his triumph, Andersson took advantage of an American tour by Hägg to eclipse the latter's 1500-meter record in the time of 3:45.

The 1944 and 1945 seasons found the four great rivals together again. In a specially arranged match race, Hägg set the 1500-meter time at 3:43.0, the equivalent of about a 3:59 mile. But 11 days later, Andersson returned the compliment by beating Hägg at the mile distance in 4:01.6, running his first half-mile in 1:57.3. Finally, in July 1945, Hägg, Andersson, Persson, and Strand were matched on the fast track at Malmo, Sweden. On this occasion, Hägg took the lead all the way. He was :56.5 at the first quarter, :61.9 (1:58.5) at the second, and :61.3 (2:59.7) at the third; and he hurried home with a sound :61.7 last lap, establishing a world record at 4:01.4. Most unfortunately, Andersson and Hägg were declared professional shortly after this great race, and the much-looked-for 4:00 mile had to wait for other challengers.

It is important to note the almost perfect pace of Hägg during the last three quarters of his race. Andersson was famous for his terrific kick at the finish of his best miles; but on this occasion he either was not at his best or the amazing pace of 2:59.7 for three quarters was just too much for even his great ability. This is one of the few examples in track history in which a strong pace runner has been able to run away from another, almost equally strong, who has a finishing sprint. One can only speculate on how it might have turned out, had these two all-time champions run again.

Though we by-pass the excellent performances of many fine milers, our story of tactics jumps 19 years to 1954 when Roger Bannister broke what had for decades been called the "four-minute barrier." The expression is a rather silly one. Four minutes, physiologically speaking, is no more significant than any other time. But the minds of track fans, sports writers, and milers as well had undoubtedly erected a "mind-block" that was most difficult to break through. After all, as we have said so often, we run with our minds and emotions as well as with our legs and lungs. Gunder Hägg wrote some months prior to the event, "I think Bannister is the man to beat four minutes. He uses his brains as much as his legs. I've always thought the four-minute mile more of a psychological problem than a test of physical endurance."

Throughout the track world there was excited speculation as to who would be the first. John Landy of Australia was favored by many. Wes Santee of the United States ran under 4:03 time and time again. Josy Barthel, the 1952 Olympic champion, trained by Gerschler, thought he had an excellent chance. There were others of great merit.

To know and understand how the "barrier" was broken would require having been with Bannister during the weeks prior to his run; to have suffered his pangs of uncertainty about his personal condition and the weather; to have heard the Iffley stadium announcement: "Result of the mile . . . time, 3 minutes . . ." and to drown out the rest in your yells of sheer excitement. It's too late, of course, to do that now but we can read Bannister's autobiography, *The Four Minute Mile* [12] and the whole wonderful story. No one could succeed as well in raising the heart beat or determination of someone else to produce a similar achievement.

We cannot repeat the story here, as much as we'd like to. It was mainly a race of Bannister against Bannister: a fight for self-control, for restraint and relaxation, for will power greater than the dragging anchors of

---

[12] Roger Bannister, *The Four Minute Mile* (New York: Dodd, Mead & Co., 1955; London: Curtis Brown, Ltd., 1955).

Courtesy of I. D. Sansom, Oxford, England

Roger Bannister is finishing the world's first mile-under-four-minutes. Iffley Road stadium, Oxford University, England, May 6, 1954. Time 3:59.4. Bannister's run was hailed as an epic in human achievement, comparable in its conquest of self to the conquest of Everest.

fatigue, all exaggerated by the absence of important competition—except the racing stop watches. Bannister had no one to be aware of except himself; nothing to think about except the enormity of what he was attempting.

Instead, it will serve our purposes better if we quote from Bannister's comments on the problems he faced in getting ready for this effort.

I prepared myself mentally in a very careful and concentrated fashion. To my mind, the necessary mental attitude to make an all-out effort—as this was—could only be developed by refusing to let anything detract from the task ahead. I tried my best to center my thoughts only on my objective. I built up this attitude for weeks previous to the race. . . .

I approached this race with the thought that this is the only chance I will have—there must be no let-up! I reminded myself constantly that the others (Santee and Landy) were getting closer and closer.

I tried to establish this "now or never" attitude because I knew that unless I was successful in attaining this attitude or mental stance, I would perhaps spoil my attempt by letting myself fall prey to the mental reaction so common to athletes: that is, thinking that there would always be a next time or deciding, perhaps, that this was not the day when things became difficult and muscles began to ache from the strain.

You see, unless there is a kind of mental attitude such as I tried to develop, it is too easy to lose your desire. I ran with complete abandon and thought only that it must be now.[13]

And it was; the first sub-four-minute mile—3:59.4.

Bannister's performance was widely hailed as an epic in human achievement, comparable in its conquest of self to the conquest of Mt. Everest, which had occurred just the year before. But once the mental mountain was conquered, its terrors dissolved. Forty-six days later, at Turku, Finland, with the help of Chris Chataway's competitive presence, Landy ran 3:58.0. Three years later, in 1957, Derek Ibbotson achieved 3:57.2, in a race which he entered for the sole purpose of getting a banquet ticket for a friend of his wife. With little thought of a world record, with no certainty even of winning, concerned but not anxious, determined but not tense, Derek exceeded the former "human ultimate" by almost three seconds!

But to return to Landy and Bannister, their world records achieved in April and June set the stage for the "mile of the century" in August at Vancouver, B.C., the site of the 1954 British Empire Championships. This race included, in addition to Bannister and Landy, Murray Halberg who had run 4:04 at 19 years of age and was later Olympic champion in the 5000 meters at Rome, and Jim Baillie of New Zealand, who two years later ran 3:58.6.

We have already emphasized the contrasting plans of Landy and Ban-

---

[13] Lloyd Percival, Report of interview with Bannister in *The Research Guide*, June 1954.

Fig. 8.4   Running style in the mile/two-mile events. The over-all action is less forceful than in the 440/880. The foot-placement is lower on the ball; the head and hips maintain a steady level; the stride is shorter.

nister in the sections on "Tactics" and "Contact." Landy felt he must somehow break contact. He therefore set pace at 1:58.2. Bannister knew he must somehow maintain contact and yet not follow Landy's exhausting pace. Landy succeeded in his plan and led by 15 yards at the half, but Bannister's mind held contact, even though his legs had lost it, and forced his unwilling muscles to make up the difference inch by inch throughout an agonizing third lap. As you read Bannister's words you realize that, in a sense, he thrust his mind and heart out ahead to Landy and they pulled his unwilling muscles after them. Landy glanced to the inside at the precise moment Bannister made his final spurt around him as they came out of the last turn. For an instant he failed to react, and in that lost instant was the race. It was one of the most dramatic races ever run, and tactics, both physical and mental, decided the outcome. Bannister's time was 3:58.8; but time meant nothing in such a competitive race.

One of the greatest competitive and tactical 1500-meter races ever run took place at the Melbourne Olympics. Of the 37 men who competed, over half had previously beaten the Olympic record. Any one of the 12 men in the final had to be rated a possible winner. In a race such as this, the man who has reserved his physical and mental energies and then releases them—with good planning or good fortune—when they are most effective, will win. As expected, Murray Halberg set pace, clocking :58.4, with Hewson of Great Britain and Jungwirth of Czechoslovakia close up, and Delany and Landy last. At the half, with a time of 2:00.1, Lincoln of Australia took the lead. The others were closely bunched with little change in position. At 1200 meters, Hewson led with 3:01.3

and with but 300 meters to go, the race for the tape was on. Landy picked up speed, stalled, then came on again for a good third place. The winner was Delany, the man with the big kick, who had probably done less jockeying than anyone. He ran his last lap in :53.8, running around the pack on two turns; his final 300 was in :38.8; his final 100 meters in :12.9! *Track and Field News,* to which we are indebted for much of this detail, called him "The King of the Finish," adding, "No one came close, and the Villanova student crossed the finish line with an ear-splitting grin on his face and arms thrust wide as he won Eire's first gold medal since 1932."

In August 1957, when Stanislav Jungwirth set a world record for the 1500-meter run of 3:38.1, he followed two "hares" for the first half and then ran on alone in what was obviously a try for the record. His times: :54.9—1:54.2—2:53.4! This was a most remarkable effort in itself, the fastest pace ever set, up to 1962. Of this performance, *Track and Field News* (August 1957) wrote,

> At this stage in the history of middle distance running, we may summarize our two cents worth of comments this way: uniform pace throughout . . . may look as the ideal solution to most observers. But in all probability, man will never be the like of a machine, and as records continue to improve, few runners, if any, will be allowed to have something left at the end of a record race. That is the chief reason why we think that the tactics calling for a faster first half will prevail among would-be record-breakers in the 1500 m./mile, at least in races where time, rather than competition, is the prime objective.[14]

The gist of the story of Herb Elliott's 1500-meter world record at the Rome Olympics has already been told in the section on "Tactics." But we do wish to emphasize here his times for each quarter of that race: :58.5, :59.5 (1:58.0), :56.0 (2:54), plus :41.6 for the last 300 meters. The crux of the race lies there. He was third at the half, running easily. But then, quite unexpectedly, he put all his energy into one tactic. The pace had been averaging 14.7 for each 100 meters. Now he spurted to run the next 100 meters in :13.2, the third lap in :56.0, and one more 100 meters in :13.6. The competition collapsed behind him. Elliott slowed to :14.4 for the last 100 meters, although he was trying desperately for the record that Cerutty had signalled was possible. He won by 20 yards over a field that was the most able ever gathered; the sixth man was timed at 3:40.9, faster than Delany's Olympic record.

The situation and tactics in Peter Snell's race in 1962 for a new mile record of 3:54.4 were quite different. The field was smaller and less talented, although the Australian Albert Thomas (3:58.6 in 1958) and Olympic 5000-meter champion Murray Halberg (3:57.5 in 1958) were there. Snell claimed he had no intention of trying for a record. For two

---

14 "Solo 3:38.1 by Jungwirth," *Track and Field News,* X, No. 7 (August 1957), 3.

and one-half laps Snell was content to follow. At the end of three, he led with a time of 2:58.0. "When I finished the third lap, I knew I was well within it," Snell said later, "I never felt better in my life so I really ran."

It is important to note in Table 8.4 that of all the world-record miles, only the best two—that of Elliott (1:58.1–1:56.4), and that of Snell (1:59.5 –1:54.9)—bear out Sid Robinson's thesis that, from a physical economy standpoint, the first half should be slightly slower than the second half. Actually the time differences are too great; Robinson thought one second would be about right, but that merely suggests what we can be certain of—better times still lie ahead.

Training of Josy Barthel

The most complete outline we have seen of careful preparation for major competition is in Josy Barthel's training diary for the month of July 1952,[15] just prior to his tremendous victory in the Olympic 1500-meter run. Barthel was trained by Woldemar Gerschler, and it is interesting to note how much woods running was interspersed with the usual interval training.

1st. Track. Warm-up for 30 minutes, with two accelerations. Three repetitions of 1200 meters. The first, 3:07.1 (62-2:06-61.1). The second, 3:12.3 (64-2:10-62.3). The third, 3:12.1 (64-2:10-62.1). Total mileage: 8¼.

2nd. Woods. Two hours of light running with three repetitions of 1000 meters, but without being timed. Total miles: 8½.

3rd. Woods. One hour and a half of light running, with two repetitions of 600 meters without being timed. Miles: 8¼.

4th. Woods. One hour and a half of light running, with five accelerations. Miles: 6¼.

5th. Rest.

6th. Competition against Germany's B Team. I won the 1500 meters in 3:51 (59.5-2:06.1-3:10). Miles: 5. I was at ease during the race, especially in the last 300 meters.

7th. Woods. One hour and a half of light running. Miles: 6¼.

8th. Track. Warm-up for 30 minutes, with two accelerations. One 600-meter run in 1:26 (57-29). Miles: 6¼.

9th. Woods. Two hours of running and walking, with eight repetitions of 300 meters, averaging about 47 seconds for each. Miles: 10.

10th. Track. Warm-up for 25 minutes. Ten repetitions of 300 meters in the following times: 40.1, 42, 41.8, 41, 41.2, 42.2, 41.9, 42, 42, and 41.7. Miles: 8½.

11th. Woods. One hour and a quarter of light running, with moderate run of 1200 meters.

[15] Acknowledgment for the use of this material is made to William G. Smith, whose unpublished master's thesis, "A Study of the Training Methods for Middle and Long Distance Running of Selected European, Australian, and American Coaches and Athletes," is an excellent summary of training problems and their solutions.

12th. Rest.

13th. Traveled to Trier, Germany. Competition over 800 meters. I won in 1:52.8 (55-57.8). I also ran a leg on the 4 times 400-meter relay in 51 seconds. Miles: 4.

14th. Woods. One hour of jogging. Miles: 6¼.

15th. Woods. The same as yesterday. Miles: 6¼.

16th. Woods. One hour and a quarter of light running, with a run of 1000 meters at a fair pace inserted. Miles: 6¼. I left for Helsinki. I am apprehensive.

17th. Arrived at 4 PM in Helsinki. Woods. One hour of light running. Miles: 5.

18th. Morning at 8 to 9 in the woods. One hour of light running. Afternoon, I trained with Lueg (One of the three world-record holders for 1500 meters), Dohrow, and Lamors. 600 meters in 1:23.3 (54.5-28.8). 800 meters in 1:58 (60.5-57.5). 600 meters in 1:27 (59-28). Miles: 11. The times were accomplished without severe effort.

19th. Morning at 10. Easy running for 45 minutes. Afternoon, track. Eight repetitions of 300 meters in the following times: 41.7, 42, 41.5, 41.9, 42, 42, 41, and 40. Miles: 11. I feel quite good from this workout.

20th. Morning at 10. Easy running for 45 minutes. Afternoon, track. A fast pace for 1200 meters in 3:06.4 (59.5-2:03-63.4). Miles: 10½. I feel tired, but am at ease.

21st. Morning at 11. Easy running for 45 minutes. Afternoon, track. A 300-meter sprint in 39.5. 800 meters in 2:01.8 (61.5-60.3). And another 300 meters in 40.5. Miles: 10½.

22nd. Morning at 8. Easy running for 30 minutes. Evening at 7. Easy running for 40 minutes. Miles: 6½.

23rd. Morning at 8. Light running for 30 minutes. Miles: 3¼.

24th. Morning at 8. Very light running for 30 minutes. Afternoon at 5. The first trial heat for the 1500 meters. Warm-up for 30 minutes. I won in 3:51.6 (59-2:03-3:08). Miles: 6¼. Despite the wind, I was very much at ease, and just rolled along.

25th. Morning at 8. Light running for 15 minutes. Afternoon, the semifinals for the Olympic 1500 meters. Warm-up for 30 minutes. I won in 3:50. (62-2:07-3:09). Miles: 6¼. I felt relaxed.

26th. Morning at 8. Light running for 15 minutes. Afternoon at 4. The Final of the 1500 meters. Warm-up for 30 minutes. I won the Olympic 1500-meter title in 3:45.2 for a new Olympic record (58.2:01.7,-3:03.3). I am inexplicably happy. And I am not tired at all. Miles: 6¼.

27th. Woods. Light running for 30 minutes. Miles: 3¼.

Training of Roger Bannister

As a basis for contrast with all others, we cannot do better than detail the training schedule of Roger Bannister prior to his history-making mile of 3:59.4 on May 6, 1954. For him the key question was, "Within the limitations of time, energy, and interest available to me from my medical school studies and the other interests I consider important, how can I achieve best possible condition for the mile run?" He had time for only about one hour of running five days a week. The slower effects of

Swedish fartlek were impossible. He couldn't even afford the long, easy jogging before and after practice that would have been helpful. All this is the inevitable burden of the real amateur.

Undoubtedly, the most reliable record of Bannister's training during this period, since he does not provide it in his autobiography, is that printed in the *Athletics World,* May 1954, by Ross McWhirter,[16] close friend of Bannister and one of track's most careful statisticians.

Knowing full well the brilliance of Australia's John Landy and that the Californian [surely they meant "Kansan"—J.K.D.] season starts two months before ours, Roger's hopes were never very buoyant. None the less he trained hard through the bleak winter on some of the more obscure of London's 22 loose and dusty tracks. . . . As the plan began to take shape in early April, Roger had not yet produced a ¾-mile time trial (always his barometer of condition) within nine seconds of that fabulous 2:52.9 of July 1952. But actually he had more training and strengthening work under his belt than ever before. . . .

Bannister's training methods are something upon which little has been written because little can be known. This is not only because his four or five times weekly dashes to London's more unfrequented tracks occur at unpredictable times, when he can squeeze in an hour away from St. Mary's hospital. It is also because as a physiologist he has a genuine dislike to mislead fellow athletes into thinking that his purely personal methods of training have any scientifically acceptable basis for anyone else.

Though perhaps more conscious than any other athlete that he is merely groping in an uncharted desert, he in fact uses quite conventional methods. This is not because he for a moment accepts their soundness, but because, in the absence of even a vestige of acceptable evidence, he finds them neither better nor worse than other methods that require longer sessions.

For the last two winters he has come to the conclusion that "interval running" is quite a rewarding system of training because of its punishing intensity and infinite flexibility. He is hoping that it will provide a firmer base upon which competition will have less of a wearing-down effect, though he seems to despair of it ever having the building-up effect that it has on others. (Landy, for example—Ed.) His favorite (if that word can be used) combinations are 15 times 150 yards, 10 times 440 yards, 3 times 880 yards, or 2 times 3 laps. . . . Long, slow warm-ups play no part in his scheme of things. Neither do vitamins nor any other dieting fads.

In the event of Bannister's achieving anything spectacular on the debut of his ninth season at Oxford on May 6th (this will depend largely upon the kindness of the wind), it may be of almost historic importance to list his immediate preparation.

Monday, April 12: 7 times 880 yards at an average of 2:10, with 3 minutes rest between each.

Wednesday, April 14: ¾-mile solo—3:02 (laps 61, 61, 60).

Thursday, April 15: 880 in 1:53 solo.

Friday to Monday, April 16-19: Rock-climbing in Scotland.

Thursday, April 22: 10 times 440 yards (average—58.9). First—56.3; last—56.3.

Saturday, April 24: ¾-mile in 3:00 in company with Chataway.

---

16 Ross McWhirter, "The Long Climb," *Athletics World,* II, No. 5 (May 1954), 35.

Monday, April 26: ¾-mile in 3:14; eight minutes rest; ¾-mile in 3:08.6.
Wednesday, April 28: ¾-mile solo in 2:59.9 in high wind.
Friday, April 30: Final 880-yard time trial—1:54.
May 1 to May 6: Rest. Six days!

Such a training schedule is in almost complete contrast with that which we have already outlined for Peter Snell, who eight years later, at the age of 21, set a world record of 3:54.4, a full five seconds faster than Bannister's "human ultimate" time. We must conclude that intensity of training in which mileage is at minimum levels can produce performances well under four minutes.

But we must also conclude that mileage training such as Snell had in 1961, in which a good proportion of sharpening speed-work is inserted, can produce even faster times. Since we have already outlined the Lydiard system by which Snell was trained and, in the discussion of training for the 880, have included his activities prior to his world-record mile, we shall not repeat them here. Since he was only 21 at the time and apparently far from his sharpest condition, we must assume there is still room for improvement.

Long Distance Running (Two miles—marathon)

To relate the history of long distance running is beyond the scope of this book. We can, however, touch on a few of the high spots which will help us understand the performances of the most outstanding men as well as of the different values they found in mileage training as compared with faster-than-pace work.

The first of these, which predates official records of running, is taken from *Walker's Manly Exercises,* printed in 1856. It tells of the methods of the famous Captain Barclay whose running feats astonished the English-speaking world for decades.

The most effectual process for training appears to be that practiced by Captain Barclay which has not only been sanctioned by professional men, but has met with the unqualified approbation of amateurs. We are here, therefore, almost entirely indebted to it for details. According to this method, the pedestrian [runner], who may be supposed in tolerable condition, enters upon his training with a regular course of physic, which consists of three doses. Glauber's salts are generally preferred; and from one ounce and a half to two ounces are taken each time, with an interval of four days between each dose. After having gone through the course of physic, he commences his regular exercise, which is gradually increased as he proceeds in the training.

When the object in view is the accomplishment of a pedestrian [running] match, his regular exercise may be from twenty to twenty-four miles a day. He must rise at five in the morning, run half a mile at the top of his speed uphill, and then walk six miles at a moderate speed, coming in about seven to breakfast, which should consist of beefsteaks or muttonchops underdone, with stale bread and old beer. After breakfast, he must again walk six miles at a moderate pace, and at twelve lie down in bed without his clothes, for half an hour. On getting up, he must walk four miles, and return by four to dinner, which should also be beefsteaks or muttonchops, with bread and beer, as at breakfast. Immediately after dinner, he must resume his exercise, by running half a mile at the top of his speed, and walking six miles at a moderate pace. He takes no more exercise for that day, but retires to bed about eight; and next morning he proceeds in the same manner.

After having gone on in this regular course for three or four weeks, the pedestrian must take a four-mile sweat, which is produced by running four miles in flannel, at the top of his speed. Immediately on returning, a hot liquor

TABLE 8.5

OUTSTANDING PERFORMANCES
IN THE TWO/THREE-MILE RUNS

Date	2-mile	3-mile	Name	Affiliation	Age	Related Data
1884	9:17.4		Walter G. George	England		
1904	9:09.6*		Alfred Shrubb	England	26	
1926	9:01.4*		Edvin Wide	Sweden		Ran 1500m. in 3:51.8
1931	8:59.6*		Paavo Nürmi	Finland	33	Three-time Olympic champion
1936	8:58.4*		Donald Lash	Indiana	23	Made while still in college
1936	8:57.4*		Gunnar Hockert	Finland		
1937	8:56.0*		Miklós Szabó	Hungary	29	Ran 1500m. in 3:48.6
1939	8:53.2*	13:42.4*	Taisto Maki	Finland		
1942	8:47.8*	13:32.4*	Gunder Hägg	Sweden	24	Best mile time was 4:01.4
1944	8:46.2*		Gunder Hägg	Sweden	26	Set ten world's records (1500m.-5000m.) during period of twelve weeks.
1944	8:42.8*		Gunder Hägg	Sweden	26	
1951	8:54.5		Fred Wilt	Indiana	31	American record
1952	8:40.4*		Gaston Reiff	Belgium	31	1948 5000m. Olympic champion
1954		13:32.2*	Fred Green	England	28	
1954		13:31.2*	Emil Zatopek	Czecho.	32	1952 5000m./10000m. Olympic champion
1954		13:26.4*	Vladimir Kuts	USSR	27	1956 5000m./10000m. Olympic champion
1955		13:23.2*	Chris Chataway	England	24	
1955	8:33.4*	13:14.2*	Sandor Iharos	Hungary	25	Held six world's records (1500m.-10000m.).
1958	8:32.0*	13:10.8*	Albert Thomas	Australia	23	
1961	8:30.0*	13:10.0*	Murray Halberg	New Zealand	28	1960 Olympic 5000m. champion
1962	8:29.8*	13:19.2**	James Beatty	LATC	28	
1963	8:29.6		Michel Jazy	France	27	Best mile: 3:59.8

* Official world record
** Official American record

is prescribed, in order to promote the perspiration; and of this he must drink one English pint. It is termed the sweating liquor, and is composed of one ounce of carraway seed, one ounce of root-liquorice, and half an ounce of candy sugar, mixed with two bottles of cider, and boiled down to one half. He is then put to bed in his flannels, and, being covered with six or eight pair of blankets, and a featherbed, must remain in this state from twenty-five to thirty minutes, when he is taken out, and rubbed perfectly dry. Being then well wrapped in his great coat, he walks out gently for two miles, and returns to breakfast, which, on such occasions, should consist of a roasted fowl. He afterwards proceeds with his usual exercise.

These sweats are continued weekly, till within a few days of the performance of the match; or, in other words, he must undergo three or four of these operations. If the stomach of the pedestrian be foul, an emetic or two must be given about a week before the conclusion of the training. He is now supposed to be in the highest condition.[17]

This all seems very humorous to us, but we should keep in mind the over-all attitudes of the 1850's toward drinking and carousing. Perhaps if we did as much, we might agree that a strong emetic and heavy sweating has its merits. But much more important is the statement that "his regular exercise may be from twenty to twenty-four miles a day. Since training was not on a year-round basis, such mileage is really quite surprising.

Alfred Shrubb

As further support of the mileage theory we have the 1904 training diary of Alfred Shrubb, who won 20 British championships between 1900 and 1904 and held all British records between one and one-half and ten miles.

During the two months prior to his setting a ten-mile record of 50:40.6 and a two-mile record of 9:09.6, Shrubb trained twice a day six days a week. For example his schedule between October 24 and November 1 of 1904 was as follows:

	Morning work	Afternoon work
Mon.	Four miles steady.	Two miles (9:17.8).
Tues.	Did not run.	Ten miles (51:02.0).
Wed.	Four miles steady.	Two miles (9:18.6).
Thurs.	Eight miles steady.	Did not run.
Fri.	Took a rest.	
Sat.	Four miles steady.	Eight miles slow.
Sun.	Took a rest.	
Mon.	Three miles steady.	Ten miles (50.55.0).

Hannes Kolehmainen

There is general agreement that the first great Olympic distance runner was Hannes Kolehmainen of Finland, who in 1912 at Stockholm won the following races within a short period of eight days:

---

[17] *Walker's Manly Exercises* (Philadelphia: John W. Moore, 1856), pp. 72-73.

July   7—Won 10,000-meter heat.
July   8—Won 10,000-meter final. Time: 31:20.8.
July   9—Won 5,000-meter heat.
July 10—Won 5,000-meter final. Time: 14:36.6—new world record.
July 12—First in a 3,000-meter team race. Time: 8:36.8—new world record.
July 15—Won 8,000-meter cross-country race.

In the final of the 10,000, Kolehmainen led throughout and was un-challenged. However, in the final of the 5000-meter run, his opponent was the world-record holder, Jean Bouin of France. Kolehmainen, though leading most of the way, was challenged repeatedly by Bouin and won, only by a desperate effort and a few inches at the tape. The time of 14:36.6 was considered "superhuman" at that time.

Despite this tremendous effort, which must have been a drain on his energy, Kolehmainen was able to come back just two days later with a second world record and first-individual place as a member of his Finnish 3000-meter team, which however failed to qualify. Even this did not satisfy him, however, for on July 15, just eight days after his first race, he again won, this time in the 8000-meter cross-country over a tough hill-and-dale course.

Coming at a time when tiny Finland, with only four million popula-tion, was breaking away from the hard rule of Russia and trying to find status in the world, these tremendous Olympic successes spread a wildfire of enthusiasm for distance running in Finland. Training paths and competitive tracks became a "must" in every tiny village, even north of the arctic circle. Between 1912 and 1956, Finland produced 21 distance champions in the Olympic Games, by far the best record of any nation regardless of size. Of the 18 races run at the 5000- and 10,000-meter distances, Finland won 10, more than all other nations added together. We must add that, unbelievable as it may seem, Koleh-mainen returned to Olympic competition in 1920, eight years later, to run *and win* the Antwerp marathon of over 26 miles in the fine time of 2 hours, 32 minutes, 35.8 seconds.

Paavo Nurmi

It is not surprising, then, that the second great Olympic distance run-ner was also from Finland—the peerless Paavo Nurmi. In the three Olympiads: 1920, 1924, and 1928, Nurmi won a total of six Olympic races, was second in three other races (twice to a Finnish runner), and was first in a team race. He undoubtedly would have added to his laurels in 1932, at the age of 35, had he not been declared a professional for broken-time payments. During his entire career, Nurmi held 19 world records.

Impossible as it seems today, Nurmi trained for and won six races, including two heats, within a period of only six days at the 1924 Games at Paris:

July 8—Won 5000-meter heat.

July 9—Won 1500-meter heat.

July 10—Won the final of the 1500 meters in the world-record time of 3:52.6. Then, only one hour later, won the 5000-meter final, in the Olympic-record time of 14:31.2. No other runner has ever equaled this performance.

July 12—Won the 10,000-meter cross-country race.

July 13—Won first-individual place in a 3000-meter team race.

During the 10,000-meter cross-country race, the temperature was over 90 degrees; of 38 starters, only 15, including Nurmi, finished. Many of the others were hospitalized for heat exhaustion. This ability of Nurmi and other Finnish runners to withstand heat and humidity has been attributed by Ernst Jokl [18] to the Finnish custom of taking Sauna hot baths once or more each week. This view is supported by the related research of Elsworth Buskirk, quoted on pages 29–38.

More than any other runner, Nurmi impressed the world with the importance of even pace in running. Much of his training took place while running to and from his work, a distance of about five miles. By placing posts at regular points and carrying a stop watch he learned to judge his pace perfectly.

It is interesting that Nurmi makes no mention of this much-publicized aspect of his training in the following excerpt written by him, published and later translated by H. Lehmusvuori, and quoted by Fred Wilt:

Ever since my childhood I have had some kind of natural turn for running, particularly for long distance. When I, at the age of 10, joined the club "Toverit" [Pals], which the neighborhood boys had founded, I usually won from the other boys of the same age and this made me more and more interested in running.

In those days there was no special training for the boys' competitions, no warming up, no track shoes or other athletic clothing.

I started really training when I joined the club Turum Urheiluliitto at the age of 15. However, I did not then take part in group training workouts with the other club members, except in gym work a couple of times a week during the winter.

The fact that I had to work at a job as early as my 13th year has undoubtedly had an influence on the development of physical fitness in my boyhood. I was an errand boy of a wholesale firm, and had to deliver goods by pushcart, as was customary in those days. I shed much sweat in taking merchandise hundreds of times up the steeply rising street to the Turku railway station. The strength of my back and legs dates from that time.

---

[18] Ernst Jokl, M.D., "Some Physiological Components of Modern Track Training," *Clinic Notes* (NCAA Track Coaches Association, 1956), p. 226.

From my 15th to my 20th year, my training was very one-sided. I practiced only in summer. Actual winter training was hardly known in those days. In general, I went directly from home to run on the road or in the woods. I had no proper athletic clothing except plimsole shoes [gym slippers]. The ordinary clothing would do. I had no idea of speed-work, so it was no wonder I remained a slow trudger for so many years! The slow progress in my results at that time was entirely due to the lack of speed-work in training!

When I was 21 years old, I entered military service. I then got more time to train and received more information about training at varied speeds, and my condition began to improve. Yet my training was too one-sided until the spring of 1924 [too much long distance running at slow speeds]. Also, between the 1920 Olympic Games in Antwerp and the 1924 Olympic Games in Paris I practiced insufficiently, for I began training each year only at the first of April. Should I have had the benefit of my experiences during the summer of 1924, I could have attained first-rate results much earlier than I did. In those days my workouts consisted mainly of walking on the road or running on the track or cross-country. Some short sprints could be included, but hard runs of 400-600m were totally lacking in the program of training.

Before the spring of 1924 my training program included a daily morning walk followed by daily running practice in the afternoon from April to September.

In May of 1924 I added one more run in the forenoon. My workout program was then as follows: An early morning walk of 10-12km with some sprints included for the purpose of getting as supple as possible for the forenoon run. After the walk I always did some gym work at home and had a bath. After about an hour I started training on the track. As my body was already suitably warmed up by the early morning workout, I could begin to sprint almost immediately. Usually I ran 4-5 × 80-120m sprints. After this a fast 400-1000m for time. Then 3000-4000m at even speed and the last lap always very fast.

My evening workout consisted of cross-country running. The distance ranged from 4000m to 7000m, the last 1000-2000m sprints. This daily training helped me to attain the condition I had at the 1924 Olympic Games in Paris.

Now as I think of my training methods at that time, I admit that it was not the correct training in every respect. In recent years it has become the fashion here to call those methods "lather methods," meaning that they were entirely unnatural. I do not understand how the word "lather methods" has come about, for as a matter of fact, those who get fit by walking "lather" much less than runners. The lack of "lather" [sweat] is the objection to walking as a means of training. The greatest weakness of walking has been that it tends to make you stiff and takes too much time. I admit that you save time by only running during training, but whether or not you enjoy the workouts as much without walking is another matter. Yet I consider walking, mixed with suitable sprints, as quite a useful means of conditioning, for a runner, when it is practiced in a terrain sheltered from the wind, at a suitable speed. I consider this essential for marathon runners. If Zatopek, who gets fit with pure running, has won the marathon at the 1952 Olympic Games in Helsinki, it could be said that I could as well have won the same distance in Paris.

The greatest mistake I made and which was formerly made in general was the one-sided training program [too much long, slow running]. It was not understood then that speed training brings endurance. Instead, the one-sided training took away even what was left of speed. It was just here that the greatest danger of training hikes in winter is located. There were 300-600 sprints included, but there were not enough of them. As I took my training hikes in winter on open, windy roads, my trouble was that I got thoroughly stiff. Therefore I could make a much better effort in warm weather. On the other hand, there was too much training done during the summer. I did not dare to risk a complete resting period, though I should have needed it sometimes.[19]

TABLE 8.6

OUTSTANDING PERFORMANCES IN THE 5000-METER/10,000-METER RUNS

Date	5000m.	10000m.	Name	Affiliation	Age	Olympic Champion
1904	14:48.2*		Alfred Shrubb	England	26	
1911		30:58.8*	Jean Bouin	France		
1912	14:36.6*	31:20.8*	H. Kolehmainen	Finland		1912
1920	14:55.6		J. Guillemot	France		1920
1920		31:45.8	Paavo Nürmi	Finland	22	1920
1924	14:28.2*		Paavo Nürmi	Finland	26	
1924		30:35.4*	Willie Ritola	Finland		1924
1924		30:23.2*	Willie Ritola	Finland		
1924	14:31.2	30:06.2*	Paavo Nürmi	Finland	26	1924 (5000m.)
1928	14:38.0		Willie Ritola	Finland		1928
1928		30:18.8	Paavo Nürmi	Finland	30	1928
1932	14:17.0*		L. A. Lehtinen	Finland		1932
1932		30:11.4	J. Kusocinski	Poland		1932
1936		30:15.4	I. Salminen	Finland		1936
1936	14:22.2		G. Hockert	Finland		1936
1942	13:58.2*		Gunder Hägg	Sweden	24	
1944		29:35.4	V. A. Heino	Finland		
1948		29:59.6	Emil Zatopek	Czecho.	26	1948
1948	14:17.6		Gaston Reiff	Belgium	27	1948
1950		29:02.6*	Emil Zatopek	Czecho.	28	
1952	14:06.6	29:17.0	Emil Zatopek	Czecho.	30	1952
1954		28:54.2*	Emil Zatopek	Czecho.	32	
1954	13:51.6*		Chris Chataway	England		
1955	13:40.6*		Sandor Iharos	Hungary	25	
1956		28:45.6*	Vladimir Kuts	USSR	29	1956
1956		28:30.4*	Vladimir Kuts	USSR	29	
1956	13:36.8*		Gordon Pirie	England	25	
1956	13:39.6		Vladimir Kuts	USSR	29	1956
1957	13:35.0*		Vladimir Kuts	USSR	30	
1960		28:18.8*	P. Bolotnikov	USSR	30	1960
1960	13:43.4		Murray Halberg	N. Zealand	27	1960
1962	13:45.0**		James Beatty	LATC	28	
1962		28:18.2*	P. Bolotnikov	USSR	32	

* Official world record
** Official American record

Emil Zatopek

Our third all-time great Olympic distance runner is Emil Zatopek of Czechoslovakia, who, between 1946 and 1954, dominated distance running

[19] Paavo Johannes Nurmi, a section from *Olympiavoittajien Testamentii (The Testament of the Olympic Champions)* (Helsinki: Suomen Urheiluliitto Ry, 1951) and reprinted in Wilt, *How They Train,* pp. 65-66.

in the world as have few others. In 1948 at the London Olympics, he won the 10,000 meters; in 1952 at Helsinki, the 5000, the 10,000, and the marathon—the first triple of this kind in Olympic history. In each race he smashed the old Olympic record. Amazingly, this was Emil's first marathon, either in competition or training. In 1938, when the world record for 10,000 meters was over 30 minutes, Paavo Nurmi predicted a human ultimate time of 29 minutes, 20 seconds. But between 1950 and 1954, Zatopek lowered the record repeatedly to a final 28 minutes, 54.2 seconds.

FIG. 8.5   Running style in the longer distances. The stride is shorter, not only because the pace is slower, but also as a means to greater economy of effort. Most men first touch the heel of the foot lightly, then roll up on the ball and toes. The kick-up of the trailing foot is less pronounced than in the shorter races. This drawing is from a photo of Zatopek, Slijkhuis, and Reiff during the 1948 Olympic 5000-meter run.

The basic principle of Zatopek's training lay in daily year-round practice. In wind, in snow, in rain, in winter's cold, in summer's heat, Emil trained without exception. When in the country, he trained in the forest or over the fields; if in town or city, he ran on the streets or on the 400-meter track. In bad weather he wore his military shoes; in good, he wore sneakers or tennis shoes. "Inexorable daily training" was his way to success.

In his biography of Zatopek, Frantisek Kozik quotes him as saying,

I took a liking to running because I recognized that it was good for one's health and fitness and gave one more out of life. But I quickly learned that conscientious and systematic training was the only way to improve one's performance. . . .

I aimed consistently at improving my performance. Even in races I never ran against an opponent merely to beat him. When I ran only against time I took every race seriously so that even when I had no rivals to threaten me I was able, on occasion, to break records. . . . I learned from all my victories and defeats and drew the following conclusion: a person shouldn't give up the fight until he's reached the finishing line. If it wasn't for this principle I would hardly have won such a difficult race as the 5000 meters in Helsinki.[20]

One other comment by Kozik is of interest.

An officer's training program is certainly a difficult one and his time for relaxation is well deserved. Even in military camp Emil found time to train, not while on duty but in spare moments. He trained all autumn along the forest paths. When snow began to fall he moved over to the road. . . . In spring he returned to the forest and not even the rain could force him away. He did this only out of enthusiasm and fervor because, after all, nobody could promise that all this effort would bring success. He ran 10 to 16 kilometers [about 10 miles] daily in heavy military boots. "It's best to get used to the worst conditions when training. A real race then seems like a relief." [21]

One of the innovations which Zatopek brought to distance running was that of deliberately uneven pace for the purpose of breaking the rhythm and control of the opposition. His training method of mixed mileage and speed-training allowed him to break down both the stamina and the morale of other runners by repeated spurts for short distances just when awareness of fatigue was highest. When training he habitually increased his speed whenever he felt tired and thus was inured to the hardship of uneven pace when racing.

However, despite these short spurts, his over-all pace by laps was remarkably steady. For example, when Zatopek set a new 10,000-meter record in 1950 of 29:02.6 he recorded, according to *Track and Field News,* the following times for each 1000 meters: 2:58.0—2:53.8—2:54.2—2:55.5—2:55.5—2:54.0—2:53.0—2:56.0—2:55.0—2:47.6. His average time per 1000 meters was 2:55.0.

It may be of value to add that, according to Archie Richardson,[22] Zatopek's pulse rates while training were as follows: before a one-hour run—68pm; just after—168pm; with four-minute rest—108pm; with ten-minute rest—98pm; and after three hours of rest—52pm.

One other firsthand account of Zatopek's training was given by him to Nick Costes, American 1956 Olympic distance runner, and cited by William G. Smith as completely authentic.

"In the year of 1945, most of my work was (1) 10 × 200 meters and 10 × 100 meters, with 100-150-meter slow jogs between the sprints; (2) or 1 × 100 meters, and 20 × 50 meters, with similar jogs; (3) or 6 × 400 meters, and 10 × 200 meters, with 150-200-meter jogs. I added two repetitions to the intervals throughout the year of 1946." As to the speed of the intervals, he would not hazard a guess but admitted that they were quite fast.

"In 1947 I ran (1) 5 × 100-150 meters (150-meter jogs), 20 × 400 meters (again 150-meter jogs between each), and 5 × 100 or 150 meters. The 400

[20] Frantisek Kozik, *Zatopek in Photographs* (Prague: Artia, 1954), p. 7.

[21] *Ibid.,* p. 20.

[22] Archie Richardson, *Archie's Little Black Book* (Hollywood: Rich-Burn Company, 1959), p. 56.

meters were between 67-77 seconds, while the initial and concluding sprints were slightly faster than the average pace of the 400 meters; or (2) 5 × 150 meters, 20 × 250 meters (150-meter jogs between each), and 5 × 150 meters. I alternated these every day.

"The bulk of my running in 1948 was 5 × 200 meters, 20 × 400 meters, and 5 × 200 meters.

"Again in 1949 I maintained the same type of training, averaging about 18 kilometers a day (about 11½ miles). On the 11th of June I set a world record over 10,000 meters in 29:28.2. But Heino, of Finland, the very next month did 29:27.0. I waited until October to step up the training to 5—30—5." During the last week before his attempt to break Heino's mark, he ran as follows: Monday, 30 minutes easy jogging. Tuesday, 10 × 200 meters. Wednesday, and Thursday—the same as Tuesday. Friday and Saturday, rest. On Sunday he ran 29:21.6 for a new world record.

"Throughout the years from 1950 to 1953, I increased the intervals to 5 × 200, 40 × 400, and 5 × 200, averaging more than 18 miles a day. As I neared an important race I would run the following in the last week: Monday, 5—40—5 as fast as possible. Tuesday, 5—20—5 slowly. Wednesday, 5—20—5 fast. Thursday, 5—10—5 slowly. Friday, 5—10—5 fast, but carefully. Saturday easy jogging for four or five kilometers with four fast 50-meter sprints. And Sunday the race."

Incited by the threat of foreign runners like the Englishman Pirie, the Hungarian, Sandor Iharos, and the Russian, Kuts, who were threatening over 10,000 meters, Zatopek launched upon a steady diet of two workouts a day. Beginning in January of 1954 he ran 5—40—5 in the morning, after breakfast was well digested; and in the evening he completed 5—30—5. The runs were interlaced with 100 meters of jogging. In March he increased the intervals to 5—45—5. Finally in April and throughout May he attained 5—50—5. He averaged more than 30 kilometers a day. The times of the intervals were mostly slow and quite irregular. Many were practically "walks" but others sprightly around 65 seconds. The plan was to cover the distance first, then to try to run the intervals faster. But always a week before the race he severely reduced the distance and speeded up the intervals.

Probably no other athlete in the world has ever run so many miles in practice. Nevertheless the records show that Pirie, Kuts, and Iharos, to cite a few, have surpassed Zatopek's best times over five and ten kilometers with training programs which cover about half the distance of the Czech's. Why is this? Zatopek was the first to admit it, "These runners have much more ability than I for they can train at higher speeds and still cover ten to fifteen miles a day." Pirie for example, training more like a middle distance runner, completed 20 × 400 meters in an average of 60 seconds. Iharos, with his two teammates, Tabori and Roszavolgyi, successfully ran 15 × 400 meters in an average of 55 seconds. Kuts's training remains obscure to the western sports world except what was seen at Melbourne. Costes personally saw Kuts do 12 × 400 meters, averaging 67-68 seconds, with a 100-meter fast jog between each. And according to his coach, he had, that day, completed two such workouts—and that Kuts was taking it easy! During a visit to the home of the 1952 Olympic 1500-meter champion, Josy Barthel in Luxembourg, he told the author he had seen Kuts run 10 × 400 meters, averaging 61 seconds with only 100 meters of fast jogging between each. Zatopek answers the question of the training methods of others, "There are certainly various ways to success, but training and more training must be the basis of all." [23]

---

[23] Smith, *op. cit.*

Vladimir Kuts

Vladimir Kuts was Zatopek's successor in long distance running, and there are those who would argue that he was his superior. Not only did this 29-year-old sailor from the Ukraine "devastate" the field of long distance runners in the 1956 Melbourne Olympics, he first set an Olympic record for the 10,000 of 28 minutes, 45.6 seconds by running the first 5000 meters in 14:06.8, just one-fifth second from the time for Zatopek's 1952 Olympic record for the 5000-meter run! Six days later he won the 5000 meters in a time of 13:39.6, over 26 seconds better than the old record!

Again we are indebted to William G. Smith:

> Few athletes have shown the perseverance and single-mindedness in their approach to sport that can match those of Kut. In an article appearing in *British Sport* magazine, his wife Raissa states, "I cannot remember a single occasion when Vladimir has started his training even 10 or 15 minutes late. In all types of weather—rain, bitter cold or intense heat—he trains regularly." . . .
>
> Said the Russian Olympic coach of Kuts's victories at Melbourne, "I believe that the stubbornness and self-sacrifice with which he had prepared for the Olympic victory were invincible." [24]

Kuts's Olympic victories were in part due to the changing tempo, the sudden bursts of speed with which he demoralized the great English runner, Pirie. These were very tough on Kuts also, but he had prepared for them physically and mentally by practicing just such bursts throughout his spring and summer training. Often Kuts's training begins and ends with calisthenics. This is typical of Russian training methods which place more emphasis than others upon body strength and flexibility. We should also note that Kuts made almost daily use of a masseur. Pirie relates that this masseur told him, "If Kuts were not to have a daily massage he would never be able to maintain such a tough training program."

Kuts based his training on that of Zatopek. Like Zatopek, he trained a lot through woods and fields with many fast-slow runs at varied distances from 200 meters to 2000 meters. His competitive racing featured running at a changing tempo, physiologically unsound but more upsetting to his rivals than to Kuts since he had trained that way. Throughout the spring months, Kuts trained in different places to break the monotony: parks, forest, fields, and rarely in the stadium. For example, after warming up and gymnastics, he might run: (1) 8 × 100 meters—gymnastics; (2) 20 × 200 meters (28-29 seconds); (3) 5 × 400 meters (68 seconds); (4) 15 minutes of easy running, springing from balls of the feet.

---

[24] *Ibid.*

Courtesy of *Track and Field News*

The 1956 Olympic 5000 meters at Melbourne. Leading, Vladimir Kuts, U.S.S.R.; second, Gordon Pirie, Great Britain; third, Derek Ibbotson, Great Britain. This picture shows the entire tactic of the race. Kuts led throughout and tried on numerous occasions to break contact with the field. Pirie, Ibbotson, and Chataway (not shown) tried doggedly to maintain it. At 4000 meters, Kuts, who had already won the 10,000 meters, broke away with a lap in 64.8 seconds and a winning time of 13:39.6, a new Olympic record.

Summer training (an average week)

Mon. In stadium. In the morning slow running and gymnastics, lasting 40 minutes. In the afternoon as follows: First, 35 minutes of warming up. Second, 5 × 80-100 meters, each done at an accelerated pace. Third, *running at a changing tempo:* 3 × 200 meters (each between 27 and 28 seconds) with 100 meters of jogging between each of these fast runs. Next, 15 × 400 meters with the runs to be done in this fashion: the first 11 runs at a time of 64-65 seconds, the next three at 67-68 seconds, and the last one at 63 seconds. Trot or jog 100 meters between each of the 400 meters. Fourth, 15 minutes of springy, balls-of-the-feet running. Fifth, close with gymnastic practice.

Tues. In forest. Work out only in morning: Run for 40 minutes right across the forest *with a changing tempo.*

Wed. In stadium. In the morning: 45 minutes of special warming-up work (slow running, and general and special gymnastics). In the afternoon as follows: First, 35 minutes warming up. Second, accelerated running, 5 × 150 meters. Third, running *with a changing tempo:* 5 × 400 meters (at 61-64 seconds); 2 × 1200 meters (each 3:12 to 3:16); and 3 × 400 meters (65-66 seconds each). Fourth, 10 minutes of springy, balls-of-the-feet running.

Thurs. In forest. One and one-half hours running *with a changing tempo:* interspersing the steady running with accelerated zestful bursts of from 100 to 600 meters. Second, 15 minutes of special gymnastics.

Fri. In forest or in the stadium. In the morning (in forest): slow running, followed by gymnastics. In the afternoon (in stadium): First, 25 minutes of warming up. Second, accelerated running, 3 × 200 meters. Third, running with a changing tempo: 6 × 100 meters fast, and after each run cover 600 meters slowly (2:42-2:46). Fourth, 15 minutes of springy, balls-of-the-feet running.

Sat. Active rest.

Sun. In forest. 30 minutes of special gymnastics in the morning. Work as follows in afternoon: First, 35 minutes of warming-up work with special gymnastics for a runner. Second, accelerated running, 5 × 150 meters. Third, running *with a changing tempo:* 3 × 1600 meters (4:40-4:47 each), and 6 × 400 meters (65-67 seconds each). Between each fast run jog 100 meters. Fourth, 10 minutes of springy, balls-of-the-feet running. Fifth, warming down.[25]
[All italics mine—J.K.D.]

Murray Halberg

Athough his victory in the 5000 meters and fifth place in the 10,000 meters at the 1960 Olympic Games at Rome were not comparable to the performances of the select group of Kolehmainen, Nurmi, Zatopek, and Kuts, I find it hard to by-pass the great running of Murray Halberg of New Zealand. At the age of 29 in 1963, Halberg had held world records for both the two-mile and three-mile runs, had run 3:57.5 for the mile at Dublin when Elliott ran his amazing 3:54.5, was holder of five New Zealand running records, and all this despite the handicap of a serious injury on the day after he was 17 while playing rugby. A large blood clot formed around the heart; for days he was near death and was fortunate to escape with a paralyzed left arm.

---

[25] Wilt, *How They Train,* p. 83.

In 1954, Murray came to the attention of the American public by running a mile in New Zealand in 4:04.4. In April he was invited to the Ben Franklin mile at the Pennsylvania Relays to run against three champions: Fred Wilt, Horace Ashenfelter (1952 Olympic 3000-meter steeplechase champion), and Mal Whitfield (1948 and 1952 Olympic 800-meter champion, and self-confessed seeker after the first four-minute mile). Despite his inexperience, Murray took the lead at the gun and led by 15 yards at the 440 and by 50 yards at the finish in 4:09.0.

It was at about this time that his coach, Arthur Lydiard, was quoted as saying Halberg would be setting world records by the time he was 27. In 1961, at the age of 27, he did just that with records of 8:30.0 for the two-mile and 13:10.0 for the three-mile.

At Rome in 1960, Halberg won the 5000 meters the hard way—he and Lydiard felt it was the only sure way—by jumping the field with a full three laps to go and pouring it on right through to the finish line. Lydiard believes he was still strong enough to have won the 10,000 meters two days later, but he had achieved his primary goal in becoming Olympic champion, and his heart was not in the second race.

9

How to Organize Your Own Training System

The purpose of this book is to help you improve your performance as a runner or a coach, not by telling you of my own well-rounded and sound training system but by explaining as clearly and completely as I can all the training systems that have gained world-wide acceptance, and, in addition, as much of the related physiological and psychological principles as space will permit.

This has been the task of the first eight chapters. They do not tell you directly or specifically how to train, but they do provide a foundation of knowledge on which you can build your own training system. I do not know how you will proceed to do this. Your own experience and attitudes, your own situation in terms of climate, terrain, competitive schedule, time available for practice, or the maturity of your runners will determine that in a way different from the systems of Holmer, Gerschler, Cerutty, or Lydiard, no matter how sound each of these may be.

I do not even know specifically how I would organize my own system, for that would depend on the same *uniqueness* of climate, terrain, and so forth that now faces you in your situation. One would not be likely

Some of the material in this chapter is from J. Kenneth Doherty, *Modern Track and Field* (2nd ed.; Englewood Cliffs, N. J.: Prentice-Hall, Inc., 1963), pp. 216-22. Reprinted by permission of the publisher.

to do well with fartlek, no matter how cleverly organized on paper, if located in a large city with no open areas for free running. Nor would one do well with Lydiard's system if time for training is confined to a few months of a few years. In summary, the "what" of my training would depend not only on a theoretical soundness and its success as used by others, but also upon the particular where-when-how-and-whom of my own unique situation.

I do know that there are certain crucial questions I would ask and that my own answers would decide my system of training. Among these would be the following:

The terrain factor. Are there one or more terrains near at hand that are both physically and mentally challenging for running? What are their natural features that might be used to achieve the basic goals of training? A sand dune was unrelated to running until Cerutty used it for his resistance training. A long hill can be just another hill, or it can be a special hill on which a Lydiard can do his valuable speed hill-training. Snow or mud can be an excuse for not running, or it can be an opportunity for basic training as was done by Zatopek and Hägg. Is a long inclined ramp in a stadium really so inferior to a sand dune in its training effects?

The time factor. *Years.* Over what period of years must my training system develop these runners? If I am concerned with their entire careers over some ten years or more, if I wish physical and mental maturity to coincide with motivational development, then I can emphasize the sounder and more gradual approaches of fartlek and Lydiard training. If I am concerned with only the four years of school or college racing, then I must adopt a more intensive training method and include speed training and interval training much earlier in each year's program.

Hours and days. Amateur running is avocational, that is, it is limited to the few hours left over from job or studies. Do these few hours total as many as three per day, seven days a week, 52 weeks a year, as was the case with Lydiard's men? Then I can consider Lydiard's system. Or are they limited to but 90 minutes from and back to the locker room on only five days per week and about 32 weeks per year? Then I cannot consider Lydiard's system and must choose one of greater intensities of running in less time. Am I certain that only these few hours are available? What about individual running before breakfast or after dark?

The competitive factor. Can I adjust my year's schedule of competitions in terms of the needs and readiness of my runners? Can I keep team scores at a secondary level and be concerned primarily with individual development? Can I consider cross-country as primarily developmental for endurance running, or is its team record of wins and losses all-important? Can I concentrate upon a few *big races* in each year's program and use all others as developmental races for them? Will my club or school schedule competitions in greater number and earlier than aids the soundest development of my runners? All these questions will influence how we train.

The individual factor. What is the maturity of these runners? What is their potential and their ambition for the future? How far am I justified in pushing my belief that running is a matter of great importance? What if they and their parents feel that running should be a matter of recreation and low-level development? If these runners are in their lower teens, how much mileage, how much intensity, how much competition should be required of them? In terms of their maturity, will they develop more from the free running of fartlek or the measured and closely supervised running of interval training?

The coaching factor. What kind of coach am I? Better, what kind of leader am I, and how can I improve my quality of leadership? I can develop leadership only within my own range of personality, experience, and attitude. What is that range? When I read the chapter on the role of the coach, did I seem to resemble Holmer, or Gerschler, or Cerutty, or Stampfl, or Igloi, or Lydiard? How I lead will inevitably influence the kind of training system I devise. The kind of system I devise will inevitably influence how I shall be able to lead.

The motivation factor. Considering the discussions in Chapter 1 on why men run and stop running, as well as the implications of Fig. 6.1, page 27, and principles 13, pages 140–144, and 18, page 148, what level of motivation can I establish within my training system? What are the attitudes of my community, of my school or club toward competitive running? How can I raise their levels of enthusiasm? The answers to such questions will determine my system and its success just as vitally as will the terrain or the time available for practice.

Having organized and integrated the answers to all such questions, I would then begin to pinpoint both the kind of running and the proportion of each kind I would use. And finally I would consider the details of the following practice procedures and choose those that fit into my system.

Time-running Procedures

Discussion. Though it makes good common sense, time running is not as commonly practiced as its values warrant. When a beginning runner first reports, or when experienced runners start a new year, it is both safe and sound to run slowly and steadily for a certain short period of time. Mileage is of little concern and the pace must be easy. As soon as the boy's muscles and tendons (the first concern) can handle that length of time, he should increase it. Arthur Lydiard urges that this be continued on a slow-pace time basis until the boy can run enjoyably for two hours.

That such a method provides a firm and injury-proof foundation for all that follows is certain. Great coaches agree that the all-important essential of distance training is the enjoyment of daily, progressive training. Time running is the best possible method to both enjoyment and progress.

The Lydiard System Procedures

Discussion. The Lydiard system, as we have already summarized it, contains a great variety of practice procedures which the sound coach would do well to consider. Marathon training, as it is sometimes called, is but one portion of these.

To base one's organization of training upon Lydiard's ideas is to move up a long 30-degree slope of progress in running. The less the incline of that slope, the broader the base of endurance that is established; the broader the base, the higher one can climb safely and surely. Since such a long gradual slope tends to be boring, Lydiard has devised a series of practice and competitive procedures which keep things interesting. At any point of the climb, when judgment or the necessities of competition require, the coach can shift to the higher angled procedures of interval training. Now the runner climbs upward faster; but keep in mind that the height to which he can climb is limited by the width of the foundation of both time and mileage on which that speed is based.

In fact, one could evaluate the Lydiard system by considering it a time-distance system in which the time factor in months and years of training is equally important to the distance or mileage factor. One cannot cover the miles of marathon training unless time—about eleven months of time out of each year—is first provided. Lydiard plans four months or more of training before the first cross-country race; six months or more, before the first track race. In addition, the early competitions are considered training trials—primarily important as they advance the runner toward his main goal, the one or two *big races.*

Before adopting the more complex and therefore more exciting procedures of interval training, the coach is urged to study carefully those of the Lydiard system.

Fartlek or Speed-play Procedures

Discussion. The principles and procedures of fartlek have already been discussed in sufficient detail to illustrate the many ways it can be used. Fartlek means to play at speed freely. Do just that, wherever and

FIG. 9.1 Exercises for increased speed in running. These are used primarily in training for the sprints and 440, but, if done carefully and gradually, they could also be of value in long distance training when increased speed is desired.

Squat and Leap

Body Flexion

Run Upstairs

Toe Bounce

Thigh Lift (rubber bands)

Bicycle

Hurdle Stretch

Sprint Uphill

Toe Raise

Thigh Lift

Bicycle

Weight Drag

High Bounding

Squat

Skip Rope

Thigh Lift

Walk in Snow

Hamstring Lift

however the challenges of speed may impel you to go. We have emphasized that there are no limitations of terrain as long as it calls for hard running and, of course, as long as its hardships do not involve danger of injury. There are no limitations on how much you run, as long as you do not do more than you are prepared to handle. Over years of effort, the ability of men to adapt themselves to the stress of running is truly amazing.

One important caution: neither fartlek nor any sound system of training will allow you to "go as you please," since you need a carefully planned program of progress and a means of checking precisely the degree of that progress. The absence of a program and checks is a weakness of fartlek as commonly used. The checks are made up of an exact dosage of work under exactly laid out conditions. These conditions can be on a sand dune, on a stretch of beach, over a measured woods path or they can be on a quarter-mile of cinder track. Perhaps for white mice or other animals, better running is the result of more running without restriction, but for the human animal, better running is the result of more intelligent running, more running according to a wise plan. "Know yourself, know what you are doing, and why you are doing it" applies even more to fartlek than to other systems, simply because it is so easily overlooked.

Interval Training Procedures

Discussion. The procedures of interval training are as variable as the ingenuity of runners' and coaches' minds can make them. But there are important purposes behind the varied approaches. The reason something is done is almost as important as what is done. Selection should follow purpose.

When an interval training program is first planned, a question always arises as to just where to start in terms of the time for each run. Usually this can be decided upon the basis of last year's experience and on the progression of times planned for the coming months. However, when a new coach or a beginning runner has no such basis for planning, he is often uncertain just where to begin. To base interval times on a man's best time for a short distance, such as a 440 or 220, is unsound. True, a man who has greater speed can run one or two or even three intervals at a given pace more easily than one who is slower. But when he runs long distances, as in 20 × 440, this advantage is of little significance.

We have emphasized the all-importance of stamina through mileage during the first months. As long as his pace is slow enough to encourage long mileage, a man will not go far wrong. Far better to begin at too slow a pace than too fast. He then has the sense of progress, rather than of failing and starting over again.

However when the time comes when he wishes to plan a progressively faster schedule of 440's, 330's, or 220's, he will want something more specific. Stampfl begins his progression schedules for 440 yards for half-milers at 66 seconds, for milers at 70 seconds, and for three milers at 75 seconds. But in each case he warns that these schedules are for runners that are mature and very fit. Bill Bowerman of Oregon lists 70 seconds as the slowest time on his chart shown on page 109. But he also works with older and well-conditioned men.

For the beginning runner we suggest 90 seconds for 440's, 60 seconds for 330's and 35 seconds for 220's. He may protest that these times are too slow, but the nettled feeling he will have at your underestimation of his condition will help build his ego.

1. *For mileage-endurance.* Total mileage per workout is the first and the most essential element in endurance training. All systems begin with an emphasis on mileage; some continue with it throughout the year, adding speed and pace only in the final months. The fixed elements are distance to be run, recovery interval, pace, and relaxation. The variable is number of repetitions. For example, a run of 440 yards in 75 seconds is alternated with a recovery interval of relaxed jogging, and repeated as many times as condition permits. Mileage is the main concern and so there is no need to be inflexible as to a fixed distance or time. "Go-as-you-please" as long as you please to increase gradually the total mileage as months go by.

2. *For speed-endurance.* As the competitive season approaches, the runner may wish to increase the speed at which he can easily handle mileage. This is especially true in the 440- and 880-yard runs. Fixed elements are distance to be run, recovery interval, relaxation, and number of repetitions. The variable is increasing pace. For example: 220 yards to be run again when the pulse returns to about 110, for a total of six times (for 880 men) or 12 times (for milers), but always within the limits of good control and relaxation. As the weeks go by, the pace at which these 220's are run is gradually increased.

3. *For minimum rest-endurance.* The recovery interval is gradually diminished. A tough program in terms of willed control. Fixed elements are distance, pace, number, relaxation. The variable; recovery interval. The example: 6 × 220 at 30 seconds, relaxed, with a decreasing period of recovery between. One might decrease the recovery period as one's rate of cardiorespiratory recovery improves, but this would be a slow progression. Pace is slower than competitive pace. (See Item 7, below.) Since this type of workout usually comes rather late in the year, men use it as an intensive trial, driving into the next run as soon as their pounding hearts permit. However, as always, runs should be made within the limits of control and relaxation.

4. *For speed-minimum rest-endurance.* This follows the same pattern as Item 3, except that the fixed pace is several seconds faster than one's planned competitive pace. It therefore combines endurance, speed, and minimum recovery interval.

5. *For pace-endurance.* Used to develop coordination and control at the specific pace at which one expects to run competitively. The fixed elements are distance, competitive pace, recovery interval, and relaxation. The number of repetitions is the variable. (Note: This is identical to Item 1, above, except that the pace must now be that of competition. In some cases, the number of repetitions could also be fixed.) Example: 10 × 440 yards with 4 minutes interval, relaxed, at competitive pace.

6. *For relaxation-endurance.* The degree of ease or sense of certain control is the criterion for judgment. Fixed elements: distance, pace, number, interval. Variable: increasing ease and sureness of control. Example: 6 × 220 at 30 seconds with three-minute recovery, employing a style showing complete relaxation and an attitude of quiet fortitude.

7. *For pace-minimum rest-endurance.* This is the same as Item 3 except that the pace is that of intended competition. The total mileage of the runs should exceed the competitive distance. Example for milers: 5 × 440 at competitive pace, relaxed, but with decreasing recovery intervals.

8. *For steady running-endurance.* One important criticism of interval training is that its runs are so short that one's feelings of fatigue and therefore the need for willed control are at a minimum. In contrast, in competition, one must run steadily for the full distance, with no stopping or easing of pace to recover. Some interval trainers therefore increase the length of the distance each time to a larger fraction of the competitive distance: one-half, three-quarters, one and one-quarter, or even one and one-half the distance. The variable can be either the number or the pace or the interval and the fixed elements will vary accordingly. An example for early season when mileage is the primary issue would be three-quarters competitive distance at a slow relaxed pace with recovery jogging until the pulse returns to about 110; and then an increase of the number as improved condition permits.

9. *For uneven pace-endurance.* Uneven running is a part of competitive running. One must move up to maintain contact. Crowded fields prevent steady running. Experienced men such as Zatopeg, Kuts, or Ibbotson put on bursts of speed in order to upset the poise and ease of pace of their opponents. Sometimes an entire lap will be at a greatly increased speed (Elliott and Halberg). Such uneven running can be practiced in various ways: by doing burst or wind-sprints for

short distances or by running the first half of each distance slowly but the last half, fast. (Called slow-fast running by some coaches.)

10. *Funnel system.* The distance of each run is increased over that of the preceding run. Example: 100-150-200-250-300-350-440-660-880. This can be varied by one's ingenuity. Or it can be repeated in reverse: 100-200-300-400-300-200-100. Or, another example would be 3 × 220, 2 × three-quarters competitive distance, 3 × 220.

11. *Interval training in sets.* Most of the items listed above can be modified so they will be run in sets of two to five runs each. Example: 3 × 220 at 30 seconds with three-minute recovery intervals, followed by 15-20 minutes of recovery jogging, and all this repeated again and again. There are many variations.

12. *Fartlek-interval training.* Interval training is traditionally run on a flat track. But fartlek's infinite variety of terrain could be added to its virtue of infinite variety of workout and thus provide even greater interest and value. Interval training, in the formal sense, must involve measurement of distance, pace, interval, and number; without such measurement, it would be fartlek. But what's in a name?

Other Procedures

1. *"Circulators."* A good warm-up procedure. Have from six to 12 men run in line around the track at a rather slow pace. The last man should always be coming up to take the lead. Warn the men against accelerating the pace.

2. *"Follow-the-leader," endurance work.* Put a dozen or so men under a leader who will determine when, where, and for what distance they will sprint. Assign two managers, one to handle the starts, the other to judge finishes. After a proper warm-up, the leader designates a start and a finish line at whatever distance he may wish. The manager at the finish picks only the last two or three men from each sprint group and tells them to jog and keep jogging together on the grass. After four or five such sprints, the best men are excused to go ahead with their individual assignments. The others who have been jogging on the grass are brought back into the game and the whole process is repeated.

3. *Competitive pace work.* (a) Run a group of a dozen or more men together, for relatively slow 220's or 440's at an assigned pace. All men will try to hit the assigned pace. Time the last man and the first man. If the last man is closer to the assigned time, cut the first two men out of the competition; if the first man is closer, cut the last two men off. Be sure to assign something to do to those who have been cut off from the competition; otherwise, they'll be wasting time. (b) Assign different

paces to different individual runners or pairs of runners, all for the same distance. Establish a penalty for missing pace, e.g., all men missing the pace by more than two seconds must keep trying until they run two consecutive races within one second of the assigned time.

4. *Competitive pace relays.* Select men for relay teams in which paired men run the same distance but not at the same speed. Assign a speed for each man on each team. The winning team is the one for which the total error from the assigned pace is the least. Obviously, it will be necessary to have two watches for each team so that each man will be individually timed.

5. *Pace work.* (a) Run the full distance by running the first half of the race at definitely less than racing speed, but picking up the second half to the pace to be run the following week-end. Repeat. (b) Run several times at three-fourths the distance. Run the first one-half at less than racing speed, but pick up on the last one-fourth. Finish up each race feeling that the full distance could have been covered. This workout is very valuable in placing emphasis upon the third quarter of a race and upon decreasing the speed of the first half of each race.

6. *Time trial.* (a) Run for time at greater than distance. Usually this is done at one and one-half times the distance: three-fourths of a mile for 880 men, one and one-half miles for milers, and three miles for two-milers. This method is occasionally used for time trials during the early season when confidence in being able to carry the full distance is lacking. It is sometimes used for pace work by having the final half of the distance run at racing speed. (b) Run three-fourths of the distance for time, all-out. (c) Run three-fourths of the distance at the pace at which the full distance will be run on the coming Saturday. Rest one minute, then run the final one-fourth all-out, or run a series of sprints. (d) Run the full distance to be run on Saturday, but run the first three-fourths at a slower-than-race speed, going all-out on the final one-fourth. This may help an inexperienced runner by giving him an idea of the distance. Under ordinary conditions, few coaches believe in running the actual distance all-out in practice. (e) Run time trials in which, for example, 880 men and milers race against each other for three-fourths of a mile. Much friendly rivalry can be established at these in-between distances, and everyone will benefit from it.

7. *Competitive relays.* These are ordinary relays in which paired men run all-out at the distance assigned to them.

8. *Repeated fast work on the track.* The distance to be covered, the speed of running, and the time interval of jogging or walking will all be specified by the coach according to his intended outcomes for the day. If endurance is the primary factor, times will be slower and the rest interval shorter.

9. *Endless relays.*   This excellent workout has in it all the ingredients of a well-rounded practice. Two or three relay teams of four, five, six, or seven men each are organized by the coach. Men should be paired off in terms of ability and told to run varying distances, i.e., the first pair will run 220's at :26 each; the second pair 220's at :28 each; the third, 440's at :60 each, and so on. Each pair will run two or three or four times, as the coach may wish. If three times, the first two will be on a pace basis, and therefore the teams will keep close together during these early runs. As the No. 1 runners come up for their third run, competition begins and the men go all-out.

For best results, two watches are needed for each team, for all runs should be timed in order to get the most benefit and the most fun out of them. Each man runs more than once and the last man passes the baton back to the first man without any halt in proceedings.

It will be noted that such a session includes pace judgment, endurance-work, speed-work, racing tactics, and baton practice. In the early season, use fewer men on each team but assign a slower pace throughout. It is then more of an endurance session. In the later season, increase the number of men on each team, making the rest period longer, but speed up the pace assignments. It then becomes a real speed workout.

10. *Sprint work.*   This consists of all-out sprinting from the starting blocks at short distances of from 30 to 150 yards.

11. *Ins-and-outs.*   While running a long distance either on or away from the track, alternate fast 220's or 330's (ins) with slow 220's and 330's (outs). Usually these are untimed and unmeasured distances. This is one form of fartlek.

12. *Wind-sprints or pick-ups.*   There are many variations of these. A man repeatedly sprints or "picks-up" until he is winded. For example a series of 220's in which the first 180 yards of each is at three-quarters speed, whereas the last 40 yards are at full sprinting speed.

13. *Four-fourths of one's competitive distance.*   Establish (1) a distance which is always one-fourth the competitive distance and (2) a pace that is faster than competitive pace. The number of runs is always four. Competition lies in seeing who can run these four-fourths in the least total time. For example, milers would run 4×440 at 63 seconds in what total time? Example for two-milers: 4×880 at 2:30 seconds in what total time? Men enjoy the challenge of this workout.

14. *Relaxed running over-distances.*   Run more than the racing distance (one and one-quarter to one and one-half the distance, for example) at only slightly less than racing pace. Maintain the pace but, above all, maintain relaxation and willed control.

10 Racing Tactics

General Considerations

Perhaps the most intriguing, yet at the same time most tragic, aspect of track athletics is racing tactics. A slight hesitancy here, a single step to the inside there, a few seconds' miscalculation of the right pace or of the timing of the final kick—any of these or other seemingly minor errors will throw away months and years of careful preparation and sacrifice. The race is not always to either the swift or the strong, but to the clever, the skillful, and the constantly wary.

The tactical possibilities in distance racing are numerous. As in a game of checkers, for every move there is a countermove; for every attack there is a defense. The use of tactics assumes similar physical abilities; otherwise there would be no need to parry the moves of a competitor. It requires mental resourcefulness, determination, courage, and quickness to take advantage of every opening, however brief.

1. In competitive running, Socrates' instruction "Know thyself" must always be supplemented by "Know thy opponent." In addition, it is important to know or at least judge what your opponent knows about

---

Some of the material in this chapter is from J. Kenneth Doherty, *Modern Track and Field* (2nd ed.; Englewood Cliffs, N. J.: Prentice-Hall, Inc., 1963), pp. 114-16, 223-29. Reprinted by permission of the publisher.

249

you and your probable tactics, for that will determine his tactics and therefore yours. Moves and countermoves should be attempted for the most part, of course, by mature and experienced runners. Bannister tells in *The Four Minute Mile* how, three weeks before meeting Landy at Vancouver, he tried to impress Landy with his great finishing speed by deliberately holding back in the British championship mile and then sprinting an amazing :53.8 last quarter, "almost as fast as I can run a flat 440 yards!" Apparently this bit of tactical showmanship reached Landy; at least he ran the first half at Vancouver in 1:57.2—too fast for either runner. At this point Bannister had lost the advantage of contact, but he had planned that this would happen and psychologically he was still "connected." He felt he had forced Landy to run too fast and in the last half held the upper hand. In races, a feeling such as this often makes the whole difference.

Zatopek's grasp of psychology and languages gave him a tactical advantage on more than one important occasion. In 1952, for example, in the Helsinki Olympic marathon, he carried on this conversation with the fine English marathoner, Jim Peters, in about the middle of the race:

Zatopek: The pace? Is it good enough?
Peters: Pace too slow.
Zatopek: You say too slow. Are you sure the pace is too slow?
Peters: Yes.[1]

Peters later related that actually he felt all in, whereas Zatopek looked "as calm and unruffled as if he were sitting down at a picnic." Thus, aside from improving his knowledge of good marathon pace, he was able to assess his rival's condition. Having satisfied himself that Peters was tired, the way was clear for him to run on and win his third gold medal.

To give one more example, in the 5000- and 10,000-meter runs at the Melbourne Olympics, Kuts first broke away from the field by setting too fast a pace, then upset his greatest rival Pirie by repeated bursts of sprinting. This was a physical waste and a mental torture to Kuts as well as to Pirie, but the difference lay in the fact that Kuts had planned such tactics for months and had inured both his body and his mind so they could maintain control. Without similar preparation, Pirie finally broke and finished third.

2. All planning must carefully consider the distance to be run, the size of the track, the number of competitors, their over-all abilities, and the specific abilities of the best runners. Planning is particularly important indoors, where straightaways are so short, position so essential, and opportunities for gaining the latter so few and so quickly lost. Even as

---

[1] J. H. Peters, *In the Long Run* (London: Cassell & Company, Ltd., 1955), p. 110.

experienced a runner as Don Gehrman suffered his first loss in the mile during the 1951 indoor season by drowsing momentarily in second position behind Stewart Ray while Fred Wilt jumped him from behind with one and one-quarter laps to go. The three yards gained thereby were enough to take the winning medal.

3. Plans must always be flexible and include at least one alternative. Not only are track conditions uncertain, but it should be assumed that the opponent is at least equally cunning. Obviously, crowded indoor tracks make all plans most precarious.

4. Once plans are made, a quiet belief in them will put the mind and emotions at ease. Worry during the few days prior to a race is certainly useless and can be a serious factor in creating fatigue. Many a man has fussed and fumed for days over his coming race and so drained his nervous energy and will to win that he made effective performance impossible.

5. The man with the best sprint is more likely to get the pole lane at the start as well as the gold medal at the finish. The pole lane, or at least a good early position, is especially vital to indoor running and to shorter runs, such as the half-mile. Therefore, practice starting with the sprinters as a premeet tactic.

6. All tacticians must agree that the man who makes the best final time is always the winner. To get out in front as soon as conditions permit and stay there all the way is certainly the simplest and sometimes the best of all tactics. However, it is a tactic in which oneself is one's strongest opponent. When heading the pack, awareness of oncoming danger and doubt as to one's ability to meet it tends to be in the very forefront of one's mind. Only by calm control of such fears can a man win a victory over himself and his opponents.

Tactics When Setting the Pace

1. The primary problem, as well as the primary opportunity, in setting the pace lies in the third phase of the race, when fatigue dulls the will and muscles feel heavy and lethargic. This is the time when the ordinary runner allows the pace to falter and lags behind, while the real champion pacemaker pours it on. This is the time when those who have filled their reservoirs of power through daily hardship in practice are able to release them in competition. Men like Zatopek and Halberg and Elliott repeatedly followed this tactic. In September 1960, *Track and Field News* reported,

The Olympic 1500 meters is traditionally a tactical race, but Herb Elliott couldn't care less about tradition. The hook-nosed, stoop-shouldered 22-year-old in the green and yellow stripes of Australia knows only one tactic—to begin, in the third quarter of his race, a relentless, man-killing drive, powered by animal strength, thousands of miles of punishing training, and a brain insensitive to the subtleties of foot racing. Herb Elliott runs to win. . . .[2]

2. An even pace makes for the best time, for it implies maximum physical efficiency, rhythm, and relaxation. However, special conditions make such a pace difficult, unwise, and often impossible:

A crowded field on an indoor track may force a man to go out fast, to take an early lead, and therefore to adopt an altogether too rapid early pace.

An opponent with a strong finish may demand a first half that is unusually fast and that may therefore discourage the others. Such an effort is likely to prove successful only against an easily disheartened competitor.

Almost universal practice sets a pace for the 880 in which the first 440 is 3 or even 4 seconds faster than the second 440. However, competitive racing conditions determine this difference, not economy of physical energy.

In actual competition an even pace seldom occurs, for excess nervous energy and the fight for position hurry the first phase of the race and feelings of fatigue slow the third phase. However, other factors being equal, every effort should be made to avoid such inefficient running.

3. In a large field of runners, the man leading at the end of the first 440 of the mile or the two-mile is certain to have gone too fast for an even pace and probably has paid too great a price for his leading position. This is particularly true outdoors, where longer straightaways make a late play for position a wiser plan. Indoors, careful consideration must be given to the relative values of the best position and a more even pace. Being well back in the field may involve a better pace, but this advantage is often lost in the attempt to gain position later in the race. However, experienced and mature runners follow this method almost invariably when running in a crowded field. They begin to move up after the first 880 and then pour it on after the mile, when men are tired and less combative. Such a practice is questionable in the mile indoors, but usually effective in the two-mile both indoors and out.

4. To discourage one's opponents, it is usually wise to pick up speed a little when a lead is challenged, but a marked change of pace can occur only once or twice without affecting endurance.

5. The use of pacemakers is a questionable practice at best, but it is certainly unethical when it deliberately slows or blocks an opponent's progress. In this case it should bring disqualification.

[2] Cordner Nelson, "Elliot Massacres Field," *Track and Field News*, XIII, No. 8 (September 1960), 7.

6. Leading is more fatiguing (at least psychologically) to most athletes than following.

7. Once in the lead, the runner should realize he is now where he planned to be and should confidently search for rhythm, smoothness, and relaxation.

8. If passed when leading, the prospective winner should immediately move a half lane out to avoid being boxed.

FIG. 10.1   Boxed   in   and therefore blocked out of a chance to win. The man in black had conserved his energies and had an excellent chance to win, but had remained in the pole lane an instant too long and was boxed in.

9. The runner should thing of others during the race—their position, their condition, their probable timing of tactics. It will keep his mind off his own fatigue and alert for quick decisions.

10. Inexperienced runners should never look around. Many of the best European runners do look back at their opponents, but only their extensive experience and skill make it permissible.

11. A runner should always sprint at least two strides beyond the finish line, regardless of the length of his lead or the certainty of his place. Many races have been lost by relaxing just before the finish line.

12. Mental alertness, which is essential to pace when leading, can be maintained only by detailed planning and experimentation.

13. Correct pace is particularly important in the 880, for lap times come too late in the race to permit a satisfactory adjustment of mistakes.

When Following Pace

1. The key question in racing is, "What is the *minimum* distance within which the athlete can outrun his opponents?" Perhaps it is the

last 50 yards, the last 150, the last 440, the last 880, or even the full distance. Every plan to win must include the answer to this question. Whitfield of Ohio State picked up his winning lead in the 1948 Olympic 800-meter run between 400 and 600 meters. Had he waited for the last 220, he very probably would have lost to Wint and Barten. Subsequent conversations with him make it seem likely that he reached this decision two months earlier and practiced accordingly.

2. Every runner should know pace, even the runner who considers himself a follower. Pace will determine the timing of his final kick, and occasionally may force him to take the lead himself through the greater part of the race.

3. A strong finishing kick means little unless one is close enough to the leaders to make it effective and in a sufficiently open position to permit one to use it when ready. The instances in which a finish effort occurs too late and from too far back are countless. They occur in almost every track meet whether in the elementary grades or in world championships.

4. When passing, never pause to ask permission or be polite. Do it quickly, unexpectedly, and with determination. "Jumping" an opponent is an art requiring study and practice, and it pays great dividends.

5. Where straightaways are short, as in indoor running, most passing should occur in the first third of the straightaway. The decision to pass must come earlier and with certainty. Come off the curve somewhat wide, *fast,* and entirely unannounced.

6. Passing on the curve means increasing the distance to be run and should occur only when necessary or when there is a certainty of successful surprise. A single curve run in the second lane adds about three yards to the race. Passing at this point produced results for Herb Barten (University of Michigan '49) over Don Gehrman (University of Wisconsin '50) in the indoor Big Ten mile championships. With Gehrman in second spot, Barten in fourth, and 300 yards to go, Barten suddenly sprinted all out in the middle of the curve, where it was least expected. In 30 yards he had a five-yard lead, enough to insure the title.

7. When following, the inside lane is usually dangerous, and in the last stages of the race it may be fatal to success. Many a potential winner running in second place, inside, has watched almost the entire field pass him before he had a chance to move out and up.

8. When following and planning to win, the safest position is in second spot, a half lane wide, about 18 inches from the curb, on the leader's right shoulder. Such a position permits one to meet every challenge, to move out and up with those taking the lead, or to feint them back into place if they are halfhearted.

9. As soon as a runner has found his position, he should search for

rhythm and relaxation. His running position, whether first, second, third, or tenth, is maintained throughout the middle half of the race at a minimum expenditure of energy in order to assure the intended final place. The best position plus maximum economy of effort brings success in this case.

10. In almost all instances, the advantage in competitive racing lies with the man running in second position, for from this spot he can control much of the race and still maintain complete relaxation. If the pace is too slow, he can, by running a little closer on the leader's shoulder, stimulate him to increase it; if too fast, the realization that he is being closely followed will cause the leader to run with greater tension and thereby either unconsciously slow the pace or incur a disproportionate degree of fatigue.

Contact

The idea of contact—maintaining a position sufficiently close to the most likely winner to enable one to overtake him when desired—is so crucial that it requires special discussion. For the inexperienced and uncertain, contact is present if you can reach out and touch your opponent. Once that distance widens to even four or five feet, it easily increases to four or five yards. Stay close so you can hear his labored breathing, so you can see his worried glances. It helps to keep your mind on him and off yourself; even more, it tends to keep him in doubt.

Actually, contact is a flexible thing that is measured by the toughness and self-control of the man maintaining it. In the 1954 Vancouver Mile, Bannister was 15 yards behind Landy at the half-mile mark. Landy was the world-record holder. Surely one would say that effective contact had been lost. But Bannister had planned it that way. He was prepared for the tough third quarter in which closer contact would have to be gained. As Bannister tells it,

> I quickened my stride, trying at the same time to keep relaxed. I won back the first yard, then each succeeding yard, until his lead was halved by the time we reached the back straight on the third lap. How I wished I had never allowed him to establish such a lead!
> I had now "connected" myself to Landy again, though he was still five yards ahead. . . . I tried to imagine myself attached to him by some invisible cord. With each stride I drew the cord tighter and reduced his lead. . . . I fixed myself to Landy like a shadow.[3]

This was truly an instance in which contact, and victory as well, were affairs of the mind as much as of the body.

Franz Stampfl makes a strong point regarding this aspect of contact.

---

[3] Roger Bannister, *The Four Minute Mile* (New York: Dodd, Mead & Co., 1955; London: Curtis Brown, Ltd., 1955), p. 235. Reprinted by permission of the publishers. Copyright © 1955 by Roger Bannister.

Contact involves mental as well as physical issues. As long as a positional runner contrives to keep contact he will continue to run with threatening determination. He knows he is still in the hunt and, while he remains so, he is capable of superhuman prodigies of endeavor. . . . But let his confidence to close the gap falter—and in this connection, where contact begins and ends is an abstract thing existing only in the man's own mind—and the inspiration he gathers from the excitement of the moment will falter too. Doubt comes to sap his determination, to bring tension in place of relaxation, and to put the brake on high-level performance. As far as he is concerned, the race is over.[4]

Competitive Tactics in the 440

Indoors. In indoor racing, a quarter-miler must almost invariably be in either first or second place throughout the race if he is to win. Occasionally, the field will open up and permit a lesser-placed runner to slide through to the tape, but one should not plan on it. In most cases, an experienced runner of lesser ability can beat a superior opponent if he has the lead throughout. By picking up the pace on the straightaways and relaxing around the curves, he can keep the following runner constantly off balance. The latter's best chance is to concentrate on a single all-out effort that will surprise the leader. If this fails, his only other chance will come on the final straightaway.

A man hoping to place only third or fourth in a field of six men may often accomplish this by relaxing in last position until the final straightaway. The other runners will have been constantly off balance and under constant tension in their efforts to improve their positions and they will have little with which to meet his challenge at the end.

Generally speaking, the race is so short and fast that a man has but one opportunity to carry out his strategy. The trick lies in determining just when and how to make the effort. When the exact spot is determined, kick with quickness and determination. Go all out with certainty; hold nothing back.

In nine cases out of ten, one should plan to complete a pass during the first third of a straightaway. If one miscalculates, there is still time to sprint the final two-thirds. However, just because this is the rule and men expect such tactics, the experienced man will occasionally upset the situation by turning it on when least expected, during the last one-third of the straightaway or even while going into a curve.

Outdoors. So many differences occur among individuals in competitive circumstances that no single statement on tactics can be accepted completely However, for races that are not run in lanes, the following points merit consideration:

---

[4] Franz Stampfl, *Franz Stampfl on Running* (London: Herbert Jenkins, Ltd., 1955), p. 31.

1. Every curve that is run 36 inches out from the curb adds about three yards to the length of the race.

2. For most men, second spot around the last turn is a more relaxing position psychologically than being in front. Actually, however, the front runner dominates the situation and has the advantage if he possesses the poise and racing judgment to make use of it.

3. The strong, slow runner will do best to concentrate on his time at the 330-yard mark and will run steadily all the way, striving for minimum deceleration during the last 100 yards.

4. The sprinter who lacks stamina has two choices, either (a) to stay well back and cover the first 300 yards as easily as possible while still staying in the running, and then to kick with whatever he has left, or (b) to use his superior speed in running a good 200 yards or so, to relax quite markedly around the curve and thus hold back fatigue, and then to sprint again at the finish. The latter strategy is most likely to pay off.

5. The sprinter who has 440 stamina has few worries. If time is important, he can go all out all the way, running the 220 within about one second of his best and the 330 within two seconds of his best.

6. Under highly competitive conditions, the race will go most often to the man who has most successfully maintained poise, relaxation, and control of both his mental alertness and physical coordination. Carr over Eastman, Rhoden over McKenley in his :46 flat effort, Wint over McKenley and Jenkins over the field at Melbourne are all excellent examples. Note that Rhoden was a front runner all the way and yet maintained control throughout.

7. The quarter-mile, when not run in lanes, inevitably produces a battle for the first turn, whether the runners come from the chute or the middle of the oval. When the field is less than five or six, position at this point is not quite so vital; but in a large field, a man hoping to place first, second, or third must secure a good spot around the curve. The energy saved by dropping back and thus avoiding jostling will be more than lost in trying to improve one's position later. Probably the best a person can do in this case is to wait until the others have lost their fight, and then go all out at the finish. Incidentally, if a man lacks the speed to secure a good position, he may be misplaced and should probably make plans to run the 880 next year.

8. If he is in the lead and thinking only of winning, the man who had superior speed will maintain his lead but he should husband his strength by easing up around the curve and just hold his lead on the straightaway. He can then outsprint the field on the final stretch. If, as so often happens, he relinquishes the lead to a stronger opponent somewhere on the back stretch, he loses control of the pace. The latter can then pour

it on all the way, hoping to build up a lead or kill off his opponent's speed. If he can maintain poise and control while doing this, the advantage is his. Of course, if he is relatively inexperienced or is "afraid" of his sprinting rival, he is in a pressure position and quite likely to tie up when the sprinter lets go at the finish. Here, as always, the twin admonitions of "Know thyself" and "Know thy opponent" are vitally important.

9. When planning to jump an opponent, do so with determination and quickness, making every effort to surprise him and thereby pick up a two- to five-yard lead before he is aware you've taken it. Usually this can happen only by starting the final sprint earlier than usual, so confidence in one's own ability to carry the pace through to the finish is important.

10. In qualifying races, always complete the last 20 yards with a strong finish. Carelessness in this regard—letting down too soon and being unable to recover soon enough—has often produced another spectator at the final. If saving energy is important, save it during the third quarter of the race.

When running in lanes all the way, three concerns are predominant: (1) the problem of pace, (2) self-control and relaxation, and (3) maintaining contact. Each of these has been discussed in this section as well as in the chapter on endurance training. One reminder: each problem tends to be at least as much of the mind as of the body.

Appendix:
More Cues
to Better
Endurance
Running

The following cues and hints to better running might well have been included in the regular text material. They are too provocative to throw away. If they provide even one insight that will lead you to better running or better coaching, their inclusion here in a special appendix will have been justified.

On Motivation

▶ The five "S's" of sports training are stamina, speed, strength, skill, and spirit, but the greatest of these is spirit.

▶ It was not the high-minded reasons of the brain that drove Jim Peters on in the marathon at Vancouver in 1954, when heat exhaustion had destroyed control and coordination. He had fallen again and again, but would not stay down. Somewhere deep inside of him, an inexorable habit of continuing on had taken over—call it competitiveness, will power, courage—what you will. That habit forced him to his feet, impelled one lurching step to follow the other until unconsciousness blacked out both the habit and the world. In this case, the brain won the race—the winner, McGhee, had stopped to cool off, but Peters and his inexorable habit won the honors—and the tears—of all who watched.

▶ Being an affair of the heart and the sensory nerves in the muscles and bowels, even more than of the brain, it is not surprising that running often occurs in ways and to degrees that the brain alone can never understand, and if it could, would disapprove.

▶ I sometimes think that running has given me a glimpse of the greatest freedom a man can ever know, because it results in the simultaneous liberation of both body and mind. . . . Running is creative. The runner does not know how or why he runs. He only knows that he must run.[1] [Bannister]

▶ What do I expect to get out of all this? That is simple: enjoyment, physical well-being, self-discipline, a sense of achievement, and world-wide friendships. Fame is merely a word. It means nothing—in fact it is far more trouble than it is worth. I do not run to hit the headlines—I run to prove myself to myself.[2] [Pirie]

▶ The toughest part of any training program lies in its early stages, before the habit of daily exertion is established, and when a sensitive body defies the power of the will to make it do more than it wants to do.

▶ Dr. Emile Coué was called a crackpot by some, but he taught that the imagination was often more effective than the will, and that what can be done by playing the role of the man I want to become is often much greater than what can be done by willing—even most powerfully and persistently—that I were the man I know I am not. The latter is aware of the luscious grapes but also the great height at which they are growing. It takes not only will but imagination to invent a ladder. Endurance running produces grapes, but they hang high.

▶ Runners are a motley lot that mill about the starting line in all shapes and sizes. Some are tall; some short. Some are thin; some muscular. A very few even have extra pounds of fat here and there. But one quality they all have in common: determined persistence.

▶ "Fain would I try, but that I fear to fail" was never said by Success in any activity, least of all endurance running.

▶ The difference between two men may not be in their physical potential so much as in what they believe to be physically possible.

▶ When, in his *Testament of a Runner,* W. R. Loader described his attitude before a race in which he ran his best, he used such expressions as, "anxious for the start," "desperate to go," "excitement working like yeast," and "confidence burned like a flame." Several years later when the competitive situation was much tougher, the tone had changed: "an irksome and monotonous chore," "dully and doggedly," "reluctantly and with forebodings," and "defeat stared at you, somberly." Truly his words described a state of mind, not the conditions that surrounded him.

---

[1] Roger Bannister, *The Four Minute Mile* (New York: Dodd, Mead & Co., 1955; London: Curtis Brown, Ltd., 1955), p. 229. Reprinted by permission of the publishers. Copyright © 1955 by Roger Bannister.

[2] Gordon Pirie, "I Run to Prove Myself," *The Road to Rome,* Chris Brasher, ed. (London: William Kimber and Co., Ltd., 1960), p. 74.

▶ Within the few hours available for it each day, endurance running is a matter of supreme importance.

▶ I believe in the intensive approach—that what we do, we do with all our heart and soul. Lift and strive, blow and grunt—whether on the sand hill or with the bar-bell.

There are those who recoil from herculean efforts—who consider possible ruptures and strains as sufficient deterrents, and overexertion the cause of weak hearts.

I hold that those who approach their exercise and goals in this way will fall short in their final endeavors and results of what they might have achieved, no matter if the achievement was a world record.[3] [Cerutty]

▶ In endurance running, nothing can be gained without effort; everything must be earned.

▶ The reason that marathon runners are older men is not just because their stamina has developed with age, but because they have acquired the patience and fortitude to accept the drudgery of such a long race.

▶ Science may in future years be able to dissect and explain a runner to the tiniest muscle fiber and nerve impulse. That will help him to run farther and faster, but it will never be able to tell him why he runs at all or why he wants to continue running—to the very best of his ability.

▶ Endurance running affords a challenge, a joy through effort, and a freedom of expression that cannot be found in the same way in any other activity in life.

▶ In the moment of victory I did not realize that the inner force, which had been driving me to my ultimate goal, died when I became the world's fastest miler.[4] [Ibbotson]

▶ When well filled by sound training, our reservoirs of energy, whether we call them stamina, speed, strength, or skill, are very deep; the level at which they can be tapped at any given moment is established by motivation.

▶ A runner who has a full knowledge of all aspects of training and racing but tempers that knowledge with timidity would be better off ignorant —if that ignorance were audacious and eager.

▶ Danger and delight grow on one stalk.[5] [Lyly]

▶ The struggle to get the best out of ourselves, painful as it may be at times, affords the greatest satisfaction in life; endurance running is one important form of that struggle.

▶ My upper body was already strong from my rowing days at Aquinas [a sec-

---

[3] Percy Cerutty, *Athletics* (London: Stanley Paul & Co., Ltd., 1960), p. 53.

[4] Terry O'Connor, *The 4-Minute Smiler* (London: Stanley Paul & Co., Ltd., 1960), p. 13.

[5] John Lyly, 1578.

ondary school], thus adding to my confidence and aggressiveness for the battles ahead.[6] [Elliott]

▶ Every good coach creates and maintains a tradition of high expectancy in effort, in off-hours training, and in competitive performance. Once established, this tradition will tend to be continued by the runners out of their own group pride, but even then, and especially in America, it will require a coach's vigilant concern.

▶ Surprisingly, weight-lifting, which once was dull, now gave me satisfaction because of the confidence it was imparting.[7] [Elliott]

▶ I have often wondered what endurance runners might achieve if they were not inhibited by the endless conditioning they receive from childhood on, from everyone, on the dangers of fatigue, exhaustion, and the stress of running.

▶ Nothing easily achieved is ever really worthwhile; nothing worthwhile is ever easily attained. This is a law of life and *the* law of endurance running.

▶ I cannot stress too much that if a youngster sets his mind to a goal with an iron determination and is prepared to accept the toil as an opportunity to show his manliness, and his courage, then he must succeed. How many times has this been said in different forms? At first I doubted it, but now I know it is the stark truth.[8] [Elliott]

▶ Turku, Finland, with a total population of only 130,000, has one "master's" track where many fast races and world records have been run, and in addition, 16 other running tracks that are kept in excellent condition. *Sixteen!*

▶ Staleness is like a heavy loaf of bread that contains too much of the flour and water of training and too little of the yeast of exciting competition.

▶ There was no limit to Mr. Reynold's enthusiasm—and no limit to his energetic slave-driving of the boys in the club. . . . The club was going to enter for the sports; we were members of the club and automatically he *expected* loyalty and enthusiasm—and equally automatically he got it from all of us.[9] [Peters]

▶ When a man conquers doubt and fear, he conquers his greatest enemy —himself; when he accepts doubt and fear, calmly and unmoved, he accepts his greatest friend—himself.

▶ Every competitor wants to win; only a few have the will to win. The will to win is as much the will to train as it is the will to compete.

▶ Indeed, immediately I find that an athlete is a "conformer," a respecter of

---

[6] Herb Elliott, *The Golden Mile* (London: Cassell & Company, Ltd., 1961), p. 46. Also published as *Herb Elliott's Story* (New York: Paul R. Reynolds, Inc., 1961).

[7] *Ibid.*, p. 62.

[8] O'Connor, *op. cit.*, p. 10.

[9] J. H. Peters, *In the Long Run* (London: Cassell & Company, Ltd., 1955), p. 16.

authority, who is diligent in doing *exactly* as he is told, just as soon do I know such an athlete is limited in his capacity and never can become truly great.[10] [Cerutty]

▶ Run for fun and from the fun will come the will to excel. From the will to excel could come an Olympic champion. Once you have found the fun there is in running, the task of training to the limits I prescribe will be much easier for you. . . . Dedication gets results, but the dedication can be heightened with the fun of living a healthy life.[11] [Lydiard]

▶ You know how it hurts the ears when beginners are "playing" a violin; and how it delights them when those same beginners have mastered it. It's the same with running. The hurting comes during the early training; the fun, with competence.

▶ The first essential is to teach the athlete to enjoy the basic exercise of running by being uninhibited in movement and thought. He will then revel in the mere rhythm of running and never tire of it. If this sounds simple I can assure you that it is the hardest barrier of all for a young athlete to surmount, and many never do. This liberated condition is one which you have to experience to appreciate. . . . When it has been achieved the rest comes relatively easy.[12] [Pirie]

▶ But if a man takes time off every time he gets a bit of an ache or pain, there will hardly be any time left for running.

▶ Once the dictum that a certain mountain is unclimbable is well ingrained in men's conscious and subconscious minds, it is unclimbable. Only when someone arrives too ignorant to know the truth, or too intelligent to believe completely that it is the whole truth, is it surmounted. So with records in endurance running.

▶ After a man has achieved his goal, there is nothing in athletics to drive him on to improve his proficiency.

▶ To Zatopek, running was always a challenge in itself and the material rewards meant nothing. He even gave away his four Olympic gold medals, saying "I do not want to be reminded of my past when I retire." When he ran his body appeared racked with pain, but this was partly due to his agonized grimace, which meant little. In fact when the pressure was on, the grimace used to vanish as he braced himself to assert his mastery.[13] [Ibbotson]

▶ How terribly hard it is to do something everyone believes is impossible.

On Training

▶ To a degree, a man can take out in competition only what he puts in through training, but training puts in far more than competition can ever take out.

10 Cerutty, *op. cit.*, p. 69.

11 Arthur Lydiard and Garth Gilmour, *Run to the Top* (London: Herbert Jenkins, Ltd., 1962; New Zealand: A. H. & A. W. Reed, 1962), p. 48.

12 Gordon Pirie, *Running Wild* (London: W. H. Allen & Co., Ltd., 1961), p. 19.

13 O'Connor, *op. cit.*, p. 149.

▶ A coach of endurance running must be an apostle of action in the here-and-now. Tomorrow may guide what is done today, but today is the only time it can be done. A mile is covered by taking about 1000 strides, one stride at a time, in rain or snow, in the dark before supper can be eaten or in the earliest morning before the sun is up—one stride at a time—NOW!

▶ Suppose that an athlete, at rest, uses 300cc. of oxygen per minute, and that, during a strenuous exercise, this consumption rises to 4000cc. Thus the consumption has been increased 13.3 times. Transportation of such a large amount of oxygen is facilitated in three ways: (1) the pulse rate increases, to speed up the blood flow; (2) the amount of oxygen taken from a unit of blood, when it passes through the capillaries, is increased; and (3) the stroke volume increases. The pulse rate is usually not increased more than two and one-half times, and the utilization of oxygen cannot be increased more than three times. A combined effect of these two factors will improve transportation only $2.5 \times 3 = 7.5$ times.

To improve it 13.3 times, the stroke-volume must increase $13.3 \div 7.5 = 1.8$ times. Since the average stroke-volume at rest is 65cc., the stroke-volume in this exercise has become 117cc. When an athlete, during intensive work, has a minute-volume of 30 to 40 liters and a pulse rate of 180, his stroke-volume must be from 167 to 222cc.[14] [Karpovich]

▶ The first rule of endurance training is that it shall proceed by gradual increments of work in which overloading in practice or competition alternates with full recovery. Overloading is the challenge; recovery the response. By work, we tear away a portion of our defenses against exhaustion; by recovery, we build them higher than before.

▶ It is no good having rest periods, because the body begins to look for them during actual races.[15] [Concerning interval training—Lydiard]
▶ Indeed we have nothing of these things [elaborate set-ups] at Portsea. It is true that we enjoy coastal scenery equal to any in our State. It is true that we are surrounded by the blue waters of ocean and of sky. But other than that we have nothing; our life is not urban: we live to the music of the sea and the birds, we train to the caresses or inclemencies of beach, sand hill and moor. How these simplicities and strengths enter the spirits, the souls of the Perrys, the Macmillans, the Landys, the Stephens, and now the Elliotts and others—no man can truly say—ever completely evaluate.

Maybe these are the true teachers; the real coachings: the School of Simplicity, Strength and Sincerity.[16] [Cerutty]
▶ There is no set rule for how you should breathe. I hold no brief for the extended rhythm system developed by the Finns, beginning with four strides to the inhale and two to the exhale and increasing until there are up to eight strides on the inhale and six on the exhale. They used to practice this assiduously but I feel that, here again, something artificial or unnatural is being

---

14 Peter V. Karpovich, *Physiology of Muscular Activity* (Philadelphia: W. B. Saunders Co., 1953), p. 166.
15 Lydiard and Gilmour, *op. cit.,* p. 132.
16 Cerutty, *op. cit.,* p. 48.

created and that it would react against the essential relaxation which is the runner's first requirement. . . . Don't worry about it. Just suck it in as you need it.[17] [Lydiard]

▶ The recognition that anything that is inhibited, mechanical, regimented, done under imposed duress or direction, even that which may be thought to be self-imposed—anything at all that is not free out-flowing, out-pouring, instinctive and spontaneous, in the end stultifies the objectives, limits the progress, and destroys the possibility of a completely and fully developed personality— athlete and man.[18] [Cerutty]

▶ One of our points of difference [with Percy Cerutty] is his addiction to weight training and my aversion to it. I doubt if Halberg has lifted twenty pounds above his head in his life and I am certain that, even if he could, he wouldn't be any faster as a runner.[19] [Lydiard]

▶ Under the system which I have developed, there is no need for guessing. You need only patience and control by training and racing at the right speeds and distances at the right times. It may involve initial disappointments. You will come to your peak slower than many other runners and you will be running last when they are running first. But when it is really important to run first, you will be passing them.[20] [Lydiard]

▶ If you can get a boy in his teens and encourage him to train and not to race until he is matured, then you have laid the foundations of an Olympic champion.[21] [Olander—Gunder Hägg's coach]

▶ How far and how fast a child runs in training should be left to his own feelings. But there is no reason why a boy of fourteen should not run 10, 15, or even 20 miles, so long as he is allowed to do it of his own free will. [This does not mean they should be unsupervised in their training, merely not pushed. —J.K.D.] Schedule training can be applied to the child most successfully.[22] [Lydiard]

▶ And I became the fastest miler in the world by using the ideas of a [long] distance runner [Vladimir Kuts]. There is no one formula that fits everyone. That is the fascination about distance running.[23] [Ibbotson]

▶ New Zealand has an event, the "everyone starts" steeplechase. A school bell calls students out for the race; a second bell starts it. Each school invents its own obstacles, terrain, and rules. Lydiard says the kids love it.

▶ This system of training [100 miles a week] tones the whole body completely. This can be tested simply by the pulse rate. I have known marathon training to bring a runner's pulse rate down from the normal 68 to 45 in three months. All the athletes I train have a pulse rate in the vicinity of 45, with Snell thudding along quietly at an astonishing 38. Their hearts recover this normal slow beat very quickly after exertion.[24] [Lydiard]

[17] Lydiard and Gilmour, op. cit., p. 56.
[18] Cerutty, op. cit., p. 68.
[19] Lydiard and Gilmour, op. cit., p. 41.
[20] Ibid., p. 33.
[21] Gosta Olander (Gunder Hägg's coach).
[22] Lydiard and Gilmour, op. cit., p. 143.
[23] O'Connor, op. cit., p. 130.
[24] Lydiard and Gilmour, op. cit., p. 73.

▶ Every man's brain knows that to feel tired is not to be tired. But every man's muscles and heart and lungs, and the sense organs related to them, do not know this truth until they have experienced it—not merely once, but again and again and again at ever-greater levels of performance.

▶ I myself offer nothing but the paraphrased words of a great war-time leader: blood, tears, sweat, and suffering. That is the formula to any and all great achievement, at least in the athletic world. I know of no other.[25] [Cerutty]

▶ To train hard, long, and enthusiastically is not enough; one must also train intelligently in terms of each competition. Perhaps we should say "conserve" rather than "train," for during the few final weeks it is conservation of energy that is needed, not the indiscriminate spending of energy; further, it is conservation of human, not merely physical, energy; mental-emotional as well as chemical.

▶ Seldom is less than twenty miles covered in the day's training [at Camp Portsea], yet it seems fun, is fun, and is as happy and pleasurable a way to live, apart from the athletic ends, as surely any healthy young man could wish for, or enjoy.[26] [Cerutty]

▶ Zatopek's training is know as "inhuman" and a "man-killer." But Zatopek did not consider it so. On many occasions he has said that he found he got best results from training when he worked well within himself. Do only so much more work today that you will do it more easily next week; and even more work, more easily, next month.

▶ An organism learns what it does and at the rate it does it. Competitive endurance running is a sustained effort at a fairly uniform pace over a given distance. For optimum training, this kind of running must be done at least part of the time in practice. In contrast, interval training, admitting its special values, conditions the organism, mentally as well as physically, to bursts of effort alternated with short recovery runs. There are no such opportunities for recovery in competitive racing.

▶ I ran hard against that wind [in major competition], thankful that I'd often run against gale-force winds in training.[27] [Elliott]

▶ A year of unbroken, unvarying training is apt to blunt the edge of one's zest for running; zeal without zest will ultimately run itself to oblivion. Each year, therefore, should include periods of freedom from all routine and tension. This does not necessarily mean freedom from running.

▶ Normally I react to my mood. Often when in London I have visited training tracks with no prearranged plan in mind. This has encouraged me to experiment with different schedules which, I believe, have helped me in my training.

[25] Cerutty, *op. cit.*, p. 46.
[26] *Ibid.*, p. 28.
[27] Elliott, *op. cit.*, p. 176.

I start with one group of runners, and then join another. This provides variety and adds the spice of competition to avoid boredom.[28] [Ibbotson]

▶ The Hungarian athletes, Iharos, Tabori, and Roszavolgyi, often trained three times a day before the 1956 Olympic Games, but I have never trained more than once a day.[29] [Ibbotson]

▶ To the spectator, the resolution with which a runner in competition drives his body onward seems almost heroic; he little realizes that the real heroism lies in the day-after-day-after-day-after-day tenacity by which that resolution is developed.

▶ Development in endurance training should occur by gradual increments of work within planned levels of effort; new effort levels should not be attempted until what is now being done is fully mastered and has become quite easy.

▶ He [Cerutty] believes that no matter how cold it is you must expose your body to the air at least once a day and surf right through the winter. Well, no one objects to midwinter swims, but one of our habits at Portsea was to work out along the beach, charge up and down sandhills until we'd got a good sweat up, and then strip off and dive into the sea. Afterwards we'd run naked along the deserted beach to the camp.[30] [Elliott]

▶ Any instruction that disrupts a natural style of running disrupts the man himself—raises a doubt where there was certainty, divides what was unified, creates tension where there was relaxation. Mechanical soundness that is "unnatural" is worse than naturalness that is mechanically unsound. Such instruction should therefore be given only after careful and precise consideration.

▶ Hard work, as typified by Zatopek's "superhuman workouts," should not be judged so much by level of energy output as by the inexorability of everyday, year-round practice. The significance of climbing Mt. Everest does not lie so much in its 30,000 feet as in the endless preparation, in the "Battle against Boredom" which was such a trial for Hillary, and in the fortitude that puts one foot above the other—endlessly.

▶ An endurance runner affirms the negative and hurtful elements that are an inevitable part of running. He does not shrink from them. He learns to accept them, to come to terms with them, in the certainty that their cost will be more than balanced by the equally inevitable elements and outcomes that are positive.

discomfort	satisfaction
discipline	freedom
concentration	relaxation
fatigue	recovery
work	fun

[28] O'Connor, *op. cit.*, p. 154.

[29] *Ibid.*, p. 155.

[30] Elliott, *op. cit.*, p. 39.

No matter how long we might extend this list, its balance of weight for endurance running, when intelligently conducted, would be on the right.

▶ We were wined and dined in America until we felt like wealthy potentates; yet I found the surfeit of luxury so tedious that I was soon craving my normal routine of plain living.[31] [Elliott]

▶ An endurance runner often thinks he is choosing a socially approved and oriented activity but soon discovers his new way of life is one of isolation and loneliness. The rest of his world finds it hard to understand a man who deliberately chooses the hard way, the way of daily rigorous routine and hardship. This alone sets him apart. But the full extent of his estrangement from his fellow men does not really hit him until an hour or so before the race is to start; he suddenly feels the enormity of the task before him. Now for the first time he understands why Alan Sillitoe called his short story, "The Loneliness of the Long Distance Runner." But there are compensations for this, for, as condition and control are acquired, the runner gradually senses that he has found a harmony within himself, and with all about him, that is certainly different and perhaps greater than he has ever known before.

▶ A modern Spartan, Cerutty still subjects himself to rigorous exercise at the age of sixty-three. That is why he is prepared to drive Elliott to an extremity which would frighten many coaches.[32] [Ibbotson]

▶ Rapid muscular movements result in a much greater increase of the cardiac output than slow movements. In part, this is caused by the "milking" action of the muscles that massage the venous blood back to the heart for a complete diastolic filling and contraction. This is a strong argument for working part of the time at faster than pace.

▶ The willingness to hurt oneself can develop during training as naturally and unconsciously as do the changes in blood chemistry.

▶ I stayed at one [an athletic training camp] called Bøson, six or seven miles outside Stockholm. It was on a lovely island, separated from the rest of civilization by a lake. . . . More breathtaking were the soft-textured paths that meandered through the fragrant pine forests skirting the camp. No athlete could resist them. I wondered why, with all these advantages, the Swedes were unable to produce more athletes of the caliber of their old heroes, Hägg and Andersson, unless it was that, like the Americans, they'd grown soft with prosperity.[33] [Elliott]

▶ Some men want victory too desperately. Fretful and overanxious, they strain rather than train. Instead of building reservoirs of stamina, self-control, and joy in effort, they allow unrestrained tenacity to tap the

---

31 *Ibid.,* p. 76.
32 O'Connor, *op. cit.,* p. 151.
33 Elliott, *op. cit.,* p. 98.

deepest depths of their strength. Tenacity is a vital trait in a runner, but it must be tempered by good judgment.

▶ When Gosta Holmer, Swedish national coach, was asked a few years ago what had happened to Sweden's distance runners, he replied,

They are still there, but they have become so obsessed by the search for greater speed that they have forgotten the need also for stamina. They now find they are so good at the shorter distances that they are not willing to undergo the more arduous training required by their proper events.[34] [Elliott]

▶ After an injury, or other forced layoff, the natural tendency is to try to make up for lost time by training just a little more, then a little more. But in most cases this loses more than it gains, and often loses a great deal. This is especially true if a race is coming up; so much energy is drained in the training that little is left for the competition.

▶ If a man's life could be planned in terms of maximum running, he would reach his peak of physical development and maturity (between 25 and 30 years of age) at the same time that he reached his peak of competitive motivation and performance. Too many are now reaching the latter peak too soon. Fortunately for men, though unfortunately for running, lives of amateurs can seldom be so planned.

▶ One thing I avoid is training always with the same people because of the tendency to run each other into the ground. This can be harmful psychologically to the one on the losing end. If you are beaten easily in training, it is difficult to imagine that the scales will change in competition.[35] [Ibbotson]

▶ A successful runner is a man who has faced great challenges and hardships, both from others and from within himself, and has overcome them by courage, sacrifice, and tenacity. Our modern world of self-indulgence sometimes lauds his achievement as though it were a path to heaven but avoids his example as though it led straight to hell. There is no short cut to endurance fitness; the old proverb, "haste makes waste," must have been coined by a distance runner.

▶ After my marathon [on Saturday—his first major victory] I had slight blisters and I was terribly stiff, but on Sunday evening I was out on the road training again, after having taken my son, Robin, in his pram for my seven-mile walk earlier in the day.[36] [Peters]

▶ Most runners suffer from too little training. So-called overtraining is usually poorly motivated training. Restore zest and competitive keenness and the sense of being overtrained will soon be gone.

▶ Rate of development is an excellent measure of the effectiveness of endurance training, but the quality or stability of development is even more so, and should come first.

---

34 *Ibid.*
35 O'Connor, *op. cit.*, p. 129.
36 Peters, *op. cit.*, p. 70.

▶ After a few more minutes' running however, I begin to feel most uncomfortable plodding along at the pace being set. I had trained to run at a fast speed, and to jog along at a rate of a mile in 6 minutes, or 6 minutes 15 seconds, when you feel well and capable of going much faster, was definitely upsetting the natural rhythm of my running. . . . I shot to the front.[37] [Peters]

▶ Overtraining will not occur so long as too much is not attempted too fast, nor too soon.

▶ Rate of recovery is a reliable guide to the stress of training. If fatigue is primarily one of oxygen debt with low motivational stress, recovery should be complete within an hour or two after the workout; if fatigue is related to fuel supply, heat exhaustion, and/or emotional exhaustion, then two or three days of easy work is not too much for full recovery.

▶ Training is mainly an everyday act maintained by dogged persistence. Nerve-muscle skill develops out of many daily repetitions; blood capillaries, out of many daily efforts—all driven by persistence, even though the work is sometimes drudgery, and the outcome seems sometimes hopeless.

▶ It is very rarely that endurance is limited by a lack of fuel for muscular contraction. When work decrement occurs in endurance running, it is because lack of oxygen has permitted an increase in the amount of lactic acid in the blood which has hindered muscle action. Such lack of oxygen is not because of an insufficient amount of oxygen in the lungs; but rather in the failure of the system of transportation—the heart output of blood and the unloading of oxygen from the blood capillaries to the muscles.

▶ A man trains at slower than pace to develop blood capillaries, at faster than pace to develop muscle fibers, at pace to develop muscle-nerve coordination; all three are essential for best performance in endurance running.

▶ A runner's body will accept and even enjoy mild activity, but step up the pace or the time and it will balk like a hungry mule heading away from the barn.

▶ My pulse rate at rest is between 44 and 46 beats to the minute, rising under extreme exertion to 198 beats a minute. . . . The average pulse beat is about 72, while the lowest ever recorded, 32, belonged to New Zealander Jack Lovelock.[38] [Elliott]

▶ Zatopek's heart beat, in moments of quiet, is 56 times a minute. The usual functional test [getting up and down off a chair 50cm. (19⅝ inches) high 150 times in the space of five minutes] shows that . . . his pulse rises to 76 and in the next minute drops to the normal level, that is 56 times a minute. . . . After breaking the world record for 20 kilometres, his blood pressure, seven minutes after the race, was exactly the same as prior to the race and his pulse, three

---

[37] *Ibid.*, p. 42.
[38] Elliott, *op. cit.*, p. 144.

hours later, was lower than we had ever measured it at any time. This is obviously because he not only enters a race well prepared but also because he doesn't completely exhaust himself and retains a reserve of strength.[39] [Kozik]

▶ Each runner must concern himself with the kind of training that is best for him, regardless of the experience of others. This means best for him from every standpoint; not merely kind and amount of work but also kind of terrain, whether alone or with others, whether in the morning or evening or both, whether under the authority of a coach or on one's own authority. Each of these conditions can produce and has produced world-level results.

▶ Each form of training (fartlek, interval training, marathon training, and the rest) has proved its value. Unfortunately we all tend to make the mistake of thinking that, if so much of a training system is good, a great deal more will be even better. The truth lies not in the name of the system, but in developing the essentials of performance—stamina, speed, pace, relaxation, poise—in the right proportions so that no one of the essentials detracts from the others.

▶ A runner must train himself to maintain racing pace after a surge of speed is completed. To burst ahead, then take it easy, is to lose more than is gained. Once breakaway tactics are started, a runner must feel certain he can hold his lead to the finish.

▶ While running fartlek, simulate the effort of your race for the length of time it takes you to run it in competition, ease off for recovery, then repeat several times. You are thus training the body and your will to control it.

▶ The most basic essential of all endurance training lies in gradual increments in both the amount and intensity of work during years of everyday running.

▶ Pushing yourself in a thirty-mile run beyond what you thought were the borders of endurance is of great moral benefit.[40] [Elliott]

▶ Of endurance training it can truly be said, "If you miss the fun of it, you miss all of it." Of course fun without training is child's play, but training without fun is drudgery, and drudgery in sport has no place whatsoever.

On Competition

▶ A runner's creed: I will win; if I cannot win, I shall be second; if I cannot be second, I shall be third; if I cannot place at all, I shall still do my best.

39 Frantisek Kozik, *Emil Zatopek in Photographs* (Prague: Artia, 1955), p. 68.
40 Elliott, *op cit.*, p. 144.

▶ Percy agrees that it's hypocritical to shake your opponents' hands and wish everybody luck. "You've got to murder them and you cannot afford any kindly thoughts," he tells his runners. "If a runner on the mark wants to shake your hand let it hang limply like a dead fish so that he has to take the initiative. He is congratulating you in advance!" [41] [Elliott]

▶ Overexposure to competition can destroy self-confidence and enthusiasm for running far faster than wise training can create them.

▶ Victory was never sweeter. I not only conquered the pain of honest effort— but I had mastered myself and won back my confidence. . . . In every race there is a crucial moment when the body wants to quit. Then it needs imagination and mental tenacity to survive the crisis. [42] [Ibbotson]

▶ In endurance running, the man with the fastest finish is the man who has the stamina to use his natural speed.

▶ I aimed consistently at improving my performance. Even in races I never ran against an opponent merely to beat him. When I ran only against time I took every race seriously so that even when I had no rivals to threaten me I was able, on occasion, to break records. . . . I learned from all my victories and defeats and drew the following conclusion: a person shouldn't give up the fight until he's reached the finishing line. If it wasn't for this principle I would hardly have won such a difficult race as the 5000 meters in Helsinki. [43] [Zatopek]

▶ Trying too hard to do well is often the main cause of doing badly.

▶ . . . This pace is killing me! Surely I shouldn't feel as tired as this! Maybe I'd better not make my break where I thought I would. Maybe I ought to wait. *No I won't.* I'll *give it a go and see what happens.* [44] [Remembered thoughts during Elliott's world-record 1500 meters at Rome!]

▶ Without competition, it is difficult to assess the benefit of a routine of training, no matter how thorough it may have seemed.

▶ This time I was happy he was with me. . . . Chataway was the greatest fighter on the track, and I wanted to conquer him at his best. . . . There is no room for the Corinthian spirit that "it is just a game." Winning *is* important. And to reach the top all one's resources of courage, determination, and even passion must be harnessed to achieve their greatest impact. [45] [Ibbotson]

▶ But most important of all is the manner of the striving—if it be done to the best of one's ability, or enough to beat the other fellow, or merely to meet the low level of expectancy from oneself and one's associates. To the great runner, it represents a declaration of himself, without reservations, without inhibitions, without apology.

▶ The aftereffects of each race should be observed carefully, though without exaggeration. Runners vary in their reactions to competition,

41 *Ibid.,* p. 146.
42 O'Connor, *op. cit.,* p. 14.
43 Kozik, *op. cit.,* p. 7.
44 Elliott, *op. cit.,* p. 175.
45 O'Connor, *op. cit.,* p. 59.

and each runner may vary in his reactions to different races. Until a man feels fully recovered and eager to run again, he will do well to avoid training that involves tension or stress.

▶ Fatigue experienced after these runs [marathons] need not cause alarm and should not cause an athlete to skip a day here and there. He may be forced on succeeding nights to run at a slower pace, but a week later he will feel the benefit of that fatiguing effort in a surge of fresh power. There is no other sport in which improvement is so noticeable.[46] [Lydiard]

▶ An excellent method of "mental training" a few days before competition is to cover the exact distance of one's race, at slower than pace, during which one concentrates on simulating the race itself: here, I shall be behind taking it easy; here, I shall move into striking position; here, I shall be doubting my condition and my ability to carry on; here, J.B. will probably be making his bid, etc. In so doing, play the role of how you will feel as well as what you will do.

▶ The most important factor in a program of training is to be able to hit the heights of physical and mental conditioning when your schedules say you should and when the *big races* say you must. Lydiard is convinced that his schedules can do just this, and that the sharpening of running fitness can be speeded up or held back as individual reactions may require.

▶ After 20-year-old Murray Halberg had won the Benjamin Franklin mile at the Penn Relays in 1954 against Fred Wilt, Horace Ashenfelter, and Mal Whitfield, he was asked by news correspondents what he thought of the American runners. Halberg replied frankly as only youth can, "I don't know; I didn't see them."

▶ I wanted to remove all uncertainty and worry except the great uncertainty of victory which is the main driving force. Only in this way could my whole being become absorbed in the struggle.[47] [Bannister]

▶ I felt joyously full of the running that I had restrained for so long.[48] [Bannister before the 1952 Olympic Games]

▶ Sometimes the terrors of impending competition can be calmed by a good dose of just plain, ordinary muscular fatigue. Even during the hour or so before post time, a man may be wiser to relax his muscles by tiring them a little than to try to rest in bed with the great burden of his tensions weighing him down.

▶ [I have a] killer instinct, which I apparently always had the moment I toed the line for a race. Where it came from, I don't know, for with all modesty, I think most people have always considered me quite a kind-hearted sort of person—until I ran a marathon. Then it was "kill" or "be killed."

---

46 Lydiard, *op. cit.*, p. 73.
47 Bannister, *op. cit.*, p. 134.
48 *Ibid.*, p. 161.

. . . I think all champions must have it, for it gives them just that extra "edge" over their opponents.[49] [Peters]

▶ The will to win is developed first by winning, later by losing; then still later, by winning over those to whom one has lost. The fibers of self-confidence grow tallest and strongest under the sun of exciting challenge but out of the soil of successful response.

▶ My normal practice is to preserve myself in absolute solitude before a race.[50] [Elliott]
▶ Similarly, I rarely like training with anybody. Even if they don't speak, their presence disturbs my concentration, so that my thoughts, which might be valuable if analyzed, are wasted.[51] [Elliott]

▶ In endurance running, an Olympic title is worth a thousand world records. To a few, a place in the Olympic Games is a great honor, but to most, even to be second—even to be second by the breadth of a single hair on one's chest—is to achieve nonentity and failure. Unreasonable? Of course—from the brain's viewpoint. But there are reasons of the heart of which the brain knows nothing.

▶ Allied to his [Chris Chataway's] instinctive athletic talent was a huge helping of that vital quality—guts. . . . I had many great races with Chataway, and lost more than I won. . . .
I was traveling at four-minute-mile speed—fifteen miles per hour—when Chataway rushed past me. If somebody had hit me in the stomach it could not have been worse. . . . So Chataway had proved decisively he was master that day. . . . The incentive to beat Chataway played an important part in my progress, and because of this I owe him a debt.[52] [Ibbotson]

▶ It is not only because of physical ability and training that a man wins in endurance running but also because he is able to assert his dominance over the other runners as persons. Psychology has now ruled that the will is an abstraction, but it is an abstraction that locks itself in conflict with the abstractions of others' wills just as forcefully as do the muscles of wrestlers in action. Men fail in running not only because of physical fatigue but also because their will to run has wilted in the fierce heat of interpersonal struggle.

▶ The timers may declare a new record; the headlines, a new champion. This is satisfying, but only a lesser part of a greater satisfaction: a resolute response to an exciting challenge, a hard victory well deserved.

▶ We've found it most advantageous to go to a quiet park a few hours before a race so that I can run spiritedly for twenty minutes or so and imagine myself winning. I become calm then and, back at my hotel, find no difficulty in

---

[49] Peters, *op. cit.*, p. 210.
[50] Elliott, *op. cit.*, p. 3.
[51] *Ibid.*, p. 67.
[52] O'Connor, *op. cit.*, pp. 51-53.

sleeping for two hours before going to the stadium half an hour before the race.[53] [Elliott]

▶ Every champion athlete must learn that press reporters are unpredictable, and that he must become indifferent to both their praise and criticism, while holding a friendly attitude toward each of them personally.

▶ Success in endurance running comes not only through physical condition, but also from quick thinking, intelligent planning, and the reckless courage to risk more of oneself in the race than will any of the opposition.

▶ Those times combined make 3:46.2, which I'm sure someone will run in the not-too-distant future. I'll go further: when half-milers start getting down to 1:43.0, 1:42.0—and it's not impossible—the 3:40.0 mile also will be "just around the corner." [54] [Elliott]

▶ The feeling a runner has when he knows he's going to run a good race is edgy, nervous, excited, and yet inside eager, certain, and relaxed.

▶ Of ten runners or more that walk up to any starting line, all have the jitters—though of course in different ways and to different degrees. Amazingly, this is a fact that each of them overlooks; all tend to assume that he alone is nervous.

▶ It was one of the most exhausting races I had ever experienced as I almost lost the desire to win.[55] [Ibbotson]

▶ Somehow I had found a mental and physical rhythm that made every demand so easy.[56] [Ibbotson]

▶ Excitement before an important race is necessary for best performance. It should be sufficient to arouse the emotions and release the emergency reservoirs of reserve energy that have been established by training. It is worry and uncertainty that drains the energy, not eagerness and excitement. The runner who has lost the stimulus of excitement before a race is either stale or too far over the hill.

▶ [During the race], my mind remained quite cool and detached. It merely switched over the lever, and well-worn channels carried to my body the extra energy that my mind unleashed.[57] [Bannister]

▶ The runner I would least like to be beaten by is the gritty little New Zealander Murray Halberg, who has the brand of determination that makes me determined to beat him. There is much that I respect in Halberg. He has extremely solid goals toward which he strides with an almost frightening degree of purpose.[58] [Elliott]

---

53 Elliott, *op. cit.*, p. 146.

54 *Ibid.*, p. 91.

55 O'Connor, *op. cit.*, p. 106.

56 *Ibid.*, p. 110

57 Bannister, *op. cit.*, p. 26.

58 Elliott, *op. cit.*, p. 154.

▶ Only those who have experienced it themselves know the emotional upheaval that accompanies most important races.

▶ A competitor's greatest asset, apart from endurance fitness, is a cool and calculating brain—calmed by confidence, excited by courage, and steeled by a will to win.

▶ They had tried to break me at the start, and now I wanted to break them at the finish. It was like being goaded by some unseen advisor back into the battle. When I regained contact, the old magic of battle flowed back into my veins. The desire for success drove out tiredness, and I managed to win by a few yards.[59] [Ibbotson]

▶ Very often a graceful and rhythmical way of running is taken as proof of natural talent. This is like assuming that a pretty face is proof of a virtuous woman. Both warrant a deeper inquiry before making final judgment.

▶ Elliott was easily converted to the doctrine that running must be "instinctive." The stop watch, so long the mentor of runners, was never used. Instead Elliott was instructed to run freely, dominated solely by the animal urge to seek the limits of endurance. In fact it might be said that the Cerutty plan was to dispense with all plans. . . .
  In races it is the same. Elliott just strives for that sensation of "liberation" or "oblivion." Midway through a race he has whipped himself into a trance and can then remorselessly pull away from the field in what has been described as "an inhuman display of speed and energy." . . .
  Together Cerutty and Elliott have brought athletics to the threshold of a new era. They have proved conclusively that not only the body but also the mind must be conquered.[60] [Ibbotson]

▶ The basis of my own self-respect had never been very secure. . . . But it was not enough for my self-esteem to do anything half well.[61] [Bannister]

▶ As Josy Barthel climbed the Olympic victory steps at Helsinki, his happiness must have outmatched even the great effort he had put into his training. As he watched tiny Luxembourg's flag go up the Olympic staff for the first time, he first wiped a tear away, then waved gaily to the tremendously enthusiastic crowd. In Olympic track and field the individual wins, not the size or reputation of his country.

▶ I was as tired as everyone else, but suddenly for the first time I felt a crazy desire to overtake the whole field. I raced through into the lead and a feeling of great mental and physical excitement swept over me. I forgot my tiredness. I suddenly tapped that hidden source of energy I always suspected I possessed.[62] [Bannister during his first Oxford-Cambridge mile]

▶ Since July I had been beaten in five major races . . . [None of them was at

[59] O'Connor, *op. cit.,* p. 117.
[60] *Ibid.,* p. 152.
[61] Bannister, *op. cit.,* p. 38.
[62] *Ibid.,* p. 58.

one mile, however—J.K.D.] though I had enjoyed them all. I was beginning to think it did not matter if I was beaten. This would have been fatal to my future as a runner.[63] [Bannister]

▶ I must admit I thought of Derek [Ibbotson] as a superman. This form of idolatry . . . is something I have now learned to hate. . . . Believe me, an athlete hates that pedestal. It takes life away from simplicity into the field of unreality; so much so that you almost wish you could become a hermit.[64] [Elliott]

▶ The attitude with which one walks up to the starting line matters above all else. At this crucial moment, the eagerness and confidence that seemed so certain can now blow away with every breath that is taken. Often the sound of the gun, or the first stride, brings it back. But sometimes a man has to reach out, as he has done in training time and again, and pull himself together.

On Tactics

▶ Tactical plans for big races have to be thought out in advance. The runner must be prepared both to meet possible moves by an opponent and to retain the flexibility to modify his scheme if something happens quite unexpectedly. The simpler such plans can be, the better, because then the mind can be free during the race. This makes it easier to relax and run more economically.[65] [Bannister]

▶ Dr. Roger Bannister apparently didn't train too well and needed tactics, as did Christopher Chataway. . . . The only tactics I admire are do-or-die.[66] [Elliott]

▶ A man is said to have contact with the leader so long as he can overtake him. Such contact is as much in the mind as in the physical distance he is behind; if the mind falters, contact is gone even when the hand can reach out and touch the leader; if the mind holds on, a hundred yards may not mean lost contact. The mind and heart have energies of which the muscles know nothing.

▶ Kuts used perhaps the toughest of all tactics—a recklessly fast pace at the start followed by violent variations of pace when the awareness of fatigue was greatest. It was even tougher physically on him than on his opponents, but he had trained for it and was doing what he planned to do. It worked.

▶ Even pace in running is not justified if it leaves a man out of contact with his rivals—worried and uncertain. It is hard to argue "economy of physical energy" when one is fretting about the nervous energy that will be needed later to catch the field.

---

63 *Ibid.*, p. 113.
64 O'Connor, *op. cit.*, p. 10.
65 Bannister, *op. cit.*, p. 226.
66 Elliott, *op. cit.*, p. 145.

▶ All passing should be accomplished quickly—perferably on the straight-away.

▶ When competing with experienced men, it is useless to take the lead in the hope of slowing down the pace; on the contrary, one should take the lead either to increase the pace or to smooth out one's own rhythm.

▶ [Fleming] was trying to anticipate everything that was going to happen in the mile, so that he could devise a counter. I told him that it was no wonder he vomited before most of his races; he was wasting all his nervous energy thinking about them. . . . Your mind is in such a jumble that it won't give your body a chance.[67] [Elliott]

▶ The possibilities for racing tactics are unlimited: as in a game of chess, every move has its countermove; every attack, its defense.

▶ In many cases, where the emotional tension of a competition is very high, the most dangerous contestant will be an unknown who can ease his way through the race and the finish line.

▶ For three vital seconds, Pirie dithered. By the time he decided to move after the Russian, Kuts had escaped, and we were never able to catch him again.[68] [Ibbotson]

▶ Every action and gesture by an athlete can have a significant and even decisive effect upon the morale of his rivals.

▶ The tactic of breaking away from the field requires great confidence but also indicates lack of it: confidence in one's ability to hold a faster pace to the finish line, but lack of confidence in one's ability to outsprint the others if it comes later. Physically, to break away is uneconomical; it works only if one is tougher than the others.

▶ From the standpoint of time spent in training, the importance of pace judgment is often overemphasized, to the detriment of other tactical factors.

On the Coach

▶ A coach's greatest asset for coaching is infectious enthusiasm. To such a man, running is an exciting challenge—personal and unique for him and for each of the men that works under him.

▶ A coach can be like an oasis in the desert of a runner's lost enthusiasm.

▶ He seemed upset when I asked him why he said this or that. I think he worked intuitively and I needed reasons for the things I did.[69] [Bannister on his reaction to his first coach]

▶ Ignore, then, whether you are tall and thin or short and stocky—whether

[67] *Ibid.*, p. 52.
[68] O'Connor, *op. cit.*, p. 90.
[69] Bannister, *op. cit.*, p. 66.

they laughed at you at home (where they are often unkind) or at school (where they are mostly blind, anyway). Indeed—to hell with the lot of them if you *feel* you can do it![70] [Cerutty]

▶ To impress others with a sense of confidence as to success and certainty as to improvement is a vital asset to every coach. It convinces others even when it is not backed up by the requisite knowledge or personal experience to make it effective.

▶ An experienced and wise coach will soon spot the man who is attracted by the bright lights, and by the simple stratagem of increasing the work load can dim them considerably.

▶ I have come to know Herb Elliott well. . . . When he came to live with us we adopted him as another of our athletic sons, for his home and his parents were three thousand miles away. . . . He has spent a fair slice of his life with us [five years]. He has learnt that his success has been our success; his happiness, our happiness; his future—and all that it conjures up—is our life, a life full of meaning to Nancy and myself.[71] [Cerutty]

▶ I educated them to use their own intelligence, to try to improve their own systems. An athlete is an individual and what suits one does not always suit others. I urged on them, as I have urged on all others since, that my schedules had to be modified by personal taste and judgment.[72] [Lydiard]

▶ Coaches hold two extreme views: (1) a team is an aggregate of separate individuals, and (2) a team is the real entity to which the individuals, as parts, should give their best: if the team wins, they each win; if the team loses, they each lose. Neither view is sound or satisfactory. A better view sees both the team and its individual members as abstractions which can be looked upon flexibly as the need may require. The team-and-its-individuals make up a system of interrelations and interactions; neither can exist in the same way without the other. In one sense, Herb Elliott was a loner, without a team. But Herb could never have been the Olympic champion without his "matey," his teammate, Cerutty; and, in a broader but sound sense, we'd have to put the Russian Vladimir Kuts on Elliott's team, since without his inspiring running at Melbourne, Herb would never have put his foot on an Olympic track. How you define the word "team" is a measure of your own awareness.

▶ I concede that many doctors understand the theory, but very few understand the extremes to which the human body can be used because they have not gained any practical experience. Without that experience, much of their theory is useless.[73] [Lydiard]

▶ Simple psychology is a big thing. Those boys [Snell and Halberg] had faith

---

[70] Cerutty, *op. cit.*, p. 41.
[71] Elliott, *op. cit.*, Preface.
[72] Lydiard and Gilmour, *op. cit.*, p. 31.
[73] *Ibid.*, p. 121.

in me. If there were any little doubts in their minds, the fact that I could tell them to do something about them seemed to allay their fears.[74] [Lydiard]

▶ The essence of athletics is the pleasure you can get out of it. I make this point no wbefore you begin to think that having a run 100 miles a week can't possibly be in the least bit enjoyable. I actually came to enjoy knocking myself about because I came to grips with myself so frequently and at such a challenging physical and mental level. . . . It is a simple unalloyed joy to tackle yourself on the battlefield of your own physical well-being and come out the victor.[75] [Lydiard]

▶ Arthur Lydiard's enthusiasm for running not only encourages but impels those around him to run. Even his ghost-writer, a 36-year-old journalist, caught the bug. After three months' training he brought his pulse-rate down from 78 to 52 and could run 22 miles without strain!

▶ No two runners will give the same reasons for their running. But among every man's reasons you will find one common element: a person —either a person who by his wonderful running inspires others to run, or an older person who by his personal devotion to running excites the young, not just to run (for they do that naturally from childhood) but to undergo the rigors of everyday training.

▶ Arthur Lydiard attributed his addiction to running to his club president, Jack Dolan.

▶ He took me for a five-mile training jog and nearly killed me. . . . [age—27] His enthusiasm for the sport was the most wholehearted I have experienced. He inoculated me beyond all expectations. Besides physically exhausting me, he mentally stimulated me. For the first time I started thinking about fitness in its true sense.[76] [Lydiard]

▶ My early training on him [Peter Snell] was tough. He was weeping with the agony of the last mile of his first run round my favorite proving ground, the twenty-two-mile Waiatarua course. But six weeks later he was coasting around. He was a very determined boy and he had to battle constantly against the troubles caused by his heavy muscle development. He took a long time to loosen up, but he never wavered.[77] [Lydiard]

On Sports Amateurism

▶ Every man in training should live a full life, curbing only the distractions that limit his achievement in running and eliminating only the joys that prevent it. Zest in life multiplies zeal in training.

▶ At the start of the 1947 track season I was just besieged with invitations to run for the AAA in various matches, but hardly had the season opened when I got badly blistered feet through wearing poorly made spikes. At this time,

---

[74] *Ibid.,* p. 44.
[75] *Ibid.,* p. 46.
[76] *Ibid.,* p. 19.
[77] *Ibid.,* p. 40.

I was still not in a position to buy a really expensive hand-made pair—even though I was the national six-miles champion.[78] [Peters]

▶ As was usual, the AAA Six Miles Championship was held on a Friday night. I had been at work all day of course, but I was still feeling in good form, even if a little nervous, for on this race depended that Union Jack. I didn't win.[79] [Peters]

▶ Running is a means of expression, just as music or sculpture: when done at its highest levels with intelligence and self-discipline, it is also an art.

▶ Fitting running into the rest of life until one's work becomes too demanding—this is the burden and joy of the true amateur.[80] [Bannister]

▶ Training for distance running is much more than a mere matter of mileage and intensity; it is best thought of as a way of life and reaches its highest level when developed within a mature and well-balanced person.

▶ When Johnny inquired about the provision of sponges [to be used during a marathon race], he was told that water would be available, but that no sponges were being provided as they were too expensive.[81] [Peters]

▶ Amateur sportsmen get their full reward directly out of what they do, and they should not be paid twice.

---

[78] Peters, *op. cit.,* p. 33.
[79] *Ibid.,* p. 44.
[80] Bannister, *op. cit.,* p. 248.
[81] Peters, *op. cit.,* p. 73.